The BLACK ELITE

The BLACK ELITE

Facing the Color Line in the Twilight of the Twentieth Century

Lois Benjamin

Hampton University

Nelson-Hall Publishers/Chicago

About the Author

Lois Benjamin grew up in Atlanta, Georgia. She received her B.A. in sociology from Clark College in Atlanta, and her M.A. and Ph.D. in sociology from the University of California, Berkeley. As a Ford Foundation Fellow (Leadership Development Program), she conducted research in Africa and the West Indies. Her publications and research interests are in the Black family, gender and racial stratification. Dr. Benjamin has taught at several universities, and is, at present, a sociology professor at Hampton University, Hampton, Virginia.

Project Editor: Dorothy Anderson

Cover Painting: *Constellations* by John Witte.

Photo of Lois Benjamin: Reuben V. Burrell

"Little Black Tombo," copyright 1968 Chronicle Publishing Company, reprinted by permission of the author.

Library of Congress Cataloging-in-Publication Data

Benjamin, Lois, 1944–
    The Black elite: / Facing the color line in the twilight of the twentieth
century / Lois Benjamin.
      p. cm.
    Includes bibliographical references and index.
    ISBN 0-8304-1215-8.—ISBN 0-8304-1303-0 (pbk.)
    1. Afro-Americans—Social conditions—1975– 2. United States—Race
relations. 3. Elite (Social sciences)—United States.
    I. Title.
E185.86.B379 1991
305.896'073—dc20   91-12016
                                                CIP

Manufactured in the United States of America

10 9 8 7 6 5 4 3

This book is dedicated to
The Reverend Ella Mae Bennett

and to the memory of my mentors and friends,
K. Z. Chavis
Josie Mae King
Mildred Williams

Contents

Foreword

The effects of racism on Afro-Americans have been the subject of numerous writers, each of whom had a unique story to tell. However, in limiting their focus to the Black underclass, each of their stories has been incomplete, a mere fragment of the ongoing saga of what it means to be Black in America. In this volume, Lois Benjamin, in relating the racial experiences of the Talented One Hundred, tells the story of the Black elite and, in so doing, completes that saga.

In this original approach to the study of Black professionals, the author challenges the widespread notion that the Black elite, by virtue of their achievements, transcend the barriers of racism. She argues very forcefully that racism, as both an individualized and institutionalized phenomenon, permeates the lives of all Afro-Americans, regardless of social strata. In identifying the subjects of her study, she has utilized the traditional objective measures of success. What sets her work apart, however, is that she analyzes the effects of the subjective components of racism on objective success.

As a departure from the usual sociological treatises on racism in America, Lois Benjamin's book is a major contribution to sociological scholarship. As a documentation of the individual experiences and the collective experience shared by the Black elite, this work helps to complete the history of the Afro-American experience in this country. As a delineation of successful strategies for coping with racial oppression, the book is a source of inspiration to all Afro-Americans in our arduous journey toward self-realization, freedom, and equality in a racist society.

Finally, for those of us who, like Lois Benjamin's Reverend Ross, have found that our stories are too much to tell and that there is not enough time to tell them, through Lois Benjamin, the voices of the Talented One

Hundred have told them for us. Lois Benjamin, bearer of the flame, keeper of the charge, has related these stories with extraordinary insight, exceptional intensity, and uncompromising clarity.

William R. Harvey, *President*
HAMPTON UNIVERSITY
HAMPTON, VIRGINIA

Acknowledgments

First and foremost, I would like to express appreciation to the members of the Talented One Hundred for their cooperation and participation in this study.

I would also like to thank the following people who offered their support during some phase of this project: Jacqueline Y. Robinson, Minabere Ibelema, Barbara J. Harris, Edward Rice, Willie J. Washington, Anne Steiner, Janet L. English, Lisa Richards, Joyce Ladner, Mary-Ann Williams, Joan Bankhead, Don Fugate, and James Maynard.

I am appreciative of the support and the helpful comments of Barbara and Charles Martin-Stanley. They always found the time to listen when I needed it the most. I am particularly grateful to Barbara who spent numerous hours assisting in the editing process.

I am indebted to the following persons for taking time from their busy schedules to read drafts of this manuscript. Their constructive and helpful comments improved the work. I always appreciated the candid comments of my friend Joyce Essien. I have learned much from our friendship. I thank my colleague, friend, and former professor Bob Blauner for his careful reading of several drafts of this manuscript and his suggestions for improving it. I also appreciate the helpful comments and suggestions from Arlie Hochschild, colleague, friend, and former professor, who provided invaluable insights and suggestions. I wish to thank Elizabeth Morgan for her warm friendship and support throughout this project. She always managed to say the right words at the appropriate moment to keep me focused. Elizabeth made several suggestions for improving the draft.

I am especially indebted to James B. Stewart, my colleague and dear friend, who has gone beyond the call of duty to lend his support to this project. He has spent countless hours of his time and energy to provide technical assistance, guidance, and support for this work. I am grateful to him for reading several drafts of this manuscript and his suggestions for reorganization. He was always critical, yet extremely supportive. His suggestions improved the manuscript. I consider our friendship invaluable.

I equate the process of writing a book with the birthing process. After several interruptions with the typing, I owe a special gratitude and heartfelt thanks to Frances H. Hawkins for salvaging the manuscript and delivering it in fine form. She took on this project at a difficult time with grace, charm, and wit. She was committed and dedicated to its completion. Not only did I find a superb typist and editor, but also a friend.

To my editor, Dorothy Anderson, who exhibited such patience and understanding during this lengthy undertaking, I say "thank you." She gave constructive criticisms, yet, at the same time, was sensitive to the author's prerogative.

Finally I would like to thank my family members for their support and encouragement throughout this project.

Prologue

Rudy's calm exterior did not mask the pain in his eyes when he spoke in disparagement, "Somebody ought to tell the story of what it is like for a Black professional in this society." Earlier that week, Rudy, a highly respected therapist in the Tampa community, appeared as an expert witness in court to testify on the state of a client's mental health. The judge ignored him, dismissing his testimony. Rudy is Black. The judge is White. His remarks struck a resonant chord, echoing my own experience as the only Black professor in the history of the University of Tampa. As we parted from a luncheon engagement on that hot and hazy summer day of 1978 in Tampa, I wondered if there were a tale to tell of two Black experiences.

In 1978, William Julius Wilson published *The Declining Significance of Race,* telling another tale. In the opening chapter of this award-winning book from the American Sociological Association, he claimed, "Race relations in America have undergone fundamental changes in recent years, so much so that now the life chances of individual Blacks have more to do with their economic class position than with their day-to-day encounters with Whites."

A plethora of academic studies seemed to support Wilson's claim, telling the tale of the objective successes and strides of the Black elite. There has been a dearth of studies, however, telling the tale of the subjective aspect of their successes. One tale was of the objective economic and educational gains made by Blacks; but there was another tale pleading, like Rudy's, for a listening post and asking questions like: What does it mean to be a marginal Black elite poised between two social worlds of class and race? What psychological roadblocks do Blacks have to overcome to "make it" in this society? What are the sociopsychological costs of mainstreaming for successful Blacks? Are there achievement-related stresses that are caused by the marginality of Blacks who are more structurally integrated in society, and if so, how do they manifest themselves? What are the mechanisms adopted by marginals in handling stress? How do styles of adaptation shape values, attitudes, and behaviors toward personal, class, and racial identity? Do high achieving Blacks experience race relations differently than those from the working class or the underclass? How do high achieving Blacks cope with racism?

Rudy's comment sparked questions about the subjective component of Blacks' success, adding a racial dimension to my own evolving interest in objective success. The pain in his eyes was indelibly etched in my consciousness, leaving no doubt that there was another tale to tell. I promised myself that day in 1978 that I would tell the collective Rudys' story of "what it is like for a Black professional in this society."

It seems a perpetual interest of mine to understand why some individuals overcame economic and psychological barriers to achieve objective success and others did not. The seed of this intellectual odyssey had been sown many seasons ago; however, the racial dimension was not primary. My friend and colleague Josie King remembers the idea fermenting during the early spring of my graduate days at the University of California, Berkeley, in the late sixties. Another colleague and friend, Elizabeth Morgan, saw some seeds sprouting in my dissertation's chapter, "Isolation and the Professional Black Woman," and concluded it was unfinished.

By 1980, race emerged as an important subjective variable in understanding the success of the Black elite. My own visceral and wrenching encounter with racism at the University of Tampa validated this interest. I wanted to tell the story of Black achievers in higher education. I shared my interest with James B. Stewart, a colleague and friend, whom I met in 1981. We considered a collaborative effort, and we scattered a few seminal grains; however, they never germinated.

During the holiday season of 1984–85 while I was visiting my family in Atlanta, the course of my long mental journey changed. I was connecting with friends to extend greetings, and I wanted particularly to greet an old college chum's mother and to inquire about Sheba [a pseudonym]. During our undergraduate days at Clark College, Sheba and I spent many hours searching for answers to life's complex questions in the philosophies of Martin Buber, Albert Camus, Martin Heidegger, Soren Kierkegaard, Plato, Bertrand Russell, and Jean-Paul Sartre, and in the writings of James Baldwin, W.E.B. Du Bois, Malcolm X, Betty Friedan, and Simone de Beauvoir. We were pioneer feminists. We were freethinkers, the gadflies of the campus. Sheba was more radical than I was in her philosophical search. She explored the Eastern philosophy of Zen Buddhism, hoping one day to reach Nirvana, a peaceful state of existence. I, sticking more with the collective consciousness of the day, read Emile Durkheim, the father of scientific sociology.

We "floated" on ideas, as we often said. But we dreamed also about academic success and "making it" in this society. We wanted to get our Ph.D's by twenty-five and write books. Though Sheba and I dreamed about success, she frequently expressed a haunting and lurking fear that she would return as a catatonic schizophrenic to the then neatly kept housing project near campus in which she had grown up. I brushed off her fear as another one of Sheba's numerous anxiety antics. I knew Sheba would be the brighter star.

After college, Sheba went to graduate school in Canada, feeling race relations there would be more tolerable. I chose Berkeley. We kept in touch frequently by long letters and occasional visits. She liked Canada during her first year. But she did not fare as well during her second year in the Ph.D. program in experimental psychology. Sheba reported racial incidents, and she grew angrier and more bitter in each letter. Finally, she flunked out of graduate school, blaming her White professors for her failure. She left Canada and entered another Ph.D. program in the same field at a university in the Northeast. Interestingly, she had chosen experimental psychology over developmental psychology; to Sheba, dealing with rats rather than humans would lessen her encounters with racism. She was singing in harmony with her new university, the professors regarding Sheba as a promising student. But soon her happy harmony with the university was disrupted. When a professor discovered she had been a Ph.D. candidate at another university, Sheba was dismissed from the program. She had misinformed the university about her previous studies in Canada. She returned to Canada, an embittered young woman, singing a sad refrain. In a final letter before leaving North America, she wrote, "Another racial blow I've suffered. I am so paranoid of Whites, I can't bear to see their frozen faces." The soil of North America had produced another bitter fruit. She married and left for Nigeria, hoping that the Motherland would extend an embracing arm and offer protection from racial strife in her womb. Eventually, she obtained a Ph.D. in experimental psychology at a university in England, returning to Nigeria as a college professor.

Although our friendship grew more distant over the years, occasionally I contacted Sheba's mother while in Atlanta. One joyous Christmas Eve, I dialed her phone and a distant, abrupt, and barely audible voice answered. I asked to speak with Mrs. Martha, Sheba's mother. The stranger mumbled, "She's not here." There was a slight hint of familiarity in the voice. "Is this Sheba?" I asked. "No, no." The phone clicked, a song of silence. I was baffled. Later that evening, I called again. Mrs. Martha answered the phone. I reported the strange scenario. She said Sheba had suffered a mental breakdown in Africa and had returned to the United States four months earlier. She asked if I could come by to see them. I agreed.

With my sister, Pat, I approached Mrs. Martha's apartment, recalling fond memories of the daily lunchtime debates and discussions Sheba and I had there. I remembered the neatly painted housing project of the sixties with it's well-manicured lawns and flowers lacing the borders. They had disappeared, replaced now by debris and barren earth, as if swarms of locusts had descended upon the green. I wanted to avoid becoming mired in this murky Georgia clay. We entered the small apartment.

My visit with Mrs. Martha was warm. I was unable, however, to connect with Sheba. How prophetic her fear! She sat in a catatonic stupor on a well-worn sofa. Her eyes were glazed. Where had the gleam in her eyes gone? Was this the Nirvana she sought? Other times, Sheba would pace the floor and mumble incoherently. Between snatches in our conversation, Mrs. Martha would shake her head. When our eyes met, hers pleaded for my help. I looked away, feeling helpless at seeing this brilliant mind lying wasted in a barren housing project, wondering if it were here many seasons ago, when the earth was green and fertile, that the seeds of my long intellectual odyssey were sown.

Pat and I left, driving in silence against the backdrop of *Silent Night,* the Christmas carol, playing softly on the radio. I went to bed knowing, "There, but for the grace of God, go I."

I paused mentally in my long journey to ponder this milestone and to search for my next guidepost. It read, "Let Sheba be the motivation and charge for your mission to tell the story. Learn the lessons of how the marginal Black elite have succeeded in the face of racial adversities and have continued to move forward—keeping their eyes on the prize and remaining active keepers and fanners of the flame. Each generation must be flamekeepers of these race lessons and stories, passing on the flaming torch."

I was still musing over this mysterious guidepost when my eyes caught a glimpse of another signpost by the roadside marked, "DO NOT ENTER! Dangerous Cliff." Had Sheba not heeded the warning sign? She had skated on the cliff of marginality all her life across three social worlds of class, race, and culture and across the three continents of North America, Europe, and Africa. But she had always "kept her eyes on the prize," remaining the dreamer.

What, then, betrayed the dream and the dreamer? I searched for the key to this mystery. Was it the lack of a supportive bridge? There were long years of separation from family, friends, and culture. Had not Mother Africa nurtured her by extending her arms across the waters, forming the bridge? Was it the bitter fruit produced from the racial soil of North America to which she had finally succumbed? Was it the scars from her childhood that took her beyond the cliff? She was born "out of wedlock" and had grown up in a housing project in Atlanta with her mother, a hardworking domestic. Sheba had been a brilliant young woman with a gleam in her eyes. She was dark-skinned with naturally curly, short hair. Her coming of age in America was before "Black is beautiful," a time when she was devalued by the Black community as well as by herself.

Finally, I asked, was it her lack of faith in a higher being? Sheba and I had challenged and overthrown, while at Clark College, our old childhood God of Abraham, Isaac, and Jacob, both claiming we would never set foot in a church again. Though we challenged the form of God and religion, could she not have been comforted by the content and substance that nourished her during childhood and our forebears during slavery and "freedom?"

I had balanced on the edge of the cliff many times. But I hypocritically drew strength from the very genre form and source I rejected. If I felt isolation in the belly of the whale, I sang the old spirituals of my mother as she prepared the daily bread—"Through many dangers, toils, and snares, I have already come. 'Tis grace that brought me safe thus far and grace will lead me home," and "A charge to keep I have." It was my way of escaping the whale. I also played church. I preached my father's sermons and the sermons of other ministers whom I had heard each Sunday, as a child, to my closest friends.

I was particularly fond of making mockery of one of Rev. E. A. Ross's sermons, "I Got a Story to Tell," that I heard when I would occasionally steal away to Antioch Baptist, a little brick, steepled church nestled deep in the wooded clay mines of Dry Branch, Georgia. I was inspired by the stories he told during his sermon and the warm communalism of the annual homecomings. But on that August homecoming in 1978, Rev. Ross was unable to tell his story. The words did not flow from his lips. They seemed choked in his throat. He would punctuate his chokes with a repeated clear calling refrain, "I Got a Story to Tell." For many years, I jokingly laughed at this sermon, not understanding what he was trying to tell that August of 1978. It took me nearly a decade to get the message. Yet, the members heard his choked voice and understood his story—the choir, the deacon board, the deaconess board, the missionary board, the trustee board, the usher board, and the congregation. They responded resoundingly, "Preach on." "Preach, Reverend Ross." "Tell the story." They sang and shouted.

When the unfinished story stopped, and the singing and shouting ceased, Mama Mattie Calhoun and the womenfolk spread the tables near the ancestral burial ground with food taken from their brown cardboard boxes. Perhaps they were symbolically offering their greens, fried chicken, biscuits, potato salad, potato pies, and cakes to their ancestors, knowing it was their nourishment that had sustained them through the vicissitudes of life. For me, this homecoming was as distant as the miles from the more austere A.M.E. church in Atlanta. Yet, it was the spiritual bridge that carried me across until the next homecoming.

Had Sheba not heard the voices of Black women, who were ripped from the soil of the Motherland and who had borne the racial crudities in America, rising from the ancestral burial ground? Had she not heard their voices singing, "Nobody Knows the Troubles I've Seen" and "Sometimes I Feel Like a Motherless Child a Long Way from Home" and rocked her weary soul in the "bosom of Abraham"?

I took a final look at the signpost. In my anger and quiet desperation, I turned to the lore of the Motherland of Africa, asking, "Did some African fetish god cast a spell over Sheba?" There was no answer, only the warning, DO NOT ENTER! Dangerous Cliff. I turned to the flashing message of the guidepost, "You have a charge to keep."

I have kept the charge to learn the lessons of how the Black elite have succeeded in the face of racial adversities and why others, like Sheba, have not.

Though Sheba's family background and psychological constitution might also have been underlying factors that contributed to her emotional collapse, it appears that her preoccupation with racial oppression and her lack of coping skills pushed her over the cliff. With Sheba as the motivating catalyst for telling the stories of the Black elite, I traversed this country for two-and-one-half years, not only spending many hours being a listening post for the stories of the psychic pain of the Talented One Hundred, but also hearing the stories of how they have coped creatively with the duality of their blackness.

This mission produced a rich harvest of stories from the best of the brightest in the race; from the best of the brightest in the nation; and from the best of the brightest in the world. I had promised to tell the collective Rudys' story that summer of 1978 in Tampa. A decade later, in the simmering summer of 1988, and nearly a thousand miles from Tampa, I kept my promise. No grant or farm subsidy helped produce and support this mission crop, only the sustainment of the guidepost's charge and the richness of the harvest.

Ten summer seasons have also passed since that August homecoming in 1978 in Dry Branch, Georgia, when Rev. Ross preached "I Got a Story to Tell." I finally heard his story. Now that I have grown a bit wiser with life's seasons, I understand that there was too much to tell and not enough time to tell it. There were many people who wanted to tell their stories, too, for this study, but there is not enough time to tell them. If somehow I missed your story, perhaps you will hear it from the collective voices of the Talented One Hundred.*

---

*All voices of the Talented One Hundred are not heard in this volume. But those you do hear are representative of my population.

Prologue

At the dawn of the twentieth century, W.E.B. Du Bois declared, "The problem of the twentieth century is the problem of the color-line." The hope of its demise lies with his notion of "The Talented Tenth," thus explaining the derivation of this volume's title.

Method of Data Collection

In collecting the stories of the Talented One Hundred, I have employed, in the tradition of Max Weber, the German sociologist, the hermeneutic approach, an interpretative understanding of social behavior and social history of individuals. I interviewed one hundred highly successful Blacks, using a purposive population. By any objective measures of success—education, income, occupation, and reputation—the Talented One Hundred stand at the apex of the upper-middle class. I chose this population because, first, I wanted a population of Blacks at the highest strata of society in order to test the widespread hypothesis that racism declines as Blacks move upward in North American society. Second, I wanted to avoid the theoretical debate over the definition of middle class and the number of Blacks in the middle class. Third, this population of Blacks would have the broadest contact with a diversity of individuals, groups, and experiences and with the movers and shakers of power in this society and in the international arena. Everett Stonequist, in *The Marginal Man,* believed also that "the life histories of marginal men offer the most significant material for the analysis of the cultural process as it springs from the context of social groups."[1] Though he was referring to Jews, I feel his statement is appropriate to the marginal Black elite in North America.

Although I consulted *Who's Who in Black America* and other references, I relied mostly on personal resources to find distinguished Blacks through professional societies and meetings, on personal contacts, and on strategically placed individuals. With some exceptions, the choice of the population was based on practical and sociological grounds—practical because of its accessibility to me and sociological because of its large representation of middle-class Blacks.

The selected population included Blacks who had obtained success by traditional avenues—having obtained at least a college degree and being gainfully employed and renowned in their professional or managerial specialty and/or their public service. I also included those who followed nontraditional avenues of success—people who achieved local, national, or international distinction in spite of their lack of educational background or income, and those persons who achieved a relatively obscure, but "special feat" in society. Most of the Talented One Hundred, however, had achieved objective success—educationally, economically, and occupationally.

xix

In general, the Black elite of this study had achieved educationally: 32 percent held doctorate degrees; 27 percent held masters degrees; 11 percent held medical degrees; 6 percent held law degrees; 13 percent held bachelors degrees; 7 percent attended college; and only 4 percent had only a high school diploma or less.

The average median personal income of the Black elite was above $50 thousand: 64 percent earned over $50,000; 18 percent earned between $35,000 and $50,000; 12 percent earned between $20,000 and $34,999; and 6 percent earned less than $20,000.[2]

The population represents prominent Blacks in a cross-section of occupations—artists, performers, brokers, financial analysts, doctors, educators, entrepreneurs, journalists, managers, administrators, ministers, lawyers, politicians, public officials, scientists, engineers, and social activists. Although athletes are absent from this population, it is not by choice. Some individuals permitted me to use their names: Jeraldyne Blunden, artistic director and founder of the Dayton Contemporary Dance Company; Dorothy Bolden, president and founder of the National Domestic Workers of America, Inc.; William Holmes Borders, Sr., pastor of Wheat Street Baptist Church in Atlanta, Georgia; Vernon E. Jordan, Jr., partner in the law firm of Akin, Gump, Strauss, Hauer, and Feld and former president of the National Urban League, Inc.; Michael L. Lomax, chairman of the board of the Fulton County Commission; Joseph E. Lowery, president of the Southern Christian Leadership Conference; James Paschal, executive vice president of Dobbs-Paschal Midfield Corporation; Joshua I. Smith, chairman and CEO of Maxima Corporation and chairman of the Commission on Minority Business Development; Bernice Sumlin, educator and past national president of Alpha Kappa Alpha sorority; Yvonne Walker-Taylor, first woman president of Wilberforce University; Vangie Watkins, social activist and community organizer in Atlanta, Georgia; the late Booty Wood, former musician with the Duke Ellington, Count Basie, and Lionel Hampton bands; and Robert L. Woodson, president of the National Center for Neighborhood Enterprise and chairman of the Council for a Black Economic Agenda.

Perhaps the age composition of the population reflects the cohort of individuals who benefited most from the gains made during the Civil Rights movement. Thirty-five percent of the Talented One Hundred ranged in age from thirty-five to forty-four; 33 percent were forty-five to fifty-four; 18 percent were fifty-five to sixty-four; 8 percent were sixty-five and over; and only 6 percent were under thirty-five.

Males are more heavily represented in my population, reflecting the social reality that males, Black or White, are more likely to be represented at the top of the social stratum. Sixty-three percent of the Talented One Hundred are males, and 37 percent, females. I recognize, of course, that recent trends in college attendance are producing larger numbers of Black women with college degrees than Black men. Thus, in the future, we may see a shift in the gender composition of the Black elite.

The population includes individuals from diverse regional and socioeconomic backgrounds. The largest number, 38 percent, came of age in the South; 32 percent grew up in the North Central region; 12 percent grew up in the Northeast; 6 percent grew up in the West; 6 percent came from outside the United States; and 6 percent were highly mobile, living in many sections of the country.

Though some individuals came from privileged backgrounds, most descended from the various strata of the working class; many were very poor. I agree with Sheridan Williams, professor of English at a major university, who expressed it best when she stated, "To discuss poverty is not even interesting when you are talking about the backgrounds of middle-class Blacks."

There is a widespread notion that the upward mobility of Blacks will affect class identity. The new Black elite, unlike the old bourgeoisie, which Frazier criticized as "status seekers in a world of make believe," is interested in acquiring power and the "social, professional, and political attitudes that are more class-linked than race-linked."[3] Traditionally, people in the higher strata of society identify with the Republican party; however, Blacks have been heavily represented in the Democratic party since Roosevelt's New Deal. In my population, this pattern prevailed. Most individuals, 67 percent, were registered Democrats, and only 5 percent were Republicans. Twenty-six percent declared themselves as independent, yet they voted overwhelmingly for Jesse Jackson in the 1988 presidential primary and for the Democratic candidate in the 1984 presidential race. Two persons were members of a third party.* In a survey of nine hundred Blacks, the Joint Center for Political Studies found that 54 percent were strong Democrats in 1984, but only 41 percent in 1987. Young Blacks between eighteen and twenty-nine were more likely to vote Republican.

In collecting the data, I used an in-depth, open-ended structured interview schedule. Because of the sensitive nature of the information I sought, a questionnaire was most inappropriate for obtaining the desired responses. I took advantage of the pilot survey approach because it affords the researcher the opportunity and the flexibility to reformulate and redirect the research as new information is obtained. The formal interviews lasted an average of two-and-one-half to three hours, often longer. They were taped. But for some individuals, the informal interviews continued for many hours, yielding more fruitful insights.

---

* A detailed summary of the Talented One Hundred's social background characteristics can be found in Appendix B.

I interviewed the Talented One Hundred in a variety of settings: their offices and my office; their homes and my home; and their hotel rooms and my hotel room. I interviewed one person in a car, while he was making his rounds of business appointments, and another at a recreational park, while we were walking along a railroad track. Although the individuals lived in many parts of the country, I conducted the interviews in the following states: California, Georgia, Kentucky, Ohio, Maryland, Virginia, and the District of Columbia. I conducted all the interviews with the exception of three. Two were done by colleagues of mine whom the interviewees trusted, and one was a taped self-interview. I promised the Talented One Hundred that their interviews would be confidential and that I would protect their anonymity. Consequently, I personally transcribed nearly two hundred ninety-minute tapes. The real names of people are not used in this book, except for those who gave their permission.

I must point out the limitations and strengths of my purposive population. First, the population should not be considered representative of all professional Blacks. However, it does contain a cross-section of professional Blacks, and thus their experiences are valid for that category. I agree with Glazer and Strauss that it is not necessary to "know the whole field" or to have all the facts "from a careful random sample" in order to discover phenomena of importance.[4] Representative survey studies of the Black middle class, like that produced by Bart Landry, offer a skeletal portrait of their objective achievements and a statistical portrait of their encounters with discrimination.[5] But those studies do not tell us much about the subjective side of how success is achieved and maintained in a racist society. While such studies focus on the structural effects of racism, they neglect its psychological impact. This psychological emphasis would require in-depth interviews, which differentiates my approach from scholars like Landry. Hence, my study is designed to contribute to understanding the psychological impact of racism on the Black elite by adding flesh and blood to the skeletal bones of survey studies.

Second, my population may be inherently biased because it includes only those persons willing to share their feelings, thus differentiating in some way those who are unwilling or unavailable to be interviewed. Third, the literature clearly points out the inherent limitations of self-reporting. The interview subject may distort reality, giving the interviewer answers that he or she wants to hear. I attempted to circumvent these limitations by using check questions to measure the Talented One Hundred's privately expressed attitudes and behaviors on the one hand and their publicly expressed ones on the other.

Despite these limitations, I hope that this study will serve as a catalyst for further investigation into the micro-dynamics of marginality and the psychological impact of racism using a more scientific random population.

The interview process, which took place between December 1985 and April 1988, in itself was revealing and thus merits comment. The cooperation from the Talented One Hundred was ideal, or as was appropriately expressed by a colleague, a "researcher's dream." Having been insured anonymity and confidentiality, they very willingly discussed candidly and openly their marginal statuses, their encounters with racism, and their feelings and responses to it.

I got beyond the mask. I know this because 35 to 40 percent of the Talented One Hundred cried, their voices quavered or changed emotional octaves, and their eyes filled with tears. They took long pauses to reflect. They laughed. I laughed, cried, and paused with them. They entrusted their emotions to me. I accepted them as sacred trusts. The Talented One Hundred described the interview as therapeutic, most indicating they had never had an interview like this one, nor ever told anyone before about a particular behavior, emotion, or event. Many recommended colleagues and acquaintances for participation in this study. When I had a four-hour interview with a well-known sociologist, I mentioned that I saw a social pattern emerging and felt I could stop at seventy-five people. He responded, "Don't deprive twenty-five people of this experience." He also expressed amazement that I had made contact with people in such high-ranking positions, feeling that this project could only have been undertaken by an ambassador's daughter, a well-known person's daughter, or an eminent social scientist. I responded, "Like yourself?" He smiled and nodded affirmatively.

Initially, when I started the interviews, I was surprised when individuals cancelled important appointments or extended the initial time given, thinking it was an idiosyncratic occurrence. By the end of the interview process, it was the norm. I wrote letters thanking them for their participation. Again, I was surprised when I received responses. One public official wrote, "I thoroughly enjoyed being interviewed by you last week. I have concluded the interview process was at least as much an educational experience for me as it was a source of research for you."

For many, the interview was a process of self-discovery and self-validation. Numerous individuals apologized for or seemed embarrassed about their feelings and beliefs toward racial attitudes and experiences. Often they wanted to know if others among the Talented One Hundred shared them. I validated their experiences, encouraging them to continue their story.

Many individuals are uncomfortable in talking about their racial feelings and behaviors, because they believe they are the only ones who feel that way or respond that way toward racism. The collective therapeutic interviews, therefore, show how their racial life history is a shared experience and is an integral part of the social fabric of the society. The way racism operates, then, is to individualize their experiences, and thus give real meaning to the concept of institutional racism. Perhaps this is the reason why William J. Wilson had a different tale to tell when he wrote *The Declining Significance of Race*. He and others missed the subjective component of institutional racism, because they lacked an experiential data base.

The Black elite experience race on an individual level, but it is a shared experience that has particular characteristics for people who are linked to society in a certain economic way. What emerged out of these life histories of successful Blacks was that they had achieved objective success—all the trappings of prestige, status, and positional power—yet it was a tenuous success. Everpresent was the subjective component of racism, reminding them of the precariousness of objective success. Despite their statuses, privileges, and successes, they were still Black in a racist society. This emphasis on the individual aspect of racism was shifted to the objective institutional aspect of racism in the sixties, thus minimizing the individualization of racial experience and the impact of its psychological damage. It is important, therefore, to see the linkage between individual and institutional racism. Hence, I shall redefine the concept of racism to incorporate both dimensions.

Toward a Redefinition of Racism

Before the late sixties, scholars focused primarily on a prejudice-discrimination model to explain race relations in the United States. The emphasis on prejudice was particularly central to earlier works of prominent psychologists and sociologists.[6] The prejudice perspective emphasized the unfavorable attitudes directed at an out-group because of real or alleged physical or cultural characteristics, while discrimination stressed the overt, unequal, and unfair treatment of an out-group member because of his or her alleged physical and cultural characteristics. This model views racism as more individualistic, episodic, random, subjective, and personal, and its effects are intended to harm.[7]

After the late sixties, Stokeley Carmichael and Charles Hamilton, in *Black Power*, expanded the focus from prejudice-discrimination to institutional racism—a pattern of racism that is embodied in the policies and practices of the folkways, mores, legal structures, and bureaucracies of social institutions that have an intentional and unintentional differential and negative impact on people of color. The following example from Carmichael and Hamilton's *Black Power* illustrates the differences between the two perspectives:

> When White terrorists bomb a church and kill five Black children, that is an act of individual racism. . . . But when in the same city—Birmingham, Alabama—five hundred Black babies die each year because of the lack of

proper food, shelter, and medical facilities, and thousands more are destroyed and maimed physically, emotionally, and intellectually because of conditions of poverty and discrimination in the Black community, that is a function of institutional racism.[8]

The concept of institutional racism, unlike the prejudice-discrimination model, shifts the focus from the individual to the system. Its effects are more covert, more systematic, more routinized, and more objective and impersonal. Its effects to harm are both intentional and unintentional.

Institutional racism has remained, since the late sixties, the dominant explanatory model of race relations among academics. However, this emphasis should be refocused to give appropriate recognition to individual racism. This redefinition of racism calls into question previous assumptions that individual racism is more individualistic, overt, episodic, random, and intentional. While these features may be more characteristic of its mode of operation, individual racism, like institutional racism, has a shared component.

Individual racism focuses more on the subjective and personal—the shared patterns of behaving, feeling, and thinking on an individual level; institutional racism stresses the objective and impersonal—the shared structural and organizational patterns on the group level that differentially affect the life chances of people of color. Hence, the subjective and objective patterns are both institutionalized; both operate as part of the basic fabric of society.

In some cases, institutional racism may be mediated through an individual, and the victim of racism may experience it as an act of the individual; however, it is really an institutional phenomenon. For instance, a personnel director acts as an agent for a major corporation which might have an explicit or implicit policy not to hire Blacks. The victim of this discriminatory policy does not have the knowledge or the empirical reference frame to separate the organizational policy from the individual act. It is, therefore, important to continue to emphasize individual racism, because although the implicit or explicit policy is embedded in the organizational structure and affects Blacks collectively, it is experienced on an individual level. Thus, the two concepts are integrally linked.

During the past twenty years, scholars have ignored the tradition of such writers of African descent as W.E.B. Du Bois, Frantz Fanon, and Albert Memmi, who stressed the subjective and psychological impact of racism. These scholars focused instead on racism's structural component. The study of objective racism, as Memmi said about psychoanalysis and Marxism in *The Colonizer and the Colonized,* "must not, under the pretext of having discovered the source or one of the main sources of human conduct, pre-empt all experience, all feeling, all suffering, all byways of human behavior, and call them profit motive or Oedipus complex,"[9] or, in this instance, I say institutional racism.

A dual heritage is common among people of color. It is the perennial Achilles heel of the oppressed. Du Bois, Fanon, and Memmi were cognizant of the conflictual nature of the dual heritage among the oppressed and the impact of its psychological damage.

Du Bois, an African-American scholar, saw this duality as a universal phenomenon that affects "the collective psyche of peoples of African descent."[10] For African-Americans, the conflict emanates from their identity as Blacks and as Americans. Du Bois, writing in *The Souls of Black Folk* at the beginning of this century, called it the double-consciousness.

> The Negro is a sort of seventh son, born with a veil, and gifted with second-sight in this American world,—a world which yields him no true self-consciousness, but only lets him see himself through the revelation of the other world. It is a peculiar sensation, this double-consciousness, this sense of always looking at one's self through the eyes of others, of measuring one's soul by the tape of a world that looks on in amused contempt and pity. One ever feels his two-ness,—an American, a Negro; two souls, two thoughts, two unreconciled strivings; two warring ideals in one dark body, whose dogged strength alone keeps it from being torn asunder.[11]

For Fanon, a West Indian scholar, the duality arises from cultural differences. "The Black man has been given two frames of reference within which he has had to place himself. . . . His customs and the sources on which they were based were wiped out because they were in conflict with a civilization that he did not know and that imposed itself on him."[12] For Memmi, a Tunisian writer, the source of the conflict is inherent in the language. "Possession of two languages is not merely a matter of having two tools, but actually means participation in the two psychical and cultural realms. Here, the two worlds symbolized and converged by two tongues are in conflict; they are those of the colonizer and the colonized.[13] He views the middle-class colonized as suffering the "most from the bilingualism," feeling that the "intellectual lives more in cultural anguish."[14]

Du Bois, Fanon, and Memmi suggest that the duality can lead to identity confusion and inherent contradictions—the collective psychological damage done by racism. It is time, therefore, to return to the study of race relations in Du Bois, Fanon, and Memmi's tradition. A redefinition of racism, whether it takes place on an individual or on a collective level, must take into account that it is institutionalized and has a subjective and an objective component. The subjective component incorporates the shared psychological effects of racism—affective, behavioral, and cognitive—on the individual. The objective component includes the structural effects of racism and its differential life chances on the group. Perhaps the empirical outcry that rose from critics of William J. Wilson's *The Declining Significance of Race* was not so much that he had missed the empirical mark; rather, he had not targeted the pain, and the cry was more a primal scream.

Racism Defined

Racism, as I define it, is a process of justification for the domination, exploitation, and control of one racial group by another. It incorporates a set of attitudes and beliefs to support the dominant group's discriminatory behavior. Racist dominance is institutionalized, multi-faceted, and all-encompassing. It aims to control the cultural, economic, educational, political, legal standing, emotional and physical health, and the sexual and social interaction of the oppressed group. Racism manifests itself intentionally and unintentionally, covertly and overtly, individually and collectively, and subjectively and objectively. At its root, and sustaining its myriad occurrences, is the unwavering belief that the definers (most powerful group—members of a socially perceived category within a nation-state) are inherently superior by virtue of their shared biological characteristics.[15]

In this definition, the key notion is that racism is a power relationship. It is exercised by the oppressor over the oppressed within a nation-state—the institution that claims a monopoly of the legitimate use of force within a given territory. Members of the oppressor group are the victimizers who derive privileges and benefits from the racial arrangements within the nation-state based solely on their membership in that category. Members of the oppressed group, on the other hand, are the victims who are accorded differential and unequal treatment from that arrangement, based solely on their membership in that category. The oppressed group has an imposed identity by the oppressor group and a sense of place in the social order.

What emerges out of this definition is a re-elevation of the psychological impact of racism. This definition helps us not only to look at the obvious victims of racism, such as William Julius Wilson's study on the underclass,[16] but also to examine the psychological impact of racism on the entire population victimized by it. Previous studies have focused on the psychological impact of racism on the underclass but have ignored the Black elite. This study is intended to close that knowledge gap.

Chapter 1, "The Color Line as Reality: Race Lessons, Patterns, and Propositions," shows how the Black elite's experiences have been shaped by race, not by the means of production. This chapter takes issue with most Western Marxists who treat race as an epiphenomenon of society. It shows that race is an important stratifying feature in this society. Blacks experience racism across class boundaries; though the experience might be different, it is still tied to the function of racism in this society. Hence, race cannot be a class phenomenon, because, in the Marxist sense, class is a collective experience reducible to the underlying social relations of economic production.

Although the reality of the color line is experienced on an individual level by the Talented One Hundred, there is a shared social fabric connecting the threads of these personal life histories. The reader will see these threads in the lessons, patterns, and propositions about the nature of the Black experience that may also help Blacks to cope.

Chapter 1 notes further that there is a dual value orientation in American society. While there is adherence to democracy, freedom, equality, individualism, progress, achievement, and success, there is also an acceptance of racism and group discrimination. Blacks are victims of these conflictual value orientations and the resulting actions emanating from them. On the one hand, Blacks have internalized the values of competition, democracy, freedom, equality, hard work, individualism, success, and achievement. On the other hand, they have overwhelmingly rejected, albeit to varying degrees, racism and group discrimination at the affective, behavioral, and cognitive levels. This dual value orientation is a source of conflict for the Black elite. They expend much energy trying to balance conflicts and concerns around issues like: universalism versus Black pride, Afrocentrism versus Eurocentrism, and individualism versus collectivism.

Chapter 2, "Manifestations of the Color Line: The Impact of Violence," focuses on the psychological impact of racism on the Black elite. This chapter shows how racism individualizes rather than objectifies their experiences. Using the universal value of individualism to contextualize the racial experience of people of color denies that there is a collective component to it. Hence, the psychological damage done by racism individualizes the experiences and focuses the problem on the individual.

This chapter also looks at how the oppressor group employs violence and three devices of power—control, dominance, and exploitation—to maintain its racial privileges and a sense of place for the oppressed group. The concept of violence is examined from a Fanonian perspective, which includes physical and psychic violence. Within the broader cultural and social arena, different realms of activities where racism operates are examined, such as: education, economics, the media, housing, and sexual interactions.

Chapter 3, "The Color Line Across the World of Work," looks at the shared racial experiences of the Black elite in the profit, public, and nonprofit sectors of the economy. This chapter notes that since the Civil Rights movement, the Black middle class has made great strides into the mainstream sector of the economy. However, these gains have been tempered by continuous battles with racism in the workplace.

Chapter 4, "The Color Line Across the World of Academe," focuses on the shared racial experiences of Black academicians in higher education. While the Black elite in academia have made gains since the sixties, they continue to face an uphill battle with racism which affects their quality of life and their retention in the halls of ivy.

Chapter 5, "The Color Line in Social, Religious, and Family Life," deals with the shared racial experiences of the Black elite away from the world of work. This chapter addresses the impact of social isolation on Blacks who live in predominantly White environs. It shows how living in a predominantly White setting can disrupt Black professionals' traditional mutually supportive familial, friendship, and organizational ties that could buffer them from their stress. This chapter also examines how they cope with isolation.

Chapter 6, "Gender Politics—Through the Eyes of Black Women" focuses on the Black professional woman and her experiences with racism and sexism. Through the eyes of Black women, we look at the issue of sexism and racism in their interactions with White men; the issue of racism in interactions with White women; and the issue of sexism in interactions with Black men. I also examine the psychological consequences of the double jeopardy of sexism and racism.

Chapter 7, "Styles of Coping," discusses the variety of shared personal and collective modes of coping on and off the job. Individuals who internalize their negative racial experiences, for instance, are more likely to see their failures as personal inadequacies. Individuals who recognize race as a reality are more likely to incorporate it as a factor in their interactions and to find meaningful ways of coping—by externalizing racism and organizing others to combat it.

Chapter 8, "Beyond the Color Line: An Alternative Vision," views the Black elite as players not only in the arena of the United States but also in a global context. This chapter focuses on duality as a stimulus in the creative process. Having a dual consciousness gives the Black elite a special way of viewing the world and a special sensitivity to the plight of oppressed peoples of the world. Thus, this chapter addresses the Black elite's views on such global issues as: global racism, human rights, and nuclear disarmament. The Black elite look at these issues primarily from an Afrocentric perspective, which emphasizes, for instance, human needs over military defense. The failure of Whites in America to benefit from the Afrocentric perspective results in a high cost to them.

Appendix A, "Exemplary Visionaries: A Candle of Collective Consciousness and Collective Action," offers four life histories of individuals from the Talented One Hundred who demonstrate a strong collective consciousness and who serve as change agents for collective action in moving beyond the color line.

ONE

The Color Line as Reality: Race Lessons, Patterns, and Propositions

The history of human relations is filled with the conflicts of peoples of different colors and races. At the conclusion of the Copenhagen Conference on Race and Color in 1965, John Hope Franklin, the Black historian, wrote, "They had learned that the specter of color and race haunts every nook and corner of the world, consuming an inordinate amount of mankind's energies and attention that are so desperately needed to solve the major problems of peace and survival." [1]

The Color Line

The color line is a major dividing reality in the United States. The Civil Rights movement represents an era of personal and collective challenge to end the color line. Jack B. Lane, a forty-seven-year-old public official and a civil rights leader during the sixties, valiantly opposed the old Black and White guardians of the dividing line. "The resistance was not just against the system of segregation and White leadership, but part of it was a revolt against the old guard within the Black community, because people said it would not work," says Lane. Most of the Talented One Hundred, like Lane, were deeply influenced by this movement, believing it signaled the demise of the color line. Joseph Lowery, the sixty-five-year-old president of the Southern Christian Leadership Conference, expressed well the personal and collective aspirations, hopes, and meaning of this era for most participants in this study:

> I felt good about myself. I guess that might have been the greatest victory of all—self-emancipation. We were free at last from inferiority. Those of

1

us who were active in the movement shared that. We were like a snake who had just crawled out of its skin. We just crawled out of that body that cramped us and that kept us fearful and inferior. We lost fear. We lost self-hatred and gained self-esteem, because we had taken our destiny in our hands. We had entered an era of self-determination.

When people stayed off the buses, it was as if to say, You can't imprison me. I don't have to ride your bus. I am free. That movement in the sixties shifted the responsibility for our destiny from others to us. Before that we depended on Congress and the courts. Now we said that it doesn't matter what the courts say; we are not going to ride in the back of the bus. So that was a very liberating experience for us. We felt that we could knock out segregation if we could open up institutions to Blacks— that we could move up into the mainstream and solve the problems of racial discrimination. No question that we were absolutely sure we could do that. Where we were wrong was the problems are deeper than that. While the overt barriers of discrimination removed the embarrassment, humiliation, and dehumanization as factors in our society, discrimination is deeper than separate facilities.

The color line is deeper than separate facilities or unequal education or residential segregation. Arthur Hoppe, an insightful White columnist, whose article appeared in the *San Francisco Chronicle* in 1968 at the height of the Black Nationalist movement, summed it up best when he tells the story of "Little Black Tombo."

Once upon a time there was a little Black boy named Tombo. He was a slave.

"All I want in life," he said, "is to be free, to be equal and to be a man."

Then one day—Hallelujah!—his White masters freed him. "Now that you are free," they said, "you must work hard to be equal to us."

Little Black Tombo nodded. "Yes," he said, "now that I'm free, I must become equal to you so that I, too, can be a man. How do I become equal?"

"The problem," said some Nice White People, "is an educational one. You must get an education. Then you will be equal to us."

So some Nice White People gave him an education. It wasn't easy. It took years and years and years. But at last Little Black Tombo had an education.

"It's funny," said Tom (for, being educated, he had changed his name), "but I still don't feel equal to you."

"The problem," said some Nice White People, "is an economic one. You must have a good job. Then you will be equal to us."

So some Nice White People gave Tom a job. It wasn't easy. It took years and years and years, but at last Tom had a job.

"It's funny," said Tom, "but I still don't feel equal to you."

"The problem," said some Nice White People, "is an environmental one. You must move out of the ghetto into a nice house like ours. Then you will be equal to us."

So some Nice White People gave him a house. It wasn't easy. They had to pass laws saying other White people had to sell him a house whether they liked it or not. But at last Tom got a nice house.

"It's funny," said Tom, "but I still don't feel equal to you."

"The problem," said some Nice White People, "is sociological. You must dress like us, talk like us, and think like us. Then, obviously, you will be equal to us."

So some Nice White People taught him how to dress and talk and think and they even invited him to their cocktail parties.

The hostess would squeeze his hand warmly (though she never kissed him on the cheek). And the men would clap him on the back and ask him his opinion (but only about racial matters).

This time, Tom didn't say much at all. He grew a beard, put on dark glasses, changed his name to Tombo X and shouting, "Black is beautiful," hit the first two Nice White People he saw over the head.

They were, of course, deeply hurt. "After all we've done for you," they said. "Don't you realize you're throwing away everything we struggled together for? Now you'll never feel equal to us."

"It's funny," said Tombo X, smiling, "but at last I feel like a man."

Hoppe concludes that the moral of this story is, "You can think a Black man is free and equal. But first you must think of him not as a Black but as a man." I would add that the moral of the story is that the color line, like sex and class, is a fundamental reality and stratifying principle in this society.

Many scholars have ignored race; particularly, Western Marxists have treated it as an epiphenomenon of society. The dynamics of society are explicable only in terms of class conflict and the mode of production. Hence, racism is attributed to the forces of capitalists. In their view, racism can disappear only after the class struggle has been won. Some scholars, like Martin and Cohen, have rejected this traditional view of race as "vestigial, transitory, and generally a disappearing phenomenon"[2]; rather, they see race as having independent dynamics of its own.

Blacks experience racism across class boundaries. Though the experience might be different, it is still tied to the function of racism in U.S. society. Hence, race cannot be a class phenomenon, because in the Marxist sense class is a collective experience reducible to the underlying social relations of economic production. The Black elite's experiences have been shaped by race, not by the means of production. Thus, the color line is a reality.

In this chapter, the lessons, patterns, and propositions about the nature of the reality of the color line in North America are examined: being

Black is to be conflictual; being Black means watching and walking the tightrope; being Black is to experience the double standard; being Black is to be on perennial probation; being Black is never to be good enough; being Black is to bear the race burden; being Black is to be always in a precarious status; being Black is to be forever in a continuous struggle, personally and collectively; and being Black is to wear the mask. Although the reality of the color line is experienced on an individual level by the Talented One Hundred, there is a shared social fabric connecting the threads of these personal life histories, as we shall see in the lessons, patterns, and propositions.

Being Black in North American Society Is to Be Conflictual

A dual value orientation exists in American society. While there is an adherence to democracy, freedom, equality, individualism, progress, achievement, and success, there is also an acceptance of racism and group discrimination. Robin Williams, Jr., a sociologist, sees the latter two as deviant and contrary to the main thrust of American society[3]; however, racism and group discrimination are the norm and are integral features of the stratification system. Blacks are victims of these conflictual value orientations and the resulting actions emanating from them. On the one hand, Blacks have internalized the values of competition, democracy, freedom, equality, hard work, individualism, success, and achievement. On the other hand, they have overwhelmingly rejected, albeit to varying degrees, racism and group discrimination at the affective, behavioral, and cognitive levels. This dual value orientation of American society is, nevertheless, strongly rooted in the Black elite's psyche, generating a source of conflict and frequently producing strange fruit.

Thus, being Black is to be conflictual in this society. There are many manifestations of this conflict, embodied in what Du Bois called the double-consciousness—the identity conflict of being a Black and being an American. Other scholars have labeled it "double vision," "dual reference group orientation," "biculturality," "diunital," and "multi-dimensional."[4]

The Double-Consciousness Revisited

When I interviewed Bernie Roberts, a prominent social researcher in his mid-forties, he reflected on the omnipresence of the double-consciousness: "The thing which is so discouraging is that when I read Du Bois' writing that he published in 1898, I would still think it is 1898 if you didn't tell me the year it was written, and that's when you feel it's sad. I got on this tie [Bernie Roberts is referring to the fact that taxi drivers in Washington, D.C. ignore him, even when he is wearing a tie], looking nice, and standing in front of the Mayflower Hotel. . . . There are little changes that have occurred now, and that tells me racism is not disappearing."

The duality evolved in Du Bois' novels, reflecting his own personal growth over fifty years.[5] Again, the duality is portrayed differently, depending on the historical and cultural epoch, by writers like Frantz Fanon and his "Manichean world," the never-ending conflict between light and dark in *Black Skin, White Masks,* James Weldon Johnson in *The Autobiography of an Ex-Coloured Man,* Richard Wright in "The Ethics of Living Jim Crow: An Autobiographical Sketch," Roger Wilkins in *A Man's Life: An Autobiography,* and John Edgar Wideman in *Brothers and Keepers.*[6]

Du Bois seems to suggest that the double-consciousness leads to identity confusion and inherent contradictions in the collective psyche of peoples of African descent. Ninety-three percent of the Talented One Hundred also believe it is a problem for African-Americans. Crystal Miller, a professor of theater in the Black Studies department at a major university who is in her late forties, feels, "It presents a divided loyalty of wanting to belong, to love one's country and wanting to be proud of it, but always being somewhat a stranger about one's own experience here. It forces Blacks to choose between [being] Black or American and being forced to choose is destroying part of one's self."

Pat Robinson, a fifty-three-year-old judge, who grew up on the West Coast, knows this dilemma. "When you think of yourself as an American, America doesn't think of you as an American. That's the problem. Sometimes you are forced to go back to your blackness, because America won't let you be an American, even though that's the way I grew up thinking. I am going to be smart. I am going to go to school and make it in society. You get a lot of knocks on your head by Whites in society, reminding you after all you are Black. Everything that's for me isn't for you as a Black. That's the real problem—a 'Catch-22.'"

Though "this system has inequities, it creates the greatest opportunities for the majority of the people. I never thought I would be saying anything like this," remarked Diane Earlinger, a forty-two-year-old pathologist and a manager in a federal agency. Johnson Longworth, a professor of art at a major university in the Midwest, agreed that America offers many opportunities, but he is still not comfortable living in this society. One senses his ambivalence and his poignancy about wanting to love his country and wanting to be proud of it, but his long racial memories have interfered.

I'll never forget that experience when I was in Brazil at an international festival for the arts, where they brought in Black folks from seventeen different countries. And we were in the hotel and different people were talking about their countries. As things developed, a Nigerian said, "I love my country." A Cuban said, "I love my country." A Panamanian said, "I love my country." I couldn't say that, and I have been here all my life. I've accomplished and I've suffered, but I would be hesitant to say I love this country.

There were some among the Talented One Hundred, like Albert Sungist, a sociologist, who remarked that the duality "produces a schizophrenic identity and conflict," the conflict of having to fight for your country during wartime, yet being denied the privilege of full participation as a citizen. To this issue, Teresa Hale responded:

Not since my early impressionable elementary school stage have I really felt pride and patriotism. The rude awakening of the need to constantly struggle for constitutionally guaranteed rights leaves a very bitter taste and a permanent sense of alienation and insecurity. Blacks constantly face issues of racism at home. This reality is so draining that I give little thought and concern for many current international issues that do not impact on my day-to-day existence—notwithstanding the nuclear arms race, the African drought, and South Africa.

Being a Black American, at some level, poses the dilemma of prioritizing being an American and being Black. Like many of the Talented One Hundred, Earnest Ross, a fifty-seven-year-old college professor, stated clearly this dilemma: "Are you an American or are you a Black American? You must decide which is going to come first." He said this choice influences the direction of how his "vote, money, or energy will be contributed."

If you decide to choose being an American, then what you do is act American, even at the expense of Blacks. Sometimes it does come to a choice. I have decided that I am a Black American. I am interested in Black things, Black women, and helping Blacks.

Although most of the Talented One Hundred admitted that they had not consciously reflected on the prioritization of their identity as an American or as a Black, they were constantly reminded of their blackness. For the Talented One Hundred to whom I posed this question, 91 percent identified themselves as Black first and American second.* Although indi-

*Whether we identify ourselves as Black first or American first merely reflects a larger collective and identity clarity issue about what we should call ourselves in America. There appears to be a continuous evolving identity. About every two decades, we change the name of our ethnic identity. In the 1940s, we changed from Colored to Negro; in the 1960s, from Negro to Black; and in the 1980s from Black to African-American. The term

viduals were not asked specifically what it means to be Black or American, they implied that being American means a sense of patriotism, a sense of belonging to this country, and a sense of sharing in the privileges and benefits of this society. For some, being Black meant claiming a geographical and symbolic identification with the continent of Africa and the peoples of African descent. However, for most others, it meant a sense of shared collective consciousness with and responsibility for other Black Americans because of racial discrimination.

The dilemma of choosing our identity is an ongoing process that forces us, as Ross suggests, to decide consciously or unconsciously the direction in which we will expend our energy. Listen to Aretha Shield, a thirty-seven-year-old artist who grew up in an inner city in the Northeast, wrestle with the conflict.

> I think it is terrible to live your life split in halves. For someone who grew up in the sixties, the questions I raise are: Am I going to be a Black artist or just an artist? What will be the content of my art? Will I be a platform for the people, my race? Am I going to go for art for art's sake—enjoying mainstream America? A lot of Black artists find themselves in this predicament which comes out of this double-consciousness. I am one of many Black artists who have this search for identity in our work. What am I going to say? How am I going to talk about this American experience? Every artist has to talk about some experience that is reflected in his art in some way. For the Black American, this double-consciousness comes out vividly. You can see it when you look at Black art. One can visualize this deep internal conflict.

Aretha is referring to the idea that in Afrocentric art, there is usually a positive reflection of the Black experience, even when the subject and message appear negative. Black art, like jazz, is improvisational, and it embodies feelings. But, even though it is improvisational, there is continuity and unity in its forms and expressions.

In her own work, Aretha said, "I thought at one point I had to solve this dilemma. I had to come up with this answer and everything would be clear, and I could be the artist that the Black community wanted. I felt that would be the thing to do; but now I don't think I can solve this dilemma. I go through periods where the dilemma of the Black/White conflict and male/female conflict come out distinctly in my work." At other times, she

---

Afro-American seems to survive through each collective identity crisis. This note is to point out the identity issue, rather than add to the debate.

I should point out, also, that embodied in this collective identity issue are such concerns as whether Afro-American Studies or Black Studies should be called Africology or Africana Studies, or whether Black, when referring to ethnic identity, should be capitalized. I have decided to capitalize Black and White to be consistent.

feels, "I need to balance the pain of that reality. I have to deal with the universal themes of the human condition, because if you cut me, my blood is red like everybody else's. I am a human being first. At this point in my life, I am focusing on universal themes—just the energy of how a flower grows; just the movement of the sky; just a feeling—nothing concrete— where you say this is a man or a woman. I have a need to deal with feelings and often you can't tell what a feeling is. I am first a human being." In focusing on those elements of her basic humanity, she hopes that the feeling will transcend her work, communicating that feeling to all kinds of people. "I am Black and female, and I hope all that will be reflected in my statement. I think that's all I can do. I want to represent the whole planet, not just Blacks. I am part of the world," reflected Aretha, as she reacted to the dilemma of being an African-American.

Jeremiah Moses, a widely respected sixty-five-year-old politician, said the dilemma is "no problem when you place your priority. . . . I am Black and I am American, so I don't see a problem. If you got to worry about whether you are Black first or American first, you have a problem."

Jefferson Barnes, a fifty-one-year-old sociologist at a major university, views the issue as an artificial separation. "I tell my Asian students if they think of themselves as first Asians—Japanese or Chinese—then they haven't been to Japan or China. If you spend some time in Sub-Saharan Africa, you'll know how American you are." For Jefferson, the dilemma is more contextual. "In America, you may feel like you are more Black American, but if you take your butt out of this country, they'll tell you this right away. In the context of this society, most of the time you are going to feel more Black than American. If you live in a White world, they are going to remind you all the time."

Hear Laverne Townson, a forty-three-year-old Black American living in Nigeria, as she groped with her contextual identity. "You look upon yourself as an American in Nigeria, but the minute you are back in America, you think of yourself as Black." Since Laverne, a successful manager of a bank, has lived in Nigeria for many years, I asked, "Do you feel more like a Black American, American, or Nigerian?" She laughed, saying, "In Nigerian society, I tell them I'm Nigerian. But I am American."

Like Laverne Townson, Teresa Johnson, a forty-three-year-old American West Indian, who was born in the Virgin Islands, has a three-way mirror to view the world. "I am West Indian and an American. I grew up as an American West Indian in the Carribean. There is a three-way cross. You are looking at yourself, and you are looking at someone looking at you as a Black person and as a West Indian. A lot of West Indians, even though they are in America, do not want to be here and don't see themselves as Americans."

In contrast to most of the Talented One Hundred, Yvonne Walker-

Taylor, the first woman president of Wilberforce University in Ohio, does not see the duality of being a Black American as presenting a problem. She felt, as 4 percent of the Talented One Hundred did, that she could not separate the two. "We are Black Americans. They go together. It is like asking which comes first—being Black or being a woman. They are so tied together to one another; I cannot separate them. I cannot separate myself from being an American any more than I can separate myself from being a woman. I cannot separate myself from my blackness and have never wanted to do so."

Though 5 percent of the Talented One Hundred claimed their salient identity as American, there is an ironic twist and ambivalence in this claim. Like Walker-Taylor, Joseph Lowery cannot make the distinction of being American or Black. "Both are being assaulted. I am assaulted because I am Black. I am not assaulted because I am an American, but because I am a Black American."

He says, "The problem with America is that we are not allowed to claim it. We are treated like stepchildren so we are without a country. And nobody wanted to claim Africa because of its presentation to Blacks as an 'ignorant, savage, and dark continent.' Now that Africa has been emancipated, we are not Africans, so we can't claim it."

Lowery rejects the Negro National anthem, even though he feels it is "a great Black hymn." "There is only one national anthem and that is 'Oh, say can you see.'" Laughingly, he says, "I can't sing it. The words are despicable and need to be changed, but as long as that is the anthem, it's mine, because America is mine. I am not going to let anybody abrogate my ownership, and I am not going to abdicate it. So it's my country, and the blackness is somebody else's problem."

He continued, "I am Black. I am comfortable with being Black. If the Lord says go back and come again in another color, I would choose Black. The only difference is I'll shave a few years off my seniority [laughs]."

Priscilla King, a social work administrator in her early fifties, also sees herself first as American and would not want to live anyplace else. But when she hears and starts to sing "Oh, say can you see" at a game, she remarks, "It's terrible to say, but I always get a funny feeling, because standing next to you at a game might be a KKK member, [wanting] to burn your house down. It's kind of weird."

When the daughter of Ruth Shelly, a fifty-three-year-old sociologist, decided not to stand for the national anthem at a baseball game, the people around her were angry. They called her names. The names that she was called had reference to being Black, not being unpatriotic.

"There may be racism and all that, but this is the only country we got. When we sing our national anthem and many Blacks sit, it bothers me," said Elizabeth Wright, a college administrator in her fifties who grew up in the South. "I feel a kinship when I stand and sing the *Star Spangled Banner.* If we are going to stay here in this country, we are going to have to relate to it. We are American and we are Black. We can enjoy our heritage and put emphasis on our Black authors, but undergirding all that, we are American. We worked to make this country what it is, and we should be proud to say we are American. I have some strong feelings about that. We need to get up and say 'I pledge allegiance to the flag' and hold up our heads." Elizabeth was initially somewhat hesitant in expressing her patriotism, remembering an incident fifteen years before when friends castigated her for having "little flags for her centerpiece" at a Fourth of July celebration.

Choosing a salient identity as an American or as a Black is one of the many dilemmas of being Black in this society. The decision is a process that invariably affects individual and group identity. The drama of the duality also unfolds in many other themes—class orientation versus race orientation, individualism versus collectivism, materialism versus spiritualism, Afrocentricity versus Eurocentricity, integration versus separation, and Black pride versus universalism.

Class Orientation versus Race Orientation

How does the double-consciousness affect the orientation of Black elite who are moving into the mainstream? Are they likely to adopt a class orientation—to identify more with the White middle class—or a race orientation—to identify more with working-class and lower-class Blacks? When a class orientation and a race orientation coexist, do Black professionals experience them as contradictory?

Martin Kilson, a social scientist, hypothesized that "status deracialization" increases as Blacks move into the mainstream. This upward mobility of Blacks will affect class identity.

> It allows, above all, new milieus to shape class awareness and identity— milieus within which middle-class Blacks derive not mere professional, but also social and political orientations. When reinforced, in turn, by the increasing shift to suburban living among upper-strata Black families . . . we have the essential ingredients of a mainstream Black bourgeoisie.[7]

But does success mean that race matters less? I asked the Talented One Hundred the question, "Would you say in terms of your values, behaviors, attitudes, and life-styles, you identify more with, that is, feel closer to, middle-class Whites or to working-class and lower-class Blacks?" Seventy percent of the participants stated specifically that they identified with the working class. However, many individuals qualified their statements, ad-

10

mitting they had, as Jonathan Mobutu, a forty-year-old director of Black Studies and an economist at a major university in the Northeast, expressed "peripheral White middle-class values, but their core values were working class." In general, they did not mention the lower class. Sixteen percent said they identified with middle-class Whites and 14 percent did not identify with either the White middle class or the Black working class or lower class. They were likely to identify with middle-class Blacks. They indicated that middle-class Blacks were very different from middle-class Whites in their values. Others did not identify with either class; rather, they emphasized their individuality.

This question generated interesting responses. Many of the Talented One Hundred often took long pauses, and I was asked repeatedly to restate the question as if suddenly they had become hearing impaired. When they recognized there were inconsistencies in previous statements, there was an attempt to align their feelings because they did not reflect their beliefs of racial solidarity. One person reminded me that this conflict was reflected in an old folk saying, "They are my color, but not my kind."

Colbert Miller, a thirty-nine-year-old cardiologist, who was still sporting his late sixties Afro hairstyle, delivered a passionate impromptu oration on the disintegration of race pride, the foibles of integration, and the need for race solidarity and empowerment of the masses.

> The worst thing that ever happened to this country is integration. As we progress, we have a tendency to try to assimilate into the other world, and that is why I think it is the worst thing that ever happened to us. It has kept us from progressing as a Black race, because as soon as one of us makes a little money or gets an education, we have a tendency not to support our own institutions, our own people, and our own businesses. People think they are nigger rich,* have achieved, and gotten over. We try to get into the other world, and it doesn't make a difference if you are an M.D., a Ph.D., a lawyer, or a major political figure, we are Black in this society.

When I asked Colbert if he identified with middle-class Whites or working-class or lower-class Blacks, he stated middle-class Whites. He took a lengthy pause and laughed. Continuing, he said, "I would like to theoretically identify with Blacks, but you gave me a group, called lower-class and working-class people on the street, with which I can't identify. I don't say to them I am better than you, but my values do not identify with theirs." Colbert is from a working-class background; his father owned a small restaurant, and his mother worked for many years as a domestic.

---

*The term "nigger rich" connotes a different standard (usually lower) by which wealth is measured in the Black community than in the White community.

11

Zora Neale Hurston, a popular Black folklorist and writer during the Harlem Renaissance, captured well the contradiction between race pride and class orientation in *Dust Tracks on a Road*.

"My people! My people!" From the earliest rocking of my cradle days I have heard this cry go up from Negro lips. It is forced outward by pity, scorn, and hopeless resignation. It is called forth by the observations of one class of Negro on the doings of another branch of the brother in black. For instance, well-mannered Negroes groan out like that when they board a train or bus and find other Negroes on there with their shoes off, stuffing themselves with fried fish, bananas, and peanuts, and throwing the garbage on the floor. Maybe they are not only eating and drinking. The offenders may be "loud-talking" the place, and holding back nothing of their private lives, in a voice that embraces the entire coach. The well-dressed Negro shrinks back in his seat at that, shakes his head and sighs, "My people! My people!" . . . What that educated Negro knows further is that he can do very little towards imposing his own viewpoint on the lowlier members of his race. Class and culture stand between. The humble Negro has built-up antagonism to the "Big Nigger."[8]

This conflict between race pride and class orientation plays itself out in other scenes, for example, successful Blacks who give lip service to supporting Black institutions, as Colbert Miller stated, but support White institutions.

Though race pride and class orientation may be in conflict, they still affect individual and group identity. In a society that values individualism, the collectivism so essential in developing a strong Black community is in opposition to the basic orientation of individualism. There is the inevitable tension between self-advancement and group-advancement.

Self-Advancement versus Group-Advancement

Benson Robinson, a fifty-two-year-old successful entrepreneur, embodied the conflictual drama of the duality. He appeared almost aracial in his orientation. Yet, he said that he identified more with working-class Blacks. He said everyone should be concerned about themselves, and there are too many Blacks on welfare, as well as too many begging in the Black community for his help. His philosophy is, "It is not what is good for Benson Robinson, but what is good for Benson Robinson's business," and "begging is not good for business." Despite his philosophy, he spent $500,000 for Black contractors in 1987 and $3 million in the past eight years. "People put me down because everybody got to have somebody to talk about. If Benson Robinson were not in business, where would people get this money?"

Tony Michaels, a fifty-year-old corporate manager, has a different philosophy. He described himself as a humanitarian and somewhat a "misfit" because he has paid a price for his community involvement. Tony said, "The corporations tell you I really want you to put something back into the community, but what they really measure you by is what you are doing in that corporation—the dollars that you bring to them. There is a tendency to write you off to some degree when you put a lot of effort into community service. They won't admit it, but it's true."

Prince Albert, a sixty-one-year-old artist of West Indian descent, feels "all professionals should be primarily concerned with their own advancement. It is an extra burden on Blacks to be concerned with the masses first and themselves second. It is the nature of people to be concerned with their own advancement. When they have security, they can help others. In the United States, you have the feeling you are replaceable. So, professional excellence and performance have to be paramount. Otherwise you might not have a job. After that, you can afford to be charitable."

Prince Albert's comments point out an additional demand placed upon the Black elite. A strong ethos undergirding the Black community is that the Black elite have a special obligation to assist the masses. This effort requires energy and commitment that conflict with a demanding career and familial obligations. Despite the fact that the Black elite must be exemplary "ambassadors for the race," proving their capabilities and opening doors for other Blacks, they still are expected to serve the community. There are often conflicting community, organizational, and professional goals. One journalist remarked that she frequently felt conflict between her sense of professional responsibility to report bad news about the Black community and her sense of obligation to the Black community. If the Black elite do not appear sensitive to the needs of the Black community, they are often the target of criticism.

Afrocentricity versus Eurocentricity: The Dilemma of the Black Elite

As upwardly mobile Blacks enter the mainstream of American society, they are likely to "confront, at minimum, two options," said James E. Blackwell, sociologist and author of *Mainstreaming Outsiders: The Production of Black Professionals*. They accommodate by adopting the Anglo-conformity model or by adopting cultural pluralism.[9] The former is the dominant group's expectations. The latter model follows the dominant group's Eurocentric expectations in language and values in the world of work and the educational process, but adheres to the Afrocentric view in other aspects of daily interaction, such as musical tastes, styles of worship, and linguistic patterns. Hence, there is always a conflict at the personal and societal level to appropriately balance this tension between the Afrocentric perspective and the Eurocentric perspective. When I commented to Clifford Warren, a prominent surgeon, about his collection of African art, he said, "I like everything Black. Blackness is my orientation. It determines where I live, what I do, and with whom I practice. I like everything Black." His sentence trailed off. Remembering that his wife is White, he looked away, explaining, "I agonized about it and how it is going to be accepted." In contrast, Graham Boston, a forty-four-year-old renowned scientist, prefers to associate, to live, to work, and to worship with Whites. He grew up with Whites in the Northeast and feels more comfortable around Whites than Blacks. But when I asked the probability of his children dating or marrying someone White, he retorted definitely, "No."

Ethel King, a thirty-eight-year-old journalist with a major newspaper, is dating a "Jewish fellow" and has experienced tension about her own degree of blackness. "Am I being a traitor because I am dating this person? Am I going to do less because I am dating this person? You wouldn't have to ask yourself these questions if you were White," said Ethel. She had dated interracially before, but was unable to handle it. However, when she met her present friend, she "liked him so much." Ethel admitted, "I started questioning myself all over again about can I do this. I realized it didn't bother me as much as it used to and that scared me. So I had to question myself about that. When you are Black, you end up doing that so many times. I don't know if a White man would question himself about dating a Black woman. I think the sense of who we are is so tied to our blackness and the Black community and what people think of us."

King added, "If you let it, the Black community will dictate everything about your life—how you write and what you write. If I spend time with this guy, there are going to be people who feel my writing is not going to be valid anymore, because I am writing about the Black experience. They will point to me and say, 'How would you know if you are with this White man?' "

There are innumerable manifestations of tension between Afrocentricity and Eurocentricity. For example, individuals who espouse an Afrocentric perspective may not desire to live in a Black community, fearing their property may be devalued. Their "creed and deed" are generally consistent; yet, inconsistencies arise when they do not want to live in a Black neighborhood, to work with Black people, or to attend a Black college, because they still harbor negative stereotypes of other Blacks, even when that environment has been nurturing. Sometimes people were embarrassed to admit these inconsistencies, and at other times they were so enthusiastic and felt so comfortable that they did not conceal their thoughts.

In general, the type of residency or workplace setting, physical appearance, style of dress, or political persuasion were not consistent indicators of Afrocentricity or Eurocentricity. Jonathan Mobutu believes, "Blacks must be bicultural to be successful, unless they function in either a totally Black or totally White world at all times. Learning to be bicultural is especially difficult for young Blacks. It causes me no specific problem, just inconvenience, because I think I understand how to use biculturality creatively as a tool to fight racism and oppression." Mobutu uses his biculturality creatively when he serves on different committees as a token Black in his university. He views his assignment on these committees as an opportunity to gain an understanding of the governance of the university and how it functions so he can better assist Blacks.

While Mobutu is managing the duality productively as a weapon against racism, over thirty years ago, sociologist E. Franklin Frazier, in *Black Bourgeoisie,* criticized the middle class for its unproductiveness. He castigated the Black middle class of his era for creating "a world of make-believe," centered around Black business and Black society, and hiding their insecurities and frustrations through conspicuous consumption.[10] Since Frazier's scathing indictment, there has been a concern over the consumptive material behavior of Blacks as a compensatory life-style in handling racism. Although material success is an important value orientation in this society, the concern in the Black community seems to be over a life-style of excessive conspicuous consumptive behavior versus a life-style of personal and collective acquisitive wealth to support and build a strong Black community. This crucial distinction is not noted when one hears the outcry that "Blacks are too materialistic."

The Trappings of Class

I asked the Talented One Hundred if they believed Blacks are too materially oriented. Twenty-one percent were neutral, believing that American society was materialistic and the behavior of Blacks was not any different. Vernon Jordan, lawyer and former executive director of the Urban League, like others, felt, "I am not prepared to make a judgment about that. This is a judgment for yourself." On the other hand, 53 percent of the individuals agreed that Blacks are too materialistic, usually offering "compensatory reaction to racism" as an explanation.

Pat Robinson thought, for instance, "Blacks put more into material things than do Whites. They want you to see the couch they are sitting on. It has to do with the Black experience and being somebody. Going into my relatives' neighborhood, you can see one or two new Cadillacs, washed and cleaned in front of their awful houses. That is the only way to be somebody. The kids will throw a rock through the window if you try to fix up the house. You can't advance at work. You can't get status there. It's too late to go back to school and get an education. So what else is there to do?"

Ferdinand Hamilton, an administrator at a large predominantly White university in the Midwest, agreed, saying, "I understand the need to compensate for a lot of inequities. I used to think about that when I went down the dusty roads in Alabama and saw television antennas on dusty shacks. I got to thinking about what else do they have."

Though Jonathan Mobutu agreed with Ferdinand Hamilton and Pat Robinson, he felt "a focus on material trappings is becoming an ideology in its own right. Having a large quantity of these trappings is becoming an end rather than a means. It is becoming a measure of self-worth and success."

Robert Woodson, fifty-year-old founder and president of the Center for Neighborhood Enterprise and former resident fellow at the American Enterprise Institute, agreed with Mobutu, but added that there is danger in this behavior. "There is really a rise in preoccupation with the objects of production, but not the means of production, and that's very dangerous when we begin to enjoy the vision of the harvest without plowing the acre."

Marla Robinson, a forty-three-year-old civil rights administrator, believes we are materialistic; however, unlike others who locate their explanation in the ethos of the American culture, Marla thinks it is a remnant of our African ancestral heritage. "We came from a kingly type environment, and there is a pride that goes way back. We buy the best, because we deserve the best. Before we were slaves, we were kingly, princely, and scholarly, and we had monuments of ivory and gold. Just like the streams, and like their rhythms, there is a pride that flows in our veins."

Although Hosea Kelley, a psychologist, also thinks Blacks are too materialistic, he disagreed with Marla's Afrocentric perspective of materialism. "Materialism is not historically one of our values. It has been one of the destructive values that we've adopted."

In contrast to this view, Jeremiah Moses does not think materialism is destructive. In fact, he believes that materialism leads to an honest work ethic to acquire goods: "I think it is a healthy thing to be materialistic. We wouldn't have so many people satisfied to be not working, because you have to work at it or do something to get it. It's a lot better than going into empty houses, stealing wash tubs and sinks, and carrying them on their backs to get $15."

Earnest Ross also feels that materialism is good. "I think we've had our shot at being too religious because that's all we've been allowed to have. So now we have a chance for a little more, and we acquire it. I don't think we are materialistic enough."

Twenty-six percent of the Talented One Hundred to whom I posed the question disagreed that Blacks are too materialistic. Often they expressed feelings similar to those of Earnest Ross and Jeremiah Moses.

Leo Aramis, a thirty-four-year-old journalist with a major daily paper in the Northeast, concurred that Blacks are not materialistic enough in the acquisition of wealth, making the distinction from consumptive material trappings.

> I don't know what is meant by materially-oriented. I don't think we are materially-oriented enough. I think that when we talk about getting gold chains and driving big cars, we call that materially-oriented. And that is not; it's trappings and a hangover from when we could do nothing else. We couldn't buy a house because they wouldn't sell us one. We couldn't invest in stocks. So the only things they would let us have were big cars. So we had big long cars and little bitty houses. And that's where they get this whole material aspect. We are not materialistic enough. We don't buy land, make investments, and perpetuate wealth for our youngsters. We need to get more materialistic and less boggler-minded.

One concern is the excessive consumption of physical assets and the lack of acquisitive behavior toward financial assets. Another concern is ambivalence about the acquisition of wealth which is deeply rooted in an ascetic Christian ethic that views the accumulation of wealth as morally suspect and is reflected in such biblical admonitions as, "The love of money is the root of all evil," "For it is easier for a camel to go through the eye of a needle than for a rich man to enter the kingdom of God," and, "The meek shall inherit the earth." In the sixties, the rise of the Black Nationalist movement and other radical groups raised the level of consciousness about the inequities in the distribution of wealth in a capitalistic society. Hence, Blacks who were upwardly mobile, acquiring physical and financial assets, were viewed as selling their souls to capitalism or betraying their Black identity.

Jonathan Walden, a thirty-nine-year-old minister and social activist, believes, "There is nothing wrong with having material goods in life. My only caution from a religious viewpoint is those things not be put before God. If God is first, we should be blessed to enjoy all that life has to offer."

John Lamont, a fifty-four-year-old physicist at a major university on the West Coast, sees an even more subtle side to the ambivalence toward wealth that emerges out of a racial ethos that somehow "wealth is not for Black people," noting, "Martin L. King, Jr., once said that the material side has its place. We need wealth in our society. Somehow there is a psychology of equating Black to impoverishment. As we develop in this society, one manifestation will be the wealth of that group. And we will somehow have to come to grips with that wealth as well as maintaining a spiritual identity as Afro-Americans."

The ambivalent values and attitudes toward materialism that evolved out of an ascetic world view of Christianity also has a racial side. On one hand, there is a feeling that wealth is unobtainable for the masses of Blacks; hence, there may be a rejection of the idea, but not the class trappings. Second, in a society that values competitiveness and individualism, there is a belief that Blacks who amass a fortune will forsake their identity and the Black struggle. Joshua Smith, chairman and CEO of Maxima Corporation, the ninth largest Black business in the United States, has captured these contradictions toward wealth among Blacks. He said, "I have witnessed a number of people who have emerged. I have noticed there is an acceptance of a White life-style—having a house in the suburbs and sending their children to private schools. The behavioral pattern of Blacks who reach financial success is that they want to be accepted by other groups. We tend to be less active in the group from which we came."

Even though Joshua is referred to as "that Black millionaire," he sees his wealth as "new wealth—on paper—but not yet established." Yet, he said, people always comment to him, "The thing I like about you, Joshua, is that you haven't changed." "I say, 'What am I supposed to change to?' I always ask them what they mean, and they comment, 'All other people I know when they get important, they change.'"

For Joshua, "wealth is a product of achievement. Wealth is a feeling of reward. Wealth is the satisfaction that I am moving in the right direction, that I am helping and will help others, and that I am making a difference. Wealth is something in time, stage, and manner that I want to achieve."

Joshua has some "basic problems about the subject of wealth and Black people."

There is a definite dogma that wealth is not for Black people. It is very clear. Our politicians talk about the large corporations without any signs or without any beliefs that we could be those large corporations. We talk about the rich as if Blacks will not be rich. Rich people are those people over there. Wealth is something for others. I think it characterizes the problem of Black people in a capitalistic society. I've said in many of my speeches, we live in a capitalistic society in the United States. I didn't invent it and you didn't invent it. It is driven by motivation to achieve wealth, and it is important that we understand that it is a measure of success. Wealth is a factor that permeates all other factors that we are lacking. We have no political clout. Jews have fewer people, but much more political clout. . . .

Wealth is something we have by the way of income. Blacks earn $250 billion a year collectively. This wealth is equivalent to the ninth largest country in the free world. There is wealth in Blacks, but the wealth is not collective. The wealth is individual, and the earnings are masked by debts. We are in debt. We do not own houses. We do not have our money in the market working for us. We do not have real assets. As a result of

18

not having real assets, even though we have the earning power, we have no influence in this country.

In general, the Talented One Hundred perceived their assets as below those of their White peers, but above those of their Black peers. A study by the U.S. Bureau of the Census in 1991 showed that the median White household net worth was ten times that of the median Black household—$43,280 and $4,170, respectively.[11]

Andrew Brimmer, a Black economist, noted that Blacks place more of their money in physical assets than financial assets. This assumption is supported by the fact that 76 percent of the total Black wealth is in homes, motor vehicles, and checking accounts, while the percentage for Whites is 58 percent. Only 11.6 percent of Black wealth is in interest-earning assets, stocks, and mutual fund shares, while 26 percent of White wealth is invested in these ways. Moreover, 56 percent of Black households own no interest-bearing assets.[12]

Joshua feels our ambivalent attitudes toward wealth may interfere with our acquiring it. "It constantly baffles me about why we refer to rich people as they, corporations as them, and wealth as not for us. We seem to bathe in being like our peers and we'll go into great debt just to impress our peers, none of whom have wealth. That seems to be our *modus operandi*. It seems the higher we go, the more debt we go into."

Reflecting, Joshua concluded, "There has to be a basic change when people say I am rich. That's good. What have I done wrong? In other ethnic groups that is why they network for the achievement of wealth."

As we have seen, duality plays itself out in many themes. While it presents a problem, unless the actions of individuals are perceived as a group threat, there is a collective tolerance level for the ambivalence and conflict. Many scholars, however, see the duality as adaptive. Elaine Pinderhuges noted, "While it requires great expenditures of energy and can lead to identity confusion, some Afro-Americans are able to become exceptionally clear about their identity and values."[13] Jefferson Barnes agreed:

It presents both opportunities and problems. The opportunities of marginality give an inside view about one's social existence that transcends the ordinary consciousness. If you have a double-consciousness, you understand those things that other people can't possibly consider. It is what happens to women who are able to see the world of men, but men can't see the world of women. Blacks can see the world of Whites, but Whites can't see the world of Blacks. [Like] any group that is disadvantaged, at any level—because we are human and have mental capacity—we sometimes get more insights into a phenomenon than if we had naked power. Naked power strips our consciousness in many ways. Du Bois was correct about that, but I don't think it should be taken to mean a negative consciousness.

Since "Blacks can see the world of Whites," the duality creates positive and negative charges when walking on racial high wires.

Watching and Walking the Racial Tightrope

"When a Jew enters a room of Gentiles, a Chicano, a room of Anglos, a Black, a room of Whites, there is a common reaction, namely, the minority member will attempt to sense out where there is severe hostility and bigotry," said Johnnetta Cole, an anthropologist.[14] Perhaps this phenomenon explains why American Blacks and Whites continue to differ in their perceptions of the treatment of Blacks. For example, in a Gallup survey of Blacks residing in predominantly White communities, 64 percent of Whites said Blacks in their community were treated "the same as Whites," but only 44 percent of Blacks believed they were treated equally.[15] Cole calls this trait the "minority sense," noting that "minority subculture teaches that one must detect or at least attempt to detect hostile attitudes and behavior in the interest of self-protection—from protection of one's pride and self-esteem to protection of one's life."[16]

Whether this trait is referred to as the "minority sense," the "sixth sense," or the "race watch," as I call it, it is the protective gauge used in navigating the racial tightrope. Many of the Talented One Hundred see race watching as a twenty-four-hour duty.

"You are on guard all the time. You run the risk of being schizophrenic. You always know you are Black, and you are always anticipating White people and how Blacks will react to you," remarked Ferdinand Hamilton. "The society is racist, and you have to figure out how to compete. In order to compete, you have to be by and large better. You have to be more conscious of details than your White peers. You know that people are looking over your shoulder. The same transgressions your White peers might make, you can't afford, because people are envious of where you sit in the first place," said Hamilton.

Agreeing, Jack B. Lane said, "We live in a racist society and we all do maintain a certain guard. Sometimes I may not be conscious of it, but I probably maintain it. I find myself in settings and meetings, and it comes to me every now and then that I am the only person of color there. I say to myself, if I were not here, they probably would be saying something else about Black folks. In my presence, they don't say this about Black folks. They only feel it, but they do not express it." Jack senses this even though he has not heard anything and has been treated cordially.

Walter Calvin, a forty-four-year-old corporate executive with an international conglomerate, grew up in the rural South, and he believes strongly that it has inured him, and other southern Blacks, giving them an edge on the race watch. "I think southern Blacks tend to have a kind of resilience to racism. You are able to almost expect it, see it, and understand it in ways that people who have not grown up in this kind of environment may not be able to catch the signals quite as fast. Once you know it, feel it, and understand it, you do not get preoccupied with it. You move on," says Walter. "You put a shield over one eye saying I know this is my racism eye, and the other eye I am going to keep on the ball in terms of where I am going."

Keeping one eye on racism and "keeping one eye on the ball" seemed to be the *modus operandi* for the Talented One Hundred. Jefferson Barnes learned very early the lessons of navigating between two worlds from growing up in a tough "working-class neighborhood of gangs and violence in Chicago." He was the valedictorian of his class, acting the "perfect gentleman" while in school. But when he left school, he acted tough like some of the gang. "I had the task in my early teens of navigating a real tightrope," he said.

Jefferson told me a story to capture the navigation. He was "captain of the boys," and his teacher, leaving him in charge, instructed him to direct the boys to the library for an assignment when he heard the bell ring. "As soon as she went down the hall, we started acting up and talking about each other's mama. I get up and I am doing my little rap. The class is quiet. I look and there is Ms. Jackson. She says, 'Barnes, I am ashamed of you. You go to the back of the classroom; you are no longer in this row.' From that moment on, my standing with the classroom sky-rockets. I learned don't go too far in that direction to make this tightrope work," he recalled.

It shaped Barnes' view of how you navigate in the world. Learning the rules of the game, he balanced a "cat-like navigational development—a difficult reign," said Barnes. Consequently, when he left his high school that was 99 percent Black and went to a 99 percent White college, he had "gotten so good at tightrope walking and so good at understanding that you had to know how people were coming at you and how they felt that going into the White man's world was one more tightrope walking."

For successful Blacks, walking the racial tightrope is another reality of the color line manifesting itself in many arenas. Marla Robinson talked about the problem of the Black administrator/manager in the world of work. Many Black administrators who head mixed or predominantly White organizations are concerned about the issue of racial balancing, because they are sensitive to discrimination and often fear charges of reverse discrimination by Whites. In her previous position, Robinson recalled, the

Black executive director of a social welfare agency "hired only Whites around her. And when she lost her job, the same people she hired generated a lot of negative publicity about her and were not supportive."

Robinson said that the executive director was "arrogant" and not sensitive to Black issues, indicating she did not need the Black community because she was supported by the Junior League. After her firing, she became very Black and very involved in Black organizations. "She is at all the banquets—the NAACP, the National Council of Negro Women, and the Urban League. When she became the executive director, these organizations were the kind I wanted her to join; they could have saved her. If she had been involved with her people, she could have cried on their shoulders and regrouped. Before her firing, I could not get her to go to a Black church, and she looked down upon Black organizations."

Ned McMillian, a fifty-four-year-old physician, agreed with Marla, saying, "Black corporations are so concerned about discrimination and racial balancing that they'll hire a White over a Black. They go beyond the call of duty to show Whites that they are okay." He thinks other ethnic groups help one another more than Blacks help each other.

John Hubbard, a forty-year-old professor of sociology at a predominantly White university in the Midwest, thinks about "balancing race all the time." Since he is in a tenure-track position, he deemphasizes race, because he doesn't "want to be perceived as a boat rocker or radical." He said, "That makes me not threatening because I don't harp on race all the time." Even one colleague commented to him, "I don't think of you as a Black faculty—just a faculty." He learned to manage race relations by toning down the discussion on the subject, particularly after his White students' evaluations reflected he "talked too much about sexism and racism."

Davis and Watson's *Black Life in Corporate America: Swimming in the Mainstream* noted the stress caused by the perplexity of deciphering race-related behavior.[17] To succeed in the corporate world, one has to skillfully navigate corporate politics and race politics. Listen to Warner Babbitt, a thirty-nine-year-old journalist with one of the most reputable newspapers in the country, discuss balancing "how to play corporate Uncle Tom without making White folks uncomfortable. . . . A lot of Blacks go into corporations blissfully unaware of political and cultural differences. We grow up being taught to carry ourselves with dignity and don't be an Uncle Tom. This is great character building, but it is bad politics in a predominantly White corporation." He thinks Whites Uncle Tom more than Blacks. "I never thought of carrying my superior's coat; to me, that was being an Uncle Tom. To them, it is using common sense. I view it as an attack on my dignity. They view it as getting ahead."

Babbitt believes that corporate Uncle Tomism is a prerequisite in his industry. He had to "figure out how to do the corporate Uncle Tom bit without becoming the Uncle Tom in the traditional sense Blacks view it. . . . You have to study it very carefully, because there is a downside to it. If you try to play the same corporate Uncle Tom as Whites, because a number of White superiors do not see you as on their par, they start seeing you in the traditional role."

There are other issues to balance in the world of work. Thomas B. Thomas, a thirty-eight-year-old marketing manager from Maryland, knows he might lose his "fair share of business" when he "dresses for success," or displays other symbols of material success. It suggests to many Whites that he is "one step closer to where they are." When he drove up in his Cadillac, a client asked, "Is that your Cadillac?" "Yes, it is my car," he replied. "You are overpaid," said the customer, "and you don't need my business."

The tightrope is not only with Whites, but also with Blacks. In her administrative position with a federal agency, Diane Earlinger feels isolated from her Black colleagues as well as Whites. Since she is in a high-ranking position, Blacks mistrust her. They see her as a part of the system, making networking to improve working conditions among Blacks more difficult. "Sometimes you are made to feel guilty because you are up there. Why can't you make the system different? Why don't you take a stronger stand on these issues? You are getting extra pressure," said Diane.

Walking the tightrope is not confined to Diane's world of work. She also finds herself balancing it for her children. "It's so difficult for parents. You are always balancing what is the right thing to do," she said. Before having children, Earlinger and her husband lived in a predominantly White community; however, they thought it was important for their children to grow up in a Black neighborhood "knowing who they are." Although advocates of public education, they were not happy with the school system, and were, therefore, unwilling to sacrifice their children's education. The compromise was to live in a Black community and to send their children to a private school "to learn to read, write, and do arithmetic and to balance that with the interaction of their cultural heritage."

Like Earlinger, most of the Talented One Hundred want their children to be citizens of the world, interacting with diverse racial and ethnic groups. Walking the tightrope requires balancing Black pride with universal concerns. "There is a need to balance special nurturing from cultural roots, but one must, at the same time, live in harmony with other people," remarked Teresa Hale, a fifty-four-year-old psychologist from California.

The tightrope walking can increase one's feelings of marginality. While growing up in the 1930s, John Daniels, a sixty-two-year-old corporate executive, had to walk between two worlds—his predominantly White school and his Black community. Balancing those concerns produced a split personality, "creating a painful marginality" that scarred his adulthood. He remembered his father saying about his success in the predominantly White school, "You are getting too big for your britches."

"The whole racism thing is incredible. There are so many things that Blacks who are in a minority situation have to deal with that other people don't," said Cassie Cooper, a vice president of academic affairs at a predominantly Black university and in her mid thirties. "If you walk into a cafeteria and find three or four Blacks at a table together and you are with your White colleague, where do you decide to eat? You don't want to give the impression that all Blacks want to be together and isolate themselves at a time when you are saying you really want to be a part of the organization."

Bernice Sumlin, educator and former national president of Alpha Kappa Alpha sorority, resolved this conflict by "sitting with her Black friends if she sees them at predominantly White gatherings. . . . When there are White friends in mixed gatherings, I'll go over and sit with them."

Being Black, one is constantly balancing on the racial high wire in some area of one's life, whether it's professional concerns versus community obligations, individual concerns versus collective obligations, Black pride versus universal concerns, Afrocentric orientation versus Eurocentric orientation, or integration versus separation. Being Black is to be keenly aware that if one missteps, there is a dual standard by which one is judged.

Being Black in America Is to Experience a Double Standard

Blacks in this society are judged by a different standard than Whites in customs, education, employment, health, and housing. These dual expectations are inherent in the nature of a racist society. In reacting to racism, Blacks also judge other Blacks by a double standard.

Since the double standard is so ubiquitous, I shall illustrate its complexities through a subject that many of the Talented One Hundred candidly discussed—Black politics, corruption, and racism.

Said Robert Woodson, "Two out of five Black elected officials are facing some legal action. Someone would look at that and say that is an expression of racism, and, therefore, focus attention on what White people are doing." With the increasing number of Black public officials under scrutiny for corruption, many Blacks adhere to a conspiracy theory. They believe that Whites are out to destroy Black leaders, diffusing their power base in the Black community. But others question the theory. "If the government targets all Blacks to be investigated, that is unfair. However, if during the investigation, they found all Blacks doing things that were wrong or in violation of the law, they should be exposed," remarked forty-five-year-old Roscoe Champion, a judge. But, he adds, "We should hold White officials to the same standards." Yet, we cannot, Robert Woodson argued, "allow racism to be used as a cover for the indiscretion of people. Blacks can exploit the whole racial issue."

Mayor Johnny Longtree, a sixty-five-year-old, knows "Black officials steal and White officials steal. And we can't steal as much, because we are not in as many situations to steal." He feels both Blacks and Whites are subjected to scrutiny, "but it's more volatile when it's Blacks."

Elizabeth Wright feels that some Black politicians have invited criticisms and investigations by their actions. Judge Champion agreed that "it invites suspicion when a part-time councilperson with a $16,000 salary drives a Mercedes-Benz. The larger society suspects Black officials. They think we want to line our pockets. They know that prior to getting elected, we didn't have anything. They don't understand how we make so little as part-time elected officials and live on the level that suggests we make $200,000."

As a politician, it is important to be economically independent, advocates Mayor Longtree, also a successful lawyer. He was invited to President Carter's inauguration and to the White House several times for dinner, and he knows one can come to enjoy "that glamorous life-style." However, he noted, "most of us who go into politics are dependent on a job. So you get a lot of pressure if you don't make money, because a lot of time must be devoted to the elected office and you can't work on that job. So with that glamorous life-style, many succumb to the temptation that is available with money."

Mayor Longtree "never took a quarter," because he understands "there is a double standard. . . . You have to be morally upright if you are Black." Joseph Lowery feels it is not "fair to ask Blacks to be more perfect than their White predecessors." Yet, he thinks "Black officials have a responsibility to live aboveboard and to recognize that they are being scrutinized more intensely than their White predecessors. Whether it's fair or not, they have to reckon with it."

Though Robert Woodson believes "there should be a single moral compass and a single means of judging misbehavior," racism has contributed to his understanding that "we have a responsibility not to be like White folks. There is too much corruption going on around Black officials. . . . I did not struggle in the Civil Rights movement to take White pigs away from the trough to be replaced by Black pigs. I fought against pigs being at the trough," said Woodson, in a rising voice.

Jack B. Lane concurred that some Black elected officials want to copy the worst habits of the majority population, like "stealing, cheating, and lying." But he did not think "we can do it," saying, "I think the young Black men and women that came out of the Civil Rights movement and got involved in politics have a special obligation—a mandate and a mission—to inject something very meaningful into American politics. We have to inject some of that ethic, some of that humanity, some of that sense of commitment, some of that sense of caring, and some of that sense of sharing, because of that legacy we have to uphold."

When Black officials fail to uphold the legacy, Lowery noted, "people always ask what is it going to do to Black leadership?" He quipped, "What did Richard Nixon's downfall do to White leadership? We have had three White presidents since Nixon—one exposed, one condemned, and one banished. I never heard anybody raise the question, Does it hurt White leadership? It is a racist notion to suggest that what happens to one Black leader, if something bad happens and the allegations are true, discredits Black leadership. It is a racist double standard."

Black leaders and Black people's trials are ongoing, because inherent in the verdict of the double standard is a life sentence to perennial probation.

Being Black Is to Be on Perennial Probation

When Judge Roscoe Champion sat in judgment of others, he, too, was being judged by his White peers and the public to see if he was fair. Champion said that he finally convinced them that: "I was not discriminating against Whites nor was I giving Blacks preferential treatment, but I was applying the law." Having proved that he was competent and fair, his colleagues accepted him. He initiated many changes in the court system. Judge Champion's experience is symbolic of another day's probation in the lives of Blacks.

To break down racial barriers, the Jackie Robinsons and the Doug Williamses had to prove themselves in sports; the Jesse Jacksons and the Adam Clayton Powells had to prove themselves in politics. In every arena, there is an admission test and an ongoing evaluation. Said Laura Price, a fifty-year-old successful gynecologist, "You can have all the credentials, have finished your internships, have been certified and re-certified, and have a successful practice, but when you go to meetings, you will not be recognized." These experiences at White medical meetings have been "crushing for me," she remarked. "Sitting at the back of the bus in the 1950s didn't bother me as much as this."

Being Black and female, Laura was sentenced to double probation. When she opened her practice in her southern hometown as a gynecologist, she noted "the community was more skeptical because I was female." Even though she described herself as "straightforward, Christian, honest, and educated," Blacks were initially hesitant to be treated by her, despite her competence. She said, "I had to work harder. I had to stay in my office and attend to my patients very carefully. I had to go over and beyond the call of duty." With her reputation established, the probation was lifted. The word spread through the Black community that "when you call, she will answer. When you go into labor, she will be at your side. She will call in other doctors or do whatever she can to make sure your health is maintained. She is a good doctor."

Laura's office is so over-filled with patients today that she has to turn them away. She has proven herself to the Black community, but she is still on probation with both her Black male and White colleagues in the medical field. She is the only Black female officer in her local Black Medical Association, and Black females are still considered to be the lowest caste of members of the American Medical Association.

Diane Earlinger also has a medical degree. Like Laura Price, she has proven herself repeatedly. However, she said, "At this point I have no interest in proving to anyone what I can do. I have no energy in trying to prove or educate people considered uneducable, and that is the average smartass White boy. [Laughs] There is no incentive for him to change his beliefs and attitudes. His beliefs and attitudes are getting him where he wants to be, so why change them?" Since she believes there is no vested interest in Whites changing, she is less interested in proving herself and more interested in "making sure the system guarantees opportunities for every Black." She knows that no matter how hard one tries to prove oneself, to be Black is to be never good enough in the eyes of a racist society.

Being Black Is Never to Be Good Enough

To achieve as much as they did, the Talented One Hundred had to be better than the best. Graham Boston, a world renowned scientist/engineer, who has been in a predominantly White environment during his entire life, remarked, "There is no one in my office who can come up to me and say that I'm not good enough. I don't take risks. So when I want something, I work hard at being better than anyone else and at reducing the risk. And it gives me a better opportunity to get what I want. My technique is to be better than anyone else."

Aretha Shield had to learn this painful lesson by trial and error. She had grown up believing, "If you worked hard and had enough talent, people would see the capability. But I live in a society that has a very strict code of passage."

As illustrated earlier in the story of "Little Black Tombo," Diane Earlinger, too, has learned that "there is no way a Black person can be successful enough, smart enough, or rich enough to be equal." Even when Blacks' intellectual capacity is individually recognized, there are other reminders, said a chief of police. "None of the men will say I am not smart enough for the position. They will come up with all kinds of other things, such as I haven't come through the ranks and I have no experience."

In areas like sports and music, where Blacks have traditionally been allowed to excel, they still have to prove themselves. Several months prior to his death, I interviewed Booty Wood, a sixty-seven-year-old former leading soloist who had a long-playing tenure with the bands of Duke Ellington, Count Basie, and Lionel Hampton. He reported that after his illness and retirement from the Count Basie band in the mid-1980s, he had to audition to play at an obscure club. Though he had an established reputation as an excellent trombone player, the nightclub manager would still "go and get some high school trombone player." He said, "Many Blacks are left out. You got to be super good to be even considered for a local band." In Dayton, he exclaimed, "they claim I can't play a show. I played shows in Paris and all over the world. . . . Years ago, they would get the least qualified Blacks and let them fall on their faces and say they can't play a show," he lamented.

In his fifty years as a member of the American Federation of Musicians union, he has received only one call from the organization. Booty threatened to sue one owner of a night club and was hired. The owner eventually told him he was the best trombone player, although he had been told by others that he could not play.

"White folks just presume Black folks are incompetent. It is an authentic presumption, wherever we go and whatever we do," claimed Leo Aramis. "Instead of getting blatant discrimination, you get that presumed level of incompetence and paternalistic kind of thing." He cited an example from his own experience. When Leo sat down to talk with a group of students about the field of journalism and asked them "questions that they needed to be able to answer," his White intern started answering the questions. "I told him to shut up. Why are you answering these questions I am asking *them?*" Repeated Aramis, "There is a presumed level of incompetence."

A "presumed level of incompetence" is the primary reason Jeraldyne Blunden, the artistic director and founder of the nationally acclaimed Dayton Contemporary Dance Company, has transmitted to her children the race lesson that she learned from her parents, "You have to be twice as good to be almost equal." This lesson was first conveyed during a prize fight in the 1940s involving Joe Louis. She remembered, "Blacks stood still to listen. There were no cars on the street. When he won, you could hear the horns blasting. The Black man had to be better than anybody else to get a chance to box."

Like Jeraldyne, Teresa Stanfield, a college administrator, also learned from her parents the lesson that "a Black person has to be twice as good to have the same job as a White person." It was the prevailing sentiment of her all-Black community in the Midwest. "You had to excel in order to be acceptable."

It is an adaptive strategy of successful Blacks to create unrealistic strivings, even when they know they are never good enough in the eyes of a racist society. But they continue to strive, because they are always "ambassadors for the race." It is a race burden each must bear.

Being Black Is to Bear the Race Burden

"Never being good enough" spurs successful Blacks to always be super Blacks. They continue to strive, because their personal success is symbolic of the achievement of all Blacks. Hence, "individual Blacks feel a significant responsibility to represent the race," said Cassie Cooper.

Agreeing, Jonathan Mobutu knows, as Langston Hughes, the Black poet, noted, "You are always an ambassador for your race." It is his strategy for dealing with racism. He said, "Whenever I am involved in something, the presupposition is going to be that I am there as a token because I am Black. I make it my business to immediately take the offensive and demonstrate that I know as much, if not more, than Whites do about their subject or whatever, and that I know about the Black experience and am able to pull it into the discussion, so it can demonstrate some additional perplexity." With his increasing confidence and his increasing awareness, he has become more aggressive in employing this strategy to "pull more information together" than his White colleagues and thus "control the situation."

In representing the race, one becomes the spokesperson and symbol for the group's failures, its successes, and its causes. Jefferson Barnes is frequently called upon to be the spokesperson on his predominantly White campus. "Whenever there is a problem involving Blacks on campus, I get a phone call. It is a case so far removed from White professors that they reach out and grab you." Laughing, he remarked, "I got a phone call at eleven o'clock at night from a high level administrator, saying 'Barnes, we have a problem.' I said, 'What's our problem, boss?'" There was a rape on campus involving Blacks and the administrator wanted to know, Should it be kept quietly out of the newspaper that they are Black? "The fact that my race is so invariably relevant that they would call me, even though I was so far from the scene is ludicrous. Why were they telling me that they had a problem?"

Over forty years before, during World War II, John Daniels was also "far from the scene" when students at his White high school attended a dance on the army base. The White school principal asked him and all the other Black students to come to his office the next day. They were reminded by the principal that Whites and Blacks should not dance together. Although the few Black students who attended the dance on the army base were not involved, Black soldiers, who were stationed in the area, had danced with White girls and the military police were called in to break up the dance. John was deeply hurt by the actions of the principal. He was the perfect ambassador for his race. John was the president of the newspaper staff and very popular, but this dance incident reminded him of the reality of racism. He always played by the rules, saying, "I was particularly bitter at the notion that the principal didn't think I knew the name of this game." He, like his grandfather, wanted to be "well thought of by Whites."

Over forty years later, Dira Ridley's thirteen-year-old daughter wants to "play by the rules" of White society to obtain success. Dira mentioned that her daughter is embarrassed by the social behavior of Blacks in her school, because they are "loud and boisterous in the cafeteria." She, herself, is also embarrassed "to go through the inner city where people are loud." "Granted, I am using a yardstick and saying that behavior is not acceptable by White standards. In the real world, based on successful individuals, you don't act that way," she said.

As a spokesperson and symbol for the race, a successful Black person is also expected to be the expert on any subject dealing with Blacks. When Robert Snow, now a city attorney, sat on the moot court as the only Black student in his law school in the seventies, he was called upon to respond to all the race questions when the moot board was accused of racism. He said, "I took the first question and the next. It was one of the few times I lost my coolness in public. I arrogantly said I was not going to answer one more race question. I was not there to answer race questions. No one had accused me of racism. If they wanted the question answered, they should ask the board members who were accused of being racist." He later found out from a White partner that there was a prearranged plan to ask him the race questions.

One of the heaviest race burdens the Black elite must bear is the notion of responsibility in empowering the masses. Du Bois espoused this idea in his concept of the Talented Tenth. His notion that the Black elite should provide leadership is deeply embedded in the Black community. This notion embodies a strongly held ethos among various strata of the Black community that Blacks who are "making it" in society have a "special obligation to uplift the masses." When I asked the Talented One Hundred how they felt about the statement, "Some people feel that Blacks who are 'making it' in society have a special obligation to help the masses of Blacks," most agreed. But they do not always feel as strongly as Jack B. Lane, who believes, "Those of us who have been blessed or given an opportunity have a moral obligation, almost a calling. It's in a biblical sense like responding to the Macedonian call. You got to do it. We've been given something special, so a little more is required of us." Having greater resources, they agree with Lane's dictum that more is required of them.

While the idea of the Black elite's responsibility for the masses is a popular one, Thomas B. Thomas, a district sales manager for a major corporation, reminds us that often their "creed is not equal to their deed." Many of the Talented One Hundred admitted they and their peers could do more. Few individuals among the Talented One Hundred subscribed to the notion that the responsibility for "uplifting the masses" lies solely with the Black elite. Rather, their views reflect a continuum in a synthesis of competing positions. One position sees Black poverty, for example, as a complex issue which requires a national solution. Thus, both the government and the private sector should be involved; but the government has the greater responsibility in the solution of the problem. Another position sees a national role for the Black elite as having a responsibility in the solution of Black poverty.

If the Black elite are expected to play a role, what should it be? There are individuals among the Talented One Hundred who think the Black elite should play a general role. One general role is political—a role of pressure and politics to make the government more responsive to the poor. Since the Black elite have greater resources, another general role is to support the economic development of Black institutions and organizations; to provide social services, like organizational skills and knowledge; and to assist in the transformation of values. And, they should serve as role models.

But many of the Talented One Hundred rejected these general roles, espousing instead a more specific role. These individuals advocated that "one should contribute according to his/her talent." For example, a physician might organize the community around health issues, while an entrepreneur can provide economic development, training, and jobs. Still others see both general and specific roles for the Black elite.

Among the Talented One Hundred were critics of the notion of the Black elite's special obligation and responsibility to uplift and provide leadership to the Black masses. Prince Albert feels that "all professionals should be primarily concerned with their own advancement. It is an extra burden on Blacks to be concerned about the masses first and themselves second. It is the nature of people to be concerned about their own advancement. When they have enough, they can help others."

Ethel King thinks it is "a racist double standard" and an "unfair burden for Black professionals to have an obligation to the masses. . . . Why should they feel that any more than a White person who has made it? It should come from the individual. No one should have to point the finger and say every Black who makes it should feel an obligation. It does not have to do with being Black, but with being human," said King. She believes there is an "inherent danger" that people may come to view the solution to the problem as lying solely with Blacks, absolving the government of any responsibility. This view is supported by Bart Landry, author of *The New Black Middle Class*.[18]

Ruth Shelly views this idea of the Black elite's obligation as elitist. "You have a special obligation to yourself, and this notion is elitist. It sounds like the master who felt a responsibility for his slaves. This is setting one group against another," noted Ruth.

Critics further point out that feeling a special obligation implies a lack of free will. If Black middle-class individuals want to contribute to the uplifting of the masses, it should be encouraged, but they should not feel it is their special obligation. This ethos may encourage the Black elite to contribute to strengthening the Black community out of a sense of guilt, rather than out of a sense of concern and commitment.

Similarly, critics say that when the Black elite feel it is their responsibility to uplift the masses, it implies paternalism. This view fails to acknowledge self-responsibility in determining one's destiny. Moreover, it suggests that leadership cannot emerge from the masses. It is argued that, while the Black elite have greater resources, strengthening the Black community requires the collective efforts of everyone, especially since the Black middle class, working class, and underclass are bound by the color line.

Ruth Shelly aptly noted that "strengthening of the Black community cannot emerge unless there is a collective consciousness." This collective consciousness can come only with a transformation of values, which involves a redefinition of priorities in the Black community. Thus, when a transformation of values occurs, a sense of concern and commitment, implied in the notion of the Black elite's responsibility and special obligation to the masses, will emerge. But this sense of commitment will be not only the group's concern and responsibility, but also the individual's.

Despite the critics, the Talented One Hundred, in general, feel a strong sense of commitment and responsibility for empowering the masses. Like others among the Talented One Hundred, Jefferson Barnes feels it is an "unfair burden" which is "true for any form of injustice. But Blacks have a special burden to deal with Black issues and how they deal with them is complicated. It is an extra burden, but we should bear it."

Pat Robinson agreed, "It is an imposing demand, but it is absolutely insidious to take the opposite view."

Being Black Is to Be Always in a Precarious Status

Jefferson Barnes, Pat Robinson, and most of the Talented One Hundred understand that, in accepting the special race burden of empowering the masses, their destinies are inextricably linked, because Blacks' success is so precarious in this society. If Benson Robinson, an entrepreneur and millionaire, can be told by his White customers whom to hire, it reflects the status of Blacks in this society. Benson told me that one White manager wanted to impress him, so he hired more Blacks. "I had six Blacks working in the same area, and a very prominent White doctor told me about two-and-a-half years ago, 'Benson, I would like to talk with you.' He had been a good customer of mine," Benson said. "You have a hell of a good business here. We are all proud of you. You are doing an excellent job, but I feel you are making a mistake. It's good you are upgrading Blacks, but I think you got too many at the door." Benson's reply to the doctor was, " 'Thank you very much. I'll take a look at it.' I get busy and I don't see a lot of things. . . . One day I decided to go out and look, and I said I do have quite a bit out here. Then I got a couple of more complaints." The customers implied that too many Blacks might scare away White customers. Finally, Benson dispersed Black employees to his businesses located in mixed or Black neighborhoods.

The following stories of John Daniels, Diane Earlinger, and Kelly Smith further illustrate the precariousness of Black success. Before his retirement, John Daniels was a senior vice president and assistant to the chairman and CEO of a major corporation. Daniels was more than an affirmative action case, stating, "I had the authority and the blank check from the chairman. I had every capacity to influence. I was on his board. I worked directly for him, and he owned 80 percent of the company. So he gave me a blank check to do anything. I came in at the top and stayed at the top."

Daniels was able to "totally integrate the company and eliminate discriminatory patterns." Before he joined the company, the chairman indicated to Daniels that he was amenable to changes, telling him, "If you say so, John, it will happen." The chairman had supported the first Black mayor of his city, and he also encouraged corporate responsibility. "I made sure all the vice presidents were lifetime members of the NAACP. [He laughed.] They would have to make speeches at Black schools," said Daniels.

The CEO died, and the company underwent reorganization. The direction of the company changed, and this affected John's influence in the company, so he retired. He had an interested and concerned mentor who was committed to effecting changes, but his untimely death indicated the precariousness of Daniels' influence.

Kelly Smith, a high-ranking manager at an international company, was greatly assisted by her mentor, the CEO, a White male, in getting a promotion, after another White supervisor discouraged her from seeking the position. Within a month of her promotion, the CEO died.

Diane Earlinger became the first top female administrator at her international agency. Although she was the "best qualified person," her White division directors were upset because they expected to get the job. "After all, they had been there for thirty years and thought they earned it," noted Earlinger. In her first meeting with the division directors, she told them, "I never had the pleasure of working with anyone like you or anyone I necessarily liked or respected, but that has never kept me from getting a job done. I trust that is not going to be a problem for you." She ended the discussion. They left. She said, "What made it tolerable at the time was the top director who supported and sustained me."

Even with his support, she "operated at a significant disadvantage, ending up working two or three times as hard to accomplish half as much." Earlinger remarked that "the sheer level of effort and energy that is required to survive reached the level at some point of diminishing return. Why am I doing it? Is it making a difference for anyone? Why am I doing that and putting up with all this crap?"

When the director resigned, a Mormon political appointee became the director. "This person could not communicate with me." Admittedly, she said, "We both have to assume some responsibility for that relationship." Five minutes before she was to receive an EEO award from her organization, the new director informed her of his intentions to reorganize her program. "Standing with a donut in one hand and orange juice in the other," Earlinger stated, "he wanted to proceed with the search process as quickly as possible. I would no longer manage that program, and it would no longer exist at the agency. That's how I was told."

When Blacks are isolated from one another, the precariousness of their success is likely to increase. While many of the Talented One Hundred understand that isolation may affect their success, there are others who relish the status of token. "They relish being the only Black. They want White people to see them in a certain way. They are not concerned about others in the group. They do not see their success as connected to group success. You cannot have individual success in this country as people think you can. It's very much related to group success," said Teresa Johnson. She believes, like Toni Morrison in *Bluest Eye*, "Some other token can always top you. Some better token can be found."

Stephanie Tahara, a forty-three-year-old public administrator from California, agrees that there is an "inherent danger" for those who relish their isolation. "They will suffer because they are going to get kicked sooner or later." She related a story about a Black male colleague who was "the least Black of anybody I've seen lately. . . . He was a computer expert, and he was their darling for two or three years. But when the computer system did not run like clockwork, he was psychologically demoted and discarded out of favor. He was a token for a while, but now he is in pain."

A colleague was promoted as boss over him. I have never known a Black to be sustained as 'darling' for very long."

Joseph Lowery castigated the token who lacks social consciousness:

> Those "bougie Buppies" [young Black upwardly mobile persons] have not yet come to realize that they need networks and that they need to be community conscious. If they haven't gotten there, they are getting there. It is just around the corner for them. Most have begun to realize that it wasn't like they thought. They are not as secure as they thought they were. And what they begin to realize is that for most middle-class Black Americans, they are one or two paychecks from poverty, considering debts and obligations. They are right back where their cousins, their mamas, and their uncles are.

It is therefore important, according to Mayor Johnny Longtree, to "always be reminded that when you grow up poor, you remember from whence you came. And if you forget that, you are never going to make it. Lots of Blacks don't reach back and pull up others. But as long as I look in the mirror, I know from whence I came. I am not too far from there right now, and it won't take too much to put me back from where I came."

Mayor Longtree knows there is a continuous struggle personally and collectively, because one is constantly reminded of one's blackness. Aretha Shield was reminded when she took her art work to her alma mater, a school that frequently purchased the work of prominent graduates. She was told by the school administrator to take her work to the Urban League, commenting, "They might like it." Aretha believed she was in this "never-never land of being colorless with the art." She realized, however, that there was "no way you could escape being Black in this country." Others are reminded of this when they or their children are stopped by the police in predominantly White upper-middle-class neighborhoods. Robert Woodson's teenage son was in Wilmington, Delaware, visiting a friend. It was night, and he was running down the street. A police officer stopped Woodson's son, placed him against a wall, and frisked him. The police thought he was a suspect in a hold-up and they handcuffed him, taking him to the 7-11 store that was robbed to be identified. The store manager could not identify him, so the police released him.

Said Woodson, "When my son called me to report the incident, I asked him how was he treated. 'Was the policeman rough with you? Did he curse you or treat you discourteously?' I was able to make some phone calls and the policeman was called into the chief of police's office. My son was not mistreated, so I didn't take any action. I had the influence to take some individual action if I had wanted to. I could have dealt with that cop and the system." Though Woodson had the personal influence to "deal with the system," it is clear from this incident that despite class or status, individual influence is precarious when it comes to blackness. Being Black is, therefore, a constant reminder of the continuous struggle of the color line both on the collective and personal levels.

Being Black Is to Be in a Continuous Struggle, Personally and Collectively

"When I wake up, I am angry. I know what is ahead of me for today. You have to get the people in the office to work on their behalf to fight the people outside the office on behalf of the people within. It is an endless struggle," said Sheridan Williams, a professor, poet, and playwright at a large university. Michael Lomax, the chairman of the Fulton County Commission, and also a professor, agreed. "I am in a world which is not going to encourage the advancement of Michael Lomax, because there are too many other individuals in that world encouraging their own advancement. I have to keep the pressure on. I can't let up. We, as a race, will have to keep the pressure on. We can't desert the NAACP and the Urban League. We went through a period where we felt we could desert the NAACP, the Urban League, the National Council of Negro Women, and walk away from Black churches, colleges, and communities." There was a feeling, after the Civil Rights movement, that "we now have the admission ticket and can go anywhere." But "we have learned," said Lomax, "that it doesn't work and we are seeing a trend of coming home or reinvesting in our institutions, recognizing that their strength is a reflection of our individual strength, and they are integrally connected, and we must keep them."

In the collective struggle, Jews are an important group role model for Blacks. Roger Johnson, a state representative from the Midwest, thinks Blacks have to be like Jews. "A group who wants to rise has to help others if they want to maintain some position of power."

"We can learn from the Jews," acknowledged Michael Lomax. "They say you will never forget the Holocaust. If you use Jews the wrong way or talk about them the wrong way, they'll be right on you. We have to be vigilant like that. It is persistence. You have to never let up."

Headlines like "Just When Civil Rights Activists Thought They Could Take a Rest"[19] and "Activists Fight Desegregation Rollback"[20] indicate the struggle is continuous. Four rulings in the late 1980s by a more conservative U.S. Supreme Court dismantled affirmative action programs designed to assist female and male racial minorities and White females. In the case of *Richmond v. Croson,* the court struck down by a vote of 6–3 the Richmond, Virginia, City Council's set-aside plan which earmarked public contracts for minority-owned businesses. In the case of *Wards Cove Packing v. Atonio,* the court ruled 5–4 that statistics showing minorities are under-represented in the workplace are not sufficient evidence to bring a discrimination suit. In addition, the court shifted the burden of responsibility to prove discrimination from the employer to the employee. In the case of *Martin v. Wilks,* the court ruled Whites may bring reverse discrimination claims against a court-approved affirmative action settlement. Finally, in the case of *Patterson v. McLean Credit Union,* the court unanimously upheld the 1866 law used to challenge discrimination in the making of private contracts, but by a 5–4 vote refused to extend the law to racial harassment in the workplace.

Many civil rights proponents view these Supreme Court rulings as signaling an end to gains won during the "Second Reconstruction" which began in the sixties. The racial battle for equality and justice is continuous for oppressed people. President George Bush's veto of the 1990 Civil Rights Bill underlines that reality.

Individuals who are likely to be in the vanguard of the racial struggle are the Black elite. Many of the Talented One Hundred, such as Vernon Jordan, have accepted this race burden, because they understand that group mobility requires their collective efforts. "The Talented Tenth have a responsibility to those not in the Talented Tenth," says Jordan. "I feel a special obligation to help those who cannot help themselves. I've spent twenty-five years trying to do that."

Joseph Lowery preaches there are biblical grounds for collective action by the Black elite. "The Bible says that the strong must bear the infirmities of the weak." He thinks "all those people who pulled themselves up by their own bootstraps have also learned to lie. We can't separate ourselves, even if we wanted to. They will put us all in the same bucket whether we want to or not."

The belief that successful Blacks must assist other Blacks in the collective struggle has kept Jeraldyne Blunden going. It is also a guiding principle by which Earnest Ross has lived. "I believe in the principle that it's only by helping others that we will make it." The collective racial struggle for him is like a "rubber band." "You have to keep the pressure on or else it goes back to its original position. In Black/White relations, the pressure must be there constantly." For Tony Michaels, a fifty-six-year-old corporate executive, the collective pressure and obligation to the Black community must come not only from the Talented Tenth but also from the Black masses. "It must exist with everyone." Hosea Kelly believes this collective obligation exists at some level. "Every Black person, whether consciously or not, has a concern about Blacks, though they may find it difficult to manifest in their behavior."

Jeremiah Moses, along with many of the Talented One Hundred, however, has doubts about young Blacks, particularly those under thirty, whom he feels "have no realization about the struggle." There is a strong sense that they lack sensitivity and commitment to the ongoing struggle for social justice, because they did not come of age during the Civil Rights era. They are the product of the "Me" generation. Hence, lacking a collective identification with the Black community, their commitment to strengthening it is not seen as a collective concern, but an individual effort to pull oneself up by one's own bootstraps. "The Buppies have bought into the philosophy that the only way to have upward mobility in corporate America is to shed one's blackness. Act White, talk White, and don't be too closely identified with civil rights organizations. You can give money, but not a check so Whites will discover you made a contribution," noted Roscoe Champion. Historian Kufra Akpan thinks that because of this absence of collective racial consciousness among young Blacks, "we are in a dangerous position in this society. . . . We are not developing the strong replacement parts for a strong Black society with a serious collective consciousness to meet the future challenge. The young people or most of them under thirty think this is 'America, the Beautiful.' "

Others are not as critical of the young, viewing them more from the perspective of a life passage and feeling they will become more concerned after their own needs have been met. One person, having criticized young Blacks, acknowledged that she "may be looking through old eyes."

Whether or not we feel there should be a collective obligation, Bernie Roberts still maintained, "We must have an obligation, because the Blacks who have made it would not have been where they are unless somebody left a legacy for them. People who were unlettered opened up the doors for us. We have an obligation to open up the doors for others."

John Hubbard knows the struggle must be ongoing because "in the eyes of the White power structure, all Blacks still are niggers because of the continuous systemic exploitation and degradation. It is the essence of nigger status. It means no matter how successful we are in terms of getting degrees and earning incomes, it is given to us by the power structure and can be taken away." Until we acquire an "independent political and economic base, what we get is at the pleasure of the master." Hence, the struggle is an ongoing personal and collective process to eliminate the glass ceiling.

Like Bernie Roberts, we can be reminded, too, of Johnny Longtree's comments, "People who think they've made it by themselves have to remember if it wasn't for your brothers and sisters down here in this mire, you might not be able to climb over their shoulders to get where you are. You see very few companies where a Black man has a chance to be president."

The Black masses who were involved in the civil rights struggle and the Black Nationalist movement, as suggested by Johnny Longtree and Bernie Roberts, helped raise the ceiling of opportunities for the Black elite. They understand, like Frederick Douglass, the ex-slave who rose to great heights as an orator and liberator, that "if there is no struggle, there is no progress. Those who profess to favor freedom, and yet depreciate agitation, are men who want crops without ploughing the ground. They want rain without thunder and lightning. They want the ocean without the awful roar of its many waters."

Being Black Is to Be Limited by the Glass Ceiling

The Southern Christian Leadership Conference has so many discriminatory complaints "that they can't cope with them," said Joseph Lowery. The Equal Employment Opportunity Commission is overburdened with racial discrimination charges. There is a glass ceiling on the aspirations of Blacks. Sometimes the glass ceiling is clear, and other times it is cloudy. It was very cloudy for a young Black woman in Atlanta, who became so enraged with the limits of the glass ceiling that she killed herself and wounded two White colleagues in 1987, when she failed to get a promotion. "The corporate community is a very tension-filled place. There is a glass ceiling and the glass is getting stained with the blood of those who have fallen by the wayside," says Lowery. "Blacks who are upwardly mobile in the workplace are finding themselves trapped under the glass ceiling and they cannot escape. If they can afford to get out, they ought to get out and do other jobs. Some are sacrificing status and salary. Others are seeking spiritual resources to cope."

In a *Black Enterprise* poll of its readers, 48 percent of all respondents said they thought "the chances for Black managers to advance up the corporate ladder were poor."[21] And more than 61 percent of the respondents said they had encountered racial discrimination in their employment.[22]

Hosea Kelly calls it the "bubble theory." He says as long as Blacks behave in a certain way, "they are allowed to live under the bubble, but they can never become a part of it. They have to be a good nigger. The good nigger doesn't challenge too much, doesn't focus on Black life too much, and doesn't tie himself to his African heritage."

There was a cloudy glass ceiling for Blacks when Claude Kent, now an engineer in his fifties, applied for engineering school in the early 1950s. He had graduated in the upper 10 percent of his class, and it was the policy of his state university to accept anyone in the upper 10 percent of the class. When he went to enroll in the university, the dean of engineering, whose name was White, did not take time to look at his transcript. "He told me," Kent said, "I could not be an engineer and the reason was because I was Black, saying, 'You people cannot be engineers.' He said I was welcomed to come there and enroll in an industrial arts course, so I can go back to teach my people carpentry and masonry."

With his mother, he drove to another university in the Midwest. Fortuitously, the dean's name was Mr. Justice. "You are welcomed to come if you want to," he told Kent. "He said I would be the first Black in engineering school, and I was going to catch hell from the faculty and students." It was not easy for Kent. He understood that his major "reason for going to the university was not to be distracted by them," but to obtain his "major goal by diversionary tactics. . . . Not having enough money or food, I risked my health to prove myself. I decided that when the going gets tough, the tough gets going. Whatever it takes to make it, I will. Since I was told I couldn't do what I wanted to do, I felt I had to overcome them."

When Graham Boston applied for engineering in the sixties, the ceiling was raised higher and its glass was clearer. He has achieved top honors in his field, but he also stands as a testament to Blacks' progress in eliminating one more barrier. He said, "I am standing on the mountain top and I have done it all. I enjoy sitting on top of this mountain. I know there are people who are trying to pull me off of it and trying to replace me." Even though he is successful, he knows the precariousness of it. His struggle must be ongoing.

While growing up, the Talented One Hundred learned a dual lesson about the glass ceiling. They were told there were limits, but they also heard, like Warner Babbitt, that "there is a world of unlimited possibilities, if you strive hard enough. . . . No one ever taught me what I couldn't do at home and school. I was always told what I could do, although the rest of the world was saying, 'You can't do these things because you are Black.' So when I met the rest of the world I said, 'Uh huh' and went on to do what I had to do."

When Jackie Robinson, Hank Aaron, Doug Williams, Martin Luther King, Jr., Mary McLeod Bethune, and Jesse Jackson "hit the ceiling," like countless others, they "went on to do what they had to do" in raising it. Since the first slave ship landed, Blacks have been raising the glass ceiling— from entertainers and servants to actors in the global arena of business, education, politics, science, and technology. They understand that raising the ceiling is a continuous personal and collective struggle. Yet, through it all, because of the conflictive nature of the duality—through the race watching and tightrope walking; through the double standard; through never being good enough; through perennial probation; through bearing the race burden; through the precariousness of their individual and collective success; through the continuous personal and collective struggle— they wear the mask.

Being Black Is to Wear the Mask

Wearing the mask is an adaptive survival strategy to conceal actions, feelings, motives, and thoughts. Uncle Tom symbolizes the accommodation to an oppressive society.

Black folk genre is also replete with tales about the rabbit trickster and about John and Old Marster, a slave who deceived and outwitted his White master. Similarly, in other areas of Black/White encounters, Blacks often do not reveal themselves to Whites. When Whites conduct research involving Blacks, for example, it is often difficult for them to obtain information. One does not reveal one's true self. Zora Neale Hurston speculates on the reason in *Mules and Men:*

> The white man is always trying to know somebody else's business. All right, I'll set something outside the door of my mind for him to play with and handle. He can read my writing but he sho' can't read my mind. I'll put this play toy in his hand, and he will seize it and go away. Then I'll say my say and sing my song.[23]

Hurston's astute observation caused me to question the meaning behind the actions of someone I observed while attending a sociological meeting in Florida, in the early 1980s. During a morning session, a respected Black sociologist, extolling the virtues of racial progress in America, used racial humor to appease and cajole his predominantly White audience. When he spoke during an evening session, Dr. Jekyll had turned to a Mr. Hyde. Before his more mixed audience, he was militant in asserting the rights of Blacks, in pronouncing Black pride, and in denouncing the evils of White oppression. Between the two sessions, during a social gathering, he played openly and affectionately with the toes of his White female colleague.

To Ferdinand Hamilton, "The worst thing in the world is to be in a position where you say one thing to White folks and another thing to Black folks. . . . You have to be at oneness with yourself to be comfortable with your own commitment." Indeed, from my observations, Hamilton seemed comfortable with his advocacy role in the presence of Blacks and Whites, not masking his personal or political posture.

Dick Godfather, a federal administrator in his early fifties, knows that Blacks mask their posture, "acting one way around Blacks and another way around Whites." John Hubbard smiles around his White colleagues, working well with them, but doesn't do much socializing. He is most comfortable socializing with his Black colleagues. "It's a matter of being comfortable around one's own kind. It's nothing that you say, it's just how you feel. It's vibes. Nothing I can put my finger on. Maybe it's the Black vernacular." He is more comfortable "talking with more expletives and profanity in a Black setting," because it would be tolerated more by other Blacks.

Marla Robinson also acknowledged that she is more comfortable relating to Blacks.

> I can comfortably relate to my Black boss, but if he were White, I would have to put on a mask or different face. People who read this in the future probably will ask, "Why don't you be yourself?" You can't be yourself. Ain't no use thinking you can be yourself. Anytime a person thinks of you as subhuman, you are going to have to reinforce that you are human, an intelligent being of a higher order. If you let your hair down, it can give them a message or another indication, because their interpretation of your behavior is so important. You can't allow it. You are constantly aware of everything. You can't relax. You can't say, "You ain't going to do it." But I won't say that with White peers, because they are going to see it as someone who does not have command of the English language.

As a journalist, Warner Babbitt frequently wears the mask as a means "to extract information from informants. . . . I understand White folks better than they understand me. I can always figure out where they are coming from, but I can confuse them when I want to," he said. In his tenure as a political reporter with a major newspaper, he "learned to handle Whites very well. I could make them love me. I could make them hate me." Sometimes he uses his cloaking shield to make himself invisible. "When I don't want White folks to understand me," he said, "I do a Ralph Ellison on them. White people are amazingly simple sometimes. They are the easiest people in the world to manipulate."

He cited the time when, as a political reporter, he was interviewing a state senator about "something he shouldn't be doing." Babbitt went into his "little invisible act with him." The senator only "saw a Black person coming. . . . The senator was going on and on. I said, 'Excuse me, Senator, I don't understand such and such.'" In a slightly Black voice, he asked the senator what he expected and scratched his eyebrow. "He fell for it and started to tell me in various and sundry ways how the program was operated. I said, 'Oh yes' and 'I don't understand.' He would make little funny ethnic jokes. I didn't react. He became so confident that he was speaking to a fool that he started to tell me everything I wanted to know."

When the story appeared in the paper the next day, the senator called the newspaper, saying, "I didn't say that." "He indicated to the editor that this young Black guy was slow and didn't understand what he was saying." When Babbitt played the tape recorder back to him, he asked as he unmasked, "Are you sure I got it wrong?" Babbitt knows, like Paul Lawrence Dunbar, the poet:

> We wear the mask that grins and lies,
> It hides our cheeks and shades our eyes,—
> This debt we pay to human guile;
> With torn and bleeding hearts we smile,
> And mouth with myriad subtleties.
>
> Why should the world be overwise,
> In counting all our tears and sighs?
> Nay, let them only see us, while
> We wear the mask.
>
> We smile, but, O great Christ, our cries
> To thee from tortured souls arise.
> We sing, but Oh, the clay is vile
> Beneath our feet, and long the mile;
> But let the world dream otherwise,
> We wear the mask.

In this society, the Black elite's economic status and achievements do not erase the color line. The acceptance of the color line and the acceptance of the value orientation of democracy, freedom, equality, individualism, progress, and achievement result in a dual value system. While the Black elite accept the value orientation of democracy, equality, and freedom, they reject discrimination across the color line. This dual value orientation is a source of conflict which manifests itself in their personal and collective identity. The way the Black elite experience the conflict of the color line is on an individual level, though it has a collective component—it is a shared experience. If Blacks understand the realities of racism, they can more effectively cope with oppression.

In the next chapter, I examine some manifestations of the color line and the impact of psychic violence on the Black elite.

TWO

Manifestations of the Color Line: The Impact of Violence

"I grew up in a very large family and a very loving home. I had an extended family of grandparents and great-grandparents. We were poor. But we had this great sense of pride and this sense that you got to make things different," said Jack B. Lane, the forty-seven-year-old son of Johnny Lane, a sharecropper and bus driver, and Louise Lane, a domestic.

His parents and grandparents valued education and hard work, frequently reminding the children, "You are not going to get anything unless you work and struggle for it. Go to school and get an education so you won't have to work so hard the way we did." His mother did not want them "to go to the field and work in the hot sun." His family also instilled in the children "a respect for people and a reverence for life. . . . My parents laid a strong foundation," said Jack.

Jack grew up with the signs and symbols of the old rural South during the fifties, a time of racial apartheid. He remembers:

> As a child growing up in rural Alabama, I've seen the signs as we would go downtown—"White" and "Colored." I've seen the symbols and signs of racism. I don't know if I quite understood racism, until I went downtown to the theater and was denied admission, or went to the library and couldn't check out a book.

In his fifteenth year, Jack saw the coming signs of change in the old South. A young minister, Martin Luther King, Jr., began reordering the signposts. He "heard King and watched the drama of Montgomery" unfolding only fifty miles from where he grew up, and he felt there was a way out and that something could be done. "This man provided for me, like he did for many young people and people not so young, a way out. He provided the instruments, tools, and techniques for dealing with the system of prejudice and racial discrimination."

King and the movement changed forever the course of Jack's life:

> Martin Luther King, Jr. and the Civil Rights movement forced me as an individual, as a Black child, as a human being, to literally grow up overnight. If it hadn't been for the movement, I don't know where I would be. It changed my life, and I know I am a different person.

Jack became a leader in the Civil Rights movement, and it gave him a sense of unlimited possibilities. He was also the first college-educated member of his family.

> The movement gave me a sense that you can do it; you can make it. If you have the sense of stick-to-itiveness and persistence, you can do it. You felt almost invincible. It created a greater faith in the possibility of change and in the possibility of seeing human beings change, grow, and develop. I would not be where I am if I had not had the experience of the Civil Rights movement.

At the time of my interview, he was a renowned and dedicated public servant who had been elected to a public office.

The Civil Rights movement, the public policy priority of equal opportunity, and the expanding economy cracked open the closed door to opportunities in the sixties and the early seventies, and thousands of young, gifted, and Black Jack B. Lanes slipped through the crack. They arrived at the door of opportunity from the cotton belt of Alabama, Georgia, and Mississippi, from the coal fields of West Virginia, Kentucky, and Pennsylvania, and from the burned-out ghettos of Watts, Harlem, Detroit, and Newark. They were the offspring of parents and grandparents who tilled the soil as sharecroppers, who scrubbed the floors as domestics and janitors, and who performed the dirty work and were the source of cheap labor in the factories, mines, and steel mills of the North and South. They were also children of doctors, lawyers, ministers, and teachers. Their traditional career choices—teaching, ministry, and the selected few occupations of medicine, dentistry, and law in racially segregated communities—were expanded to more diverse career options for the first time in racially integrated communities.

With this burgeoning middle class, William Julius Wilson, in *The Declining Significance of Race*, asserted that "many talented and educated Blacks are now entering positions of prestige and influence at a rate comparable to, or, in some situations, exceeding that of Whites with equal qualifications."[1] For many academics, including Wilson, this expansion of

Blacks into the middle class heralded the decline of racism. But some eschewed this positive prognosis of the state of race relations in America. Sociologist Charles V. Willie, one of Wilson's strongest critics, using data on family income, provided empirical support for the inclining, not declining, significance of race. He argued in the late seventies that not only was racism increasing, but it was especially so for upwardly mobile Blacks. He asserted that "middle-class Blacks in racially integrated situations at this period in American history are almost obsessed with race."[2] And, "The people who most severely experience the pain of dislocation due to changing times are the racial minorities who are talented and integrated, not those who are impoverished and isolated."[3]

The debate over the significance of class and race as factors in the upward mobility of Blacks continues and is likely to persist in the 1990s. In this debate, generally, the Talented One Hundred take the position that race is a more salient factor in their life chances than class. When I asked them if racism was declining in the 1980s, 92 percent said it was not. They did believe overt racism has declined since the 1960s, however. While 8 percent of individuals felt racism would eventually disappear, the majority believed it is a permanent stratifying feature in this society. Thus, whether overt or subtle, racism aims to rule the cultural, economic, educational, political, legal standing, emotional and physical health, and the sexual and social interactions of the oppressed group. The dominant group wants to maintain a sense of place for the oppressed group. Hence, the oppressor group employs violence and three important devices of power—control, dominance, and exploitation—to maintain racial privileges.

The concept of violence is examined here from a Fanonian perspective, which looks at human violence in situations of oppression. It incorporates violence that is defined as legitimate or illegitimate, intentional or unintentional, instrumental or expressive, individual or collective, overt or covert, and physical or psychic. According to Hussein Abdilahi Bulhan, in *Frantz Fanon and the Psychology of Oppression,* "violence is any relation, process, or condition by which an individual or a group violates the physical, social, and/or psychological integrity of another person or group." He states:

> The proposed definition rests on several assumptions. First, violence is not simply an isolated physical act or a discrete random event. It is a relation, process, and condition undermining, exploiting, and curtailing the well-being of the victim. Second, these violations are not simply moral or ethical, but also physical, social, and/or psychological. They involve demonstrable assault on or injury of and damage to the victim. Third, violence in any of the three domains—physical, social, or psychological—has significant repercussions in the other two domains. Fourth, violence occurs not only between individuals, but also between groups

and societies. Fifth, intention is less critical than consequence in most forms of violence. Any relation, process, or condition imposed by someone that injures the health and well-being of others is by definition violent.[4]

Bulhan's definition allows us to look at violence from a broader perspective and to extend the taxonomy of violence to include personal, institutional, and structural violence. Bulhan notes that "institutional violence and structural violence involve more complex relations, processes, and conditions than personal violence. Personality and temperament are more likely to gain primacy in personal violence than institutional and structural violence. Ordinarily, institutional and structural violence span individuals and generations. . . . Structural violence in particular imposes a pattern of relations and practices that are deeply ingrained in and dominate everyday living."[5]

Since structural violence is so much an integral feature of the attitudes, values, and mores of individuals who are socialized into the system, it is sometimes difficult to detect. Both the oppressor and the oppressed often construct their social reality around daily interactions or somewhat "ascribed" roles that are taken for granted. Social oppression involves all three forms of violence. "Oppression and one of its expressions, racism, legitimize structural violence, rationalize institutional violence, and impersonalize personal violence," writes Bulhan.[6]

In this chapter, I examine how the violence of racism is used as an important mechanism to maintain control and a sense of place. The oppressor group aims to control, dominate, and exploit in every major institution and in every facet of social interaction. In attempting to impose a sense of place and identity, the actions of the oppressor have important psychological consequences for the oppressed group. The violence of racism manifests itself physically, culturally, and socially. Within the broader cultural and social areas, I look at how racism manifests itself in the realms of economics, education, housing, the media, and sexual and social interactions. I also examine how these racist manifestations in these areas have changed since the 1960s.

The Impact of Physical Violence

The most common and fundamental control device is reliance on physical violence. The oppressed are kept in their place by threats of physical injury or actual acts of violence. The history of Black/White relations in this country is replete with physical violence—floggings, lynchings, whippings, murders, and police brutality.

Prior to the Civil Rights movement and the opening up of equal opportunity, the members of the traditional Black elite were confined to segregated environments. They lived and attended schools in primarily segregated communities. They were generally employed or self-employed in institutions serving the Black community. The racism that the traditional Black elite experienced was overt, and it was supported and sanctioned by the folkways, mores, and laws of the larger society. This overt form of racism empowered White individuals to have personal power over any Black person. Thus, individual acts of physical violence were more rampant among the traditional Black elite, as we can see in the stories of Lee Watson, Yvonne Walker-Taylor, Joseph Lowery, and Ned McMillian. Though individual acts of physical violence are not as pronounced among the modern Black elite, violence still remains an important feature, as illustrated by Renee Stone's story (p. 50).

Lee Watson, a fifty-nine-year-old college administrator and realtor from Virginia, heard stories of physical atrocities suffered during and after slavery from her great-grandmother, an ex-slave, who lived to be over one hundred years old, and from her grandmother, who lived to be ninety-four:

> In slavery, White men feared the slaves' ability to communicate with God. If they were caught praying, they were whipped. They were hanged from their hands with their feet hanging down. They were whipped with a horse whip until the blood ran down their backs. They would scream, "Oh pray master." And the slave master would scream, "Oh pray yourself, damn nigger," and rubbed salt in their wounds. After freedom, the Black woman would not be allowed to be seen with a calico dress and the Black man with khaki pants. They would be flogged by the patrol.

Her great-grandmother was "taught by White children to read the Bible in the loft. If their parents had caught them, they would have been whipped," said Lee. She was greatly inspired by the stories of her great-grandmother and her grandmother, who reared her, and by their philosophy "to walk like you have something to do; act like someone has a string on you, pulling you forward. Never drop your head. Keep walking." Her mother died when she was four. "Without having a mother, I could have been a prostitute, drunkard, or dope fiend, but I chose to follow in my great-grandmother's tracks as a person who could stand up and be counted," said Lee, as tears overwhelmed her.

When she wiped away her tears, she said, "I knew I was placed on earth by God, and I intend to take my place." Her place in society turned out differently than her great-grandmother's. At seventeen, she started working. "Calling myself a woman, I took my place in this world and in this society. I had $13 in change in a tobacco bag. Today, at the age of fifty-nine and divorced, I feel comfortable to say I am more than a millionaire," said Lee, who keeps walking like someone has a string pulling her forward.

While Lee Watson's story illustrates how acts of physical violence are transformed through time and continue to impose psychic trauma in the next generation, the story of Yvonne Walker-Taylor, the seventy-one-year-old first woman president of Wilberforce University in Ohio, one of the oldest historically Black colleges and universities in the country, gives us a glimpse of the pre–Civil Rights violence in the 1920s.

In that era, the Ku Klux Klan was very active. Walker-Taylor, who was from a socially and economically privileged background, said that "when the cooks didn't come and the horsemen didn't show up, it meant the KKK would parade" in front of their home in Raleigh, North Carolina. Although she was born in New Bedford, Massachusetts, her family lived briefly in Raleigh. Her father was an A.M.E. minister and an outspoken social activist who urged his congregation from the pulpit to vote. "While lying in the attic" at age eight, Yvonne was told by her parents that "they were playing a game, and they were going to watch those people."

> I looked out and saw all those white robes and pointed hats. I thought it was the cutest thing. I thought they were clowns. They looked so funny. They planted their cross down in the yard and stood looking at the house and burned that cross. All the neighbors pulled their shades and nobody walked up and down the street. I remember hearing nothing but the crackling of the fire. They all marched away and daddy breathed a sigh of relief and brought us downstairs. He made a couple of calls to the press and the police, but no one did anything about it.

She and her mother were sent back to Massachusetts after Whites attempted to kidnap her. "They were trying to force my daddy out of Raleigh, because he was 'too big-mouthed,'" said Walker-Taylor. Her father wanted to be a part of the American dream to vote. Even in the face of violence, he aspired to a higher place for Blacks, and he inspired her to fight for the civil rights of Blacks.

It was during the Depression of the 1930s that Joseph E. Lowery had his first encounter with racial violence in rural Alabama. It was a bad time economically for Whites and Blacks. The bad times accentuated the competition between Blacks and Whites and Blacks' sense of place.

> When I was quite a young lad, I came out of my father's business—a little ice cream parlor. I was three-fourths the way out and this big White policeman was one-fourth in the door, and he jabbed me in the stomach with his nightstick and said, "Get back nigger. Don't you see a White man is coming?" I ran home to get my father's pistol and as God would have it, my father came home when I was on the way out of the house.

49

He had never been home that time of day in my lifetime, except on Sunday. But he was there and saw the tears running down my cheeks, and he made me tell him what the problem was. I told him. I finally admitted I had come to get the gun, and he took the gun and said he would handle it.

He made a complaint to the chief of police and the mayor. Both told him they understood his problem, but the best thing was to forget it for two reasons: (1) nothing they could do about it, and nothing they would do about it; and (2) that was the only person they could hire in a small southern Alabama town. I grew up bitter for a while about that. But as I experienced the Christian religion, my bitterness faded into determination to do something to change that system and to work with hearts and minds. It was an important event for me because it brought home for me, in a very traumatic way, race relations.

During the mid-forties, when Black men were fighting in Europe during World War II "to make the world safe for democracy," Ned McMillian, then a twelve-year-old boy, did not feel safe in his small Georgia hometown. He learned early his sense of place from the lessons of his parents, who told him, "This is a White man's world, and if you are going to live in it, you are going to live by the rules and regulations that he has set up." His father owned a small restaurant, and Ned saw those rules and regulations when he was working in his father's kitchen. Ned was often "perturbed because every weekend, the police would come down to the restaurant, but no one would call them." He added, "One Saturday night, one hit my father, and I'll never forget that. The policeman drew his gun and my father couldn't hit back." He repeated, "I'll never forget that."

"How did it make you feel?" I asked.

"If I had a gun I could have gotten to, I would have blasted them. I felt there was nothing I could do. I felt bad, because my father didn't have an even chance. I didn't feel he was a coward. He was overpowered. They had the gun. He did not. They had the badge. He did not," said Ned, now a prominent doctor and a social activist for the Black struggle.

Not having an even chance has been the norm for Blacks from north to south, and from east to west, and from the dawn of slavery to the dusk of the twentieth century. Renee Stone, a perky twenty-six-year-old professor and the youngest among the Talented One Hundred, knows firsthand what it means not to have an equal chance for the American dream. Her perkiness seemed to belie the nightmare of her racial experiences. Perhaps she learned from her parents, both professionals, that "to be successful, you have to wear the mask." The mask was off when she talked about the pain of her elementary school days in the mid-sixties in an upstate New York all-White neighborhood and her post-Civil Rights experiences with physical violence.

50

It was Ku Klux Klan territory and my life was being threatened every day and our house was bombed. I remember sitting on the playground for over an hour on a rainy day, while my parents were trying to get me into this public school. When I was admitted, the school bus would not pick me up.

On my way home from school, a high school kid grabbed my shoulder and said, "Nigger, if you go through these woods again, I am going to break you and throw you in the swimming pool." I ran home crying.

Stone's family was highly mobile, moving across many states. In each move, her father challenged the limits of "place." And each challenge brought reprisals. When they moved into a White neighborhood in the 1980s in the Midwest, they were harassed. The neighbors and their dogs would harm their farm animals. On one occasion, her father, a minister, "blew a dog's brains out." She said, "The White folks did not like it, and they threatened to bomb us. They started a fire on the grass." She ended our discussion of her racial experiences by saying, "We had to fight battles with the White folks, the fire department, the health department, and the police department. The fire department excused the fire as 'they were not trying to burn down the property.' There are so many racist things, I could go on and on."

I could "go on and on" relating the stories of physical violence among the Talented One Hundred, but I shall pause here to reiterate the major points of the story lines.

Reliance on physical violence is the most fundamental control device used by Whites to maintain a sense of place for Blacks, in order that Whites may continue their domination and exploitation and maintain racial privilege. Control, domination, and exploitation take place in every major arena of this society, and personal physical violence is an integral feature; but it is less prevalent today than before the Civil Rights movement.

Race privilege is, as in the story of Lee Watson, Whites preventing Blacks from praying or reading during slavery years. These practices were used to keep slaves from organizing and revolting. To maintain a cheap source of labor, it was essential to have uneducated and passive slaves. Whether racial privilege is to keep Blacks from voting and organizing to obtain power, as in Walker-Taylor's story, or to keep Blacks from being economically independent, as in Lowery's and McMillian's stories, "race privilege is not simply economic. It is a matter of status also," says Robert Blauner in *Racial Oppression in America*.[7] To indicate differential social status, it is important for Whites to keep Blacks out of certain neighborhoods or schools, as seen in Renee's account, or to keep Black women and men from wearing their calico dresses and their khaki pants, as described by Lee.

Some of the Talented One Hundred who participated in the Civil

Rights movement encountered personal and institutional violence. However, they have rarely encountered it as professionals during the post-Civil Rights era. But the rise of physical violence in the nation during the past few years, perceived by many as "gone with the wind," may once again subject the modern Black elite to physical violence. While the recent incidents of physical violence have been primarily directed at the Black working class and underclass, as the Black elite move into predominantly White suburbia, they, too, may become victims. The probability of encountering physical violence is increasing, given the rise in campus violence in the late 1980s and the early 1990s. College-educated individuals who participate in campus violence represent the most "enlightened" members of society and thus the hope of a more democratic society. Their overt racist behavior has surprised and shocked those in academe and others throughout the nation.

However, given the fact that most college-age students were not born yet when the Civil Rights struggle was going on and given the shrinking economic opportunities, campus violence should not shock or surprise us. Physical violence seems to be related to the downturn in the economic cycle and to the segment of society in which the economic threat is most visible. With the tightening job market among college graduates, racism is a reaction by some White students to protect their interests and to maintain their statuses. Before the late sixties, there were very few Blacks on White campuses. At the time they entered in larger numbers, the economy was expanding. The individual physical violence on campus or in other segments of society is not overtly sanctioned and supported by the larger society, and it is a rarity among the modern Black elite. Though a few Black elite continue to be physically threatened, like Renee Stone and her family, who live in a White neighborhood, others have not experienced such threats in the past twenty years. But they are still affected by earlier experiences which have left psychic scars.

Most of the Talented One Hundred avoided the closed doors of segregation while growing up in the South. But, in the face of physical violence, some were made stronger in their convictions to change the system and their place in it. At the beginning of this chapter, we met Jack B. Lane, who said that the violence he encountered during the Civil Rights movement made him stronger in his religious convictions and faith.

> It convinced me that I don't know what the end is going to be. I don't know the outcome. I don't know whether I am going to live or not. But I am going on anyway. I am going to take the leap of faith and go. You may get arrested and jailed; you may be tear gassed and bull whipped. But I am going on anyway. You felt like you were involved in a holy crusade, and you came to the point where you were prepared to stare

death in the face to arrive at the prize. And that's why we would sing "keep your eyes on the prize—hold on, hold on."

The Impact of Cultural Domination

The most effective way to win allies among the oppressed is to control their belief system—the way one perceives the world and thinks about objects and events. Cultural domination is more subtle than physical violence, and it is employed as a means of social control. It defines the backdrop for the important socialization process. Language becomes that backdrop and the important symbol and defining tool for the transmission of culture. Language is used to define, validate, and invalidate the oppressed and their customs, rituals, values, and institutions by negating and denigrating them. This integral and universal feature of culture influences people's thoughts and experiences more than is recognized.

The old proverb "Sticks and stones may break my bones, but names will never hurt me" is not an accurate reflection of reality. We recall that Renee Stone had vivid memories of physical violence while growing up in the 1960s. Yet, she could also clearly recall the psychic impact of her elementary school days of being ignored, ostracized, and called names. She said:

> Children would take apples to school to give to their teacher. I would take pretty little maple leaves that I had found on the way to school. The teacher would look at them and throw them in the trash. The teachers never let me assume leadership roles in their little chicken skit. The children teased and called me "nigger."

Such language as "nigger" is used to divide people into categories. Thus, language is pivotal to understanding Frantz Fanon's theory that a Manichean world view undergirds human violence and oppression. Hussein Bulhan notes in *Frantz Fanon and the Psychology of Oppression* that:

> A Manichean view is one that divides the world into compartments and people into different "species." This division is based not on reciprocal affirmations, but rather on irreconcilable opposites cast into good versus evil, beautiful versus ugly, intelligent versus stupid, White versus Black, human versus subhuman modes. This duality of opposites is not dialectical and hence not an attempt toward a higher synthesis. Its logic is a categorical either/or, in which one of the terms is considered superfluous and unacceptable. Yet in reality, this duality of opposites in the Manichean outlook are [sic] interdependent. Each is defined in terms of its opposite and each derives its identity in opposition to the other.[8]

Out of a Manichean world view a duality has emerged between the values of Western and non-Western people. In the Manichean world view, the Western world defined its values as good and superior, and consequently these views were to be extolled. Non-Western values were defined as bad and inferior, and these views had to be denigrated. The cultural transmission of a Manichean world view has a major role in perpetuating racism through the socialization process, whether consciously or unconsciously. The process of cultural domination for White American children begins when they first hear the nursery rhyme, "Mirror, mirror on the wall, who is the fairest of them all?" They begin "feeding and cutting their teeth on the milk of Mother Racism," said Ruth Shelly, a fifty-three-year-old sociologist. Black, Brown, and Yellow children have already been weaned from the benefits of its nourishment, because the mirror does not reflect them.

Thus, the oppressor aims to define the reality of the oppressed group, which incorporates, at some level in its ways of thinking, acting, and feeling, both consciously and unconsciously, the definition of the oppressor group. It is necessary for their survival and success in an oppressive system. It is *The Mark of Oppression,* as Kardiner and Ovesey recognized nearly forty years ago.[9]

Michael Lomax, the first Black chairman of the board of the Fulton County Commission in Atlanta and a professor of literature, in his early forties, expressed well the psychic impact of the mark of oppression. While growing up in Los Angeles, California, in the 1950s, the son of a journalist and a lawyer, Lomax watched the drama of the Civil Rights movement unfolding from his integrated environment. He knows how racism rules emotional health. Although there was the positive side of seeing Blacks "standing up for their rights," there was also a "downside of the movement" for Lomax.

One downside effect of the Civil Rights movement was particularly traumatic for him. Between the ages of fourteen and sixteen, he visited Alabama with his family. His mother covered the Civil Rights movement for their family-owned newspaper. He recalled, "It was a very painful experience. I grew up in an integrated environment where I had protection from such overt hostility and violence. When I went South in the early sixties, it was very violent; Black people were vulnerable. It was traumatic, and it took a long time [for me] to recover. My brothers and sisters still refuse to visit the South."

Another downside of the Civil Rights movement for Lomax was seeing the "negative images repeated over and over again on television" of Black children trying to enter integrated schools and being met with White hostility. He said, "These negative images were confusing and harmful and gave a low self-image. It was damaging to the ego. It took me a long time to understand that the negative things that were said by White people about us as a people had unconscious implications. We internalize a lot of it, and we do not realize how strongly we internalize it, until we think about it." He pointed out that:

> From day one, my mother may tell me Black is beautiful and my church may say that. But every time I turn on the television, everything that is beautiful is White. Everything that is ugly is Black. Everything that is good is White, and everything that is sinful is Black. These are the values that our society promotes. When I see a beautiful woman on television, she is more likely to have blond hair. When I see a strong, assertive man in a position of power, he is more likely to have blond hair and blue eyes. So all of these images wind up consciously and unconsciously causing conflict in a Black person's mind.

The preoccupation with skin color created a conflict for him, even within his family. Though Lomax is "fairer" in complexion than most Blacks, in his family, he was the least "fairest of them all." "My grand-mothers looked like two little old White ladies. I was considered dark-skinned in my family," he quipped. When I asked how his family treated him, he responded, "To be honest with you, there was a conflict. Because of my grandmother coming out of a social hierarchy, which was in part based on skin color, I was not high on the totem pole. I was not as high as my baby brother who's got blue/green eyes, sandy brown hair, and a white skin tone." He laughed again, saying his brother has a problem trying to figure out who he is.

Lomax said the psychic effect of the mark of oppression was "harmful." "I wanted to change and be like my brother." Lomax never thought of himself as light-skinned. "I always thought I was dark; my complexion is a relative matter."

Lomax knows, like Ethel King, that if Blacks internalize those negative images, it can have devastating consequences for their self-esteem. Ethel, thirty-seven years old, is a successful journalist with a major newspaper. But her road to success has been paved with pain, her path deviating more than others among the Talented One Hundred. Although most of Ethel's formative years were spent in a small town in the South, the family traveled a lot with her father, a career military person. She grew up in a supportive and loving family who told her she could become the president. When she was in the eleventh grade, she was among the fifty Black students bused to an all-White school with a student body of two thousand. She said:

> I didn't want to be at that White school, because I felt I wasn't wanted. I was always a person pretty much into emotions, and I wanted to feel I was needed and loved. It was very important to me. The way I acted out was that the White teachers didn't think I was so bright, so I acted out in total confusion and ended up skipping classes. No one understood what

55

was happening to me. There were a lot of other things going on, so the teachers only saw me as this problem child. At the time, I didn't understand myself.

Her image of herself was poor, even though she defiantly said, "I didn't believe I was less than a White person. I think I had bought into it without realizing it until I went to school with Whites. I was believing in some of the things I said I didn't about myself. I was shocked at myself—afraid to raise my hand in class for fear I wouldn't know the answer and embarrass not only myself, but every Black person in America."

Ethel King left school and ended up pregnant. Her plans to go to college were put aside. She got married and moved to North Carolina, but she soon separated from her husband. She said, "Things got progressively worse. I became a very confused teenager and got into lots of trouble. I got involved with drugs and the wrong crowd. I got arrested for shoplifting and arrested for possession of drugs." The major turning point for Ethel came when she was arrested in North Carolina for the possession of drugs. She vividly recalled the incident which led to her turning point:

> I was about twenty-two years old and my daughter was about three. While waiting for my trial, I spent the summer in jail. I remember looking out the window and seeing my relatives carrying my daughter. They pointed up to the window and waved, as if to say, "That's your mother up there." I said to myself, this is crazy. I don't want anyone else to raise my child. That was always clear, when everything else was muddled. I wanted this child to do well and I thought I could raise her. I said I am not going to go to jail. I didn't change overnight. It took awhile. I had to look at myself and look at life to try to change myself. I asked, What is this thing called life? How did I get to this point? What is wrong with me? I had to go through a long internal process to change.

After reflecting on this period in her life, she remarked, "I used to associate being Black with being down and out and being cool. I used to be ashamed that my family had a lot more than other Blacks. When I lived among Blacks while growing up, I was uncomfortable with my privileged status, but I didn't feel that way when I lived among Whites. I only associated being Black with being down and out. So to prove myself as a regular Black person, I had to hang in the streets."

"I can look back and say I came a long way," said the sensitive young journalist. Indeed, she has. But there are thousands of young, gifted Blacks who never make the return trip from the psychological damage of racism.

Like Lomax and Ethel, Teresa Hale, a fifty-three-year-old psychologist now living in California, grew up in Louisiana and also knows the emotional legacy of racism. While growing up, she learned to protect her self-esteem by ignoring racism.

I grew up under highly discriminatory circumstances and later worked in institutions that did not serve Blacks, both during my early childhood and later on as an adult in California. It was the order of the day, whether overt or covert. There had not been specific incidents aimed directly at me, but overall pervasive, restrictive discrimination. I was accustomed to it. I had developed an armor—blindness. Discrimination was expected and accepted by me as a reality. It still surrounds me. I now know that there are legal approaches which may, with enough time, money, and effort, be effective.

The racism contributed to her feeling "demoralized and ineffectual," but, she said, "I had learned to live with it and, at the same time, to seek dignity, meaning, and self-validation. I am sure this repressive approach has been detrimental to both my mental and physical well-being."

Though the mark of oppression left its psychic scars on Teresa, Ethel, and Lomax, Ethel appeared to sustain more emotional injury. While growing up, she seemed, more than Lomax and Teresa, to internalize the negative emotional pain emanating from racism. Lomax's mother tried to balance the negative images he saw of Blacks by instilling positive images to insulate him against emotional injury. Teresa, on the other hand, chose to ignore racism as a way of insulating herself from psychic injury.

The examples of Ethel, Lomax, and Teresa illustrate the psychic damage sustained by the Black elite while growing up in America. Most of the Talented One Hundred expressed similar experiences and feelings, depending on their level of tolerance, racial sensitivity, and awareness. Although a few of the Talented One Hundred claimed that they had *never* experienced racism, they described virulent incidents that sounded like those experienced by other participants. While the racial experiences of their youth continued to "touch" the Black elite, they faced more psychic pain from racism as they moved into the mainstream as professionals.

Leo Aramis, a thirty-four-year-old journalist, argued that "racism touches everyone. You can't grow up in this society without it touching you." Leo believes that the Black elite who lack identity clarity are more likely to deny racism. To succeed by the majority standards in this society, some token Blacks feel it is necessary to negate their racial identity. What are the psychological consequences?

The Token Black Elite: Dilemmas and Contradictions

Some Black elite, in the quest for success, negate their racial identity. Robert Snow, a city attorney for a large metropolitan city in California, feels this could lead to the denial of racism, which manifests itself in negative attitudes and behaviors toward other Blacks.

People who make it all the way to the top ignore a lot of racism. They refuse to deal with racist acts, or they don't see them as racist acts. They don't put any color attachment to it. Even if they do, they don't deal with it. They skirt around it. They have come to the conclusion that they are not Black or it is not good for them to identify with being Black. It is not uncommon to go to functions and you are the only Black. If another Black shows up, it is likely to produce hostility. They will avoid you. I sense that many times, even though they are similar in terms of background, education, and income. They see Blacks and deny them. There is a recognition, but a sense of avoidance and denial. They believe it is necessary to get where they are going. And some people genuinely believe there is no racism. They believe we bring all the problems on ourselves; therefore, racism is hardly worth talking about. If you are in the process of denying the importance of it, it is hard to admit racism.

Sharla Frances, a forty-two-year-old chief administrator for a large metropolitan area in the South, also questioned the integrity of tokens who deny racism or who say they feel comfortable being "different" in White environs.

I think they feel isolated, but behave in a different way. They know they aren't any different from other Blacks. Their success suggests they are. But in their hearts, they know they're not. They pretend they like being a token but in their hearts, they can't stand it. The people I know in this situation live lives of alienation and frustration. They are angry, hostile, quick to blow up, and standoffish. They are professionally competent, but mopish. In fact, that is the way they may behave in a close context, but from afar they act as though they love it and brag about it. They tell you "I am comfortable being different," but the way they behave is "I hate it."

Graham Boston, an internationally renowned scientist/engineer, admitted that he did not like being different, but he was accepting it. "I come into an environment and somebody says, 'Hey, you are different.' It makes me look at myself and recognize that I am different now."

John Hubbard, a forty-year-old professor of sociology at a predominantly White university, was also doubtful about the token Black who enjoys the status of tokenship.

I think most token Blacks are miserable, whether they admit it to themselves or not. Any token Black by definition is separated from the collectivity of his or her kind. When you are separated from the collectivity, you are alienated. Separation from others of one's kind, as Karl Marx calls it "species being," is to be alienated. When Blacks are taken apart from other Blacks in the work setting, they are estranged from other Black people. In this estrangement, alienation, and separation from one's own kind, the individual ultimately, in a spiritual sense, winds up committing suicide, unless they maintain contact with other Blacks. I say those who enjoy the status of being a token are fucked up in the head. I see people who enjoy the status of being a token reject themselves and their blackness.

Whether or not one relishes being a token, there are a number of dilemmas and contradictions of being one, says Rosabeth Kanter in *Men and Women of the Corporation*. Her assumptions about token women are applicable to the male and female Black elite in predominantly White settings. The social isolation of the Black elite, if they lack proper coping skills, contributes to psychological damage and the individualization of experiences. Psychic violence is also imposed when the Black elite are denied a reference group with whom to identify. Let us look at some ways the Black elite may be affected.

First, the experience of being a token and the lack of self-validation, if one lacks a support system, contributes to isolation and loneliness. Yet, as Kanter notes, the "dynamics of interaction around them create a pressure for them to seek advantage by disassociating themselves from others of their category."[10] The Talented One Hundred reported that in their interactions with White peers and colleagues in formal and informal settings, they are constantly doing a balancing act. Should they speak to or sit with another Black at lunch or at a professional gathering? If they sit with Blacks, how will this be interpreted by their White colleagues? It is okay if Whites sit together. If two or more Blacks sit together, it was reported that Whites get suspicious. Blacks are also concerned with how other Blacks will interpret their behaviors. My participants often reported noticing the lack of eye contact or other body language signalling discomfort displayed by another Black while in the presence of Whites, suggesting a level of discomfort when other Blacks are present. Even in predominantly Black settings, there are similar dynamics, but not nearly as frequently as in predominantly White settings. Blacks are more likely to include or defend Whites than Whites are to include or defend Blacks in White settings. It seems Blacks emphasize fairness more, perhaps because of their greater sensitivity to oppression.

Second, although the Black elite are aware of their racial differences, because of their underrepresentation in organizations, they deny racism or do not talk about it, particularly in the corporate setting. If they do so, they are seen as "too sensitive." They have to play the role of "entertainer" to some extent, that is, they have to "fit in." Blacks often have to be nice, friendly, and cheerful. If Blacks express too much confidence, it is defined as arrogance. In general, never mind how unpleasant a White may be to Blacks, Blacks should be nice to Whites. If Blacks complain, they are viewed as disruptive and not a "good fit."

Often the victim is made to feel like the victimizer. For instance, when Diane Earlinger filed suit against a former employer, she felt like the victim. Before her employment as the first woman in her present position in a federal agency, Earlinger filed a suit with E.E.O. against a major corporation for discrimination. She said:

> I became aware of how difficult a decision that is. I only understood at that time why people have a difficult time acknowledging discrimination in an overt way. It's almost as if you are guilty about how you've been treated. It is a strange set of dynamics. I tended to feel guilty, which sounded stupid as if to say "Gosh, I really should be grateful for what they've done for me."

She concluded, "The other thing that happened is that you almost have to acknowledge that you haven't escaped. You are just like every other nigger. You may think for a period of time it is different for you, because you've done certain things. But it isn't."

Earlinger was victimized twice. She suffered guilt because she filed a suit against the company that hired her. And even though the E.E.O. found reasonable cause for discrimination in Earlinger's case, the agency was underfunded and thus unable to act on her case.

When Earlinger filed her discrimination suit against a former employer, she had no idea that in her present position she would one day be charged with reverse discrimination. When Earlinger hired a Black person, a White female felt that she should have been hired for the position, so she filed suit against her. (Interestingly, Earlinger was defended by E.E.O. lawyers in her agency.)

Third, although Blacks are highly visible as tokens and may be used to support an organization's image as an equal opportunity employer, they often do not get to participate in major decisions that are made informally. Walter Calvin, one of the highest ranking Black CEOs in the United States, said, "The greatest source of current discrimination that I experience is that, even though I am active at a level in the organization that demands exposure to the best country clubs, because I am Black, I am not invited to play golf. I have to join a club that is of a lesser quality. I will invite them to play on my course, but I don't get an invitation."

Fourth, when Blacks participate in informal gatherings of colleagues, they cannot let their guard down and relax too much. There is a sense that they are being tested. Warner Babbitt said he is convinced that Whites have a "drink test, and if you let your tongue get loose," some judgment will be made about that behavior and eventually held against you.

The informal flow of information is another way to neutralize the authority of Blacks. Frank Russo said that when he issues an organizational policy, his White assistants frequently withhold information from their subordinates.

Fifth, in the realm of interpersonal interaction, Blacks reported, as did Rudy in the prologue, that their positions, status, or ideas were constantly being invalidated. When Diane Earlinger attended meetings, it was often assumed that she was a secretary. In one meeting, the minutes were never taken. A White female who had been sent to take the minutes assumed Diane was the secretary. In another instance, Jefferson Barnes, chairman of a department at a major university and in his early fifties, said that when he wanted to use the library stacks, he was asked to present his ID, even though he identified himself. Pat Robinson, a federal judge, told me that three or four times a year when he called attorneys for a conference and asked their names, they responded to his court clerk by asking, "Where is the judge?" The first time it happened, he said, "I lost my coolness and stared at the attorney." The counselor responded, "You don't have on a robe." His friend suggested that the next time he should handle it by saying, "The judge only handles important cases, and I am the janitor, so I'll handle these crappy little cases," he said, laughing.

Crystal Miller is a professor in the department of Afro-American Studies in a university in the West. Even though she has published extensively, Crystal knows what it means to be invalidated. "As a professional Black woman, there are numerous instances in dealing with Whites where they are making the assumption that Blacks are not quite as equal as they are. There are many subtleties." I probed for an example, and she said:

> The White person you are interacting with is not allowing you the validity of your own experience. I was teaching a workshop in liberal arts, as a faculty member, and there were only two other Blacks, the only minorities out of 150 participants. We were having dinner—my husband, the two Black participants, and myself. The table was comprised of four Blacks and one White, which was unusual. We were talking about several things, and we noticed the person who was serving the table was slow in doing that. We were talking about racial issues, and one of the Black men said that when slow service happens to him, because he is a Black person, he suspects it has to do with race. The White person at the table kept saying, "It may not be that—it may be something else." The Black man kept trying to get him to understand that it may not be prejudice on the part of the waitress, but because of the nature of his experience in this society, it was natural for him to consider that. The White person simply could not understand that. He kept saying, "Sometimes I get slow service, so it could be that."
>
> Not allowing that person to have the experience, interpret it, and

understand why that person is making that interpretation, and the White person not extending himself to understand that, is an example of a subtle racist manifestation of invalidating experience. The Black person was not saying he was being discriminated against—he was saying that this is what goes through his mind.

Crystal further stated, "Professionally, people make assumptions about what you know and don't know. Whenever I introduce myself as being in Afro-American Studies, the lids go down. The assumption is made that you are pigeon-holed in a box. Obviously, you don't know anything, and you are inferior. You are an idealogue. You are an affirmative action case."

Many Whites say to Blacks that they are in their position because of affirmative action; this is a double-edged sword. The affirmative action policy did allow Blacks to enter the mainstream. However, the credentials and integrity of talented Blacks who are qualified and who have achieved meritoriously are called into question. Although Black achievers have benefited from the policy of affirmative action, some individuals remain ambivalent, because it does not acknowledge individual merit. Furthermore, the charge of reverse discrimination, arising from the affirmative action program, has become the new ideology of White males to maintain their privileges.[11]

So when she was ignored as an affirmative action quota in Black Studies, Crystal Miller said, "it takes some discussions with the person [to establish] that you are a human being and you follow a discipline as well as anybody else. I don't make assumptions about people who are in the English department. If you say you are a historian, I want to know more about it. It is the kind of subtlety that people don't always recognize. They are making assumptions based on what you look like. Blacks make the assumption that people in Black Studies don't know anything either."

Ideas and suggestions are also picked up only when Whites present them. Often, if Blacks want to get a suggestion enacted, they may get a White colleague to present the idea. The rejection induces anger, frustration, and a sense of helplessness. If Blacks do not understand this racist pattern, they will internalize it and decide something is wrong with them.

Sixth, the Black elite are symbols of their race and also the exceptions. "You are different from other Blacks" is a comment often heard by the Talented One Hundred. It serves to individualize their experiences; however, if one of them fails, then he or she becomes a negative embodiment of characteristics attributed to the race. The Black elite are under much pressure to be "ambassadors for the race."

Graham Boston, who was raised in a predominantly White setting and who prefers to live and work in one, knows what it means to be "different" and to be a "symbol for the race."

I may be attending a party, and I am the only Black person there. Some White people come up to me and say, "Some of my best friends are Black." When they say that, they say I am different. So if I am in a situation where someone comes up to me and says I am different because I am Black—that isolates me. I will walk into that situation and say I am like everybody else, until somebody comes up and reminds me that I am different. I don't look at myself as Black and everybody else as White. There is a bunch of people out there. I am one of them and that's because of the way I was raised.

Boston said that when he became world renowned,

people reminded me I was Black. Everybody did. The public did because I was unique. The neighbors said I was a unique person. I recognized I was different. Surprisingly enough, I thought it was bad. It made me feel different. And I wasn't used to feeling different. I felt the same as everybody else. [Did you feel like a symbol representing the race?] Yes. But I wasn't used to that. I was accustomed to just being Graham, just the average person. I don't look at myself as Black and as different from other people.

Even though Graham Boston doesn't look at himself "as Black and as different from other people," a racist society does. No matter how brilliant, talented, or world renowned, the color line is a reality. As Leo Aramis reminds us:

Racism touches everyone. You can't grow up in this society without it touching you. It's like being in a room with people who are throwing mud. Even if you don't choose to throw mud, you are backed up against the wall, even if you choose not to be involved. The nature of mud is that it will splatter on you. There will be mud on your shoes, pants, and skirt, because that is the nature of racism. Blacks who deny racism are either fooling themselves or they have been somewhere I haven't been.

The Impact of Social Domination

Like cultural domination, the violence of social domination is more subtle than physical violence. Social dominance is employed by the dominant group as another way to maintain racial privileges in the socioeconomic arena.

Each year, the *Annual Report* of the Urban League on the state of Black America begins with an objective statistical portrait of discrimination in unemployment and education, and the impact of racial discrimination on the life chances of Blacks—the racial landscape of America. It does not tell us much, however, about the racial layout of the raceway. Is the path smooth or rough? Is it straight or curved?

For many of the Talented One Hundred, the raceway is rough. Roscoe Champion, the soft-spoken honor graduate in high school and college and a backstage organizer in the Civil Rights movement, described his journey. Champion, a forty-five-year-old judge, grew up in a large Southern city. He knew about discrimination and what it meant to be defined as inferior. His parents explained to him very early that "Whites felt superior to Blacks and there was a considerable effort to keep Blacks down," and he was going to "have a difficult time as a Black person." Hence, his mother encouraged him to be successful and to go to college. He had been among the first four Black law students admitted to a predominantly White university in the South in the late 1960s. He did well in law school, though he encountered the usual discrimination—being graded unfairly and being ignored or dismissed by professors and students. After finishing law school, he passed the bar and went to work as one of the first Blacks in a district attorney's office.

Shortly after this appointment in the late sixties, he was drafted for the Vietnam War. He thought he would "automatically be assigned to the Judge Advocate General's office, the legal unit of the military," because of his background. He knew it happened to others who were drafted—the doctors went into medical service and his White lawyer classmates had been assigned to the JAG office. But he was given the classification of MOS rifleman. The army's plan for him was "to go to Vietnam and shoot."

This racial arrow left Champion wounded—his blackness invalidated any sense of privilege gained from his status as a lawyer. "It was my first visceral encounter with racism. I got incensed. I was so hurt. I felt an injustice had been done to me. This was the first time I had experienced what other Blacks had." When he saw the classification, he assumed it was an error, but it wasn't. He complained to the first sergeant, but there was no result. He wrote to his senators, but they could not assist him. He wrote to the NAACP, the Urban League, the SCLC, and the Civil Rights office.

He said, "When the first sergeant got wind of my trying to get my MOS changed to a classification consistent with my training, he called a special formation and announced, 'We have someone with a law degree who thinks he is better than the rest of us and should not be made to carry a rifle and go to fight in Vietnam like men fight.' "

Everyone was aware that Champion was the object of this ridicule, since he was the only one with a law degree. The sergeant continued tauntingly, "The person I am talking about should know that someone long ago went to war with a rifle and had a law degree and received a congressional medal of honor—he thinks he is too good to do it."

Roscoe felt good when the Black GIs supported him 100 percent.

"They felt the sergeant was after me and it was wrong. They were upset that he had called a special formation to ridicule me. That is why I believe in my people, because they could have taken a different position—that you are no better than I am." He had gotten along well with the GIs, remembering that his mother always told him to "respect others and you'll get respect."

One night, while on duty, the first sergeant said, "Corporal Champion, catch the next bus!" Champion said, "I knew I was leaving. God told me. I believe in God—my prayers had been answered." The sergeant was angry and tried to detain him in the rain.

The next morning, he went to the JAG office and the major said, " 'They've been raising hell in Washington about you—the Urban League and the NAACP. I didn't know that you were here with a law degree. We would have sought to have your classification changed, because we don't have any Black lawyers.' He asked if I wanted to become a JAG officer. I turned him down because I wanted to get back to civilian legal practice. I will never forget that experience," said Champion.

Although Champion's racial encounter took place in the late sixties, after the Civil Rights movement, when Blacks had supposedly gained legal and social rights, it was more typical of the overt racism experienced by the Talented One Hundred before the movement. Overt racism is still, however, very much a part of the cultural and social landscape. When the Talented One Hundred grew up in the South with *de jure* segregation and in the North and West with *de facto* segregation before the 1960s, the racial waters were more turbulent. Since then, the racial waters have calmed.

Within the broader cultural and social areas, it is important to recognize different realms of activities in which racial violence manifests itself. By way of illustration, I have chosen to explore the realms of education, economics, housing, the media, and sexual racism, for examples of racial violence.

The Educational Realm

Racial privilege and dominance are not only economic, as Blauner reminds us; they are also a matter of status. Thus, they are an integral part of the educational landscape. While growing up, the Talented One Hundred were likely to have experienced overt racism. Those Black elite who grew up in the South experienced legal segregation in education. Although the facilities were generally inadequate, dedicated Black teachers, who were denied entry into other occupations, used their creative energies to nurture the aspirations of Black students. The Black elite who came of age in the North and West were usually gerrymandered into Black schools, and their White teachers, with the exception of a few, were often not supportive of their aspirations. In general, the Talented One Hundred who attended predominantly White schools reported exclusion from extracurricular activities. They also often had separate athletic programs, segregated student councils, and/or separate proms.

Take Albert Sungist, a minority officer at a major university on the West Coast, for example. He has strong memories of his experience in a predominantly White school in a large city. "The most vivid experience I had was with White teachers." He had been speaking softly, but his voice rose several notes when he said, "Sometimes I felt teachers singled me out for special treatment, but I can't put my finger on it. It was most uncomfortable. It created a lot of doubt about my intellectual abilities." His aunt kept up his spirits, reminding him to be "patient, understanding, and strive for what you want." His self-confidence was not restored until he entered college as an adult and was influenced by his White sociology professor. He eventually went on to achieve a Ph.D. in sociology at a major university.

Timothy Brownlee, a forty-eight-year-old public official, and Ronald Fellows, an educator and entrepreneur in his early fifties, had similar experiences with their respective high school counselors. Black males in their schools were discouraged from going to college because of their supposed lack of intelligence. Instead, they were encouraged to become firemen or policemen, to go into the army, or to go to work in a local factory. "I was skinny, nearsighted, and half-deaf; I knew no cop was going to put me on the force. The counselor would show us the test scores. I knew he was wrong," said Fellows. The negative encouragement was also mitigated by his parents who "wanted me to do better than they." Brownlee, who enjoyed reading René Descartes, Charles de Montesquieu, and Adam Smith, found himself tracked with the "really slow students." The slow classes were all Black except for one or two Whites. After a few weeks, his teachers could see that he did not belong in this class. His parents and grandparents were the "striving force" that kept him motivated in school. Brownlee and Fellows did not know it at the time, but they discovered many years later during their class reunions, that their White counselors had told all Black males in their classes the same thing. Both had attended different schools in different cities in the Midwest.

As we have seen from the above examples, in previously segregated or integrated environments before the 1960s, racism in education was more overt than today in affecting the life chances of Blacks. Now, it is more subtle. When Blacks enter, in any significant numbers, previously closed arenas, the qualifications become higher. (There were, however, temporary measures in the late 1960s and the 1970s to reduce qualifications as a result of political pressure by Blacks.) The screening and tracking process is used to disqualify Blacks and poor people from the system. The process begins as early as kindergarten with IQ tests and continues through graduate and professional training with admissions tests. Since the tests are based on White middle-class norms, they are designed to eliminate minorities and the poor from having access to privileges. Blacks are overly represented in basic educational classes as a direct result of the intelligence tests. National intellectual torchbearers, like Arthur Jensen, an educational psychologist at the University of California, Berkeley, provide the ideological support to sustain racism.[12]

In addition to the tracking system, which results in Blacks being overly represented in vocational rather than college preparatory classes, the curriculum is also Eurocentric oriented. Hence, the culture of other groups is negated and/or denigrated. Black children see few positive role models in their textbooks. The Black history that is presented is often distorted. Blacks are viewed in stereotyped ways or studied as a problem. These educational policies have a negative impact on the self-concept and success of individual Blacks.

Sharla Frances, a forty-two-year-old public administrator for a large city in the South, remembers walking out of her graduate class at a major university in the Northeast in the late 1960s when she read what in her perception was a racist question, "What was the effect of the rising underclass on the state?" The racist atmosphere affected her decision not to obtain a Ph.D. in sociology. Even though her father was a lawyer and her mother, an educator and administrator in the public school system, her White professors assumed, she said, that "I was a deprived Black female, disadvantaged, and an unlikely candidate for graduate school, even though I had been admitted solely on my test scores." On one occasion, she complained about an unfair grade; she knew she deserved an A. The professor said, "'Given your background, you should be pleased with your success at the university.' This was a Jewish professor and I was very quick to tell him my parents were educated when his parents were still coming over on the boat," said Frances.

In addition to the curriculum, there is also the problem of counseling—academically, financially, and socially. There is a dearth of sensitive and responsive student support services and personnel in predominantly White educational settings, whether at the elementary level or at the university level, for Black students. As the only Black on her university counseling staff, Teresa Hale has to be "both an advocate and teacher of Black interests and concerns. There is a lack of knowledge and sensitivity to Black issues." Teresa said:

> Being a Black spokesperson is an awesome responsibility when trying to represent the highly varying values and concerns of Californian Blacks. When I speak of diversity within the Black community, White opponents

who are against special assistance for minorities often seek to use this diversity argument as proof that there are no Black values or special needs.

The shortage of relevant personnel has made my work extremely draining and usually misunderstood and unappreciated by White colleagues. The never-ending education, advocacy, and jack-of-all-trades aspect of my work has been devastating to my psychological and physical health. I had to take a disability leave. Fortunately, now there are more minority professional organizations and conferences than when I started in the field. They are a big help, but they are inadequate for the day-to-day, on-the-job lonely struggles.

These more subtle examples of racism can be documented by showing their differential impact on the life chances of Blacks. Blacks experience these discriminatory acts by agents of institutions on an individual level. Sometimes they expend much energy analyzing the sources of oppression that adversely affect their self-images and their successes.

The Talented One Hundred are baffled about whether an act is race related or not. Though they observe differential treatment, they also question whether it is their politics, their personality, their physical appearance, their sex, their race, or some combinations of these characteristics. Their "minority sense," as Johnnetta Cole, an anthropologist, called it, tells them race is always a relevant factor.

John Daniels, a sixty-two-year-old corporate executive, remembers that in his predominantly White junior high school in Indiana,

> the teacher would seat you alphabetically, but I always wound up in the back of the room, and others would be sitting right in front of the teacher. It became clear there was some fiddling with it. In one line, you'll have nine people and the other line, you'll have five people. They deliberately put me in the back. I told my mother and she gave them hell when they moved my seat. It affected my performance in the class in a negative way.

Rosenthal and Jacobson show how subtle attitudes of teachers can affect the performance of students. They told teachers in their study that certain children (randomly picked) were "potential academic spurters." On the basis of tests administered at the beginning of the year and other occasions over two years, "the children from whom teachers expected greater intellectual gains showed such gains." Not only did students perform better on the IQ tests, but also the teachers felt they had a better chance at success in later life. They were seen as "happier, more curious, and more interesting than other children." [13]

The children involved in this study were White. One can only imagine the detrimental and traumatic effects on Black children. The insidious patterns of nonverbal behaviors of teachers, like dismissing or ignoring, were constantly reported by the Talented One Hundred who had attended predominantly White elementary and high schools. Their White teachers' silent language was a constant invalidation of their blackness and their sense of selfhood. (I could easily predict, by the twenty-fifth interview, that individuals who had attended predominantly White or integrated schools were less likely than those who attended segregated schools to say their teachers had been the most important influence outside the family.)

Sometimes the insidious effects of the silent language are so damaging that Blacks react in a manner that is unpredictable to them. Frank Russo, a health administrator, was the first of two Blacks to be admitted to his medical college in the late sixties in the South. He recalled some of his negative racial experiences in medical school. While he ignored some experiences, he confronted others. He was accustomed to being ignored by professors and by fellow students who did not want to study with him or to be his lab partner. But, when a professor "flashed up a picture of an obese nude Black female and everybody laughed," he walked out of his class and complained to the dean, his White mentor. Russo said, "One of my professors in the lab was so prejudiced that he would not even answer questions I addressed to him. And I was a student. When I had to give lectures and teach the class in lab, he would not look under my microscope to see if I had the right slide. So naturally, I spent a lot of time and did a lot of extra work to make sure it was perfect." His experience is similar to those of others among the Talented One Hundred. They complained of studying and working in isolation. Often they did not have a supportive faculty mentor to successfully guide them through graduate or professional school.

Russo recalled one incident which had a major impact on him and almost caused him to leave medical school. A certain professor had stretched his patience.

> One day I was lecturing and every five minutes, he would interrupt me and ask a question. He was trying to be disruptive. I understood temporary insanity. I felt myself getting hot, and he kept on interrupting and interrupting. The next thing I knew, I had him around his neck, pinned against the wall. I never remember walking from the front of the class to the back to get him. I had knocked over pots and pans with hearts and lungs all over the floor. I didn't remember any of that. After it was over, it kind of frightened me because I didn't remember. I went to the Dean and told him I was going to leave before I killed somebody.

Russo laughed as he recounted the story. He said that he can laugh now because he has learned to better navigate the "racial course."

The Economic Realm

The Talented One Hundred made it through the educational hurdles. But they still had to face the job market.

Though overt racism still rules the economic landscape, it is not as blatant now as it was in the 1930s. John Lamont, an eminent physicist, discussed his father's experience with racism during the Depression. Although John's father had only an eighth grade education, he was a brilliant, self-taught aeronautical and aviation engineer, who supported the family for a time as a cook on an estate of a wealthy White woman. During his leisure time, he developed inventions in the field of aeronautical engineering and received a patent related to aircraft engines. When the Depression was over, he was unable to pursue his avocation because of his nine-to-five work schedule as a janitor at a gas company in Washington, D.C. He had aspirations to move up from janitor to craftsman at his workplace. But his ambitions were not the order of that day. He "went to the foreman one day and told him he would like to try for a job as a machinist. The foreman laughed at him and said, 'How do you know how to operate those devices?'" His father said, "I'll show you." It turned out that he knew how to operate them, because he was a skilled craftsman. The foreman became so enraged that he fired him on the spot.

Since the late 1960s, the racial climate has changed. There is legal recourse if one is fired solely on the basis of race. Yet, Ferdinand Hamilton, the highest ranking Black administrator at a major university in the Midwest, knows there is still a ceiling in the 1990s. "I've been here sixteen years and I've done my job well," he said. He has lots of respect from his White colleagues, Black faculty, staff, and students. His White colleagues comment on how proficient he is as a writer. "Niggers are not supposed to write," said Hamilton. "Even at this stage, you have to prove yourself." Though he has worked hard and earned respect from his White peers, "no one has come and said, 'I've got an opening as vice president of communications.' No one has asked me to apply for it. As long as I am dealing with the Black man's issue, I do an excellent job there and that's fine." His White colleagues cannot, however, trust him outside the Black perimeter and put him in a "more global setting." Hamilton, the assistant to one of the top White administrators at his university, added, "There is an assistant-to-the-provost phenomenon in higher education."

Though the economic cast of racism has changed since John Lamont's father played the supporting character of the janitor in the 1930s, the leading players remain White. Blacks, as (mostly) employees, are often the supporting cast in every major occupational arena.

As a result of the Civil Rights movement and the opening up of equal opportunities, most of the Black elite became employees in predominantly White settings rather than employers. This shift reflects the trend of the larger society as it moves from a manufacturing to a service-oriented economy. There is often a barrier encountered in the recruitment and screening process—an implicit policy not to hire Blacks. The informal interview becomes a way of screening Blacks out. Individuals who do not have access to this information may interpret the discrimination on a personal level.

The Recruitment and Screening Processes

The subtle racism found in the recruitment and screening processes eliminates many talented Blacks. Studies have found that white-collar workers, like blue-collar workers, obtain their jobs through informal personal networks more than by any other method. More importantly, one study found the best indicator of the rate at which Blacks applied and were hired for white-collar positions correlated with the Black racial composition within the organization.[14] In fact, the study suggests this may be more important than the attitudes of personnel officers. Since job advertisement is usually by "word-of-mouth" or by other informal organizational processes, Blacks are often excluded if their numbers in an organization are low or nonexistent. A job may be advertised in agencies where minorities are not well represented. And often, when a job is advertised, an employment decision has already been made. Black applicants can have the same or better education or training as White applicants, but their qualifications remain suspect. The usual assumption is, if you are White, particularly male, you are qualified. Finally, since the classification of "minority" was legally defined to include White women, Orientals, and Hispanics as well as Blacks, the chances of Blacks, who struggled in the sixties more than other oppressed groups to gain opportunities, are greatly diminished.

When a job is available to Black professionals, sometimes the qualifications and standards are increased for Blacks. There is an interest in hiring the "super Black," while the hiring criteria remain lenient for Whites.[15] Thomas B. Thomas, a district sales manager, observed that "Blacks must have a law degree from Harvard to work in the legal unit of my corporation, while the majority of these White guys have degrees from mediocre law schools. These White lawyers would have a hard time trying to make it in private practice, so they work in corporate America or as public defenders."

Leo Aramis said Whites manifest an attitude of "presumed incompetence" toward Blacks. In the eyes of Whites, Blacks never measure up. Hence, their credentials must be beyond the requirement of Whites. Although Jesse Jackson was the most articulate presidential candidate on issues facing this country, receiving over 7 million votes in the 1988 presidential primary, he still had to constantly remind the American public, "I am qualified to be president."

Even when the Black elite have met the objective criteria for a position—educational training and experience—there is an informal interview. Many subjective factors come into play in an interview, such as: physical appearance, height, style of dress, mannerisms, speech pattern, and skin color. In major corporations, Black professionals must represent as closely as possible the organizational norms of middle-class Whites. Hence, Black males and females may be discouraged from wearing their hair in an ethnic style, for example, braids. If their physical appearance, dress, or speech pattern is "too ethnic," it is viewed negatively. When Thomas B. Thomas, for instance, hired a promising salesman, a muscular, dark-skinned man with a "jheri curl," his supervisor did not look favorably upon the hiring. Although the young man performed extremely well on the job, Thomas's supervisor constantly harassed him. The supervisor did hint that he was uncomfortable with the hair style and the physical appearance of the salesman.

An abundance of studies have been done on the correlation between physical attraction and life chances. People who are perceived as attractive have more opportunities. Since there is a differential racial standard of beauty in this society, racist attitudes and practices may be manifested through "attractiveness prejudice." [16]

If Blacks and Whites are not sensitive to the subjective factors in the informal interview process, the Black elite's chances of being hired are reduced, despite qualifications. Whites, consciously or unconsciously, identify with persons with whom they feel more comfortable. Since Whites are likely to feel more comfortable with other Whites, Blacks may be eliminated from the pool of applicants because of this comfortability factor. When Blacks are in a position to hire, they can see more clearly the way in which the interview process operates to exclude them.

Frank Russo, the highest ranking Black in a public health agency, said, "There was a vacant position in the agency and the applicants were a very qualified Black woman and a very qualified White woman."

> We were supposed to get together and talk about the two most qualified candidates—the administrative staff—and then vote. There is only one Black and that's me. Naturally they voted for the White woman. When I asked the basis for their decision, they started out by saying both were qualified for the job. They thought, however, the White woman would fit in better and a few other nebulous things. I told them, "Let me tell you how it is going to be. We are going to hire the Black one if things are that equal between them. While I am here, a Black will get the job."

He added, "I knew they had gotten behind my back and decided to get the White one. They sat there and voted in front of me, and it was done strictly on race." Russo knows there is an implicit policy not to hire Blacks in management, and the informal interview is a way of screening Blacks out. Individuals who do not have access to this information may interpret the discrimination on a personal level. Russo's decision to hire the "qualified Black woman" over the "qualified White woman" was also a race-based choice. But he felt it was the only way to increase the number of Blacks in the agency.

Kelly Smith, a corporate executive with a major firm and in her late thirties, asked, "Do you think another White will give us a job if a White boy is sitting near?" She noted:

> In graduate school, I learned about something called "nonpecuniary gains" that White people derive from working around, being around, and living with other White people. If you have two employees, one Black and one White, the Black employee has to give something more in order to get the same kinds of benefits that the White employee gets, because the employer gets another benefit from his White employee. This is the nonpecuniary gain, and this is why we are fighting all the time.

Since Kelly is a manager, she has seen firsthand the discriminatory process of the informal interview. She was required to take a course in "The Targeting and Selecting Process." According to Kelly:

> There are all kinds of legal mechanisms found in the interview process that people say are objective, while it turns out to be all subjective. It is very discriminatory. There are objectives for interviewing applicants now that are supposed to be legally defensible. They measure people based on a point system with several interviewers asking specific objective questions. But the problem with the "objective" process is that the rating on the answer that the applicant gives is a subjective process. People put in their own biases about how a response should be rated. It boils down to people's biases incorporated into an objective process.

When Kelly was clear on its intent, she stated to colleagues, "It appears that this is nothing more than a legal mechanism to continue discrimination." (Kelly asked me not to print her quote about the targeting and selecting process because she feared that because there are so few Blacks in her position, she would be recognized and punished. I decided to print the quote, not to violate her confidentiality, but to show that the informal process is a standard practice in many organizations and, thus, it would be difficult to identify her.) When I asked how long this process had been used, she reported, "In the last two years." This informal selection process has in actuality been used for many years. Perhaps it is being more finely tuned to avoid lawsuits. What is clear from Kelly Smith's comment is how racism operates to individualize a shared process.

Blacks may also be eliminated from the hiring process because their presence might affect business. Thomas B. Thomas was almost eliminated from a company until he convinced the employer to give him a chance. He stated, "When they hire someone White, they don't ask why you hired that White guy or if you think your client base will accept him. That is not even a question." When the company hired him, he broke all previous records. However, his achievements did not provide an inroad for other Blacks to enter the company, because they did not measure up to his success. Thomas said, "There is a double standard of measuring Blacks. On a group level, Blacks are measured against Whites, usually negatively. On an individual level, Blacks are compared with other Blacks." Hence, if an average or above average Black does not measure up to the "super Black," it becomes another way of controlling opportunities. When another Black employee was hired but did not perform as well as Thomas did in the company, he was terminated. The failings of one Black symbolize a collective failure of the race.

The "super Black" also serves an additional function. That person is a cheap source of labor. Warner Babbitt, a thirty-nine-year-old journalist, said he travels all over the country and has more assignments than a White colleague in his department who writes only one column a week. Yet they receive the same salary.

Sometimes the authority of super Blacks is diffused because their energy is diverted to many projects. Frank Russo said:

> When I do something, I try to do it well. Sometimes you have to be careful that they don't keep adding things on to you deliberately, and you can't do them well. I have begun to wonder if it is a deliberate act—all in the name of "you are doing a great job." So you have to be on your toes to know that. What it does is to dilute you too much, because you have to delegate. You can delegate yourself totally out of it. You need to have time to monitor all of your monitors.

In a *Black Enterprise* survey of readers, 60 percent of those who responded said they were "underpaid considering the level of education, skills, and time logged on the job."[17] There may be explanations for the survey's findings. First, when Black achievers are hired for a position, they have to confront an internal tracking system. There is an entry level "place" for minority men and women and White women, although occasionally they are placed on a fast track. In the downsizing of a corporation or a downturn in the economy, those positions are the most vulnerable. Blacks become "the last hired and the first fired."

The Black middle class is also more heavily represented in sales and in staff positions in human resources than in the mainline positions in corporations.[18] They are also heavily represented as academics in Black Studies programs on White campuses or are concentrated in Black colleges. And, they are overly represented in jobs that are dependent on federal support.

Many Black elite are trapped on the lower rung and become frustrated. The internal training programs are not targeted for the entry level. So when it comes to promotion, the emphasis is on the "best qualified." This usually means the White male who is at the upper level of management and who has acquired the experience. The individuals in my population escaped entry level positions through the sheer force of their personality, their work efforts, their determination, their acceptance of greater work responsibility, and self-responsibility. And perhaps having the support of a mentor also contributed to their accomplishments.

For instance, when Kelly found out about an opening for a better position in her organization through a friend, she went to her supervisor to indicate her interest. He responded, "I don't think they'll give it to you, because you do not have the international experience." Kelly knew her supervisor had recently brought in a colleague with the same experience she had and he was in a position two steps higher than Kelly. Fortunately, she had worked with a CEO who recognized her abilities. The CEO wrote a letter to her supervisor, stating she had "done a wonderful job and had international experience at a city bank in New York." She eventually *got* the promotion for which she was next in line.

Another explanation for the results of the *Black Enterprise* survey is the lack of mentors. The Talented One Hundred frequently indicated that they did not have a mentor. They pulled "double duty" trying to perform their duties effectively and trying to learn the politics of the organization. In particular, Black women expressed more difficulty finding a mentor. For a Black woman in a predominantly White male-oriented setting, social interaction is constrained by the negative, historical, sexual racism between Black women and White men. Dira Ridley, a physical chemist for an international corporation, attends group luncheons with her White male colleagues but limits evening functions or personal interactions to avoid rumors that might affect her career.

For Clarence Pinkney, a forty-three-year-old manager with a major corporation, who arrived from the segregated South in the mid-sixties, not having a mentor meant "a sink or swim approach. . . . More personal initiative was required for the job," said Pinkney, who now ranks among the top Blacks in this international corporation. He told me that there was no one to validate whether he was doing a good job. At the time, he was the only Black. Others reported similar experiences.

Despite the barriers that talented Blacks encounter in the economic arena, their incomes give them more options in the marketplace. However, the option to live where they want to may be denied because of skin color.

The Housing Realm

Racist dominance and privilege are a part of the housing pattern. An analysis of government records of $1 trillion in loan applications by the *Atlanta Journal-Constitution* found that Blacks were rejected more than twice as often as Whites when they applied for home loans at America's savings and loans. This study showed that the Black/White discrepancy in loan rejections was definitely more prevalent in the Midwest and the plains states than in the South. Throughout the country, high-income Blacks' loan rejections were greater than low-income Whites in "85 percent of the one hundred largest metro areas in at least one of the past five years. . . . In thirty-five of the one hundred areas, high-income Blacks were rejected more often than low-income Whites in at least three of the five years."[19] Michael Lomax, a highly esteemed public official in Atlanta, was rejected for a housing loan.

Prior to the sixties, most Black elite lived in segregated communities. Now, most of the Talented One Hundred who live outside the South are in integrated or predominantly White neighborhoods. Finding adequate housing has presented problems for many at varying points in their lives. In fact, housing was the one area where the Talented One Hundred had encountered the most discrimination. Sometimes the signs were blatant, and other times, they were more subtle. Jefferson Barnes received his degree and "headed for route 66" in the 1960s, but, he said, "I couldn't spend the night until I got to Amarillo, Texas, in a Black part of town." When he reached California and searched for an apartment, the for-rent signs were taken down. When he parked his car, the sign said, "No niggers here."

The signs are not always so blatant. Blacks are often steered toward neighborhoods that are designated as mixed or changing. Black brokers, who could assist them with available housing, may be denied membership in the National Association of Real Estate Brokers or full participation in real estate firms to discourage them from selling homes to Blacks.

Sometimes when Blacks want to move into a White neighborhood, their housing loans are not approved, even though they are fully qualified. When Leslie Glouster, a health administrator in her early fifties, and her husband applied for a housing loan in a predominantly White community, they were told they did not qualify. But a Black real estate broker informed them that another Black client, a service station attendant whose wife was unemployed, had received a loan for a house in a Black neighborhood. When Glouster challenged the president of the bank, he said ("after fumbling with the paper"), "I'll go over it again." "We were granted the loan," said Glouster. The analysis of the *Atlanta Journal-Constitution* concluded that race is a better predictor of a loan application's success than sex or marital status.[20]

The Media

The message of the media is both overt and subliminal. The effects on an individual depend on factors such as the level of racial awareness and the amount of time spent watching television or using other media forms. Some studies show Black children spend more time watching television than White children. Television is the most popular medium and the bellwether for interpreting and defining the popular culture. Television contributes to the individualization of the Black experience, because there is the absence of an incentive to obtain information about the experience of Blacks. Since Blacks are underrepresented on television in programming or in positions of power, this medium contributes to cultural denigration of Blacks and other people of color. Other media forms also have the same purpose as television.

The Jeffersons, a Black television comedy appearing in the 1970s, and *The Cosby Show*, a Black comedy in the 1980s, show how the Black elite have been portrayed by the media. In the pre-1980s on *The Jeffersons*, the Black elite were portrayed in the tradition of E. Franklin Frazier's *Black Bourgeoisie* as materialistic and as status seekers in a tenuous socioeconomic position. George Jefferson, the leading character, is depicted as the "Kingfish" on *Amos and Andy*, but in middle-class trappings. George is short and nonthreatening. He plays the role of a greedy, insensitive buffoon who wants to forget his humble origins. He is dominated by two strong, aggressive Black women—his wife and the maid.

On the other hand, *The Cosby Show* projects a positive image of the Black elite as having made it. The Huxtables—Claire, the lawyer/wife, and Cliff, the doctor/husband—are egalitarian in their social interactions. The show, however, lacks a race consciousness, and there is a benign view of the Black experience.

While these shows project different images of Blacks, the genre form is comedy. Blacks are still viewed in the role of entertainers. Putting these comedies aside, the truth about how Blacks are treated by the media lies somewhere in-between these comedies. How the media handled Jesse Jackson's campaign by defining and invalidating his candidacy illustrates this point.

In 1984, the media asked, Should Jesse run? Note that the media frequently referred to Jackson by his first name and White candidates by their last names. In 1988, the question became, What does Jesse want? The media ignored him, because they assumed he was "unelectable." They were not presenting his political agenda and issues; instead, they were comparing him, as a Black leader, with Martin Luther King, Jr. Black leaders and other individuals are compared with one another, not with Whites. When the media mentioned Jackson, it was usually because of his view on Palestine and his remark about "hymie-town."

In the meantime, other candidates began to incorporate Jesse Jackson's populist themes and issues—South Africa and drugs—into their campaigns to dilute his strength. Even when he came in second or third place, ahead of other candidates in primarily White areas, he was ignored as a part of the political analysis. The question became, Can he win White votes?

Finally, when Jackson won the Michigan primary, a stunning victory over Dukakis, the media asked, Can Jesse win? The media claimed that they were soft on Jackson, blaming him for their failings and implying Jackson had gotten away with minimal criticisms. He was then bombarded with much critical coverage to make up for the previous failure to recognize him as a viable candidate.

Along the way, the media were defining, interpreting, and setting limits on the aspirations of Blacks. Jackson did represent the aspirations of Blacks and a large segment of other Americans, even though the media individualized that by asking, What does Jesse want? When Jesse Jackson received 7 million votes, came in first or second in forty-six contests, and elected over twelve hundred delegates to the Democratic National Convention in Atlanta in 1988, he had made an impact. His issues on South Africa and drugs became part of mainstream debates of all candidates—Dukakis labelled South Africa as "a terrorist nation," and Bush labelled it as "a racist nation."

At the Democratic convention, the media commentators asked if Jesse would disrupt it or disrupt Dukakis's campaign. They followed with questions like, How can Jesse be controlled or kept in line? Peter Jennings, anchorman for ABC, asked during an evening coverage of the convention, "Can he be contained on the reservation?" Jackson was aspiring for the highest office in the country, and agents of the media were so intimidated that they did not even conceal their feelings.

Jackson's electrifying and candid speech during the 1988 Democratic National Convention caused a temporary paralysis in analysis by the articulate Dan Rather, Tom Brokaw, Walter Cronkite, and Eric Sevareid; even Ted Koppel lost his train of thought when Jackson appeared later on

Nightline. On the major networks, ABC, NBC, and CBS, no one could provide insight into this historical occasion.

Jackson's ideas were powerful, and perhaps, as he often said, his time had come. White commentators could not overlook their own personal responses or those of the audience—Black, Brown, Red, Yellow, or White. Some, like Sevareid, wanted to confine the impact of Jackson's speech to the "articulation of his people's needs." On the other hand, Walter Cronkite recognized that Jackson had gone beyond this. However, he viewed Jackson as the conscience of the nation, providing moral leadership, and Dukakis as the managerial leader. Seemingly, Blacks could now play in this new arena, but only in the role of a moral leader, not as a manager of the country. Finally, Cronkite validated that Jesse Jackson was the best orator in the country. While this is a noble recognition, it has its downside. Other Blacks, not Whites, will be compared to him, like the athletes and entertainers who are now recognized as among the best, because they proved themselves beyond a reasonable doubt.

The next question the media posed was, Can Jesse reconcile with the Democratic party to win the election? The media will continue to raise questions about Jesse Jackson and other Blacks who move beyond the color line. However, the media have not yet raised questions about their role in perpetuating the color line by denigrating and/or negating an accurate collective portrayal of the Black experience.

Sexual Racism

Lisa Allen, an attractive forty-one-year-old professor of history at a major university in a border state, is well-liked by her colleagues. Yet, she has to carefully tread the tightrope with her White male colleagues on the issues of being collegial and being aware of the unspoken dynamics of sexual racism. While speaking, her White male colleagues may touch her hands, arms, or back. Though "the touch" may be a mere friendly gesture from colleagues, she is still somewhat wary. Admittedly, only one colleague has referred to her "dark beauty as mysterious and exciting," but being touched still makes her wonder. She is also reluctant to go out to lunch or dinner alone with her White male colleagues.

Lisa is addressing the dynamics of sexual racism in this society. The relationship between Black females and White males has a long history of negative familiarity—a history of sexual exploitation by the White male. The Black woman in this society has been portrayed as sexually exciting and unrestrained. So Lisa is unsure whether "the touch" from her colleagues is a part of that negative history or whether it is a friendly gesture from a warm colleague.

Sexual racism is also a part of the landscape of the color line. Calvin Hernton, in *Sexual Racism in America,* and Charles Herbert Stember, in *Sexual Racism,* have dealt candidly with sexual racism between Blacks and Whites and its impact on Blacks.[21] Along with sexual myths about Black women, Hernton and Stember also discuss the preoccupation of Whites, particularly the White male, with supposedly Black male super-sexuality and the sexual purity of the White woman. These are myths that govern interactions between the races and among Blacks. The construction and manipulation of the myths by those in power have functioned primarily to maintain their social and economic privileges.

Although attitudes toward interracial sex vary by race, religion, occupation, education, age, region of country, and sex, sexual racism is embedded in the fabric of this society. When Thomas B. Thomas, director of marketing and the only Black in his position at a major company, is away on business with his White colleagues, they feel comfortable in telling racial jokes; Thomas seems "different" from other Blacks they've heard about, because he is smart and hard working. The common racial joke in his workplace is, "When you get out of the shower in the morning, there are three wet spots on the floor," said Thomas, who appeared very embarrassed as I probed. (The three wet spots supposedly left by a Black man are two footprints and the print made by his very large penis.) He also mentioned that sometimes when he is on business and is assigned a room with his White male colleagues, "they try to sneak around and catch a glimpse of me, so they can go and tell if it is true"—the myth of the Black male's extraordinary anatomical sexual endowment.

The myth applies not only to adult Black males, but also to children. One story told to me during this research took place in Huntington, West Virginia, in 1987. There was a conversation among White nurses in the local hospital about Black males' penises. One nurse took out a ruler and responded to a newborn Black male's cry, "If you cry or need attention, you are so beautiful and gorgeous, and with what you got between your legs, you got it made."

Although interracial marriages have increased since the 1967 Supreme Court ruling that struck down state laws prohibiting such marriages, the mores are still strongly against them. Thomas said, "You can commit corporate suicide if you bring your White mate to visit the company or marry a White woman." He said that some Black males think it helps them advance, but he has seen the careers of Black men, who had been placed on the fast-track in the corporation, halted. The White woman becomes a source of rivalry between Black men and White men. "Once a White woman goes Black, she can never come back," said Thomas, indicating that she is stigmatized for having any sexual interaction with Black males.

"I can't have White women talking to me too long about anything, because rumors will spread, and they will hunt around and try to catch you," said Thomas. Two well-known politicians echoed similar feelings. One sixty-five-year-old mayor said, "I don't fool with White women. I stay away from them if they get too close. I limit their time." The other sixty-five-year-old politician said, "I am scared of them. They'll trick you." He thinks that White men use them to entrap assertive Black men who have openly challenged the system.

The comments of Thomas and the two public officials reflect some of the collective dynamics of sexual interaction. On an individual level, however, many of the Talented One Hundred had dated interracially and reported mostly positive experiences. Ten percent—mostly males—were married to or had been married to a White person. One professor described his marriage as "stormier than most." Others had long, stable marriages, like the jazz musician and his White wife of twenty years, whom I interviewed separately and together.

But there were many contradictions and ambivalences surrounding interracial sex, dating, and marriage. They were especially pronounced when I asked, "What is the likelihood that your child/children will marry or date someone from a different racial background?" While a minority strongly disapproved, in general, the majority gave a restrained and tacit acceptance, saying, "I'll respect their choice. It's their decision, but I prefer that they marry Black." They cited difficulties their children might encounter with society, the problems their interracial offspring might encounter, and how these issues might affect their racial identity and consciousness.

Veronica Pepper, a psychologist in her late fifties who is interracially married, did not like it when her son by a previous marriage to a Black man married a Hawaiian. "My husband is White, so I am not a good one to talk about this. I was very upset when he married. I felt rejected. There are not enough Black men, so I am saving one for another Black woman. I think men choose more, initiate more, and so it reflects your choice. I felt personal rejection as well. My grandson is multiracial. He got some Black in him, but you would not necessarily see it. I have two White grandchildren, but I want a Black child," said Pepper. She stated that she had expressed those thoughts only to her husband, but "my son knows how I feel about interracial marriages."

Pat Robinson's ex-wife was White. He told me he was very concerned when his son would date only White girls. But recently his son has been dating a Black girl. "I am very pleased," said the judge, smiling. "I don't know how I would feel if my son got married to a White woman." I asked, "How do you think you would feel?" He answered, "I would be open because I married a White woman. If I had a preference, I would rather for her to be Black. I think he would be happier." He thinks his son has a "racial identification problem that kids of interracial families have."

Sexual racism, like the racial landscape of education, economics, housing, and the media, was more overt prior to the 1960s, when conventional mores and legal restrictions limited interracial marriage and sexual and social interactions between Blacks and Whites.

The Response of the Black Elite to Oppression

How does one respond to oppression? Does one deny it? Does one ignore it? Does one accept it? Does one withdraw from oppression or reject it? Is there a dominant mode of adaptation or a mixed mode?

When I approached Ruby Dee, actress, poet, and writer, for an interview and explained my project, she said, "I am more concerned with justice than racism. I keep my head above the clouds and choose not to deal with racism, and I look beyond it." Although she agreed to the interview, I never had the opportunity to find out how she kept her head "above the clouds."

Individuals among the Talented One Hundred are diligently ignoring, denying, avoiding, and withdrawing from racism and "keeping their heads above the clouds." But as the sensitive young journalist said, "The nature of mud is that it will splatter on you," even when one does not *choose* to throw it or to be involved with it.

While the Talented One Hundred may ignore some acts of racism, they may be particularly sensitive to others. Bernie Roberts, a social researcher, is rather adept at handling racism. But he admitted that he is very sensitive to taxi drivers in Washington, D.C. who ignore him.

> The thing that bothers me, as an adult, is that here in Washington, I can't deal with not being picked up by a taxi cab. It has blown my mind. I still have to deal with that. But I haven't recovered from it. It is the one act of discrimination that I can't figure out. It baffles me. But I have to explain why Blacks don't want to pick me up either. My friend tells me, "They think Black males will accost them." But I observe Black taxi drivers passing Black women to pick up White women.

When Pat Robinson was growing up in the 1940s, he coped with racism by avoiding it. Yet, it did not avoid him when he became the first Black member of a varsity baseball team in the early 1950s. The coach wanted his players fit. In his apparently customary pep speech, he somehow forgot that Pat was a member of the team when he said, "I want all of you to run around the field five times and the last one back is a niggerbaby." Robinson says, "I was stunned and there was clear silence. It was one incident I'll never forget." The university named the baseball field after the coach and wanted the players to attend a dedication ceremony in his honor. "I would not show up to honor that son-of-a-bitch," Robinson said. "To them, he is a good old boy. For me, [that incident] left its scars and seriously interfered with my affection for the school." This had a real emotional cost for Robinson. He had been very involved in extracurricular activities, feeling fully included then, but now dubbed himself as the "official Negro." "It seemed as though they said we ought to have a Negro and I was that Negro," he said of his predominantly White alma mater.

Over thirty years elapsed before Robinson reassessed his way of looking at his college experience. "I got angry at myself for having such little insight back then. It took me thirty years to realize this was not what I thought it was." He had played football during his freshman year, and the death of a player brought the college teammates together in 1985. He looked forward to sharing fond memories. When they gathered, "there was a lot of drinking and war stories and what you've been doing all these years." Robinson's voice lowered to a whisper. "I had the weirdest experience, because I realized I never belonged there. I didn't realize it back in 1951 when I played with them. When the other players were recalling incidents, I said, 'I never did that with you guys. I didn't know about that.' I played football and kind of goofed around a little with the guys, and then went to this rooming house where other Black athletes stayed, and it was nothing like that." The highly esteemed public official's voice trailed to silence. When his thirtieth year graduation anniversary came up in 1986, he recalled, "I remember I didn't go and I had planned to. I said it is going to be just like the other one—why should I go?"

Denial is a way of masking the pain. It is time-consuming and unproductive for many to remember the painful incidents. Ethel King "did not remember" two important discrimination lawsuits she had filed. It was only through extensive probing that I found out about them. One suit was filed against a restaurant that did not serve "colored people" and the other was against a realtor. "It was one of the most heartbreaking cases for me. I would cry and couldn't get over the fact that the realtor had been so blatant." When the court found the realtor not guilty, she remembered that the realtor "jumped up and said, 'Justice has been served.' My girlfriend was in tears, but I couldn't cry. I was so angry, I said this is why people throw Molotov cocktails." Tears flowed freely from her eyes as she recalled this incident thirteen years later.

"For what reason do you think you had difficulty in recalling these experiences?" I asked. She replied, "I was so angry and hurt. I could see the power of that anger. If I could get that angry, I couldn't live with it, and what happens is you put it so far back, it doesn't immediately come to mind. But you never, never forget, and once I start thinking about it—it's amazing." There was laughter when I told her others had done the same. "I thought I was the only one," Ethel responded.

Claude Kent, an engineer, is good at ignoring the impact of race.

When I asked the racial composition of his neighborhood, he said repeatedly, "I don't know." I became impatient with his unusual response. Finally, I asked, "Do most of the people in your neighborhood look like you or do they look like her?" I pointed to a White female who was within view of his office. Finally, he acknowledged his neighborhood was predominantly White.

Denial and avoidance are coping mechanisms used in handling racism. They may be functional or dysfunctional to individuals, depending on the situation. There was a feeling among the Talented One Hundred that "they could not dwell on racism; they must move forward." They use a mixed mode of coping, depending on situational factors.

We can, nevertheless, see, through the experiences of Pat Robinson and Ethel King, how the psychological effects of racism are deep and lasting.

Occasionally, individuals accept the blatancy of racism without questioning. Benson Robinson, a fifty-two-year-old successful entrepreneur, grew up in a predominantly White community. He is among the wealthiest of the Talented One Hundred and among the wealthiest in the country. For Benson, race is not a salient issue in his life. His mother taught him that "people are people regardless of their race," and he responds to people on that basis. He was among the few individuals who stated that they had never encountered racism. However, during our interview, Benson recalled that a competitor who heard he was opening a new business said, "Doesn't that damn nigger have enough money?" Benson hires mostly Whites in his business. (You may recall that when Benson's White manager hired six Blacks, some White customers complained he had too many Blacks working for him.)

When I asked Benson if he had ever hired a Black manager in his business, he said that he had hired two. But they did not work out, because they stole from him. "I have a problem, and it's my biggest problem that I'll share with you. Black people, for some reason when they get in a position, they get slick. They don't want to work anymore. They try to find an easy way to make it," said Benson, who works a fifteen-hour-a-day schedule. He likes to deal with people in an honest manner. Turning the question, he asked, "Where do we get that mentality? You are a sociologist; tell me."

Benson's son, a college student with whom I had a chance to interact, does not share his father's philosophy. He said, "I would assess my target market, but it would not deter me from hiring qualified people, and if it turns out they are Black, I would hire them. If they were not qualified, I would not. If they were White and not qualified, I would not hire them. I would certainly not hire them just because they were White!" We were out of the earshot of others, but the son whispered, "My father is a compassionate person, so I know that prejudice has to bother him." He cited examples of his father's White employees who left racist notes, like "Nigger, clean up," in the bathroom for the Black janitor. (I did not have a chance to ask the father about such notes because I spoke with the son after our interview. I also did not want to violate the confidentiality of the son's conversation.)

Benson's candid response to racism reflects a lower level of racial awareness and sensitivity, unlike most of the Talented One Hundred, whose levels of awareness were higher. In general, they rejected many detrimental aspects of the Eurocentric perspective and incorporated an Afrocentric one to buffer them against racism. They emphasized the importance of maintaining Black institutions, preserving Black culture, and teaching Black history. Their responses were not, however, unidimensional; at some level, they were multidimensional.

The Talented One Hundred expressed contradictions and conflicts in the three components of their personality—cognitive, behavioral, and affective. Individuals who had a higher level of self-awareness sought to justify their inconsistencies and bring them in line. Multilevel conflicts and contradictions are endemic to a racist society.

The individual awareness level—shaped by such factors as age, regional differences, racial composition of environment in formative years, racial experiences, and academic discipline—is along a continuum. Racial responses are multidimensional, depending upon the situation and the historical time period.

Let's look at Dira Ridley's response to racism. As a physical chemist in her late thirties, she is strongly influenced by her academic training. When

A Black Elite's Racial Response Model

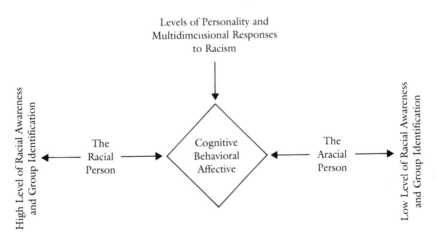

85

I asked if she had ever been discriminated against, she responded, "Yes, I have felt discrimination, but I can't scientifically prove it to you." Although she intuitively senses racism, she needs hard empirical data to prove it. She feels also that "scientific data will lead to greater enlightenment," particularly among natural scientists. Dira strongly believes in science solving problems. Interestingly, in the light of Dira's analysis, the data show that in the natural sciences, Blacks are the most underrepresented racial group.

The concept of the "race man," as Alfred Moss noted in *The American Negro Academy,* was more prominent before the rise of specialization in the academic disciplines. Black professionals had a greater allegiance to ameliorating race conditions than advancing in their particular discipline.[22] Jonathan Mobutu feels this emphasis on greater specialization by Black professionals will lead to individualization of the Black experience and, hence, a more aracial orientation.

The individualization of their experiences may not allow the Black elite to see their individual fates as being integrally linked to one another and to the masses of Blacks. Moreover, the individualization of racial experiences may contribute to psychic damage. For instance, the Black elite may become gatekeepers preventing other Blacks from achieving. Michael Lomax, who was extremely candid in our interview, wanted me to use his real name. Perhaps he felt his candor would assist others to examine their actions. He said, "At an earlier point in life, I tried being a gatekeeper. I've gone through periods where my self-esteem was not high enough that I felt comfortable having other Blacks around."

Lomax, the chief architect for the inaugural National Black Arts Festival in Atlanta, is now working to change the image of Blacks. He is addressing not only the external issues of blackness, but also his internal conflict, although it has taken him a while. He said:

> I am angry about the conflict inside of me or angry that I am Black. I have a legitimate reason to be angry, but I am not going to change my racial identity. So I have to learn to accept myself and determine whether it is appropriate to fight against those negative images and to recognize them and not allow them to seep in and affect those positive images of myself.

If Blacks do not understand this hidden agenda of racism, the result is inaction. If they do understand the hidden agenda of racism, they can externalize it and create messages from their subjective and objective experiences, as Lomax did, that will lead to action.

The following life histories of Lula Brown and the Reverend William Holmes Borders, Sr., two of the oldest individuals among the Talented One Hundred, show that the modern Black elite's experience is a continuation of the same type of psychic violence experienced by the traditional Black elite. Since there was less specialization in the 1920s and 1930s, the traditional Black elite used a wider arena to fight the range of oppression and brutality. The modern Black elite, on the other hand, are more likely to fight in their professional arena.

The Life and Times of Lula Brown

Lula Brown, a social activist and the oldest among the Talented One Hundred, was born in 1901. Her youthful appearance and energy belie her years. She was temporarily immobilized from an arm injury incurred while playing tennis when I interviewed her in August 1987. She welcomed me into her home.

We had an informal chat about the intent of the project before the formal interview began. It was her way of finding out if she would feel comfortable sharing her life. Her long history of social involvement, no doubt, taught her to be "on guard." When the guard came down, she told a passionate story.

When Lula was four, her mother, a young woman in her twenties, ended her marriage with Lula's father. Lula and her mother left Chicago and headed west to Seattle, Washington. For the next twenty years, she and her mother were disconnected from family. She said, "My mother must have been heartbroken. I saw no relatives and I knew no relatives for over twenty years." In those twenty years, she said, "we rambled the West. I lived first in Seattle and then Nevada during the famous silver and gold strike. We lived in Utah, Idaho, and the State of Washington." For the most part, her formative years were spent in Oregon. At fifteen, she and her mother moved to California, where, for the first time, they lived in a Black community.

Lula Brown's experience of wandering over the West was not a pleasant one. When I talked with her, she was in the process of writing her memoirs, recreating "what it meant to grow up as a Black woman living in a racist society in a western state without friends, family, church, or other Black institutions." When I asked her what it was like, she responded, "Hell! What I think I would like to compare is growing up as a Black child in an alien, hostile White racist society to growing up in the South. It is my feeling that it is far worse, because you have no friends, no playmates, and no history."

At this point, she showed me a picture of her mother, who looked White. She continued, "My mother was as White as any White person." Her mother's family was very fair-skinned. Although they came from Kentucky, her family settled in Ohio, and later some family members went to

Chicago. The family was split in Ohio. Her mother's seven brothers went White, cutting themselves off from the family, while the sisters remained within the race. "Did your mother pass for White?"

> No. She was very conscious and protective of her Black child. I imagined my father was brown-skinned. My mother's hair was as straight as my hair was kinky, so I had no identity with her. We had no knowledge of Black history and all I know was that I was called nigger every day of my life and names like chocolate drop.
>
> I remember my first racial experience in the first grade in Nevada. It is the reason why I am starting my memoirs there. I don't remember anything, but a teacher sitting at a desk, having a pile of white envelopes on the desk, calling out each child in the room, and giving each child an envelope except me. It was an invitation to one of my classmate's birthday party. That was my first consciousness about race.

She asked her mother, "Why don't children play with me? Is it because I am Black?" Her mother would only say, "Don't pay any attention to it." Her mother would also cry when her daughter told her about her educational experiences. Lula did not like to see her mother cry, so she did not tell her about the incidents. She said, "That is what I am talking about, the cruelty of being the only one. It is like being a leper, a pariah." She was reliving, through her memoirs, how "a child survived such an experience." These incidents were typical of her experiences during her educational process. "I knew I was Black, but why? All I could hope for was to be White." The only way she knew how to handle racism was to be the best student. According to her, when recess came, "the kids played, but I could not be a part of it. For a child, it is the most miserable childhood you could ever possibly have. It's only when I got out and learned something about my history and my people that things changed for me."

The only Black history she learned in school was that Blacks were not good. "I used to stay home from school when we studied the Civil War, and they showed all the happy Blacks on the plantations, dancing, doing the cakewalk, and showing how happy we were, laughing in the history book. When we studied geography, savages were in grass skirts, going around the White man. I didn't know about Harriet Tubman and Sojourner Truth," she said. The only Black man she had heard of was Booker T. Washington. When he visited Washington State during her childhood and she went to hear him speak, she was disappointed. "All I remember is he told jokes to White folks and they laughed." One joke she remembers is the one he told about a Black woman who was going somewhere and she met her "massa" and he said, "Where're you going?" The Black woman responded, "Massa, I forget where I gwine."

When she went to college, few Blacks in California attended at that time. W. E. B. Du Bois spoke at her university. Her voice lowered to a mere whisper as she recalled his impact on her life. "He stood up in the auditorium and spoke. There were three or four Blacks in there [ages seventeen or eighteen]." She said, "I am trying to evolve something out of this. I am talking to myself about my memoirs as I talk with you. What Du Bois meant to us was like Jesus Christ."

She graduated from college with honors in business administration. But she was unable to get a job because of her color. The university did not help. The only job the university offered was baby-sitting (taking care of White children). "I could not walk around with a little White child under my supervision," she said. This period began her rebellion. Her minor was Spanish, so she got a job in San Francisco, passing as a Hispanic. But she could not live a double life, so she quit her job. She left for Chicago. She met, for the first time, her mother's family and friends. Although her complexion is fair, she was the darkest among them. She asked me, "Did you ever hear someone say 'She'll do well in Washington, D.C., because the girl has straight hair and fair skin'?" Washington, D.C., was a center of fair-skinness, as well as Charleston, Boston, and New Orleans.

Lula left Chicago because she had different aspirations than her friends. She wanted to travel and see the world. She wanted "to know people who were doing things and to read books and not just get married. I had begun to see the world and learn about Black history. I wanted more."

She got her first chance to meet Du Bois at an NAACP convention, where, at age twenty-four, she had the opportunity of dancing with him. She described him as a "happy, gay [cheerful] old man." He invited her to come to New York and see him. Along the way, she met and became the friend and colleague of the "Who's Who" of the Harlem Renaissance: Alain Locke, Paul Robeson, Langston Hughes, Zora Neale Hurston, and others. Rufus Osgood Mason, a White philanthrophist, was Lula's patron, as well as the patron of Zora Neale Hurston and Langston Hughes—Lula's experience with "philanthropy" turned sour when she denounced Zora as "not being a true Negro." She said Zora Neale Hurston, the writer, was for Mason "the ideal primitive. . . . She was nature's gift to the unspoiled and undressed-up of White folks—a real gem." She stated that Hurston knew how to "pull their leg," to obtain material resources from wealthy patrons. Lula could not wear that mask.

The seeds of her rebellion against racism that started when she met Du Bois in college were taking hold. She became very active in social movements that fought against classism and racism. She joined the Communist party and organized a committee of twenty-two to go to the Soviet Union.

Langston Hughes and Whittaker Chambers were among the committee members. Her friends, like Mary McLeod Bethune, the educator, said, "What's happening with you?"

Her perceptions about race relations changed after she visited Russia in the early 1930s. She felt the United States had to change from being an exploitative society, and socialism was the answer. She was deeply involved in the struggles of the Civil Rights movement, encountering many racial incidents in the movement and along the way as an adult that affected her life. But it is the impact of her childhood experiences that she is still assessing. "What does it mean to grow up in the Far West as a Black?"

The Life and Times of Rev. William Holmes Borders, Sr.

Rev. William Holmes Borders, Sr. was eighty-three years old when I interviewed him in June 1987. He sat comfortably eating his breakfast in the parsonage of Wheat Street Baptist, the church he had presided over for the past fifty years. I apologized for disturbing his breakfast. "I prefer talking to eating," he said. And indeed he does.

I did not ask many questions of him or of Lula Brown. Instead, I turned on the tape recorder, sat at their feet, and drank deeply from their fountain of knowledge, wisdom, and life experiences of nearly one hundred seventy years. Their lives, however, are a study in contrast. Rev. Borders, unlike Lula Brown, grew up among Black families, Black friends, and Black institutions. He came of age in the segregated South. Although he has travelled around the world four-and-a-half times, he has remained close to his Georgia roots. He was taught at an early age his family history and the history of Black people. His grandfather was an ex-slave who had worked himself and his family out of slavery. "They bought their bodies by working overtime, sometimes a full day on top of a day," he said. His father was a minister, and he described himself as being a fighter like his father and also just as stubborn.

The family valued education and hard work. He went to Morehouse College, graduating in 1929. He received a B.D. degree from the predominantly White Garrett Theological Seminary, Evanston, Ill., in 1931 and a masters from Northwestern University in the 1930s. Though he worked on his doctorate at Northwestern, he did not finish. He responded to his calling to preach. He was the first Black to receive an honorary doctorate from Garrett, his alma mater. So far, he has received thirteen honorary doctorate degrees.

When he left Morehouse College for Garrett Theological Seminary in the late 1920s, he said, "I was treated better than I had ever been treated by White people." To prove his worthiness, he said, "I had the people that I worked for send money to the treasurer of the school. It was to prove to them that I was worthy of being there. What I proved was that I was more worthy than the White boys who were there."

While William Borders attended Garrett, Booker T. Washington came to speak, and Borders was deeply influenced by Washington's industriousness and self-help philosophy. He also respected W. E. B. Du Bois. "The two persons offered solutions that people thought were clashing, but they weren't. Each was approaching the problem according to his philosophy of life." He had an opportunity to work with both men personally, and they influenced his life, along with people like Mordecai Johnson, a famous Black minister, and Thurgood Marshall, a Supreme Court justice.

Rev. Borders is a lifelong member of the Republican party and has even run for a political position. He said, "It is the party of Abraham Lincoln. He is the greatest president we've ever had." (He was referring to Lincoln's freeing of the slaves. But Lincoln's decision to free the slaves was not related to any kindly humanitarian feelings toward Blacks. Lincoln stated clearly his feelings. "I am not, nor have I ever been, in favor of bringing about in any way the social and political equality of White and Black races; I am not, nor ever have been, in favor of making voters or jurors of Negroes, nor qualifying them to hold office. . . . There is a physical difference between the White and Black races which I believe will ever forbid the two races living together on terms of social and political equality. And inasmuch as they cannot so live, while they do remain together, there must be the position of superior and inferior, and I, as much as any other man, am in favor of having the superior position assigned to the White race." [23])

The crafty Rev. Borders, who has interwoven the ideals of Booker T. Washington and W. E. B. Du Bois, knows that "Whites have always thought they were superior and you fight like hell to change it." He has fought to change the system. He began the efforts at voter registration in Atlanta, many years before Martin Luther King, Jr. "There is a role for Black ministers in the struggle," said Borders. "They have to lead their people. We aren't going to do to White people what they've done to us. We are going to walk over them and make stair steps out of them and stand up tip toe and talk about the rising sun. I won't talk about the moon because he doesn't even know the moon. The reason he doesn't know the moon is because he is so moony," the witty minister laughs.

Rev. Borders has been a repository of Black cultural heritage and Black pride throughout the country. Members of his congregation have heard him say for the last fifty years, "You are the finest people in the world. I love you—every one of you." He composed the poem "I Am Somebody" when the Wings Over Jordan, spiritual singers from Cleveland, came to the University of Georgia in the 1940s, and he was asked to speak to the group. He said he does not mind Jesse Jackson using it, "because he is doing a good job and there is no need for two Negroes to be quarreling about a piece of poetry. . . . What was I to do to prove that I wrote it? It was no big thing for me. All us Negroes better stick together."

He straightened his back, and his waning physique was again made strong when I asked him to read his poem, "I Am Somebody." (Rev. Borders corrected me immediately when I said "I Am Somebody." He stated, "Here's the way I say it—'I'm Somebody.' I cut out the A.") This was the voice that Martin Luther King, Jr. heard every Sunday morning in Atlanta while growing up, and he was influenced by it. The children who play in the street of Auburn Avenue hear him and say, "I'm Somebody."

I am Somebody—I am a poet in Langston Hughes.
        I am a creator of rhyme in Paul Lawrence Dunbar.
        I am a Christian statesman in J. R. E. Lee.
        I am a diplomat in Fred Douglass.
I am Somebody—
I am Somebody—I am a soldier in Colonel Young.
        I am courage in Crispus Attucks.
        I am a humorist in Bert Williams.
        I am a radio artist in Dorothy Maynor.
        I am a world-famous tenor in Roland Hayes.
        I am a contralto in Marian Anderson.
        I am a baritone in Paul Robeson.
I am Somebody—
I am Somebody—I am an athlete in Bennie Jefferson.
        I am a sprinter in Ralph Metcalfe.
        I am an intelligent pen in the hand of Du Bois.
        I am a college president in John Hope.
        I am a fighter in Samuel Howard Archer.
        I am a breaker of world records in Jesse Owens.
I am Somebody—
I am Somebody—I am an orator in P. James Bryant.
        I am a preacher in C. T. Walker and L. K. Williams.
        I am a composer in Nathaniel Dett.
        I am an actor in Richard B. Harrison.
        I am a boxer in Armstrong Williams.
        I am a knock-out punch in Joe Louis.
I am Somebody—
I am Somebody—I am a scientist in George Washington Carver.
        I am an industrial educator in Booker T.
           Washington.
        I am a congressman in Oscar Depriest and Arthur
           Mitchell.
        I am a skin specialist in [Theodore] Lawless and
           teach what I know at Northwestern.
        I am a pathologist in Julian Lewis and serve on the
           University of Chicago faculty.

I am the first successful operator on the human heart
in Daniel Hale Williams.

I am Somebody—

I am Somebody—I am a marksman in Dorie Miller.

I am a register of the treasury in Judson Lyons.

I am loyalty in the Armed Services.

I am insight in Sojourner Truth.

I am an advocator of justice in Walter White.

I am a leader in A. Philip Randolph.

I am Somebody—

I am Somebody—I am a moulder of character in Nannie Burroughs.

I am a banker in R. R. Wright and L. D. Milton.

I am a certified public accountant in Jesse Blayton.

I am a sculptor in Henry O. Tanner.

I am a business man in Alonzo Herndon.

I am a grand specimen of womanhood in Mary
McLeod Bethune.

I am Somebody—

I am Somebody—I am an insurance executive in C. C. Spaulding.

I am a biologist in Just of Howard.

I am a historian in Carter Woodson.

I am a lover of education in Charlotte Hawkins
Brown.

I am a beautician in Madames Walker, Washington
and Malone.

I am a trustee in slavery—I protected my master's
wives and daughters while he fought to keep the
chains of slavery about my body.

I am Somebody—

I am Somebody—I am a bishop in W. A. Fountain.

I am a ball of fire in Richard Allen.

I am a laborer in John Henry.

I am a Christian in "Tom," for indeed, I practiced the
religion of Jesus at points better than my master
from whom I learned it.

I am Somebody.

Rev. William Holmes Borders, Sr.

Summary

This chapter focuses on the psychic impact of the color line on the Black elite, in the cultural and social area and within the different realms of activities where racism is manifested, such as education, economics, housing, the media, and sexual relations. The oppressor group aims to impose a sense of place for the oppressed group by employing violence and three important devices of power—control, dominance, and exploitation—to maintain racial privilege in every social institution and facet of social interaction.

The concept of violence is examined from a Fanonian perspective which looks at human violence in situations of oppression. This definition extends the limited concept of physical violence to include psychic violence.

An emphasis on individualism, a major value orientation in the United States, contributes to individualizing the racial experience. Using this universal value of individualism to contextualize the racial experience of people of color denies that there is a collective component also. Individuals sometimes do not link "the personal troubles of milieu" and "the public issues of social structure," as sociologist C. Wright Mills noted in *The Sociological Imagination*. If Blacks do not understand the hidden agenda of racism, reactivity may result. If they do understand the hidden agenda, the Black elite can externalize their response and create messages from their subjective experiences that will lead to proactivity. Two life histories illustrate the manifestation of psychic violence in the lives of traditional Black elite and modern Black elite.

THREE

The Color Line Across
the World of Work

The door of opportunity swung wide for Jack B. Lane and other talented Blacks in the late 1960s and early 1970s. The winds of change, spurred by the Civil Rights movement, an expanding economy, and the shift from a manufacturing to a service-oriented economy, produced the largest Black middle class, in America, by any definition, in nearly four hundred years. It also created unprecedented career choices. Blacks could now sit on corporate boards to school boards, and choose from a range of careers, from architect to astronaut, corporate manager to mayor, and scientist to school superintendent. Bart Landry, for example, found "no less than sixty-five different titles held by Black males" in a 1976 national survey of middle-class Blacks and Whites.[1]

The old Black middle class, unlike the new Black elite, was confined to traditional occupations of teaching, ministry, social work, medicine, dentistry, and law in segregated communities. The new Black middle class is increasingly in the White suburbs, where the majority of new, white collar, middle-class jobs are being created. A *Washington Post* article, "The Integration of the American Dream," noted that this new Black middle class, unlike the old Black elite, is "emerging and succeeding by the standards of the majority White culture in mainstream American careers. One result is that class is becoming a more important predictor of behavior than race."[2]

Though class is an important predictor of some behaviors, race continues as a salient variable in the lives of the Black elite. Such articles as that in the *Washington Post,* describing the success of the Black elite who are moving into mainstream careers and into corporate boardrooms, reflect an accurate surface portrait. "But scratch the surface and another reality appears," says Bart Landry, a sociologist, in *The New Black Middle Class.* He knows the workplace "is still not color-blind."[3] Acknowledging that the "racial climate has greatly improved," Landry senses too, as illuminated by the following vignettes, that there is still a chilly racial wind, swinging back the door.

Although Jackie Robinson broke the color barrier over forty years ago, becoming major league baseball's first Black player in 1947, there is still a deep racial freeze when it comes to hiring Black managers. Black players did not need Al Campanis, the former vice president of the Los Angeles Dodgers, to say that Blacks "may not have some of the necessities to . . . be field managers, or perhaps a general manager." They had heard many times the stereotypes of Black players on the baseball field. They also did not need a survey to tell them there were few Black managers, but it nevertheless provided statistical evidence to support their observations. A *USA Today* survey in 1987 found that of the 879 top administrative posts in major league baseball, only 17 were held by Blacks and 13 by other minorities. Since baseball reflects a microcosm of the larger society, it signals the racial ceiling in other arenas of the social structure.

Blacks comprise only 3 percent of all lawyers. Only a small fraction are invited to practice as partners in White law firms, including those who graduated from Ivy League law schools.

Black entrepreneurs find it difficult to obtain sufficient capital from banks to start up or expand their businesses.

Black visual artists find it difficult to exhibit their works at major museums and galleries, while Black performing artists have limited, stereotyped roles.

Black elected officials have increased [in number] dramatically since the 1960s, but they are often kept off important committees and are rarely appointed to chair them.

Black medical researchers find it difficult to secure adequate funds to study diseases, like sickle cell anemia, which primarily affect the Black population.

Blacks have moved into corporate America as managers and executives. But too few Blacks have reached the level of board member, president, and vice president of major companies. At this writing, there is no Black CEO of a major American industrial corporation.

The "Gilded Ghetto": Blacks in Corporate America

When Clarence Pinkney, a forty-three-year-old, started at X Consumer Products Company in the mid-sixties, he was one of the first Black professionals ever hired. Now Blacks comprise 7 percent of the management, and the company is listed as one of the fifty best places to work by *Black Enterprise*.

The popular literature about the triumphs of successful Blacks furthers the perception that profound changes in the boardrooms of corporate America have taken place. For instance, in 1988, *Black Enterprise* ran a cover story on "America's Hottest Black Managers," stating:

> They represent some of the most powerful men in corporate America. Their decisions determine whether the world's largest corporations will reap millions—even billions—of dollars in profits. They influence what the nation eats, buys, and drives, as well as how it communicates. They are America's twenty-five hottest Black managers and they are putting their bold signature on big business.[4]

Evidence from the Equal Employment Opportunity Commission supports the significant growth of Black officials, managers, and professionals in corporate America within the last two decades.[5] Clarence Pinkney exemplifies this trend. In more than twenty years with the X Consumer Products Company, he has moved from an assistant advertising specialist to a top position in personnel management. He expects to continue his progress in the company.

For a brief period, it seemed corporate America held promises of unlimited opportunities for young Blacks. But during the Reagan era, these triumphal opportunities began slipping away. From 1980 to 1985, the number of Black male managers only slightly increased from 2.7 percent of white-collar managers to 2.9 percent, a decrease in the rate of growth from the previous five years.[6] The retrenchment in the commitment to affirmative action by the Reagan administration and corporate downsizing were clear signals that Blacks were losing ground and experiencing added trials. A conference board survey of business leaders ranked affirmative action for minorities and women as twenty-third out of twenty-five human resources management issues.[7]

Not only has the rate of growth for Black employment in corporations slowed down, but even fewer Blacks are moving up the corporate ladder, particularly into the senior executive level. There is a sense of ghettoization of Black professionals working in corporate America. Many Blacks who enter the corporate world remain at entry level positions. They are also likely to be employed in staff positions rather than line positions. They are channeled into such human resource areas as: community relations, public relations, and personnel relations. These jobs are the most vulnerable to shifting economic winds. Moreover, they are less likely to prepare Blacks for upward mobility or the fast-track positions.

The Talented One Hundred who are employed at the senior executive level in corporations confirmed the earlier assessment of John P. Fernandez's work, *Black Managers in White Corporations,* published in 1975, and Edward W. Jones, Jr.'s research on the status of Black managers, which appeared in an issue of *Harvard Business Review.*[8] According to Fernandez, Jones, and the Talented One Hundred, there are several shared concerns in such areas as: (1) recruitment, retention, and retrenchment; (2) quality of life; and (3) the balancing of the role strain and role conflict sometimes inherent in their political and professional positions.

Recruitment, Retention, and Retrenchment

Many barriers exist for Blacks entering corporations. As noted, the literature supports the importance of informal networks in obtaining a position among both blue-collar and white-collar workers. In addition, corporations are most likely to hire individuals with whom they feel more comfortable. The lack of commitment to affirmative action by the federal government and the private sector helps ease the pressure to hire Blacks. Also, there is still a reluctance on the part of some corporate managers to recruit Blacks. They feel their clients are unwilling to accept Blacks, and they are uncomfortable about taking risks with their own careers. Thomas B. Thomas, a thirty-eight-year-old regional sales manager for a large corporation, said senior executives in his company continue to use this rationale, despite his success.

> Some corporations do not hire because they feel their client base will not accept a Black expert on any topic. The White person who hires Blacks puts himself in jeopardy. If the Black person doesn't work out, not only are you out the door, but also the person who hired you. There is a slim chance that a White manager will put his hands out, knowing his arms will be cut off in the process and risk his career. If the Black guy fails, the manager was not making his point to the corporation about equal opportunity and fairness.

When Thomas went to work as a sales manager with a major corporation in 1971, the district manager did not want to hire him, because he felt employing Blacks would affect the company's White clientele base. Thomas convinced the manager to hire him. "You are either the biggest 'bull shitter' I've ever met or the best sales manager," the district manager said to Thomas. "The only way you can find out is to hire me," retorted Thomas. He broke all previous sales records in the company in an all-

White area, and each time he broke a record the White district manager "moved up a notch." Thomas thinks Whites "measure the successes or failures of all Blacks by one another," so he always works hard and performs better than others to cope with racism. "If I were of Caucasian descent, there would be no stopping me in the market, but I lose my fair share of business because they know I'll move one step closer to where they are," concludes Thomas. He believes it is important to have more Blacks in the corporation. Hence, Thomas has actively recruited other Blacks, but has not met with much success.

In contrast to Thomas, Duane Dennis, a thirty-two-year-old stockbroker for an international investment firm in the South, did not have any difficulties in the eighties being hired in an industry that has until recently excluded Blacks. Less than a dozen investment banking firms in the nation are Black-owned. In 1987, only one Black firm had a seat on the New York Stock Exchange.[9] "It is an industry," Dennis said, "that survives by the confidence of people investing a large sum of money with brokers to manage." Since there are negative stereotypes about Blacks being poor managers of money and incompetent business persons, I asked if he thought it mattered being Black in this industry. Dennis does think "it matters a lot." He believes, like Thomas, that he has to be better than other brokers to succeed. While he has been successful with both Whites and Blacks, who comprise 60 percent and 40 percent, respectively, of his clients, he has encountered racial incidents. Said Dennis:

> When I talk with White clients on the phone, they are receptive. [He said his speech pattern does not sound typically Black.] But when I go to the office to pick up the check, they are taken aback. I remember only one incident in which a client wanted her money returned, an older White female, who was going to invest a large sum of money. In the course of two months, we had spoken four or five times on the phone, building up rapport. Once I got to her place and she saw I was Black, she literally developed heart trouble at the door. She said that she had chest pains and would mail the check, but would need time to recuperate. Needless to say, the check never came. A phone call beat me back to the office. She indicated that she never had any professional relationships with Blacks, and that she prefers having an older White male to manage her money.

To minimize such overt racism, Dennis learned to appear in person to meet his clients, commenting, "I want them to make sure they know with whom they are dealing. I don't want any more surprises."

In contrast to the response of his White female client, Dennis had a favorable reaction from clients who live in an all-White community renowned for its overt exclusion of Blacks. When his White clients offered to mail a check to him after a phone consultation, he wanted to make certain they knew he was Black. He said, "They were initially shocked, but they ended up telling me that they felt more comfortable with an honest Black broker than a dishonest White one." When other White clients meet Dennis in person, they make comments like, "I thought you were Jewish over the phone," or "I thought you were short and Italian." Dennis does not think these comments are inappropriate or racist. "I smile when they say that. I think it's a way of establishing rapport. If they say something that is offensive or inappropriate, I'll let them know. I react to the comment, not the person behind it. I would react the same way if the person making the comment was Black." Black clients have also been surprised to see a Black stockbroker, but upon further probing, he admitted, "No Blacks have ever made such comments."

Many competitive and highly skilled young Blacks, like Duane Dennis, are entering new career paths in finance. Previously, not only did they lack information about career opportunities in finance, but racism was primarily the major factor blocking their paths. Prior to the election of Black mayors and the appointment of Black public officials, White investment firms were selected to manage municipal accounts, even though Blacks contributed a large portion of those funds. However, in the 1970s, these investment firms discovered the need to hire Blacks as entrees to Black mayors. Thus, greater opportunities in public finance have become an avenue of upward mobility for many Blacks, but still the more lucrative business in corporate finance continues to elude them.

Although some corporations, such as accounting and investing firms, have aggressively recruited Blacks, there is still a problem in retention. In a *Black Enterprise* report on corporate racism, Joyce Johnson, chair of the National Association of Securities Professionals, noted, "It's almost like a blood bath [is taking place] in some of these major firms. . . . They are hiring minorities left and right, but they're firing them within six months."[10] These issues of evaluation, promotion, and retention concern many Blacks in corporate America.

Evaluation, Promotion, and Retention

Having acquired the proper credentials to enter corporate America—maybe even M.B.A.'s and Ph.D.'s from Ivy League schools—Blacks still find the workplace is not color-blind in its evaluation, promotion, and retention. A survey conducted of Black M.B.A. alumni of the top five graduate business schools found that 84 percent believe that considerations of race have a negative impact on ratings, pay, assignments, recognition, appraisals, and promotion. Ninety percent of the participants also agreed with a statement that subtle racism pervades their own companies, and more than half said the racism is overt.[11] Thus, the evaluation, promotion, and retention process may be affected by these conscious and unconscious racist attitudes and behaviors, as indicated by a 1982 survey of the class of 1957 Ivy League graduates. When asked if Blacks are as intelligent as Whites, only 36 percent of the Princeton class, 47 percent of Yale, and 55 percent of the Harvard class agreed with the statements.[12] These graduates are now in the age cohort to be promoted into senior corporate positions. One can speculate about the impact of their belief not only in hiring, but also on evaluating and promoting.

The Talented One Hundred who work in corporations frequently reported experiencing or observing overt discrimination in the appraisal and promotion process. Thomas B. Thomas mentioned that his wife, a regional manager for a major company, earned excellent ratings, but just prior to evaluation and promotion, her personnel file was partially destroyed. Usually, appraisal and evaluation take more subtle forms. For instance, when a White manager behaves assertively within the corporation, it is often interpreted as positive. But if a Black manager acts similarly, this may be negatively interpreted as arrogant. This racist perception and interpretation adversely affects evaluation. The person may be labeled "not a good fit," thus impacting his or her chances of moving up the corporate ladder. More importantly, however, the Talented One Hundred reported that supervisors often stated that the reason for nonpromotion was a lack of qualifications.

Take Kelly Smith, a high-ranking officer in an international corporation, for example. She knows that she was qualified for the next rung on the corporate ladder, the highest position in her field. Even her boss maintained that she is better than others, although he claimed she didn't have the qualifications for a position in international affairs. "I have more qualifications than others. The only advantage they have over me is that they've lived abroad. My qualifications are in excess," said Smith, who has an M.B.A. from a prestigious university. She thinks it is very difficult to distinguish corporate politics from racism. She admits that "many bosses keep their subordinates behind because they feel the promotion will have a negative impact on them. This, I feel, is corporate politics." But she thinks it was racism when her supervisor said she did not have the qualifications to do the job. "It is very difficult to assess corporate politics; often people get muddled and don't know how to behave. It gets mixed up in terms of the subtleties of corporate politics and racism."

Since Kelly was promoted to her present position, she has seen many persons, several steps below her level, promoted to her level. She even hired a man and a woman who are now at her level. "I have not been promoted, and the reason is that the next position is a big step," said Smith. She does not think the company is ready for a Black, particularly a woman, to be promoted to the high-ranking line position. While there are two Blacks in the corporation who rank higher than she does, they are employed in staff positions. Kelly said:

> They've been given the position of external affairs, basically where you give money away. They do not have line functions where corporate decisions are made. So you can see it is a very powerful position, and many people would not want me to have this high-ranking line position. What I think the company is likely to do if they promote me is to ship me out to some country to be in charge of some division of a country. It would be a position of authority, but it would take me out of a line position, and I may be out there for life.

A disproportionate number of Black managers are in staff positions in the field of human resources. Many Blacks who entered corporations in the late 1960s and early 1970s had liberal arts degrees. Thus, they were more likely to be hired in staff positions as affirmative action officers, community relations experts, or personnel managers. Since Blacks are disproportionately in human resources areas, they are vulnerable to downsizing in the corporation. Equal Employment Opportunity officials who are in the human resources are also being phased out or have little power. They, too, have to walk the tightrope in protecting their own positions by not pushing too fast and too far in helping other Blacks. Although Blacks entering corporations today have a greater chance than ever before of being promoted, they may be ghettoized in entry level positions. In such industries as banking and finance, they are often stuck in public finance rather than corporate finance, where the opportunities are more lucrative. Being clustered in certain positions limits their chances of upward mobility.

Quality of the Workplace

The literature on Black managers suggests they experience alienation, isolation, loss of identity, and culture shock in varying degrees. In his research on Black M.B.A.'s, Edward W. Jones found that 98 percent of the participants believed that corporations have not achieved equal opportunity for Black managers; 90 percent perceived the climate of support as worse than for their White peers.[13] Rosabeth M. Kanter, in *Men and Women of the Corporation*, found that the culture of corporate administration is influenced by the numerical dominance of men, while the quality of life for women was influenced by their proportion in the organization.[14] It was not surprising when the Talented One Hundred in the corporate world said they lacked supportive mentors and informal networks in assisting them to reach the next step of the corporate ladder. Since the middle management level has very few Blacks, their numerical minority affects their chances of finding a mentor. Kelly Smith sees it as "unfortunate that Blacks in the corporate world have very few mentors they can count on." She feels fortunate in having had them: "I've had people who have served as mentors to me—one was an Egyptian CEO—but the others were White. I have been very fortunate to have had them, but I don't have any at this point."

Even though Kelly has climbed the corporate ladder by her own merit and with the support of a few mentors, she found that the competition becomes keener and fiercer at the top rung. A *Black Enterprise* survey of readers supports Kelly's experience, indicating Blacks who have the highest level of education and income were the most likely objects of discrimination.[15]

Kelly feels she has reached an invisible ceiling and the possibility for her promotion is slim. She described the organizational climate in the United States as not supportive. However, when she travels abroad, her clients and staff treat her courteously and respectfully. Kelly reiterated that her colleagues and supervisors think she has too much power. "They want to dilute my power, undermine me, or ship me off to another country." One means of diluting her authority was to ask her to share her Cuban secretary, whom Kelly had hired and promoted to executive secretary. This presented some serious problems. Said Kelly, "She was extremely loyal to me. Now that she reports to two other men, her allegiance is to them. I have asked her to do certain things for me and she has gone behind my back to my boss to tell him she does not want to do these things, prior to discussing them with me. That is totally unheard of." Kelly maintained that a White secretary, whom Kelly described as "an envious little White girl," helped "pollute the mind of the Cuban, who has a Latin mentality that says if she works for a man, she owes him more allegiance."

In describing further the quality of her life in the workplace, Kelly pointed out that she is hassled by her boss and others about the way she dresses and about the type of car she drives.

I am a very bright, confident individual and qualified for the position I have. But the White folks on the job can't stand the fact that I have the money and the material goods. My dear boss mentioned this to me. Some of my colleagues are on my level, some beneath, and a few above. It is not that they can't afford them. It is just that they don't think I should have them. About three years ago, I bought a Mercedes Benz. I am an officer of this company and paid to make financial decisions. How on earth do they think I can make a better financial decision than I make for myself? I invested my money in a Mercedes Benz, which I thought was a reasonably good investment.

Since her White colleagues were envious of her, the new boss appeased them by restructuring her department. When Kelly asked:

Why are you restructuring the department? He replied, "People are envious of you. It is not that you can afford to buy a Cadillac and others can't afford to buy a Cadillac, it is just that others think you should be driving a Ford." He didn't say my Mercedes Benz, because that would have been too clear. The people are envious of the way I dress, the way I look, the car I drive, my behavior, and the power I have. I am an officer and make a lot of decisions. They would like to find something wrong with what I do. But they can't, because I know it better than they know it. They are constantly looking for something to nitpick.

When Kelly leaves the workplace, home is not a total refuge from racism; not even the nightly comfort of her bed brings her peaceful sleep. "I can't sleep—my mind is racing—because I can't figure out how they are going to come at me next. So I have to work twice as hard to think about this person and what is going on and to try to figure out what they are going to do next."

Even though Kelly is unable to sleep some nights because of the race watch, she warned, "Blacks could destroy themselves if they internalize the stress from racism." To cope with racism, she said, it is necessary to always "be the best at what you do and to be persistent, because you never know who is watching you." She reminded me of the CEO who noted her performance and promoted her just one month prior to his death. Though Kelly, a political moderate, understands the importance of working hard, being competent and independent, she is also keenly aware of the political landscape. It is important for Blacks not to "confine all their energies to working within the corporation," said Kelly. "Blacks should have outside contacts with political organizations of strength and power. If you can't get what you need on the inside, you need to develop an external base in order for someone to think twice about doing something adverse to you." Kelly lives in a politically active Black neighborhood in the South where many public officials also reside. "Although the corporation where I work is powerful, my colleagues do not know who I know and what power I can engender."

Like Kelly, Walter Calvin, also a top-ranking Black senior vice president in an international conglomerate, has had "to figure out what they are going to do next." In fact he became so "fed up" with trying to figure things out, he told his superior, "Include me in this act or move me." He was transferred from the domestic to the international side of the parent company. Walter has not encountered much discrimination as an executive within the international side of the corporation. However, he still faces it when he represents the company. He said:

Even in Europe, where Whites are not accustomed to Blacks getting off a corporate jet, they stare at me as though I am a ghost. I can be in a crowd of my White counterparts in London or in Frankfurt and it is as though I am—[He did not complete the sentence]. I've had instances like this happen to me. It goes something like this: [A waiter asks] "What would you like, gentlemen, to drink?" And everyone answers and he says, "And you, sir?" [Laughter] It is as though I am the guy who is carrying everyone's bags. In many instances, I've been the senior officer in that setting and that has happened here and abroad. As a senior vice president of a world class corporation, I should be able to go, because of the stature and the status of this job, anywhere on earth I might choose. But because of the color of my skin, I am being denied access to the privilege that this job affords me.

Prior to his transfer, he had no mentor and was not a part of the social and informational network of the organization. This was a serious problem for Walter, who described his life as "a constant daily trauma of literally chipping away at a block, just trying to get your foot in the door, and getting around the table where decisions are made. I went through this experience for three years, and it affected me psychologically. This experience nagged at me for over a year. It took me a long time to get over it." Walter recalled one experience.

I shall never forget one incident where I felt extremely isolated. There was a marketing meeting in Chicago, and the marketing segment leaders had to make presentations before our colleagues. I kept asking the team leaders who were talking about how the presentation should be made, "What are you looking for?" I never received an answer. I came to the meeting with all my storyboards for advertising and storyboards for marketing strategy. I found out when I got to the meeting that it had started thirty minutes before I was told it would. I was scheduled to be the second person to make a presentation. Yet, I was put on hold until the next day. You can imagine what this does to you when you're ready for a presentation. I never got the rules for the presentation. Everybody else had the rules except me, even my White marketing groups who were at a lower level. I was never invited to sit in on the marketing strategy meetings.

In spite of the frustrations, Walter succeeded. His success in the corporation in the early 1980s epitomizes the aspirations of Blacks seeking to move up the corporate ladder. But he felt that he could not share his "daily traumas" with other aspiring Blacks, so he coped with his racial traumas alone. Now he feels it is important for Blacks to maintain outside networks to relieve stress encountered on the job. Walter, a liberal Democrat, has "gotten his foot in the door" and, finally, he can take his place "around the table to influence decisions." He is working internally and externally with groups and individuals to divest his company's vast holdings in South Africa. Walter's and Kelly's experiences are typical of the Talented One Hundred in the corporate world.

Looking inside the newsroom, we get another glimpse of the quality of life behind the scene from Warner Babbitt and other journalists. Life in the newsroom can be difficult if one does not understand the interfacing of corporate politics and racism. Said Babbitt, "I had a White woman editor who had an absolute attitude about Black men who had balls. She could only deal with a eunuch, but not a Black who is a man and enjoys being a man. She took great pride in berating me in front of the entire desk, chiding, 'That is your problem, you always think small and here you are focusing on that small union. You must think big and have bigger stories.'" He didn't listen to her, but continued to pursue the story. When the story became an international daily headline, he said, "I beat everybody with the story." Yet, he didn't get any credit for his work. Instead, Babbitt said, "I got constantly reprimanded by her. . . . I couldn't figure her out. I was doing my work." Not only did he feel the editor was racially biased, he admitted it did not help her attitude toward him when he "screwed up politically with her." Unknown to Babbitt, his editor and another editor were competing for the same story. One asked him to do the story, but when he completed it, he gave it to the other. "*They* thought I was playing both ends of the stick," said Babbitt.

Politics interface with race in the newsroom, affecting the quality of life for Black journalists. "You are seen as a Black first and not a reporter," claimed Babbitt. Hence, this perception strongly influences the life chances of Blacks in the print or broadcast media. "[Black] reporters do not get the good assignments, the meaty or plum stories, the front page stories, the foreign desk and national assignments, the positions as editors, managers, and publishers, or enough feedback on their work," said Leo Aramis, an associate editor with a major newspaper. These limited assignments and opportunities obviously affect their evaluations and their chances for moving up the ladder.

The quality of life in the newsroom is further affected by the nature of the work. Journalism, one of the most stressful occupations, is extremely competitive, and being Black increases the stress. "People will cut you in the back; they do play politics," said Babbitt. "I went around thinking that if I were smart, they would let me do what I had to do. They didn't have very many Black reporters on the national desk. Only one at the time. Even now, the desk is called the White Citizens Council. This paper has never been able to maintain more than two Black reporters out of a staff of forty or fifty on its national desk. Only once briefly did they have four, and I was one of them."

Caustically, he asserted, "We were all doing nothing, covering what I call RUMP and RUIN. RUMP is refugees, urban affairs, minorities, and politics. RUIN is refugees, urban affairs, immigrants, and Negroes. The only difference is when we weren't covering RUMP, we covered RUIN. The White folks wanted to know how the Negroes were going to vote." A colleague, who left the national desk, forewarned Babbitt, "You can stay here on this national desk, but the White folks aren't going to let you go very far, because they consider politics and the state department their property." "It turns out that he was exactly right—all the things that have to do with the running of 'Great White America,'" remarked Babbitt. "I always ended up working on Sundays, and it was considered penalty work. Their stars do not work on Sunday, and the paper does not have a fair way to allocate Sundays. One Black and three White women ended up running the national desk. I would call it 'Affirmative Action Sunday.'"

Ethel King, also a journalist for a major paper, agreed with Babbitt, but pointed out, "I used to think the media were leaders because we pointed the finger at everybody else. Many people think that, and I try to clear up that misconception. Racism is everywhere." For this reason, Ethel does not pour her whole heart into the corporation as she feels most Black males do. It is important for her to maintain outside interests in writing and in a supportive network of family and friends to sustain her in the newsroom.

Supportive mentors or a network on the job would have greatly assisted Walter Calvin and Warner Babbitt; however, their experiences are typical of others in corporate America. According to a *Black Enterprise* poll of its readers, participating in a survey on working in America, 66 percent said they didn't have a mentor to assist in advising them in their careers.[16] A similar finding among the Talented One Hundred showed that 62 percent of them did not have a mentor. Bebe Moore Campbell, writing in the *New York Times Magazine* on "Black Executives and Corporate Stress," noted, "Blacks are trying to learn an ingrown system without coaching and mentoring. They can do it, but it takes longer. And some are paying a heavy price in stress."[17]

Unlike most of the Talented One Hundred, Tony Michaels, who entered the corporate world in the late 1950s in the Midwest, has been fortunate in having many mentors to guide his career. "I had people willing to go to bat for me," said Michaels. Earlier in his career during the late fifties, when Michaels faced racial discrimination, he was confrontational in coping with it. His mentor, having risked his own position in hiring him, advised him, saying, "I know your make-up, drive, and competitiveness. Anytime you do anything different, be sure you are right. People all over the country are trying to prove you are wrong. You know you are right. I am right, and we are going to show them we are." So he persuaded Michaels not to be confrontational, imploring, "Let me do your fighting for you."

Jews and White women, having their own history of marginality, were identified as the most likely mentors for the Talented One Hundred. Jeraldyne Blunden, a dancer, was the first Black student of her Jewish mentor. "She was a big influence on what I did," said Blunden. Certain White ethnic and religious groups, like the Mormons, were the least supportive. Three of the Talented One Hundred reported negative experiences with Mormons, who comprise a small percentage of the White population in the United States.

Leo Aramis views the role of a mentor differently from others. He said, "We got to stop this nonsense about a mentor being a surrogate parent or buddy. A mentor is someone who can help you do what you need to do, so you can do your job better. If that person can be a surrogate relative, that's fine. But if not, that's all right, too." Warner Babbitt sees merit in this position, though he has had mentors. "Several editors helped me out and moved me along," remarked Babbitt. One woman assisted him "to write and conceptualize a story and not be satisfied with 'he said, she said,' and how to grasp the context." Yet, it was a White colleague who gave him the best strategy for survival in the corporate jungle of journalism. "You see yourself as working for this newspaper. You have to see yourself as working for Warner Babbitt, who is selling something to the newspaper. And if you see it that way, your job would be a lot more fun," advised his colleague. He started to work on stories on Fridays to "hold them away from the great White male editors. [When] my good lady friend editors would come on Sundays, I would spring the story on them. Since Sunday is dead, it was a great idea. The story always went up on page one on Monday."

There may be a greater expectation among young Blacks of having a supportive mentor and network. Blacks who were directly influenced by the Civil Rights and Black Nationalist movements may view themselves as more willing actors and initiators in the face of adversity, thereby feeling more undaunted by obstacles of racism. A discussion among journalists during an annual meeting of the Association of Black Journalists illustrates the differences between professionals who came of age during the Civil Rights era and those of the post-Civil Rights era. During the conference, young journalists who had worked five years or less in the profession were invited to share their concerns and to obtain feedback needed to upgrade their technical skills. Leo Aramis discovered "some young people came close to having psychological problems, despite the fact that they had grown up in integrated neighborhoods, gone to integrated schools, gone to the best journalism schools in this country, and had been accepted by Whites in those settings. They went into the newsroom and got hit by racism. We had one girl sitting there crying, 'They never invited me out to lunch.'" Leo retorted, "I told her she was not there to go to lunch and somebody should have told her." Other young journalists complained they did not get the best stories, assignments, or promotions. Responding to the young journalists, Leo reminded them that, "I had to fight for it. . . . They came in thinking if they busted their butts, they would be accepted by White folks. I came knowing I would never be part of the group. I had to demand it."

Leo also found that some of the younger journalists who had been in the profession as long as four years "still could not write a story lead and did not grasp or didn't even know how to organize a story." They felt they were in a position to move up. "But they weren't, because no one in their shop was helping them," said Leo. "They weren't telling them you are doing this wrong and you need to work on this. Either their copy was changed on the desk or the people would print it the way it was written." He strongly believes "they need to find someone to look at their work" and "there is someone they can find."

In spite of the lack of mentors and supportive networks, the Talented One Hundred are succeeding and functioning in corporate America. As Leo suggested, most came to corporate America "knowing they would never be a part of the group." But they continue to view themselves as actors of their destiny, in spite of racial roadblocks. They understand that as ambassadors for their race, they must bear its heavy burden of continuing to move forward.

A myth runs through corporate America that companies are "color blind." A silent conspiracy of both Blacks and Whites pretends race is not a factor in the workplace. "Discrimination is ever present but a taboo topic. . . . If you want to move up, you don't talk about it."[18] Hence, some Blacks feel that to associate with other Blacks or to hire a Black secretary or a Black manager is viewed as suspect by Whites or is seen as "too Black." Dira Ridley, a physical chemist in a major consumer products company, thinks "if you are seen with another token Black, it may be okay. However, if you are outspoken about race and you are associating with other Blacks, it weakens your security. The crumbs thrown out are like a bird in the hand, whereas the collective power of Blacks might be far away. " So, many Black elite do not wish to upset the status quo, even though their inaction may conflict with their political orientation to assist other Blacks move up the corporate ladder.

Dira Ridley, who described her political orientation as vacillating between moderate to liberal, did not fear risking "the bird in the hand" when she helped to organize professional Black women in the corporation where she works. Dira understands the importance of the collectivity, asserting:

> I am a firm believer that while one individual may progress, it is important for the group to progress. I didn't think Black women in the organization had anything to do with what I was doing. I was doing extremely

well. In fact, one of the reasons I signed the letter to investigate the attrition rate of Black women in the company was because my manager said I was doing extremely well. I didn't sign it out of spite; I think I could have progressed in spite of getting a consultant to come in to evaluate the status of Black women. I think I am that good. If I put into perspective what it takes—not only knowing something, personal interaction, and that comfort factor—I could have made it. The question is, Have we made this true for the broader group? I was interested in Black women and not Dira Ridley, knowing that if the environment of Black women changes, it would help me as well.

When greater numbers of Blacks enter the workplace, race issues become more salient, and the quality of life seems to improve. The larger the number of Blacks, the greater the likelihood of having supportive networks and mentors who can assist in learning corporate politics. When *Black Enterprise* selected the twenty-five most successful Black managers in corporate America, it was found that Black and White mentors who were well placed had a major impact in shaping their careers.[19] Many of these managers were employed by companies listed by *Black Enterprise* among the fifty best companies for Blacks to work. As Blacks move into positions as managers, they can hire and mentor other Blacks. Leo Aramis believes it is easier to fight his battle against racism because 18 percent of the professional staff in his company is Black. If you challenge the system alone, you are likely to be isolated. Leo challenged an editorial endorsement by his newspaper of a White mayoral candidate over a Black one. He challenged it because a Black mayor was being compared with a Black candidate. (The comparison involved the late Harold Washington of Chicago.) "I saw it in the computer and thought it was racist. I put a note on the end of it and told them I thought it was patently offensive and shouldn't be in the paper. We don't compare Jewish mayors, Polish mayors, and Italian mayors. The editorial endorsement was stereotypical, and I wouldn't work for anyone where that would appear in the newspaper. It was rewritten." Of course, he admitted, "I had to be prepared to quit if they didn't change it. . . . But it helps being at a paper that has as many Black folks as my paper does," said Leo. "One of the Black editors came to me [after the editorial incident] and said, 'You know, man, I really enjoy being at a paper where once in my life I don't have to be the only one to fight every fight.' I fought this one, and the next one he might fight. Next time somebody else might fight one. It's not just always one person who is picked out as the rabble rouser who jumps up and down every time so he can be ignored, pushed out, or sabotaged. So that makes a difference."

Despite racial obstacles, the Talented One Hundred continue to work diligently to move up the corporate ladder, believing they should be promoted on merit, instead of patronage. They also expressed the fervent belief that if you work hard enough and do your job efficiently, "someone will recognize your abilities." The Black elite learned to cope with all the contradictions inherent in the workplace by treading the tightrope carefully. Edward W. Jones, in "Black Managers: The Dream Deferred," captures well the role strain and dilemmas of Blacks in corporate America.

> Running the gauntlet means smarting from the pain of prejudice even as White colleagues deny that your reality of race has any impact. It means maintaining excellent performance, even when recognition is withheld.
>
> It means being smart but not too smart. Being strong but not too strong. Being confident but not egotistical to the point of alienation. Being the butt of prejudice and not being unpleasant or abrasive. Being intelligent but not arrogant. Being honest but not paranoid. Being confident yet modest. It means seeking the trust and respect of fellow Blacks and acceptance by Whites. Speaking out on issues affecting Blacks but not being perceived as a self-appointed missionary or a unifaceted manager expert only on Black subjects. Being courageous but not too courageous in areas threatening to Whites.
>
> It means being a person who is Black but not losing one's individuality by submersion into a class of "all Blacks," as perceived by Whites. Defining one's self while not contradicting the myriad definitions imposed by White colleagues. Being accepted as a leader for Whites and not being seen as an Uncle Tom by Blacks. Being a person who is Black, but also a person who is an authentic human being.[20]

For some, "running the gauntlet" is physically and psychologically risky. In increasing numbers, the Black elite are going to work for Black corporations. More importantly, however, some are using their expertise and skills gained in corporate America to start their own businesses.

Entrepreneurship: Fortunes and Frustrations

Reginald Lewis, the mega-deal maker, made a fortune in his buyout of the billion dollar Beatrice International Corporation. It catapulted him from number six to number one on *Black Enterprise*'s list of "The Top 100 Black Businesses" and to perhaps being the most influential Black businessman in America. His success signaled a shift in the role of Black entrepreneurs as national and international players in the marketplace. Since the Civil Rights movement, some top Black businesses have expanded to the general market in construction, automobile dealership, manufacturing, and computer systems. Others continue to serve primarily Black clientele, particularly those in the cosmetic industry, publishing, and real estate. The vast majority of Black businesses still cater to Black clientele. These businesses are mostly sole proprietorships which are service-oriented, such as automotive repair shops, beauty parlors, grocery stores, and cab companies. According to the Bureau of the Census, individual proprietorships accounted for 95 percent of all Black businesses.[21] Black businesses increased about 50 percent from 1977 to 1982, but sales receipts declined during this same period.[22]

With the decline in sales receipts, there is an increasing concern that Black businesses might disappear unless more of African-Americans' estimated income of $250 billion is recycled back into the Black community. Having greater options in the consumer marketplace, Blacks do not exclusively patronize Black businesses. Also, Asians and other minority-owned businesses have begun to replace establishments owned by Blacks, eroding further the wealth in the Black community.

Black Enterprise magazine's board of economists sees the low level of self-employment as a primary obstacle to creating wealth in the Black community. These economists claim that individuals who own equity in businesses are more likely to have higher incomes than the general population. "People who are in business have five times the net worth of people who work for salaries. So if you are going to improve the wealth base of a people, you have to have more entrepreneurs and successful businesses"[23] said one *Black Enterprise* economist.

Many impediments exist for Blacks who would like to become successful entrepreneurs. Like others among the Talented One Hundred who are self-employed, Joshua Smith, a nationally known entrepreneur who owns a computer services company, pointed out some common concerns and obstacles of Black entrepreneurs. He asserted that "race plays a major role in business development." First, he said, "Race is critical because when we had major businesses during the period of segregation, we also had a Black business market that was a captured market. That market was there because Black people were unable to choose where they could buy. So in order to meet the supply side of things, Blacks had to develop businesses. We did develop businesses to fit an available consumer market that couldn't go anyplace else to do anything. People can be successful entrepreneurs when conditions are right to support them." However, as a result of integration, he thinks "the rug to the consumer market was pulled." Blacks "went everywhere and bought everywhere. They have got to get away from that freedom consumption. It means the markets for Blacks have completely gone in terms of any loyalty to Black businesses."

Black consumers' estimated total income is $250 billion. However, said Joshua, "less than 5 percent goes to support Black businesses. We have reached a chicken and egg situation. If we don't have businesses, we can't create the business, and that must change." In order for Black businesses to thrive, "they must produce or provide a service to the overall society, basically to the White community. [My] business is not unlike other businesses; we don't have Black customers yet. We have basically institutional customers and federal government customers." He believes that "there is a heavier burden on Black businesses than what exists in other ethnic communities. If the community supports the business, it has a chance to grow up. No one is going to tell me that every Chinese who opens a Chinese restaurant knows how to run one. You can't tell me that every Vietnamese who goes into the market has a family background in that area. That is not true; but they have in place a support system to buy from one another." Joshua thinks that "since Blacks have no loyalty, they will patronize a Korean or Vietnamese restaurant that has taken over a Black restaurant in the Black neighborhood. We are so used to exercising freedom of buying that we haven't gotten out of this pattern. Now we have gotten so accustomed to not seeing Black businesses that we don't expect to see them."

Tony Brown, a television personality and columnist, organized the Buy Freedom national campaign to promote Black businesses and to challenge the Black community to move from freedom consumption to stewardship. Blacks, he asserted, spend almost 95 percent of their income on goods and services controlled by non-Blacks and thus "export 1.7 million jobs annually from the Black neighborhood and import unemployment, welfare program dependency, and a defeatist attitude."

Not only is there a relative lack of support for Black businesses within the Black community, Blacks find it difficult to acquire the necessary capital for investment from both the government and the private sector. When Thomas B. Thomas was self-employed, for example, one reason for the failure of his business was the lack of capital to bid on federal contracts. "You had to put up 10 percent to bid. If the bid is a million dollars, not many small businesses have the capital to let you hold that amount for ninety days until the final bid." Thomas mentioned that when he tried to get private funding, the funding company wanted to take 60 percent of his company. He claimed that some supposedly joint ventures of minority-owned enterprises are actually owned by major White corporations who have financial control.

While there are various set-aside programs in the federal government for minority businesses, according to Joshua Smith, "When we get outside that set-aside market, we fall flat on our face, and that's unfortunate," because often small businesses lack capital. Approximately 80 percent of all Black businesses fail. But, Joshua pointed out, "80 percent of all small businesses fail, and Blacks have primarily small businesses. Hence, they are no more likely to fail than White businesses."

Joshua agreed with Thomas that when an entrepreneur wants to generate capital to start a business, the finances are often not available to Blacks. "Black people do not have assets. We own only one-tenth of one percent of the assets in this country; even though we have income, our assets are abysmal. So there is a perception that the Black person is not a good risk in the banking or financial services. If such a perception exists, you would not want to loan money to that person either." He claimed, "These perceptions are not only in the White community, but in the Black community. Black people are the harshest critics about Black businesses; therefore, the perception is simply prolonged and enhanced. So Blacks have a harder time in gaining access to capital."

Joshua noted that although the negative perception about Black business is strong, it is inaccurate.

> There is a definite perception in this country about Black businesses. It is unfortunate that no one goes back to the days when businesses were thriving. Who the hell did Black people buy from when they couldn't buy from White people? They bought from Black businesses. There were role models in Black businesses. People expected to see successful news-papermen, insurance people, restauranteurs, grocers, and furniture deal-ers who supplied all the needs to the Black community. We are losing those role models today. So there is a perception out there that Black businesses are inferior businesses and Black business people aren't very businesslike people—none of which is true.

The truth is that Black businessmen, like James Paschal, a successful restauranteur in Atlanta, have been serving the Black community for years. When the Paschal brothers wanted to expand their restaurant business and build a hotel and lounge in the early 1960s, they were able to obtain the capital from a Black bank. The renowned Paschal Brothers' Restaurant has been in business for over forty years. Several presidents and international dignitaries have visited the restaurant. It has been called the place where "politics get under way in the morning." James Paschal said Martin Luther King, Jr. held several of his strategy meetings for the Civil Rights marches at his restaurant, including the Selma march. The Paschal Brothers' Res-taurant was deeply involved in the Civil Rights movement, providing food and getting students released from jail. There is a saying around Atlanta, recalled James, that "when election time comes, the local politicians who do not meet at Paschal Brothers' restaurant in the morning can rest assured that they won't be elected." Though Blacks are still supportive of his busi-ness, he admitted, we "have lost support to White establishments."

Joshua Smith sees another important factor contributing to the diffi-culties of entrepreneurs, and that is the loss of incumbent rights.

> As a result of desegregation and the breakup of Black businesses, we lost something that is so critical to competitiveness. We lost incumbent rights—that is, the company that has the contract or the job. It is the organization on the inside, the company that is working every day with problems and the future needs of the client. The incumbent is breaking

bread every day with the client and is developing a sense of comfort with the client. When it comes to bids on new opportunities where there is an incumbent already present, it poses a basic obstacle to Black businesses. We are not incumbents. By virtue of not being incumbents, we don't have the comfort or confidence. We haven't had that opportunity to build up relationships. We are new, unknown, small, and Black. All these factors are negative in terms of who will be the winning contractor. So when Black businesses submit their bids, it is very unusual for a company who has not dealt with a Black business to throw out an incumbent that they've been dealing with for years to get this unknown with all the perceived negatives. So, by lack of incumbency, we suffer a lot. Incumbency is very important to understanding how a market reacts and what a market does to any kind of opportunities.

Thomas B. Thomas can relate to Joshua's comment about incumbent rights and the difficulty in obtaining contracts from White businesses because of the negative perceptions about Black businesses. When Thomas was in business, he had to "hire a White bird dog to sniff out business. Whites go out and develop an interest in your product and service, and we would come in and close the deal. The reason we have to do that is because if we go after clients who are Caucasians, they have a real problem with giving you a piece of the pie." Thomas admitted that "some Blacks have been very successful at playing the government game. How they do it, I can't speak for them. But I do know they have made a lot of money. For me, I had a horrible time."

In contrast to Thomas, Joshua has "made a lot of money" from federal contracts. But he has not hired a "White bird dog." Despite some difficulties, Joshua has been able to sniff out his own business prior to and since his graduation from the Small Business Administration's 8(a) program in 1986.

Joshua attributes his success in part to his ability to take risks when he sees an opportunity. He said that "the only things that will show up on your doorstep are trouble, mangy dogs, and other people's opportunities." He feels that Blacks do not want to take risks in entrepreneurship.

> Black people, to a great extent, are unwilling to make the transformation from secure corporate positions into the entrepreneurial role. That is driven a lot by our standard of living. If we have things tied up in homes, we obviously have to make the mortgage payments. We are strapped by other financial limitations in terms of our standards of living. So it makes it very difficult to make that move from the secure to the unknown, because we've committed ourselves to our yearly outlay. So we don't have the flexibility to make a move nor do we have the assets. Our families are not wealthy. We do not inherit money. So we lack the financial support to provide the security to take risks. We are cautious about what we have

and want to maintain that. The end result is that Black businesses are small and these businesses have an abysmal mortality rate.

Having said that, the only way Blacks are going to secure any kind of position of autonomy is through economic avenues. The power base of economics is entrepreneurship, which has a spirit that is driven by the attitudes on the part of the people that it is something that we must do. So there is a need within the Black community to produce more successful entrepreneurs and larger Black-owned and controlled firms. It is a matter of resources, role models, perceptions, and access to capital. All of these factors make it difficult for Black businesses to make it. It seems inevitable that if Black businesses don't become a priority, we are guaranteed to continue to slide into dark channels.

Joshua said he is also successful because he carefully plans his career paths.

> I planned my career. I said if I were going into business, I needed to know about the business, management, marketing, operations, and finance. I needed to understand what the market was all about, and I needed to pick a business where I could take those accumulated experiences and turn them into opportunities. I spent twenty-five years in the field, but I planned ten years before starting a business. I picked a field that is growing and that I had knowledge about and felt that I had something to offer. I was able to identify a concept that was workable in the growing environment of information. It is basically planning, capturing what you need to know, surrounding yourself with the right kind of people, developing your reputation, and being able to move ahead. I think people who do that are successful.

Joshua cautions aspiring entrepreneurs to avoid "starting a business and learning while you are on the job, because it is too costly. You have to learn on somebody else's operation. You have to bring people into your business that have knowledge that you don't have. So many businesses fail because of the ego of the person who started it. You bring people in who will challenge you and not acquiesce to you. In order to attract good people, you have to have integrity and a good track record yourself."

In building a business, Joshua feels it is important to "have high goals" and to climb the mountain top. But he, too, has seen the valley in the first few months following his graduation in 1986 from the 8(a) program. The Small Business Administration retroactively disallowed over $100 million in contracts his company, Maxima, had won, threatening the company's future. Joshua, therefore, cautions that "one must have plateaus within those goals. So if one falls, it will not be a total disaster. Success is a staging process. Thus, the biggest part of mountain climbing is not the steps you take, but the steps you hold onto."

Joshua, a moderate Republican, was appointed in 1989 by President George Bush as chairman of the Commission on Minority Business Development. It is his goal to set policies that will have a positive impact on minority businesses.

Still, no matter how talented one is and how hard one works, opportunities for Black entrepreneurs like Joshua Smith seem inextricably linked to the public sector, particularly those opportunities provided by the federal government. But the recent Supreme Court ruling in January 1989 on set-aside programs may have a continuing negative impact on Black businesses. Two months after the Supreme Court ruling, the Georgia State Supreme Court struck down Atlanta's affirmative action program, one of the most effective programs in the nation. Only days after the Georgia ruling, Michigan's set-aside program was declared unconstitutional.

Public Service: Public Servant or Puppet?

With the equal opportunity policies of the federal government in the 1960s and the increasing political control of large cities by Blacks, the ranks of middle-class Blacks in public service began to swell more than any sector of the economy. Yet, even before 1960, the government was an important source of Black employment and upward mobility. In 1960, for instance, 13 percent of White managers and 21 percent of Black managers and administrators were employed in government. The proportion of Black managers and officials was 62 percent greater than that of Whites. By 1970, 27 percent of Black managers and 11 percent of White managers and administrators were in government. The proportion of Black managers and officials increased to 133 percent greater than Whites, noted Sharon Collins in "The Making of the Black Middle Class."[24]

A significant number of Blacks have benefited from the federal government legislative policies to gain economic parity. But, according to Collins, the "structure of opportunity within which the middle class has grown is still characterized by inequality. The Black middle class emerged from special political and legal protection, and it occupies a useful but powerless market position in U.S. society."[25] She argues that the opportunities available to Blacks are more dependent on political pressure than economic trends. Moreover, Blacks are overly represented in positions dependent on federal funds, positions that are most vulnerable to shifts in the political winds. Middle-class Blacks are in positions in those sectors of the economy that serve the needs of Blacks. Since these positions are heavily dependent on federal funds, they are also vulnerable to political winds and pressures.

The number of Blacks holding senior policy-making and managerial positions in the federal government rose during President Jimmy Carter's tenure, but dropped when President Reagan took office. The number of

Blacks holding presidential appointments dropped from forty-four in 1950 to twenty-one in 1981; from nineteen in 1982 to fifteen in 1983; and climbed from nineteen in 1984 to twenty in 1985, remaining at that level until 1987.[26] In 1988, Reagan appointed the fifty-one-year-old Lt. Gen. Colin Luther Powell as the national security adviser, the first Black ever to serve in that position. Subsequently, Powell was appointed by George Bush as the first Black to head the Joint Chiefs of Staff, and the president has continued to appoint Blacks as senior policymakers.

Seemingly, whatever gains Blacks have made since the 1960s are the result of race-oriented policies. Collins maintains that researchers often ignore the types of organizations in which Blacks earn their income. "Black workers' functional relationship" is to "Black consumer networks and the dependency of class mobility on government rather than free market forces."[27] The government-supported jobs created new opportunities for Blacks, but Collins maintains they were the result of "a policy-mediated situation—not a market-oriented situation."[28] She indicates four federal policies that created opportunities for the growth of the Black middle class: the Equal Opportunity Commission, the Office of Federal Contract Compliance Programs, the federally funded social welfare services, and the federal contract set-aside programs. Many of the Talented One Hundred, who had high level positions as officials and managers and who benefited from the federal policies that created opportunities for the Black middle class, found themselves at the mercy of political tides. When the federal funds ceased or decreased, so did their economic security.

Blacks who are in mainline positions in government are not immune to racism. While the government has sometimes vigilantly served as a watchdog for the enforcement of equal opportunity policies in other sectors of the economy, it has not guarded its own door. Like the Black elite in the private sector, those who were public servants repeatedly reported feeling powerless even when they were in mainline positions as opposed to administrative and staff positions. Often those individuals in mainline positions were reclassified, removed, or ignored. The Talented One Hundred reported that another common discriminatory pattern is to restructure departments or divisions to neutralize the authority and power of Black managers. Stephanie Tahara, for example, works as an administrator. She managed ten divisions for a county government before a reclassification and reorganization of her division. Her experience was typical of the isolation and the quality of life for Blacks in public service. She remarked:

> If I succeed in managing well ten divisions without turmoil, I am not recognized. If a White person does it, he/she will get a promotion. The criteria are always changing. I was given a huge division to manage with a reclassification, but it never materialized. The person to whom I re-

ported was an assistant director, and he was evil. The director was neutral, but he allowed certain things to happen, and that made him evil. The director had wanted me to take this job, but he allowed this man to persecute me. The assistant director never gave any positive reinforcement, and he was forever finding the most nitpicking issues to be concerned about. He would arbitrarily assign an impossible deadline for a project. One way to deal with it was to be superficial, but that was a "Catch-22" and another set-up.

Since there was a pattern of systematic discrimination of Black professionals and managers in her county government, Stephanie, who described herself as sometimes a political radical, was instrumental in helping to organize a Black Managers' Association to combat racism.

When Dick Godfather, the highest-ranking Black civil servant in a federal agency, was removed from a position, his response was more accommodating. He received outstanding evaluation and performance ratings by his superior. Yet, he was removed from his position, "so a White boy could have my job. . . . No one said anything was wrong with my job performance. They just transferred me to a less satisfying job, saying it was for the sake of the organization." At first Dick got very angry "and began calling people that precious name that Black men have a way of calling people. . . . Then I just felt hurt," he said. Having a strong racial consciousness, Dick realized he "could not give up." He felt, "Black men get caught in that situation." Masking his feelings, he decided to "accommodate to make sure a Black remained in a position of authority." Eventually, Dick said, "the other guy screwed up the job, and three years later I got the job back—it became a more powerful position."

At the time of the interview, Dick administered about thirty different national educational programs. In his position, he has assisted numerous Black educational institutions.

Sharon Georgia, a forty-two-year-old city attorney for a large municipality, believes "if you mask your feelings, you can move through the system." But the situation is so intolerable that she cannot wear the mask or become a puppet. Sharon, an outspoken activist, made a guest appearance on a radio program to discuss how she was treated by Whites. She said, "The city manager raked me over the coals for 'playing politics.' You know they [her White supervisors] don't listen to Black radio stations on a Sunday afternoon. But the next morning, they were calling in to request the tape." She was angry. Unlike Dick, Sharon is unable to mask her feelings.

> I won't go anywhere in this job because of my personality. White folks consider me as arrogant and caustic. My bosses, Black and White, don't like it. If they are bull-shitting, I might tell them. When you are in a corporate environment, there is a certain way you act. I don't fit into my

job because of my personality as well as race, but I can separate personality from race and sex. For example, I have a White colleague who was given a higher position, more money, and better equipment than I. That is partly racism, or maybe partly sexism. When that happened, I got upset and angry, but I didn't internalize my anger. I know I am going to face racism, so I move on and don't get locked into the system. I will tell the motherfuckers to take this job and do what they want to do with it—but there is a price you pay and you got to be willing to pay that price. It can be termination or ostracism from the community. When I first started to practice law, I was recognized as an outstanding young Black woman. Now I am seen as that wild woman—that witch—because I will tell White folks to kiss my ass. Some Black folks say be careful. White folks can hurt you if you move on to another job.

Sharon's response to this warning was, "When I came to city hall, I had a reputation, and when I leave, I'll have one." Historically, Blacks who were unable to wear the mask were killed off, isolated, or labeled "crazy nigger" or "bad nigger." Yet, they were often instrumental in initiating positive social changes that moved Blacks forward.

The Nonprofit Sector: Victories and Vicissitudes

Some problems cited in the corporate sector are applicable to the public sector as well as the nonprofit sector. There are, however, distinct concerns associated with the nonprofit sector of the economy.

In 1968, Jeraldyne Blunden founded the Dayton Contemporary Dance Company in Ohio, a nonprofit, tax-exempt corporation with the commitment "to enrich the cultural environment of the Dayton community through the art of dance." Having performed at the American Dance Festival, her company is now nationally acclaimed, and her goal is to "establish and maintain a world-wide reputation with strong capabilities in the fields of jazz, ballet, and modern dance." She is victorious, in spite of the vicissitudes she has encountered over the past twenty years.

Like Blacks in the for-profit and public sectors of the economy, Blacks in the nonprofit sector, too, are ghettoized and stereotyped in roles and positions, whether as visual or performing artists, as administrators/managers, or as social activists. Blunden speaks to the issue of stereotyping Blacks in certain roles, saying:

The professional dance world was not ready for Blacks to do anything other than tap dance, jitterbug, swing their hips, tap their feet, and pray. [Laughs] When I joined the regional National Association for Ballet, we were the first Black company that did straight modern dance. It was different. They weren't used to seeing us do that. And little by little, we were accepted, because we could do other things than tap dance. That was something we had to prove. If we had a dance or piece based on spirituals, Whites loved it and we would get a standing ovation. If we had a piece from Western Europe or something from the Renaissance or classical music, there was little said. The fact that we danced it well was accepted, but more audience members would say, Why didn't you do something that was finger-popping? They are now getting over that because companies like the Dance Theatre of Harlem and Alvin Ailey do everything. They can do finger-popping type pieces and the German composer's *Streams*. It is important that we keep those two Black companies and their international focus so people will know that we can do other things.

Securing and distributing adequate funds are issues for those employed in nonprofit agencies, whether service-oriented or concerned with the arts. When Blunden started going after corporate money, "funding corporations decided they could not support two dance companies and indicated they didn't need two." The intention was to eliminate funding for her dance company, considered in the top five Black dance companies in America, and continue to fund a White company. "The percentage of funds the White dance company receives is higher. There is an inequity in funds. The artistic performance and reputation should have some merit," said Blunden. "Our needs are just as great as other arts organizations in the city, but we are treated differently. They make you jump through more hoops." In order to become a part of a mainstream funding source, the dance company was required to move to larger headquarters. The company is still not a full member of the arts organization in the city. "When we first applied for membership, they turned us down, in 1982," said Blunden. "We kept applying, but instead of making us a full member, they created a [new] category, calling us an associate member. Never before or since has anyone been an associate member of the arts organization in the city. I don't think they will ever use it again. There are always new criteria. No matter how good our artistic product, and I do think we have a good one, it will never be equal in the eyes of the people who have the money. I personally feel Whites see us first as a Black organization, not as an arts organization. If they could wash away the color, we'd rate very high."

Since those in the arts community will not "wash away the color" of her predominantly Black dance company, Blunden selects influential Black community leaders as board members to fight funding battles. This allows her to devote her energies to the creative process and to actualize her dream "to have an internationally known company that works fifty-two weeks a year." She knows "being successful is part and parcel of surviving in doing what you really want to do. So you must rely on yourself. That is where the motivation, ideas, and creativity have to come from, and in my business you start with a dream."

Since the Civil Rights movement, Blacks have made great strides in the mainstream sector of the economy. However, these gains have been tempered by continuous overt and subtle battles with racism in the workplace. In spite of Black professionals' credentials and career experiences, they are more likely than Whites to be ghettoized into staff positions in human resources. They also have several areas of concern in workplaces: (1) recruitment, retention, and retrenchment; (2) quality of life; and (3) the issue of balancing personal stress and role conflict inherent in their professional positions and their personal politics.

Entrepreneurs find the negative perception about Blacks in business makes it more difficult for them to obtain capital for expansion and start-up. In addition, since the Civil Rights era, the support of the Black community has eroded, because Black consumers have more options in the marketplace.

Because of the triumphs and trials of life in corporate America, the fortunes and frustrations of Black entrepreneurs, the public servant or puppet role of Blacks in the public sector, and the victories and vicissitudes of Blacks in the nonprofit sector, the Talented One Hundred are politically sophisticated and cosmopolitan. They understand both the political and the racial landscapes, which help them to more effectively cope in the workplace.

FOUR

The Color Line Across the World of Academe

Jefferson Barnes, a fifty-one-year-old tenured professor, is head of an academic department and a research institute at a major university. Having published widely, Barnes is respected by colleagues within the department and in the larger academic community. Barnes serves on several key committees within the university. He is very political, describing his present political orientation as liberal to radical on most issues. With a direct line to the chancellor, he has been successful at obtaining more funds and equipment for his department, recruiting more Blacks on campus, and improving their quality of life. Barnes exemplifies those Blacks in academe who have successfully negotiated the professional, political, and racial landscape in higher education since the sixties.

Prior to World War II, Black faculty and administrators were deliberately excluded by law or tradition from predominantly White universities. William H. Exum, in an article, "Climbing the Crystal Stair: Values, Affirmative Action, and Minority Faculty," noted:

> The first few Blacks to be accepted as faculty were obvious anomalies. For example, in the 1850s Charles L. Reason became professor of arts and letters at New York Central College, a school founded by abolitionists. Later exceptions were clearly "superstars." A Black Jesuit priest, Father Patrick Healey, who rose from instructor to become president of Georgetown University in 1873, is one example. On the other hand, W. E. B. Du Bois, the internationally acclaimed Black scholar, held a position as assistant instructor of sociology at the University of Pennsylvania from 1896 to 1897, but was never offered a permanent post there or in any White college or university. When Blacks did begin to receive faculty status in the twentieth century, recognition was belated, or dependent upon

123

special funding. William A. Hinton began as an instructor at Harvard in 1918. He spent twenty-six years at the rank of instructor and three as lecturer before finally being appointed professor in 1949—the year before he retired.[1]

Black administrators and faculty are a relatively new phenomenon on predominantly White campuses. Prior to the Civil Rights movement, they were largely confined to Black campuses. As a result of the Civil Rights movement, the enrollment of Black students increased. With the rise of the Black Nationalist movement and the assassination of Martin Luther King, Jr., colleges and universities began recruiting Black students aggressively.

When Black students arrived on White campuses, they found a dearth of role models; they protested and called for more Black faculty. The Black colleges were a major source of talent from which Black faculty and administrators were drawn, creating a brain drain in those schools. Many Black academicians were lured away by the promise of greater research opportunities, higher salaries, more leave-time, and reduced teaching loads. In addition, some believed they were playing a viable role in furthering the process of integration and equal opportunity. However, in contrast to Barnes' success in academe, a disproportionate number of Black administrators and faculty hired since the late 1960s and early 1970s have found their paths of opportunities littered with perils.

Blacks in academe, like those in the private and public sectors of the economy, continue to face obstacles in their effort to attain a higher quality of life, cope with the strains of role conflict in the workplace, increase their numbers in academe, and obtain tenure. While only a few Blacks successfully find their way to traditional departments in White academia, the career paths of many Black academics are blocked at the lower ranks in nontenurable positions that are affiliated with special programs for minorities.

In higher education, Blacks represent less than 5 percent of the total faculty. It is estimated that from two-thirds to three-fourths of Black faculty remain concentrated in historically Black colleges and universities, and since the late 1960s, in Black Studies departments on White campuses. They are also less likely to be employed in the most prestigious colleges and universities.[2]

The problem of recruitment of Blacks in higher education in predominantly White colleges and universities relates in part to supply, demand, and distribution. Though the concentration of Ph.D. holders in historically Black institutions decreases the available pool of Black faculty, a survey of minority Ph.D. recipients found several other explanations why this pattern of supply and demand exists. First, there has been a sharp decline in the number of Blacks receiving doctorates. The sharpest decline occurred from 1977 to 1986, when the number fell from 1,116 to 820.[3]

Second, Blacks, as well as Asians and Hispanics, are entering academic employment at a smaller percentage than ten years ago. Third, Black Ph.D.s have the lowest faculty promotion and tenure rate of any group. A nine-year longitudinal study of minority Ph.D. recipients revealed that Black faculty were less likely to be promoted and/or to receive tenure at the same rate or in the same time span as Asian-American or Hispanic faculty. In fact, Asians' promotion and tenure rates were higher than the national average. Promotion and tenure are affected by the quantity of research in higher education. The data indicate Blacks are predominantly in administrative and teaching positions, Hispanics are in teaching and research, and Asians are in research.[4] Thus, the differential rates in job assignment may explain in part differences between ethnic groups.

Blacks are also distributed disproportionately in education and the social sciences, while their participation in the natural sciences and engineering is minimal and appears to be decreasing. Black students earned only 222, or 1.8 percent, of 12,480 doctorates awarded to U.S. citizens in graduate science and engineering programs in 1987. In contrast, in 1978, there were 278 Blacks who received doctorates in science and engineering, 2.1 percent of the total doctorates awarded.[5]

Although there is a problem of supply, demand, and distribution, Jewel Prestage, in "Quelling the Mythical Revolution," notes, "The institutions in quest of Black faculty are the sole source of such faculty. The dearth of available Black academic talent is a direct consequence of their failure to produce such talent."[6] Often, commitment to and leadership in equal opportunity is also lacking from administrative officials. One reason is that, in higher education, "the ideologies of merit and autonomy provide a legitimate 'nonracist' basis for resisting demands for racial change as embodied, for example, in affirmative action programs."[7] In the search and recruitment process, there is the issue of how to estimate the pool of available racial minority candidates; an underestimation of applicants will result in lower hiring goals. Potential candidates are often overlooked, because of the way in which the position is advertised. In evaluating and processing candidates, universities desire "minority superstars, but may be less willing to gamble on minorities than on Whites."[8]

Even when Blacks are invited for interviews, they are frequently treated insensitively, which discourages them from accepting a position. According to Lisa Allen, a forty-one-year-old Ph.D. from a major university, who interviewed at a large, predominantly White public university in the Northeast in the late seventies, the climate was hostile. She declined her faculty appointment.

> I learned from a more humane colleague that others in the department felt I had an advantage over White candidates, because I was Black and

female. It was their reason for giving me a hard time. The department scheduled a grinding agenda from 8 A.M. to 11:30 P.M. without a break. I had to meet with each faculty (about fifteen), to teach a class, and to make a two and one half hour presentation. During the presentation, I was constantly interrupted with snide remarks about my findings and methodology. I was angry and frustrated. I felt [that] if this interview was any indication of how I would be treated in the department, I didn't want to be here. So I accepted a more congenial college.

While Lisa Allen was able to glean the quality of her academic life during the interview process, others do not feel the impact until their arrival on campus as faculty and administrators. The quality of life is related to the number of Blacks. When there are fewer Blacks in a predominantly White institution, there is greater social isolation.

Role Strain and Role Conflict in the Academic Marketplace

Black academicians like Jefferson Barnes have integrated into predominantly White university settings; yet, they maintain their Black identity. Understanding the political and racial landscape, they are able to work with Whites. They expect racism. Barnes said, "I am never surprised by racism. I never assume there is a minimum of racism among White colleagues and friends, so I don't get angry when it comes up. My question is, How is it going to be manifested? Is it going to be with a billy club or with knights in hoods or will it be subtle discrimination of talk at the faculty club?" Understanding that racism exists, Barnes acts with political expediency when "it doesn't override Black concerns." While he has learned to negotiate the political and racial tightrope in academe, there are others who are apolitical and aracial. They enjoy their status as a token Black in the university and ignore racism.

For most academicians, however, the social isolation in predominantly White universities is an issue. "It is tough for the individual who is a pioneer," said Cassie Cooper. Having worked at both Black and White institutions in higher education, Cassie, vice president for academic affairs at a Black college and in her late thirties, feels that there are more identity conflicts in White settings.

> It puts the person in a position of cognitive dissonance. There is a lot of pressure to perform well that I don't think you find for a White person in the same situation. A Black must represent the whole race. You want to do a good job and not let the race down. There is tremendous pressure for an individual to stand out. Not only do you want to do well for yourself—whatever the position dictates—but you are doing it as the first or

126

only Black person. There is only the problem of trying to fit in. What do you do? On the one hand, if there are other Blacks in the situation, you want to be a part of the Black group. However, if you are going to be successful, you have to be a part of the White group. You have all these identity issues to deal with. You want to move upward, doing the things that any person, Black or White, in that situation would do to be successful. Yet, you don't want your Black colleagues to think you are out for your own selfish motives, because you identify with them.

When Black colleagues are perceived as concerned solely with their own professional self-aggrandizement at the expense of their Black identity, social pressure is frequently brought to bear upon them. They are reminded that, although they may have achieved meritoriously, they owe a great deal to "the blood, sweat, tears, and the backs of the student movement"[9] in the 1960s and 1970s. Hence, they have an obligation to share their knowledge and to participate collectively in the empowerment of Black faculty, staff, students, and the larger community.

The literature on the quality of life for Black academicians indicates that there is limited social interaction between Black and White colleagues. Black administrators, however, do appear to have more contact with Whites. If academics limit their interaction with White colleagues, their access to important networks of mentors and sponsors is affected, thus impeding their upward mobility in the university. Having powerful allies and advocates can assist them in getting their research published with established journals and publishing outlets. Mentors can also assist new academicians in learning how the system operates. While some of the Talented One Hundred in academe had White mentors at some point in their careers, they were the exception rather than the rule. And there are few Blacks in top positions to act as mentors at White colleges and universities; when they do exist, they are often isolated from one another because of their heavy involvement in academic activities. Even when Blacks are teaching in Black Studies, Crystal Miller, a professor of theater in Afro-American Studies, noted, "it doesn't mean everything is peachy creamy. There are problems we have with one another, like not supporting each other, jealousy, envy, and sexism. It may be exacerbated because we are in a powerful White setting."

Not having mentors and supportive networks can impact on the evaluation process, preventing individuals from successfully climbing the academic ladder. Jonathan Mobutu, an economist and director of Black Studies at a predominantly White university in the Northeast, attributes the difficulties of a Black professor, who was denied tenure at the university in which he teaches, in part to not knowing the system. He maintained, "There are other factors going on in higher education. Once you get tenure, you can goof off; so you have people coming in reading the *New York Times* and *Wall Street Journal* and going to lunch. The brother is doing that too; but as an assistant professor, you don't do that. Your behind is supposed to be over in the laboratory demonstrating how hard you are trying to get publications. It illustrates the need for a Black network to facilitate new faculty entry into higher education, to let them know about the culture and the informal agenda as opposed to the formal agenda." Professor Mobutu, who has a progressive political orientation, is working to create an office of minority faculty development to assist the newly arrived and those who are not fully established in buttressing their credentials for promotion. This office will also provide them with mentoring and garnering support for research, travel funds, and grants.

Mobutu also feels that Blacks do not get support from White colleagues because Whites have a "lack of respect for the academic and service activities of Black faculty." This colors the perceptions of White faculty and students toward Black faculty. Having a negative image and lower expectations of Black faculty, Mobutu asserted, "any White student feels he/she has the authority to challenge one's credentials, while they will never do that for a White faculty member." Students feel "more comfortable challenging a Black woman" than her male counterpart. There is still "the macho image of the Black male that if you get in my face, I'll knock you down."

The barriers Black faculty encounter are as much with their colleagues as with White students, maybe even more so, claimed Mobutu. Colleagues assume that the expertise of Blacks, unless they are in the natural sciences, is limited to the Black experience. Mobutu cited a personal encounter in which he sensed disrespect from a White colleague and how he coped with it.

There is a course taught at the university on nuclear war, and it involves the invitation of guest lecturers to come and talk on specific topics. I got a call from the coordinator saying that he heard I knew about the economics of war and the defense build-up. Since you are an ambassador for your race, I always arrive early. "There goes those Negroes again; they are always late." So I arrived early and sat in the front row. There are no Blacks in the class. This guy walks in the class; he has never seen me before and he looks around and says, "Well Professor Mobutu has not gotten here yet, so we'll do this . . ." I said, "Wait! I am here." I am sitting with a suit on. [Since the professor could not readily identify Mobutu, he assumed Mobutu had not arrived, which indicated his tendency to stereotype Blacks as always late.] The White students' perception was to pick up what was going on. The guy started to hem and haw. So I do my thing and whatever I am talking about I try to make sure I bring a correct and comprehensive perspective to bear and the students appreciated that. They wanted to continue the discussion.

The lack of respect and sensitivity toward faculty may be expressed in overt ways. In the late 1980s, when Mobutu and his boss had a luncheon engagement with the director of a project to improve science education, this stereotype was evident. During lunch, Mobutu asked the director if Black secondary teachers were a part of the science education program. The director answered, "We had one, but she dropped out. I don't know if Black folks aspire to know anything about science." "This statement was made to my face," remarked Mobutu. "It is personal racism, but it projects a broader stereotype." The stereotype is that since there is a paucity of Blacks in the natural sciences, it is the result of a lack of interest or intelligence. "In that kind of setting, you can't always respond to it the way you like. I wanted to reach across the table, snatch him, and beat his butt. But I had to handle it in a different way and that exacerbates the frustration. It is part of what Black males and females experience daily on White campuses." Mobutu handled the situation by trying to correct the perception of the project director and convince him that Blacks were indeed interested in science.

In facing social isolation, a lack of respect, the lack of support services, and taxing professional obligations, Black academics are still expected to perform their "buffer" role in the university with Black students and with the Black community. It produces a dilemma, creating role strain and role conflict. Sense the tension and conflict from walking the academic tightrope as both Teresa Johnson and Crystal Miller articulated the dilemma. Said Teresa:

> Blacks have to do more. We have to develop a department, participate in the community, and involve ourselves with our students. I don't think most people do that. We wear tons of hats in order for us to keep what we think we have for our folks on campus. So you have to do double duty all the time. There are committees on affirmative action, graduate minority, etc. There are only forty-fve or fifty of us in this university of 40,000 population. Can you imagine how overwhelming? There is a continual amount of energy being exerted. They need more of us. They are getting a lot more [for their] dollar [from] each of us, and they are overworking us.

Teresa, a political progressive, copes by attempting to balance her professional obligations and service activities.

Crystal Miller, a radical Democrat, echoed the sentiments of Teresa Johnson, raising questions about the expectations of Black professors on predominantly White campuses.

Minority people who work in White universities are a rare breed. It is important to our community that we interact and provide service in some way, help out in the school system, work with community groups, and speak to various groups. In a university, that is translated into community service. How much do you do? How do you value that when it comes to evaluating someone's work for promotion? Community service is not as valued—for example, as giving a talk at a church versus presenting a paper at the MLA, though it may be more effective in the long run in helping young people. However, a promotion depends on standards set by the university. What do you do when the church calls up and asks you to give a talk? Do you say, "I am sorry but I have a paper I have to give." Can you take the time to do it, or do you find a way to do the community service as well as academic work? You have double demands placed on you; you have a choice to ignore one and go with the other or try to satisfy both. I try to satisfy both. I don't believe I would be here without the support of the community of people who didn't have the opportunity I had. I feel I have an obligation and debt to pay to my community.

William Ofodile, a Nigerian professor of anthropology in a traditional department at a large, predominantly White university, acknowledged that the demands of the educational systems are in conflict with those of the minority community.

The minority community expects you to do more applied things, but the academic community is not looking for that. I serve on committees that convey to the Black faculty whether he or she is making it. I feel Black Americans see things in a different perspective. The Black candidates do not publish. They want to solve problems rather than deal with theoretical and methodological problems. Sometimes Blacks have difficulties in balancing the two things.

Ofodile does not try to balance professional obligations with community concerns. Instead, he has chosen to concentrate his efforts on research and publishing.

For administrators like Ferdinand Hamilton, who is also a well-known scholar, there is a constant balancing of professional growth and administrative duties. Black administrators are hired as interpreters for the needs of Black students, faculty, the Black community, and those of the White administrators, faculty, students, and the larger society. "It presents potential problems, anytime you have to serve two masters or wear two hats," said Ferdinand, a vice provost for minority affairs and special assistant to the president of a predominantly White university in the Midwest. It requires constantly walking a political tightrope to be recognized by various factions within and outside the academic community. "There are certain expectations the university has and certain expectations my Black constituents both on campus and within the community have. They can be counterproductive to what you are doing. You have to do a lot of in-fighting." So he finds that the most productive way to balance on this tightrope "is to let people in the community do the fighting for you or whatever is necessary. Otherwise, you cut your nose off to spite your face, and you won't be here to do what you can do," said the politically active liberal Democrat.

Black administrators in higher education are likely to be "a special-assistant-to-someone phenomenon."[10] Most Black administrators in predominantly White universities are denied access to power and have limited authority, except for Black Studies and minority affairs. Ferdinand Hamilton has used his position to influence university policies. He has recruited minority administrators, faculty, and students and improved the quality of their lives on campus. These changes have also improved the overall quality of the university's educational process through cultural diversity.

The quality of the environment affects the retention of Black academicians. Much talent is lost from higher education when they are unable to successfully function because of the role strain and conflict and the impact of social isolation inherent in their predominantly White settings.

Although retention of Black academicians is affected by quality of life, there is also a formal process which factors importantly in retention. Once Black academics enter the halls of ivy, the issues of evaluation, promotion, and retention become important. John Lamont, a tenured professor in the physics department at a major university, for example, has been recognized by the university for his brilliant contributions to the scholarly community and to all humankind. In his case, the goals of academe, which subscribe to the "pursuit of knowledge," "fairness and reason," "free inquiry," and "value neutrality," have been realized. But too often this is not the case. Since universities are bureaucracies, these ideals do not mesh with the reality of how bureaucracies function. (We sometimes forget universities are bureaucracies with their own goals, needs, and norms.) Most colleges and universities have a merit system for hiring, promoting, and retaining. However, "it is not an objective, competitive system, but rather a patronage system of merit. Publication, achievement, and performance are important in such a system, but so are ascriptive traits, personal qualities of style and manner, conforming behavior, mentors, and sponsors."[11]

Even though there is an "objective system" in place for the evaluation of scholarship, how is it derived and from what source? At the core of the evaluation process are epistemological concerns about the nature of knowledge itself—such questions as: What is knowledge? How is knowledge generated? Who are the dispensers of knowledge? What knowledge becomes the acceptable truth? And by what mechanism does it become the acceptable truth?

Evaluating the Black Scholar and the Afrocentric Perspective

Though Blacks, like Jefferson Barnes and John Lamont, are hired in traditional departments in predominantly White universities, most Black faculty are concentrated in Black Studies programs or they hold a joint appointment in a traditional department and Black Studies. One reason for hiring Black scholars is that they offer a new source of knowledge. Yet, some of these scholars face the problem of how that knowledge is evaluated and how it impacts on the promotion and tenure process.

Black scholars often challenge the traditional body of Eurocentric knowledge and scholarship in terms of content, theoretical paradigm, underlying world view, and methodology. Consequently, they produce knowledge that is new and is derived from an Afrocentric perspective. Hence, in evaluating the scholarship of Blacks in academe, the traditional Eurocentric producers of knowledge are in conflict with the emerging Afrocentric perspective. There are problems created by this divergent world view. Professor Jonathan Mobutu, a director of Black Studies, discussed the differences in the Eurocentric and Afrocentric perspective in scholarship and the problems it presents in the evaluation of that scholarship.

"In the Afrocentric perspective, Blacks define themselves relative to the continent of Africa and our origins in Africa as a principal point of Black Studies," said Mobutu.

> It means building upon the knowledge that we have a classical African civilization and Blacks have always been actors, shaping their own destiny, as opposed to being victims at the hands of other powers. Black people have been the ancestors who produced the major contributions in the modern world, even though Europeans have been co-opted into making believe that somehow Greece and Rome emerged out of the sky. It also means that in trying to improve humanity, a principal focal point is those activities which focus on trying to re-elevate African people to their former role as teachers of the world, as opposed to being treated like children of the world.
>
> One historian once said that "Africans are certainly my brothers, they are just two hundred years my younger brothers." We are correcting that notion and getting people throughout the African diaspora to understand that the situation people of African descent find themselves in is only temporary and simply not consistent with the historical record of the Black experience.

Mobutu also believes:

> Western science has created the strength and feasibility to manipulate the environment to achieve social ends. The hallmark of Western science is

prediction. If you can predict phenomena, you can control and change them. All sciences, natural and social, are geared toward prediction. We develop models to explain phenomena in terms of complex realities; certain types of responses are based on control variables and dependable variables. Western science is good as long as you have a value structure that focuses on change to improve humanity as opposed to using the ability of science to control as a way of promoting inequality or power imbalance. That is what Western science does that traditional ways of understanding didn't do. Traditional ways of understanding focused more on the harmony of the environment, and control was outside. The gods control. So it limited the way one could change the environment.

However, one of the problems that emerged in Western scientific tradition is the fragmentation of knowledge. It is a system [by] which more and more people know less about the global picture. They are trained to be specialists and are not trained to look at how their area of knowledge connects to other things. In the traditional Afrocentric perspective, things were connected regardless if they were verifiable. If you were sick, somebody put a curse on you. Western science has not attempted to connect these interdisciplines.

On the other hand, Black Studies has attempted to interject the study of wholeness into the human condition. Beyond that, there is also the task to do the same thing for the natural and the physical sciences, that is, try to reinterpret and see how they impact one another in meaningful ways. This world view contradicts the Western way of thinking, because we don't have the tools to prove it. Western science requires that you come up with some kind of symbolic representation, using some kind of number system. If you are talking about consciousness or one's connection to a broader reality, you can't measure them. So you have to choose some other way of understanding that you can use or evaluate, other than the Western science way of manipulating the environment.

Out of the Afrocentric perspective, we get important information about the Black experience through oral traditions—art, music, etc. The data are embedded in there and not reducible to numbers. It is data on what people are thinking and what they want to achieve. All religions, for instance, have visions about what's going to happen under certain types of conditions. These sources of knowledge have been relegated to a subordinate status by Western science, which suggests that this is the best way of knowing something and understanding something. It's Western science that comes up with replication, verification, and falsification.

Western science also has inherent limits to understanding and examining patterns of causation. What you have to assume in science is the directions of the causation. If you are talking about a system with circular causation, there are no techniques. The bottom line is that you make some assumptions about what is causing what. The nature of what is causing what is limited to what you can observe and measure. In the Afrocentric perspective, there are spiritual ways of knowing things that do not get factored into the process of science or its application, and thus science generates a lot of biases. The scientific model tends to be ahistorical in focus. It is tied to the notion of free will. The Black experience says you don't look at conditions now without understanding how they evolved.

Mobutu concluded that scholars in Black Studies are trying "to understand and link African ways of understanding the universe as opposed to Western ways. It is a challenge because it is not acceptable to traditional science. It depends on who is in academe and who decides what constitutes knowledge and what isn't knowledge."

Like Mobutu, Tefe Fusi, a renowned ethnomusicologist at a predominantly Black institution, understands and needs to vigorously defend these fundamental differences in world view and philosophy of the Afrocentric and the Eurocentric perspectives. The Afrocentric sounds and elements of music—time, rhythm, and form—for example, are often misunderstood in the context of the Eurocentric tradition. Listen to Fusi as he discusses some differences in world view.

Western orientation is intellectual, and the African orientation is intuitive and wholistic. And there is always a conflict. The world view is different. The African concept of sound is totally different from the Western world's. Traditionally, African sound is considered as a wave length that establishes a link between the visible and the invisible worlds. And that is why we are able to use music, the raw material of sound, to put into structural patterns. Those patterns are meaningful to those societies in which the events are taking place. We are able to use the medium of organized sound as a link between the invisible world and us. Music, to us, is not art form for entertainment. It relates directly to the psyche and is, therefore, psychologically conceived. Thus, music becomes a spiritual element in our lives.

Fusi, an African, selected his doctoral thesis at a predominantly White university in this country. He said, "The White faculty members were against my doing something on my own traditions. At first, I didn't understand their reasons, but later I concluded they wanted to remain the experts, and it would have been a challenge to their authority." There was resentment when he decided to study his own culture. He believes this was the reason for the subsequent denial of the assistant professorship, which had been promised to him upon completion of his doctorate.

Now that Fusi is a widely respected ethnomusicologist, lecturing across the country, he constantly stresses to his White colleagues that a knowledge of African philosophy is crucial to understanding the significant difference between African and Western elements of musical expressions and styles.

> You see, this is my argument with White folks about the philosophy of Africa. How are they going to argue and tell me how I feel about my music and what constitutes what I feel about it? I am in the middle of the stuff. I have experienced rituals in which people use music, and they've gone nuts listening to a particular type of song. Who is going to tell me— a White person for that matter—that because of this element and that element, that is why people are going through that state of mind! There is no way any White man in this room—I say when I go places—[can say that it is] because of this rhythmic element or melodic element in music that we feel that way about it! They don't like it; but there is no way I am going to stop telling it the way it is. All we are trying to do is develop an African philosophy.

In "The Study of Music as a Symbol of Culture: The Afro-American and Euro-American Perspective," Robert W. Stephens, a musicologist, concurs with Tefe Fusi that the musical traditions and styles of Afro-Americans and Euro-Americans are different. For instance, the former traditions arise from an oral culture and are more spontaneous and intuitive, while the latter derive from a literal culture and are more structured. "Many implications flow from this observation; the most crucial is that products of the literal culture may misunderstand products of the oral culture, or vice-versa." Not surprisingly, "such misunderstandings have occurred and played a central role in the relationship between Afro-Americans and Euro-Americans."[12] The differences in these cultural traditions affect musical styles and the use of musical elements. "Since the dominant group reflects Western European musical values, it views them as the benchmark by which to judge all others,"[13] thus adopting feelings of cultural and musical superiority.

Similarly, misunderstandings and negative interpretations within the context of traditional academe are made about the professional discipline of Afro-American Studies that has emerged within the past twenty-five years. While a number of Black Studies programs proliferated during the campus upheavals in the late 1960s and early 1970s, few developed into full-fledged university departments with control over budgets and faculty. Critics of Black Studies continue to challenge their academic validity, refusing to accept the discipline as having a legitimate place in higher education. This results in "the failure to understand fully the emergent field of Afro-American Studies and the special circumstances of its professionals that leads to failures of fair and accurate assessment of the nature, scope, and quality of their work both as academicians and as administrators."[14]

Hear Teresa Johnson, a professor of Afro-American Studies at a major university in the West, discuss the demands, problems, and responsibilities confronting Black professionals in the field of Afro-American Studies.

> I am in Afro-American Studies and Afro-American literature. It has been a field that has been resisted by the educational system here in this country. So you need to do three times as much as other people around you to make whatever you do count. It's not that you have to do more publishing, but you have to do a lot more work to publish.

The many obstacles for Black academicians who want to write about the Black experience, she believes, are "a major factor why many bright young people are not choosing academe." Teresa pointed out, "When I did my first book on Black women novelists, colleagues sent out queries to other White scholars, and the overwhelming response was there was no such field. So you overdo the proving. You have to really make it clear that it is a scholarly field. You have to go out there and educate people who think they are educated."

The university holds a regent professor's position, an appointment that is reserved for exceptional people in the arts. James Baldwin, the renowned novelist and essayist who died in 1987, was a regent professor. But Teresa asserted, "We had to persuade the educational establishment that James Baldwin in 1978 was really a fine writer. We had to convince them that he wasn't a radical browbeating crazie." When she invited Paule Marshall, the African-American writer, to the campus, most of the committee was unfamiliar with her. "I literally gave them lectures on who she is. Not until recently did people here admit that we have great Afro-American writers. Not until Alice Walker won the Pulitzer Prize was she recognized by this university. . . . It makes her established." Teresa said:

> It has taken years to make it clear to people that the writing I and others do is to acknowledge the great Black writers. It is a continual plugging away. So if I write about those writers and their works are not considered great, now what would *my* work be considered. I think that is the trial of people in other fields of Afro-American literature. People will discuss race relations, but they won't necessarily see that there are great writers and thinkers among Black people. They may be interested in whether Blacks and Whites can get together, or they can think of us as problems. But when we talk about our contributions and the things we do and the way we set our standards, that's another matter. There is a continual striving that we have to do here to make this point clear. I really do think given my attributes, if I were in a more racially-privileged situation, I would be far beyond where I am now.

Teresa senses "there is a ghettoization of ethnic studies." Other departments within the university resist accepting courses from the Black Studies program. For example, "The English department doesn't want to accept Black literature." She also noted that when scholars are in an ethnic field, "it is not considered an important field. . . . even though the person may be a first rate mind." Because they are in the ethnic field, they are not chosen for positions in other departments. She raised the question, "Why aren't there any Blacks in history?" There are "top White scholars in Afro-American Studies at this university. But it doesn't mean you don't hire a Black in history." She wonders if it is a threat to hire a Black scholar in the same department with a White scholar whose field is in the Black experience.

It is clear from the responses of Jonathan Mobutu, Tefe Fusi, and Teresa Johnson that the emergent discipline of Black Studies challenges the state of Western knowledge, its paradigms, and its philosophies. The new knowledge, paradigms, and philosophies that evolve out of this new discipline are unfamiliar to traditional academe. Problems exist in evaluating this new scholarship, but not because it lacks merit. "Black Studies" has a negative image in traditional departments not only because it is new, but also because it is associated with a less powerful group in the society. A lack of sponsors in established fields to serve as advocates for this new scholarship adds to the problem. Hence, since publication of research is an important criterion for evaluation in promotion and tenure, Black faculty members are not retained or promoted at the same rate as White faculty.

Promotion and Retention

Even when Blacks are engaged in research, promotion and retention may still be difficult to obtain. Said Mobutu:

> White faculty do everything they can *not* to tenure a Black faculty. They come up with every excuse they can, such as, not a good colleague—meaning you didn't go to their parties and get-togethers and your research is not mainstream enough. If you do research on the Black experience, it doesn't count or it is not published in the right journal, like the *Western Journal of Black Studies*. It is not the same as if published in the *American Journal of Economics and Sociology*.

He cited an example of a colleague who had been denied tenure because of the nature of his research. "This professor is doing path-breaking research in hypnosis, using a Black and White sample. He published in Black journals." But his White colleagues are saying "he has not published enough."

Even when one has "published enough," there is still the issue of quality. One case which received national attention supports Mobutu's contention. Dr. Sandra A. O'Neale, a forty-nine-year-old former professor at Emory University in Atlanta, Georgia, was twice denied tenure in the English department. The Phi Beta Kappa graduate from the University of Kentucky doctoral program, filed a civil rights lawsuit against the school, alleging race and sex discrimination.

Dr. O'Neale, whose areas of interest are in nineteenth century American literature, African-American literature, Biblical literature, and Black Feminist Studies, has published twenty-nine articles on Black Americans. While some colleagues contended she was denied tenure because her research is too Black-oriented, other faculty and administrative officials maintained "the decision to deny tenure was [based on] the questionable quality of her published articles." One tenured White professor stated, "There are members of the English department who do not regard the works of the authors she writes about or the periodicals in which she publishes as important."[15]

William Ofodile has published extensively in mainstream academic journals and with major publishers. But when his tenure was initially denied by his department, unlike most African-Americans, he did not attribute it to racism. Said Ofodile, "I was turned down for tenure the first time I applied because I had been there only four years. It hurt me. It wasn't how long you've been there, but what your productivity was, and I had met that. I don't think it was racial, but a growing glut in the marketplace." After another reputable university offered him tenure and a professorship, the university reversed its decision, giving him tenure and promoting him to full professorship. "I didn't ask for it. It was due to the quality of my work and the offer from the other university," said Ofodile. He has a different perception of race relations than his African-American colleagues. Ofodile said he has not experienced racism. "I will not say it's because of the quality of my work, but I have done well as far as my work is concerned." When I broached the subject of racism with another African professor at a Black university, he mentioned that he had to be resocialized like African-Americans to be sensitive to racial cues. It was not a part of his socialization process in Africa. Perhaps Ofodile has not learned the subtle racial cues or has chosen to ignore them. Some academics, particularly Blacks, are critical of Ofodile's research on minorities and the educational process. They reject his idea of blaming the victim and criticize his lack of an Afrocentric perspective. Said Ofodile about his critics:

> I am not angry with anybody. The acceptance of my work is split with both Blacks and Whites. There are Whites who support my work as indicated by invitations to speak and to contribute to journals and books. They think it is new and needs to be listened to. People who are involved in solving social problems—Blacks, Whites, Hispanics—have problems

with my work. I can understand their positions intellectually. Since I am from Nigeria, I can stand back and look at the issue as a marginal person. I can ask questions that both Blacks and Whites don't ask. Since there is a pressure to solve problems, some people don't go beyond that. And I do feel victims sometimes contribute to their own demise. I want to explain why that is as opposed to letting the differences be explained biologically. My good friends no longer talk to me because they think I am blaming the victim.

Walking the Academic Tightrope

Although publishing is more important than teaching and service as criteria in the evaluation process for promotion and retention at most colleges and universities, Blacks are still expected to fulfill an important service role. Minority academicians are "buffers, mediators, and interpreters between students and institutions, expressing the needs and interests of each to the other."[16] However, "the institution puts pressure on you to provide services without including it as a part of the evaluation process. And now it comes from the top position of president, so you can't say you prefer not to serve, because you are not tenured. He makes the final decision on tenure. So you are caught between a rock and a hard place," asserted Mobutu.

Albert Sungist understands what it means to be "caught between a rock and a hard place." When he was denied tenure, he was a faculty member in an experimental ethnic college in the West that was strongly interested in recruiting minorities and the poor. He said many faculty were recruited "under the rubrics of affirmative action, giving us a negative label. . . . Most of us in that college were not viewed favorably in some corners of the campus because we were minorities. There was a minority person who headed the college; many people hated the college as well as the Black provost," said Sungist. "I got caught between the old and new policy with this experimental college. The old administration emphasized service; the new administration emphasized publishing." He attributes his tenure denial to the confluences of racism, elitism, and changing standards.

Sometimes changing standards occur at "a time when new groups of populations are moving into academe—Blacks, women, and Hispanics. It is a tool to control a subset of a population," claimed Mobutu, adding, "in the fifties and sixties, you didn't have to be a good researcher or an excellent teacher to get job security. But these same people are now changing the standards to judge new faculty under the guise of quality education. You have to publish or perish. If you look at them, they don't have the publications." It is no coincidence that standards change when a diverse population enters academe or any new marketplace. A *Newsweek* report noted that as Asians enter American universities (particularly prestigious universities) in increasing numbers, administrators are beginning to change the standards. Instead of looking at their high test scores and grades, they are adjusting admission criteria to keep Asian-Americans' numbers low. Berkeley, for instance, revised its procedures in 1983 to give more weight to essays and extracurricular activities, areas in which Asians have generally not fared well.[17] Because of protests from Asians, this overt policy was changed.

Black academicians in predominantly White colleges and universities often serve two masters. Many Blacks hold joint appointments, for example, in the English department and Black Studies or Ethnic Studies. Having to fulfill two separate roles and requirements may affect their tenure and promotion at review time. Serving two masters can produce a conflict over academic standards. Crystal Miller described such a conflict:

> What is valid scholarly work? Is it valid to do an anthology of a work or one of your authorship? Some disciplines in the university would say an anthology is less valuable. Do you accept these values or do you challenge them? These are the pressures Blacks are under. When you don't agree with these values, you can be punished or fired. I don't fight all the battles, but there are some that are too important not to fight.

Retrenchment in affirmative action, along with problems in the evaluation process, results in the loss of many Black faculty from the halls of ivy. Though some Black academicians are in traditional departments, most are concentrated in Black Studies or hold a joint appointment in a traditional academic department and Black or Ethnic Studies. Administrators usually are in staff positions related to minorities. The Black academicians often experience social isolation because of their low numbers. They also have to balance their professorial duties with service oriented concerns related to Black students and the Black community.

Academicians who want to offer a broader vision of knowledge often find that the Afrocentric perspective is rejected. This impacts upon the retention process.

Despite the perils, the Talented One Hundred in academe continue to cope successfully, because they have learned, like those individuals in other sectors of the economy, to successfully negotiate the political and racial landscape. They also know the importance of a political and social network.

Kanter states in *Men and Women of the Corporation:*

> There is a small positive psychological side to tokenism: the self-esteem that comes from mastering a difficult situation and getting into places that traditionally exclude others of one's kind. If the token can segregate conflicting expectations and has strong outside support groups with

which to relax, then perhaps a potentially stress-producing situation can be turned into an opportunity for ego enhancement.[18]

This benefit may accrue only if there are buffering networks to shield the impact of social isolation and of the tokenism found on the job.

FIVE

The Color Line in Social, Religious, and Family Life

Bernice Jackson, fifty years old and a social work administrator, is among the few Black managers employed in a racially mixed social services agency in a large midwestern city. Her relationship with her White colleagues is warm and cordial. They work cooperatively as teammates on joint projects. They participate in the office celebrations of birthdays, promotions, and bon voyage parties. But this work-inspired congeniality does not extend beyond the work day. Bernice Jackson returns to her Black neighborhood and her Black friends.

Twenty years after the death of Martin Luther King, Jr., *Newsweek* ran a cover story on "Black and White," asking, "How integrated is America?" Did the winds of change that brought many Blacks into the mainstream of the world of work also take them into the educational, political, and residential arenas and the social and intimate spheres of Whites? After twenty years, some sectors of the workplace have become "more neutral meeting grounds" for Blacks and Whites, but the winds of change left a chill in their social and political worlds. Churches, neighborhoods, and schools are largely divided by the color line. Few work-inspired friendships go beyond the workplace.

Unlike Bernice, who returns to her Black community after work, increasing numbers of Black elite find themselves living and working in a predominantly White world. One consequence of this is a growing sense of social isolation. For Blacks who live and work in communities where there is only a small Black population, this social isolation can be intense and stressful.

An article, "Young, Black and Bored," in *Providence Sunday Journal Magazine,* raised the question, "Where do you go after work if you're a

142

Black professional in Rhode Island?" The retort, "Home—to call the moving van?"[1] A similar article in *Ebony Magazine* asked how Blacks fare in Vermont, "The Whitest State," which is less than 1 percent Black.[2] Although most middle-class Blacks live in states with a higher percentage of Blacks, isolation is a concern for those who are moving into the mainstream.

The expanding economic, educational, political, and social opportunities for Blacks have resulted in greater opportunities for mobility and interaction in the White world, thereby creating new sources of stress. Sociologist James Blackwell, in *City, Suburbs and Blacks,* notes that as Blacks move into the mainstream, isolation is an increasing phenomenon, resulting from the disruption of social ties to the group of origin.[3] This pattern is typical of the persons I interviewed. Seventy-one percent of the Talented One Hundred grew up in Black neighborhoods; 15 percent in White neighborhoods; and 14 percent in racially mixed or transitional neighborhoods. At the time of the interviews, only 44 percent of the Talented One Hundred lived in Black neighborhoods; 35 percent in White neighborhoods; and 21 percent in racially mixed neighborhoods, usually over 70 percent White.

This mobility pattern is different from that of previous generations of Blacks, who migrated to the North during the great migration or to the West Coast during World War II seeking jobs in the defense plants in California. While they were uprooted from their southern origins, many extended-family members moved together, usually settling in predominantly Black communities. The Black elite, on the other hand, often settle with their immediate family or alone in a White neighborhood. Overwhelmingly, the Talented One Hundred felt that when you live and work in a White community, isolation is likely to increase. In her dissertation, *Life in Isolation: Black Families Living in a Predominantly White Community,* Beverly Tatum, studying upwardly mobile Blacks, reported that "some parents lamented that they no longer experience that collective community spirit and cohesiveness."[4]

Many salient factors contribute to the isolation of the Black elite in White settings. One is the issue of balancing Afrocentric and Eurocentric concerns. Blacks who work in the corporate world spend an increasing amount of time nurturing their careers. To climb the corporate ladder, it is essential to interact socially outside of the workplace, where important business transactions take place. If Blacks expect to be successful in the workplace, they have to increase their interactions with Whites outside the office. These social functions are more instrumental than expressive. In their quest for upward mobility, some Blacks feel they must assimilate totally, adopting the life styles and values of Whites. Hence, their business and social contacts become increasingly White.

Joseph Lowery sees an inherent danger in this isolation. Said Lowery, "There are people who choose to be isolated. They live in White neighborhoods, join White churches, send their kids to White schools, and completely divorce themselves from the Black community." Whether or not the Black elite freely choose an all-White setting, it can be stressful, particularly since there is no reprieve from the continuous onslaught of racism. While the Black elite may be accepted on the job, they may not be accepted in their community. If the Black elite patronize a neighborhood restaurant, they may be concerned about whether they will be seated near the kitchen or be treated courteously. (When an acquaintance of Jonathan Mobutu, for example, went to her neighborhood restaurant, the waiter brought her a slice of watermelon along with a glass of water.) Some of the Talented One Hundred reported that when they go to their neighborhood stores, more identification may be required of them to cash checks and the police may stop or follow them to see if they live in the neighborhood.

Even on vacation, the Black elite might not find relaxation from racism. While Diane Earlinger's family was vacationing at a beach resort in the South, her teenage son spotted a White female classmate. They started conversing, and Diane observed the scowling faces of Whites. She felt uneasy about their expressions, fearing for her son's safety.

These continuous bouts with racism, on and off the job, can put the Black elite who live in isolation from other Blacks "at high risk for emotional collapse," said Joseph Lowery. "Those folks are taking off all their shields. And they are going totally out there, exposing themselves to the atmospheric pressure, and many collapse. They have become very frustrated, because sooner or later, they are wrong about their acceptance. They hit that ceiling, becoming frustrated and not knowing where to turn." Sometimes, Lowery said, they return to the Black community; other times, "they stay there and live in anguish."

Blacks are concerned about the danger that Lowery posed; they want to retain their balance on the tightrope between Afrocentric and Eurocentric concerns. Having come of age during integration, many of the Talented One Hundred are reevaluating, over twenty-five years later, the impact of integration. They understand the need to keep their racial identity by maintaining a strong Black support system in their familial, educational, religious, political, personal, and social spheres.

Living in a Predominantly White Neighborhood

While many Black professionals live comfortably in the Black middle-income neighborhoods dotting the suburbs of many large cities of this country, there are still not enough homes for the expanding Black elite. In other smaller communities, the Black population may not be large enough or may be too dispersed to form a Black neighborhood. Greater opportunities in the workplace along with the increased options in housing resulting from fair housing laws have had a major impact on residential patterns. Many Blacks look to predominantly White neighborhoods for housing. But Blacks in predominantly White communities interact less with their neighbors than Blacks who live in Black communities. If other Black families live nearby, they are more likely to interact with each other than with their White neighbors.

Increasingly, middle-class Blacks live in isolated White communities, away from their extended families, their Black peers, and their Black communities. Often this pattern disrupts ties with their traditional support system. The strong extended family has been recognized as an important feature of the African-American tradition.[5] It is an important source of emotional, financial, and social support. Shimkin, Louie, and Frate's research on the Black extended family found that the family network served as a facilitating agent in migration and urbanization and fostered educational and economic advancement.[6] The extended family continues to be a significant resource for the Black middle class. According to sociologist Harriette P. McAdoo, "Whether or not they had moved up recently, and whether they had moved out to the suburbs or stayed in the city, today's Black middle-class families have kept an important part of their roots, the networks of mutually helpful family and kin who helped them rise."[7]

Pat Robinson, like many others among the Talented One Hundred, lives in a predominantly White neighborhood and is geographically distanced from relatives. Sometimes his desire to help the "Black masses" and his relatives creates a dilemma for him. "I have a lot of poor relatives back home. The question I face is, 'Where does it go? What do I do?' I can spend my time helping my relatives. I am a federal judge, but I have to remind people of my roots."

Since many Black elite are the first generation to succeed in the professional mainstream, they "assume an important position in their family hierarchy," said Bebe Moore Campbell in an article about the plight of "Black Executives and Corporate Stress." They are frequently called upon by family members for "financial assistance, career guidance, and even psychological counseling."[8] This expectation of mutual aid can sometimes be a drain on their resources. They may find themselves assisting siblings and relatives who may be on welfare or drugs or who may need their financial or emotional assistance in other ways. While the Black elite might value family ties, these often conflict with personal aspirations. While some Blacks remove themselves from their familial network, others remember their own precarious success, a mere stone's throw from poverty.

Blacks who live in predominantly White communities miss being in the presence of relatives, sharing and supporting one another. Many of the

Talented One Hundred expressed concern about relatives, particularly elderly parents whom they left behind to fend for themselves. Jonathan Mobutu lives in a comfortable, predominantly White college community, but he is concerned about his widowed mother, who lives over 250 miles away in a large city. Since she lives in a high-crime community, his own comfort is disturbed by her lack of security. She protects herself with a gun, which almost cost him his life. During a weekend visit to his mother's home, Mobutu sat in a chair where a gun was placed in a ready position for any intruders.

It is the "dichotomy and tragedy of being a so-called successful Black," remarked Johnson Longworth, because "you always have that string tied to that other reality. You cannot do things comfortably knowing that other reality exists." Longworth cited an example of a Black vice president of his university who was chairing a meeting when he received an emergency phone call. "He came back with a long face. Later we learned that his mother had been mugged in Chicago. A vice president had to jump on a plane to Chicago because his mother got mugged." Thus, while the Black elite might be geographically removed from their social origins, they are emotionally wedded to the daily struggles and concerns of their extended families, Black friends, and the Black community.

Friendships and Social Networks

Since the amount of interracial contact outside the workplace is limited, peer networks are important support buffers for the Black elite. Here they can have the conflicting expectations inherent in their racial status validated by others, thus reducing the stress of isolation. The Talented One Hundred seek validation from Black friends and close associates, even when they live and work in predominantly White settings. When I asked individuals if their friends or social contacts were Black, White, or racially mixed, 62 percent said their friends were primarily Black. They reported feeling a greater level of trust and comfort with Blacks. They also wanted release time from "race watching," as expressed by one individual. "You always have to watch what you say and what you do in the presence of Whites, whether it is in a social or business environment. You can't be free. There is a sense of being watched."

Marla Robinson agreed, asserting, "I would share some things with Blacks that I would not share with Whites. I don't believe in discussing my private life with White people. I don't want them to know me that closely. I don't trust what they'll do with the information. I have never leveled with a White person, despite having had close friendships with White women."

Thirty-four percent of the Talented One Hundred had friends and social contacts of different races. Many reported having very close White friends, but indicated their closest friendships were with other Blacks. Remarked Robert Woodson, "I have Black and White friends, but I have a deeper relationship with my Black friends than my White friends. We share more in common. There is much more to talk about, for example, a common culture and childhood experience. You can share, and the range of things you can explore from someone of your culture is greater. There are nuances and subtleties that you accept that become a part of you and the interchange." Woodson perceives there are distinct differences in the way Blacks and Whites conduct themselves in social settings in his environment. "We can drink, dance, and be very friendly with somebody else's woman, but there are acceptable limits no matter how much you have been drinking. Your hands do not suddenly wander, nor do you begin to take certain liberties . . . in the name of comrade or good times. We are conservatives when it comes to that. Whites are freer. I am always on guard for Whites maybe exceeding the boundaries of kidding, comradeship, and saying and doing something that breaks across the imaginary boundaries."

John Daniels, who also has racially mixed friendships and social acquaintances, said his five or six best friends are the Blacks with whom he grew up. He and his wife are comfortable with both Blacks and Whites. But his Black and White friends may not be comfortable with one another. Therefore, his racially mixed affairs are usually small dinner parties. When he had a surprise birthday party for his wife, it was all-Black. "If we had Whites, it would not be the same. The mixing capacity of my Black and White friends may not be compatible. They are not comfortable with one another. So the party takes on a different tone," said Daniels.

The social contacts of the Black elite are primarily Black, while the business and professional contacts are 12 percent Black, 60 percent racially mixed, and 26 percent White. This pattern suggests that there is exclusion outside the workplace that operates in both directions.

In his study of *Black Managers in White Corporations,* John Fernandez found that the "percentage of Black and White managers who belong to racially mixed and unmixed organizations are quite similar," but "there is a large difference in their degree of contact at social functions. The Black managers have a great deal more contact with Whites at functions not related to work." Moreover, White friends of Black managers are usually not from their workplace.[9]

I found that most of the Talented One Hundred belong both to racially mixed and to all-Black organizations. They hold memberships in Black sororities and fraternities and civil rights organizations, which Daniel Thompson, in his book, *A Black Elite,* categorized as: (1) Black caucuses—established by Blacks who belong to predominantly White organizations; (2) parallel organizations—established by Blacks to enhance professional advancement outside of the main parent organization (e.g., the Association of Black Psychologists); and (3) the traditional civil rights organizations (e.g., the NAACP).[10] Some Blacks belong to a number of organizations, but others are not active, often because of the demands of their jobs.

Blacks have historically used their fraternities, sororities, lodges, and civic and social organizations to solve personal and community problems. They serve as "service centers, information exchanges, forums for jobs, and business-related and support mechanisms in personal development," noted sociologist Lawrence Gary.[11]

Political Consciousness and Political Affiliations

The Talented One Hundred have a high degree of participation in social and civic organizations and they are politically conscious and very active. Among researchers, there is a strong perception that as Blacks move upward in the social structure, their social, professional, and political orientations and affiliations become more class-linked than race-linked. This perception is fueled by the fact that increasing numbers of Blacks have moved into the middle class since the 1960s.

With the rise of a significant Black middle class, there is growing concern within the Black community that it is becoming two separate societies. One society is an affluent middle class that has moved to the suburbs. This group feels isolated from the Black masses. The Black elite sense a lack of support from the Black community and feel "put down" for their achievements.

The other society is an inner-city underclass that feels trapped by poverty, crime, drugs, violence, rampant teenage pregnancy, and high unemployment. They feel deserted by the Black elite and resent them for moving up and leaving them behind. The result has been tension between the two societies, a troubling concern for many. Leo Aramis, a thirty-four-year-old journalist, who lives in a predominantly White neighborhood in the Northeast, expressed this troubling tension between the two strata of society. While Leo would prefer to live in a predominantly Black neighborhood, he chose a White neighborhood because, in part, he said:

> I can be close to work, and in part, I don't want to come back and all my stuff is gone. It is obvious that Black on Black crime is a severe problem. It is often that Black professionals are unwittingly the buffer zone between lower income and less educated Black folks. So the next time there is a riot, the neighbors are going to come and get middle-class Blacks. They aren't going to come and get White folks first. I think we have unwittingly put ourselves in that position. It is that distant feeling that [explains why] brothers in the neighborhood are saying the niggers can't relate to this person, and he is no more than a honky to me. And he got

148

more than I got. The divide and conquer mentality never existed like this before.

I think it is one of the reasons our cities and neighborhoods have dissipated. As professionals, we have moved out to the suburbs to get away. We have taken that "Talented Tenth" that led our neighborhoods away from Black neighborhoods. It used to be doctors, lawyers, teachers, and preachers could not get away. They had segregated housing patterns, and they had to live there. So you take all these leaders away and what you have left is not the most positive leadership. And so we have rampant drug use in our community, drug sales, and gangs running things. You got little girls and boys with no positive role models.

While pointing out the tension between the Black elite and the underclass, Leo affirmed, "I am not going to move into the Black community because it doesn't work. But it does not stop me from being deeply involved in the community."

Middle-class Blacks do become the buffer group between the dominant White group and the Black masses. Hence, we can see that individual success contributes to individualizing of racial experiences; it prevents Blacks from seeing the hidden agenda of the dominant group. This hidden agenda is manifested, for example, in the social policies created by the government, which have primarily benefited middle-class Blacks. Such public policies, like the equal opportunity policy of the late 1960s, created an available job pool for middle-class Blacks during a period of social unrest and during an expanding economy. Affirmative action was one program which resulted from the public policy priority of equal opportunity. Robert Woodson feels that "the affirmative action program is only useful to some Blacks, not all Blacks."

It is only useful to Blacks in the first two tiers of the work force, but it doesn't have a damn thing to do with the unemployed dishwasher who needs training and economic development. So we have to be clear and not use all Blacks when it is convenient; but when we talk about crime, only some Blacks commit crime. But when we talk about affirmative action, we are talking about all Blacks. I think the middle class needs to be truthful in advertising. We need to be accurate and not make these pervasive statements. We tend to disaggregate when it is convenient to us, for example, crime. But we aggregate when we say affirmative action helps all Blacks. I think the civil rights leaders are engaged in a bait and switch game. We use the conditions of poor Blacks to say we need affirmative action. But when we look at who it helps, it is middle-class Blacks. The Black middle class may not be conscious of its attitudes and behaviors, but it is a consequence.

On the other hand, the benign policy of the welfare program, which is designed to benefit the poor, expands in times of social and economic upheavals and contracts in times of stability.[12] It also serves the function of reinforcing the values of hard work inherent in the Protestant ethic. Welfare recipients are viewed as deviants because they do not conform to the norm; thus, they are treated like pariahs. This group also creates a source of cheap labor and is exploited economically in other ways by the dominant group, and, as Robert Woodson noted, may be consciously or unconsciously used by the middle class to maintain its status. Since more Black women than Black men are on welfare, there is not only the question of class but also of gender. Woodson, like others, castigated the Black middle class for its lack of involvement in "changing economic policies so the flow of investments can come to low-income communities" and its lack of involvement in identifying policies that are beyond class and race. Instead, middle-class Blacks are likely to focus on setbacks in affirmative action policies or race-oriented policies that are likely to benefit them. This is the reason why Robert Woodson feels "there is a growing schism between the middle class and the growing underclass." The consequences of these social policies reflect the underlying tension between the rising Black middle class as a buffer group and the underclass and how this tension has been diverted from interactions with the dominant White group.

The members of the buffer group, despite their privileges, are likely to occupy positions that are vulnerable to a downturn in the economy. It becomes clear how the individualization of the Black elite's experience prevents them from seeing that their own precarious status as members of the buffer group is intertwined with the masses. If they understand the hidden agenda of racism, the Black elite can externalize it and create messages from their subjective and objective experiences that will lead to action. But if they do not understand the hidden agenda of racism, reactivity and inaction result. Nowhere is the issue of reactivity and inaction more pronounced than in the tension created by the widening gap between the Black middle class and underclass, diverting energy from strengthening the Black community.

Although there are class distinctions, in general, the Talented One Hundred felt that living away from the Black community would not stop them from being deeply involved in it. They strongly identified with the social concerns of the masses of Blacks. About 75 percent of the Talented One Hundred have a liberal political orientation; they manifested that concern in their vote for Jesse Jackson in the 1984 primary and stated they would vote for him in the 1988 presidential campaign. They believe that the government should be more responsive to the poor by developing social and economic policies to ameliorate their social conditions.

Research shows that, whatever their economic status, Blacks are more liberal on social issues than Whites. A 1986 Gallup poll, commissioned by the Joint Center for Political Studies on the attitudes of Blacks and Whites, found that "eight in ten Blacks, compared with three out of ten Whites, believe the federal government should make efforts to improve the living conditions of minorities, and about 86 percent of Blacks, but only 55 percent of Whites, feel the government should spend more on social programs."[13]

In general, the Talented One Hundred wanted more progressive policies in welfare reform, involving meaningful training, more child care, and improved medical benefits for recipients. In voting for Jesse Jackson's progressive social and economic agenda, they symbolized their collective identification with the masses. There does not appear to be a mass defection from a liberal political orientation. (My interviews with the Talented One Hundred suggest that equating political orientation and political party affiliation is too complex a correlation. However, I found, like Daniel Thompson's study on the Black elite,[14] that the Talented One Hundred are largely affiliated with the Democratic party.)

Since the New Deal, the Democratic party has espoused more liberal causes, while the Republican party is viewed as more conservative. Only 5 percent of the Talented One Hundred identified themselves as conservative; 28 percent claimed to be moderate; 38 percent, liberal; 13 percent, radical; and 14 percent said mixed, meaning they were liberal on some issues and conservative on others. The 5 percent Republicans among the Talented One Hundred reported their political orientation as conservative or moderate. Thus, the perception that as Blacks move upwardly in society their political orientation is more likely to become class-linked than race-linked is unfounded, judging by the Talented One Hundred.

I found race still an important factor in the voting behavior of the Black elite. As suggested in a *Washington Post* article on the Black middle class, there was much disillusionment with the 1988 presidential election.[15] With the election of President George Bush, the Republican administration has expressed an interest in recruiting Blacks into its party. Those middle-class Blacks under thirty-five appear more receptive than older Blacks. Whether such an emerging pattern materializes, the shifting of political orientation and affiliation among young middle-class Blacks from a race-linked to a class-linked orientation remains speculative.

Since there appears to be a changing political orientation among the young Black elite as a result of social isolation, the Black church becomes the critical institution that continues to bridge the gap between the classes.

Religious Affiliation

In *Strengths of Black Families,* Robert Hill notes the importance of a strong religious orientation. Being in a hostile society, "Blacks have used religion as an important coping mechanism."[16] Said Bernie Roberts, a social researcher, "The more I see Black people, the more I see we got over because of our religious orientations. We talk about the material aspect of blackness, but Black people are religious people. Religious people do not put their emphasis on material things. We are religious people, even if we don't go to church."

The church has historically been an important resource in the Black community. The church is a status giver for those with a lowly status in the larger society, thus affirming their dignity and worth as human beings and serving as an anchor for those with little support. "The Black church is my anchor and it is for a lot of Black people. When you go to a Black church, you will be on the same level with Ph.D.s, maids, farmers, street sweepers, and you are home," noted Jack B. Lane.

William D. Watley, in the *Roots of Resistance: The Nonviolent Ethic of Martin Luther King, Jr.,* agrees, noting that "The all-pervasive character of racism . . . brings together in Black congregational life a unique blend of persons from various walks of life who have not only the same ethnicity, history, and culture, but also a common oppression by racism. It is not unusual in the Black church to find the 'Ph.D.'s and the no D's' sitting on the same boards and exercising the same power."[17] Hence, the Black church is the place that provides a safe harbor and spiritual refueling to anchor Blacks in the racial storms.

The church provides many additional functions. Said Benjamin Quarles, a Black historian, "The church served as a community center where one could find relaxation and recreation. It was a welfare agency, dispensing help to the sicker and poorer members. It was a training school in self-government, in the handling of money, and in the management of business."[18] The church also acts as a training center for intellectual and moral leadership. Noted Bernie Roberts, "I can speak well because I learned to do so in church. I learned poems at a very early age. I feel comfortable speaking, no matter how large the audience. I saw Martin Luther King, Jr. and Andrew Young speaking at my church. It is a training ground."

Because the church serves so many vital functions, Marla Robinson, who lives in a predominantly White community and whose son attends a White school, insists on going to a Black church. "It is very important for [my son] to have a kinship with the Black church and the Black community, because of the whole ceremony of the Black church, its hymns, and its spirituals. The church has impacted upon us politically, economically, and socially, and it has provided a leadership role. He does not have Black friends in the neighborhood. He does in school, but they go their separate ways." It is the reason for Jack B. Lane's strong belief that the church should be there for a young Black person to "have something to lean on."

More than 95 percent of the Talented One Hundred had "something to lean on" while growing up. The church served an important function in their lives. Seventy-one percent held membership in the Baptist or African Methodist Episcopal denominations, 49 percent and 22 percent, respectively; the other 25 percent membership was about evenly distributed among Apostolic, Roman Catholic, Congregational, Episcopal, Christian Methodist Episcopal, United Methodist, and Unitarian churches. And there was one Christian Scientist. The few who claimed no church affiliation acknowledged that they attended church. Presently, 69 percent of the Talented One Hundred are members of predominantly Black churches.

Many of the Talented One Hundred, such as Laura Price and Yvonne Walker-Taylor, have grown more committed to their faith. Price, in addition to her medical practice, is an ordained minister in her Baptist church. She has no ambivalence about her practice of medicine and her religion. "There is no separation of the physical and spiritual being." Said Laura, "I have always thought of my medical practice as the ministry because of the type of work I am doing. I sincerely believe any good work that you do and you are dedicated to is God's work." Yvonne Walker-Taylor, a life-long member of the A.M.E. church, attributes her success and tenacity to the church and to her father, an A.M.E. bishop. She thinks her strong spiritual A.M.E. background has given her "that impetus and added confidence in self."

John Daniels agreed with Walker-Taylor. That is his reason for maintaining a dual affiliation with the White Unitarian church on the West Coast and the A.M.E. church of his childhood in the Midwest. He became a member of a Unitarian church "because the belief system was close" to his own. Yet, he maintains his alliance with the Black church. He said, "It had a major influence on my early development. . . . I don't want to conflict with my mother, my brothers, and sisters who are A.M.E. I feel very much at home in Black churches."

So does John Lamont, an eminent theoretical physicist, who, like John Daniels, maintains his Black church membership in his southern hometown. He also attends a mixed church in his West Coast community. As a young adult, he explored many faiths, including the Baptist, Catholic, Episcopal, and Methodist. But as an adult, he realized that his southern family church was "used surreptitiously as a school where family members learned to read during slavery years while White people thought it was used for church." As a young adult going through an intellectual odyssey, he said, "I began to think of myself as a member of my forefathers' church, the little colonial church in the rolling hills." He started to identify with this concept of family religion. "What I was looking for was just right in my family."

Twelve percent of the Talented One Hundred, like John Daniels and John Lamont, attend a predominantly White or mixed church in their present communities. Sometimes, Black people attend predominantly White churches because there is no Black church in their community or no Black church of their religious preference. Both a decline in overall affiliation with church denominations and changes in denominations were prevalent among the Talented One Hundred.

Those individuals who grew up as members of the Baptist or A.M.E. denominations had the greatest decline in membership. The former declined from 49 percent to 37 percent; the latter from 22 percent to 16 percent. The Presbyterian denomination gained the largest number of converts, from 3 percent who had religious origins in this denomination to 8 percent of individuals who presently are members. The change in religious orientation may account for a significant drop in church attendance and membership. Seventeen percent of the Talented One Hundred claimed they had no church affiliation at the time of the interviews, as opposed to less than 5 percent while growing up. Others said they were members, but attended infrequently or not at all. Teresa Hale, who lives in a predominantly White community and seldom attends church, explained how her religious orientation evolved.

> I grew up in a hell and brimstone religious atmosphere where there could be no joyous living. God was fearsome, awesome, and all judgmental. My baptism was largely motivated by fear of hell and fear of God—not from the love of God. Once on my own, I left the church. It had never been a true resource for me. However, I paid a high cost for this separation. I was plagued by fear of impending doom, loss of soul, extended burning in hell, and separation from my family and loved ones. At times there were transitional value changes—agnosticism and attempts to stand wholly on my own two feet. At this point, my spiritual development is a high priority. I no longer see God as a White father in Heaven. Growing up in the racially segregated South with a tradition of White supremacy, getting those little Sunday school cards picturing Jesus (who was White in terms of my Louisiana reality) and understanding God as exacting, watchful, and all judgmental was somehow alienating to me. I never felt that I was a real member of this family. I never felt "saved."
>
> I now realize I want and need a spirituality that speaks to day-to-day living rather than a focus on the hereafter. I am presently much attracted to Eastern doctrines, especially Buddhism, as well as Christian teachings that deal with living and coping with daily life. I am also much sustained by many of the hymns and gospel songs recalled from my early Christian affiliation. Now, I pray a lot, seeking Christian fellowship with others.
>
> I am contemplating joining a Black Baptist church, but am somewhat concerned about the inherent petty politics as well as the church

covenant that forbids the use of alcohol, even though I drink very sparingly. It is mainly a matter of principle. In any case, I feel that I am deeply religious. God is the major force ultimately.

While some of the Talented One Hundred have left the church because of changes in their religious orientation (e.g., the service was too emotional and anti-intellectual and too concerned with spiritual fulfillment at the expense of social and political empowerment), others, like Teresa Hale, continue to maintain strong spiritual beliefs. Now in their mid-lives, they are seeking religious affiliations, because they feel the need for a spiritual resource and because they have a better understanding of the role of the Black church. Moreover, having rejected their traditional faiths, they are now reevaluating their importance politically and as a foundation for their children's ethical and moral growth. They want to provide their children with an identity and a moral and social support system that is unavailable in their predominantly White world.

Jonathan Mobutu, forty years old, exemplifies the return of the Black elite to the church. He said, after twenty-three years, "this is the first time I have actively participated in church. It happened because of a better understanding of the roles played by the Black church. I am also concerned about the socialization of my children." He is now a trustee in a new Black church started in his predominantly White town. The church is affiliated with both the Baptist and the Methodist denominations.

Jonathan Mobutu grew up in the Baptist church in a large inner city. At eight years old, he was a junior deacon. He attended church on a regular basis until he was about fifteen. Though his estrangement from the church started when he was eleven years old, he was forced to attend. At fifteen, he left the church, "dissatisfied with its beliefs, doctrines, and values." He maintained that even prior to the emergence of his Afrocentric consciousness, he was uncomfortable with a White Jesus. Since he did not understand the role of the Black minister and the church in African-American society, he felt alienated. "I didn't understand the role of the minister until I undertook Afro-American Studies. The minister is a spokesperson for his congregation and a buffer for the White community and unemployment. The church had to provide spiritual rejuvenation in order for Blacks to get through another week of racism or through other problems." Being an inquisitive young man, he didn't think the "minister was bringing a level of intellectual discussion to the sermon. . . . There were questions I would ask and the minister could not provide appropriate answers. I thought I was smarter than he was; I wasn't getting what I wanted." Mobutu was also uncomfortable with his "uneducated minister," who used phrases like "more better" and would mispronounce words such as Job, saying *job* as in work instead of *Job* as in the Bible. . . . "I am no longer embarrassed by my childhood minister. Having studied Black religion, I can appreciate both him and the church," said Mobutu.

During his twenty-three-year break with the church, Mobutu continued to search for a spiritual base. He left home to attend a White college, and there were no nearby Black churches. He attended a White church one Sunday, but, he said, "the service was so different that it alienated me. It was a Baptist church, but the emotions, the feelings, and the call and response dimensions of the service were not there. So it projected nothing of the Black experience and the church with which I was familiar." After his marriage, he occasionally attended the Catholic church to which his wife belonged, but he could not "buy the theological presupposition." He therefore played the albums of Malcolm X, claiming "that was my religion." Mobutu continued to explore different philosophical and religious orientations—Muslim, the philosophy of Ghandi, Eastern philosophies, and African ideology and traditional religions. "These religious and philosophical inquiries laid the foundation for exploring the spiritual dimension of my personality," Mobutu said. His spirituality evolved more, he stated, "when I started to appreciate and understand better some Eastern philosophies about how life can be intertwined and how life paths can connect for specific reasons."

In blending diverse philosophical and religious orientations, Mobutu has acquired a measure of inner peace. Unlike the "hell, fire, and brimstone" church of his youth, his present church is Afrocentric and its minister a Pan-Africanist. In his sermons, he emphasizes human liberation and Black liberation. The minister is actively involved in the South African movement, including leading protests. At last, Mobutu has found a comfortable shelter in which to retreat from the oppressive storms, a sanctuary where he can be comforted and challenged.

However, Mobutu is concerned about his children, who live in a predominantly White neighborhood, because they have not found a sanctuary where they can be comforted. Like Mobutu, others among the Talented One Hundred who live in White communities are also concerned about their children and the impact of social isolation on their identity in the community, the school, and the social sphere.

Black Children in White Communities

The world of the Talented One Hundred differs significantly from that of their parents and their children. In general, their parents had minimal or no contact with Whites in an egalitarian environment. On the other hand, their children have greater contact with diverse groups. The degree of assimilation increases with each generation. Robert Woodson, fifty years old, discussed his parents', his own, and his children's interactions with Whites and how the three generations differ. This pattern is typical of many families who live in racially mixed or White communities.

> I guess my mother never had to adapt. [His father died when he was nine.] They just worked for White folks and they went their way and did their work and came back to the Black community. White people were never discussed in the family, in the neighborhood, or in the Black community. Race was never talked about. They listened to Joe Louis [the boxer] on the radio and celebrated the victories of Roy Campanella [the baseball player].

They accepted the values of the Black community. Woodson agrees with the "values and perspectives" of his parents. But he also differs from them, claiming, "I have to interact in a much larger way with the White society. My interaction is going from home out there and coming back. I pretty much have the same social milieu of my parents inside. The definition of my social life is all-Black."

On the other hand, Woodson's children have "Whites as playmates. You do what you have to do in your environment. If the only kids your age are White, then you play with those kids." Yet, he admitted that "even though the kids play, the families are not as close as they would be in an all-Black community. We are cordial to one another, but we very seldom visit back and forth, except that the Black families do. My children go to a Black church and interact with other Black families. We have our own Black enclave in suburbia." Woodson's neighborhood is one-fourth Black. In greater numbers, middle-class Black children will be born in predominantly White settings; they will live, work, and die in these settings.

Elam Coke, a dentist, in his early forties, thinks it is good that Blacks are mixing more with Whites. He feels "it helps people think in terms of individuals rather than Black/White." Timothy Brownlee, a public official, concurs that integration has its virtues. While his integrated experience has made him cautious, it has prepared him to "deal with people on a one-to-one basis and you get to know them well. . . . Blacks and Whites in segregated settings have a distorted view of Black folks and White folks," and racially mixed environments seem to lessen this perception.

Jack B. Lane also likes the idea that his son has the "freedom to choose" from a predominantly Black, a racially mixed, or a predominantly White setting. Yet, he wants to shape that preference by the type of neighborhood he chooses. For himself, Jack would prefer a Black neighborhood, but he does not have a preference for a workplace setting. He would have liked a mixed educational setting for himself, feeling it would have prepared him to "cope to live and serve in a mixed environment." Jack feels that if he had gone to a racially mixed school, he would be "in a better

position to understand the make-up and mode of the majority population." But, on the other hand, he is not so sure, saying, "I would not be
who I am and what I am, if I had attended a mixed school. I am what I am
because, to a large degree, I came through an all-Black school. Because of
the situation of segregation, it made me tougher." In his early days in the
Civil Rights movement, he stated, "I wouldn't say no. I wouldn't say yes.
I wouldn't give in. The guards said they were going to arrest me; they
would arrest me. I would come back the next day. . . . I wouldn't have the
appreciation for Black history or wouldn't be collecting Black books if I
had grown up in a mixed setting." Increasingly, with global communication, Jack feels he must prepare his child to adapt to a world that is different from that of his youth. But he is concerned that more cultural and
structural assimilation will be at the expense of his son's cultural heritage.
"It is important for Black children to know something of their past. When
children forget their past, they don't seem to be anchored. They live between two worlds and sometimes three worlds." Jack has "seen young
people get away from the Black world. They become marginal people. It is
very important for all of us, particularly a young child, to have something
to lean on."

When Black children do not have "something to lean on," such as not
being securely grounded in their cultural heritage, an identity crisis is
likely. Mobutu said his oldest daughter "got messed up in terms of trying
to deal with her identity. It was a very painful process, but she came
through it." His daughter was reared in an all-White environment, and she
identified with her "classmates and their families, and not with her own."
But when it came time for dating, her White girlfriends "didn't worry
about her." Since she, like her father, attached herself strongly to people,
she was "devastated by her friends." He had to seek counseling for his
daughter. Mobutu said the White counselor wanted to ground the problem in a family crisis, rather than understand the impact of racism on her.
As his daughter became more Afrocentric in her perspective, she developed an organization to help other Black children to cope.

The literature supports the view that a racially homogeneous environment appears to have positive effects on the self-esteem and the group and
personal identity of Black children. Frank Russo, a forty-three-year-old
public health administrator, did not need any studies to confirm his convic-
tion that "children in predominantly White settings have a tendency to
place more value on not being Black." He related the following incident
about his three-year-old son.

> When I wanted to buy my son a Black male doll, he became very adamant
> about not having one. His home is in a White community. He attends

nursery school in a White community, and his teachers are White. The Black male people he sees in the environment are not on the same level as Whites. I am sure there are some intangible things that went on in my three-year-old, but the bottom line is that he was adamant about not having a Black doll. My wife, who is fair-skinned, said to him, "Daddy is Black. Don't you love Daddy?" It was almost as though he went into a still pause, as if he were thinking. It means even at that age level, there is some unconscious programming going on in that environment.

Tefe Fusi, an African, is aware of the negative "unconscious programming" of his children in this country. The children in his predominantly White community refer to his children as "Black African potatoes" (African-American children also call his children names). When they come home crying, Fusi tells them, "You have to understand that you are in this society and you are Black." Tefe Fusi sends his children to his African country every two or three years in the summer. "It gives them a positive self-image and reinforces their Africanness."

Many Talented One Hundred were ambivalent about the impact of a predominantly White setting on their children, recalling the impact it had on them. Mayor Johnny Longtree, sixty-five, and Judge Jeannette Gear, in her late thirties, feel that being in a predominantly White environment affected their personalities. "It warped my personality, making me introverted. It's not natural for a man or woman to want to be alone. Even today I don't like a lot of people around me. I was alone during most of my years of growing up in a small White community," remarked Longtree.

Whether The Talented One Hundred grew up in Black, racially mixed, or White settings, they understand that racism is persistent. Unlike Tefe Fusi, who can send his children back to Africa, they have no place to go to reinforce their African-American heritage. Hence, most parents find it necessary to inculcate in their children "race pride" and the "race lesson." On the one hand, they identify imposed limitations because of race, and on the other hand, they encourage unlimited aspirations and being equal as an American. Often, the young offspring of the Talented One Hundred have encountered limited experiences with racism in their predominantly White setting. Yet, the parents feel they should prepare their children for a larger society that may not be as accepting of them.

Cassie Cooper, for instance, likes the idea of her child living in a mixed setting and sees advantages in it. "I was making an observation recently when she attended a birthday party as the only Black child. She was quite comfortable and happy, seemingly unaware of her blackness. I think there is something to be said for the positive side that race is not a factor. At her age, had I been the only Black child at the party, I would have been most uncomfortable." But Cassie also feels uneasy about her child's assimilation.

She does not want her child to "lose sight entirely that she is Black," because her race will be a reality in this society. "No matter how stable the community and educational situation you grow up in, you are going to have to deal with problems of a racial nature, and you can't get around that. I want her to understand the history of Black Americans and what they have been through. I want her to understand the situation her dad and I have been through and how the situation has improved, but to understand why that is. Even though it has improved, it is not what I would like it to be," said Cassie.

Dira Ridley, like Cassie Cooper, said her daughter is also further along in race relations. "I am there intellectually," Dira said. However, her daughter "doesn't see Black as different from White, and that is good. . . . In junior high and elementary school, people tend to look at factors other than color. But I tell her that in the twelfth grade when people are competing for the National Merit Scholarship, it might be different. If I tell her about race, it will not be an abnormal data point." Dira's daughter has only one Black among her circle of friends. Her interaction with other Black children is limited, because her Black community is small, with an older population. A top-ranking student in her predominantly White school, she does not interact with the Blacks who are in lower tracks (toward whom she harbors some negative feelings because of their boisterous behavior). However, Dira thinks her daughter's views will "broaden about Blacks when she meets more middle-class Blacks with attitudes like middle-class Whites."

In fact, where Black children have limited contact with other Blacks, they have a sense of discomfort in their presence, particularly lower-income Blacks. This problem may be accentuated if the child is an offspring of an interracial union. Pat Robinson noticed that his son had some racial identification problems when he was about thirteen years old. "He started acting really strange after the busing of Black kids to his White junior high school. The tough Black kids were doing a number on him, taunting, 'Are you with us or against us? Are you White or Black? Who are you with?' "

Jeffrey Falcon, Kevin Poston, and Regina Moon are children of interracial unions, and they have asked those questions many times of themselves.* They have walked between two worlds, sometimes feeling they belong to neither. While they were growing up, Blacks called them "half-breed," "honky," "spic," and "zebra." Whites just called them "niggers." Whatever racial identity they have personally assumed, they have been frequently reminded that they are seen as Black by the larger society.

*I conducted personal interviews of children of interracial unions in May 1987.

Jeffrey, a very fair-skinned, twenty-one-year-old junior at a predominantly Black college and the offspring of an Italian mother and a Black father, grew up in a racially mixed neighborhood (65 percent Black; 35 percent White) in a small midwestern city. He came to grips with his identity very early. Said Jeffrey, "I have always felt closer to Blacks than Whites." His racial identity has solidified since he attended a Black college and learned more about Black history. While he was growing up, he was acutely aware of the identity crisis in himself and other children of interracial unions. Many of his mixed friends identified more with Whites. They wanted also to excel academically. Jeffrey said, "By excelling, they wanted to further distance themselves from their Black heritage, thus decreasing their chances of being stigmatized as dumb and inferior by Whites."* At school activities, when asked to identify relatives, his racially mixed friends would point to White aunts, uncles, and grandparents, wanting to be associated only with them. Pat Robinson learned from his mother, a domestic, only a month prior to my interview with him in 1987, that his son, then a twenty-six-year-old, had denied his grandmother when he was thirteen years old. While Pat's mother and her grandson were strolling in the park, he saw some White friends nearby. Pat reported that his son started "acting really strange, like he didn't know my mother. He didn't want them to know his grandmother was Black." I asked, "When you heard this story thirteen years later, how did you feel?" "I was furious. I don't know what I would have done then. I probably would have cried rather than being furious," said Pat.

Kevin Poston, a twenty-three-year-old senior at a Black college and the offspring of a White mother and Black father, grew up in a predominantly Black neighborhood in the Midwest. He, too, agonized over his identity. He said that one day in elementary school, "I looked at Whites and saw that I wasn't that color, so I put down Black on my school form." His racial awareness grew after attending a Black college and learning of the "oppression of Black people. . . . I became angry and my relations with my mother became rocky. I started treating her like other White people. It was very traumatic. I told her things I can't say on this tape. But I can kill myself now for saying them." Kevin has come to terms with his racial identity and mixed heritage.

Regina Moon, a fair-skinned twenty-year-old, on the other hand, seemed to be struggling even harder with her identity than did Kevin or Jeffrey. Her mother is White and her father, Black; they are divorced. She grew up in a liberal, racially mixed community in Ohio and attended a

---

*Alvin Poussaint, a psychiatrist, notes that children of interracial unions are high achievers, as quoted in Lynn Norment, "A Probing Look at Children of Interracial Marriages," *Ebony,* September, 1985.

Black college. She identified herself as mixed and accepts herself as "an individual, identifying in some circumstances with Blacks, other times with Whites, and sometimes neither." She feels closer to Black men and White women than to White men or Black women. While growing up she felt that Black girls were jealous of her and White men found little interest in her as a dating partner. But Regina feels closer to her Black relatives than her White relatives, irrespective of their sex. When her mother and father married, her mother's parents and relatives did not "talk with their daughter until after she divorced her Black husband." Regina said she feels like an outsider with her White grandparents and relatives. She has heard them say "nigger" too often. "Once my grandmother told me, 'You are really pretty.' But she said it like a Black person couldn't be pretty," said Regina.

Although Regina, Kevin, and Jeffrey have had their racial identity conflicts, they see advantages in their mixed heritage. But Pat Robinson thinks being racially mixed has left some confusion in his son. "He is not scarred, and there are not any heavy psychological problems, but it shows in his dating. He tends to date more White girls. Recently, he has been dating Black women," said Pat.

To many Black parents, selecting a person of another race signals an identity crisis in their children, even when their dating opportunities might be limited, especially if they live in a predominantly White community. Hence, the issue of interracial dating and marriage is a sensitive one with Black parents. This topic surfaced frequently during the interviews. The Talented One Hundred know the likelihood of their children dating interracially is greater than their own, since there is more extensive contact with other ethnic groups. For parents who live in a predominantly White community and who would like their children to date Blacks exclusively, it becomes a quagmire. Take Ellen Strawberry, an administrator in a non-profit agency in the Midwest, as an example. She wants her children to date other Blacks, but there are few Black teenagers in their predominantly White neighborhood and school. She commented, "If some White person approaches them for a date, they are quick to tell me, 'Mom, you should have thought about that when you placed us in this setting.'" Her son, who recently started to date, boasted to a friend, "I am going to the good life now," by which he meant he had a chance to date White females.

Historian Kufra Akpan has a daughter. When she went to the prom with a White boy, Akpan was upset. "I said to her, 'You couldn't find a Black person? You have humiliated everybody and Black people everywhere. You are stepping on them and your dad. How would you feel if I dated a White woman?'" He attributed her action to an integrated environment. "I thought she was weird. She's coming around now. She married a Black man. The children evolved over a period of time. While living in a Black community, they were race conscious. But they became integrationists after we moved into this mixed neighborhood. I think their integrationist mode had to do with their living in an integrated community. They got socialized in spite of me in that White community. My children's friends were uncomfortable with me. I didn't encourage their friendship. They were trying to be human, trying to be racially unconscious, and trying to act like they were growing up in the racial melting pot of America." Yet, he believes that subconsciously they always understood their blackness. "They had a reminder because I was always negative," said Akpan.

Encouraging Afrocentric behavior and identity can prove expensive, especially if there is a limited pool of Blacks from which children can select a dating partner. Jonathan Mobutu's daughter and her friend could not find Black dates in their high school to take them to the prom; Mobutu had to import their dates from another state, providing for their transportation and other expenses. His daughter is particularly interested in attending a Black college after this and other experiences in the White community.

Diane Earlinger's children attend a predominantly White school, but she makes it clear to her children "that the only thing they are to bring from this environment is reading, writing, and arithmetic. I don't expect them to bring home a White girl, and I certainly don't expect them to bring home a White value system."

The Talented One Hundred who reside in predominantly White communities are particularly sensitive to the importance of imparting the race lesson to their children, who often identify themselves as being "only American" and who sometimes resist this lesson.

Said John Hubbard, echoing the feeling of other parents among the Talented One Hundred, "Strangely enough, I think my children are happy with Black/White relations. They think I talk too much about blackness and point out too much discrimination. When I look at television, I point out the subtle racist messages that come across. I point out racism in advertisements and comic books. I point out all the incidences of institutional racism. They acknowledge it exists." But his children say, "It is not important, Dad, not to us." "They want to be accepted by their White friends," said John.

John and his wife are very race conscious, but his children, admitted John, "see us as going too far. They feel we overplay the issue of discrimination in this society, mainly because they haven't seen it on the personal level as we did. My wife's father's barn was burned down by some jealous Whites. She has seen what hostility can do when directed toward Blacks. Our children haven't experienced discrimination firsthand. They think everybody is equal, and we're all the same." John and his wife raised their children in the teachings of the Bahai faith, which advocates that everyone is like "waves of the sea, leaves of one tree, and flowers of one garden. . . . Race doesn't make a difference in one's worthiness in the sight of God and in the sight of each other. We've taught them that and they've taken it to heart." While they stress the universality of humankind, they also impart another message. Though universal human acceptance is a part of the Bahai faith, "the larger society still sees [Blacks] as second-class citizens and their options are going to be limited based on their race. I have told my children and shown them about racism, but they don't quite believe it or accept it yet." John's children have mostly White friends, and John is concerned about their lack of contact with other Blacks and is considering moving to a Black community. He feels his all-White community has contributed to an identity crisis and psychological problems in his youngest daughter; she has been involved in shoplifting.

The conflictual dual message in the socialization process is viewed, nevertheless, as an important adaptive strategy. But it is sometimes cumbersome to impart this dual message of survival. Marla Robinson, whose teenage son lives and attends school in a White neighborhood, said,

> I am seeing my child as not willing to be accepting of what you have to do to survive. My child is unwilling to bite his tongue, and it is unfortunate that he has to do it. I tell him in the real world, it is a game, and you have to learn how to play it. It goes against my grain, and it annoys me that I have to talk like this, but in reality it is true. I would not be a good parent if I didn't tell my son those people he will be dealing with see him as Black first, and I don't want my son to go out there and think he will be equal to them from their perspective. I want him to feel he is better than the element he is dealing with, but he is not a free spirit in America. He should work toward being that, but in the interim, he has to survive and learn how to deal with them, but not give up everything.

Diane Earlinger thinks today's young people feel entitled to education and jobs. "If that is not turned around about the time these children are twenty to twenty-five, they aren't going to do as well as they did in the 1960s. These kids aren't going to take it. There is a built-in inherent right that they expect with their generation. I am very concerned about my kids."

Some Black elite feel that this sense of entitlement stems from parents' failure to discuss racism with their children. Many parents, having escaped poverty, feel embarrassed by their negative, overt racial experiences prior to the Civil Rights movement. They never confront the issue of racism with their children or discuss their social hardships, thus contributing to their children's lack of social consciousness. Still others believe that the Black elite have become "so preoccupied with materialism and being White, they fail to pass on our noble heritage." Lacking a sense of Black struggle and not feeling as eager for success as their parents, they are therefore not as motivated to achieve and/or work as hard. The Black elite are concerned that the young Blacks—the children of the elite—who have greater resources and privileges, will not pass on the wealth, knowledge, and skills to their children or to the Black community, this society, and the world.

The Black elite's children must be aware that to be Black and to work toward being a "free spirit in America" means a continuous struggle with oppression and to establish one's identity. It is essential for parents to transmit the "race lessons" and "our noble heritage" as coping mechanisms. In an integrated environment, particularly an educational setting, some parents fear that these race lessons are not being transmitted, resulting in "confusion among young people under twenty and contributing to their lack of sensitivity to the race struggle." Though Frank Russo sees advantages and disadvantages of a diverse setting to educate Black children, he thinks students should be in a "setting where they can emphasize their total blackness as opposed to dealing with everybody's value system, since we have a tendency to get lost." His children live and attend school in a White neighborhood.

Benson Robinson, Jr., the twenty-four-year-old son of a successful entrepreneur (introduced earlier), agreed with Frank Russo, responding quickly when I asked about his educational experience in an exclusive White private school. "I wish somebody would write a book about the danger of steeping Black children in predominantly White settings." He thinks there are "some real dangers in terms of identity and being different." He recalled his first day of school as a first grader in that setting. "I remember the experience like it was yesterday. I was the only Black in a class of thirty-five Whites. The teacher asked the students to introduce themselves. Since I was so preoccupied with playing, I was the last to stand up. When I stood up and introduced myself, the students and teacher sighed." During the break, "I remember the kids running over to me and rubbing their hands through my hair. . . . Am I that different from the rest of them to cause this reaction?" he thought. His parents made him feel "good enough" about himself "to ward off the feeling of being different."

Benson remembered feeling uncomfortable about being different in the third or fourth grade. "It was during the time when you begin to notice little girls and Valentines with I love you," he said. "I noticed I didn't get as many Valentines as other kids, and I was not included in their activities. That was a rather difficult experience for me." But, he noted, the isolation was "offset by my participation in the Jack and Jill," a social club for the children of middle-class Blacks. The organization was very important to him because it "reaffirmed that your values are correct and those differences that are so apparent do not really mean anything. The group also reaffirmed the fact that Blacks are capable of professionalism and can perform the same as Whites. In the White environment, I was just there. The environment addressed their needs, not mine." Yet, he admitted, "the White environment helped me to relax and not pay attention to color barriers all the time." But on the other hand, "you were always reminded that they were there." Benson cited the advantage of having equal opportunity in instructional development, but noted the disadvantage of not having positive role models and "not having access to one's Black cultural heritage."

Suddenly, he shifted again to the emotional impact of his educational experience. "In any society or time period, the worst crime is to be different. I was different. Even though I was different, I spoke the same as Whites. I could afford the same toys and better. I enjoyed skiing. The more I think about it, the more I feel someone should address the dangers of being in that environment, where there is no reinforcement." It is a contradictory situation. "Every day was spent in a see-saw way. It gets to be confusing after a while, and that's where the danger lies."

Black Children in Predominantly White Schools

When Teresa Johnson's daughter performed extremely well on a national mathematics test, Teresa felt extremely proud. She also felt "much pain" when her daughter cried "because she would be in a class with no Blacks." She is not in mathematics anymore, since she did not want to be set off from her Black peers.

The Talented One Hundred were concerned about the quality of their children's educational environment. Like Teresa Johnson, they were aware of the inherent danger of denigration or negation of the Black cultural heritage in White schools. Marla Robinson's sixteen-year-old son, for example, was "kicked out" of his private White high school for challenging his teacher about her lack of knowledge. Chiding her, he said, "I don't believe you are a biology teacher who is teaching a unit on blood and you don't know Charles Drew, the Black scientist, who discovered blood plasma!"

At least 79 percent of the Talented One Hundred reinforced the importance of Black history and culture in their interactions with their children. In addition, 78 percent said they keep in contact with relatives who live in primarily Black communities to reinforce a positive group and personal identity in their children. The school, one of the important agencies of socialization, can have a powerful impact on children. It mirrors the societal values. Education is seen as an avenue of upward mobility and "the great leveler," as Michael Lomax believes, but it also preserves the status quo, directly and indirectly reinforcing discrimination toward and stereo-types about Blacks in the classrooms and in the curriculum.

Warner Babbitt, a journalist, has three children in an upper-class, pre-dominantly White public school. "White folks who are accustomed to Black people not achieving believe, whether they admit it or not (as nice as they are, when they smile in your face and say all the things they are sup-posed to say), that Black folks are inherently inferior. It doesn't matter about your background. They know Black middle-class children are differ-ent from Black lower-class children, but still, deep down inside, they really believe they are inferior." His thirteen-year-old daughter is the only Black in a program for gifted students. But, he said, "she constantly runs into the problem, more than the White kids, that she couldn't have written a partic-ular essay, because Blacks don't write that well. She is treated as special, like she is some kind of affirmative action quota, although she scored in the 99 percentile on the SAT. They can't take that away from her. We have to explain to the teachers that she is where she is because she works hard and is intelligent. Whites are accustomed to teaching bright White kids, but not bright Black kids who want to excel. However, if Black kids have par-ents who will kick the school's ass, they also get taught."

As the twentieth century draws to a close, Black children are still being called names like "nigger," "pickaninny," and "chocolate mousse" by Whites, just as Lula Brown was taunted in the beginning of this century. They have been discouraged from taking mathematics, though their par-ents are doctors and scientists. Some White teachers feel Black children aren't capable of handling it. Marla Robinson, who pays $5,000 a year to send her articulate, bright son to his White private school, said his White teachers asked him "if his parents spoke ghetto English or regular English." Black children have also been discriminated against by classmates with the tacit approval of teachers. Michael Lomax's daughter's experience clearly illustrates this point. He said, "My daughter attends a very exclusive pri-vate school, where there is a waiting list. It has an open-class system, not structured. Even without that structured element that is associated with private schools, there is a race and class structure in the school." One day, his daughter came home very upset, saying, "[So-and-so] is having a party at school and I am not invited." I said, "Who is [so-and-so]? And she said, 'A little White girl.' I said, 'Who is invited?' And she said, 'Everybody ex-cept me and [she named a little girl who is an East Indian].' The only two kids not invited were girls of color. I was mad. I had a long talk with her and indicated, 'There is a lesson you are going to have to contend with because wherever you go, there are going to be people who treat you badly or hurt you because of the color of your skin.'"

Lomax wanted to make certain that invitations excluding children of color would never be sent out through the school's mail. "I am going to be really mad if you do that again. I am going to scream and yell," said Lomax to school officials. He observed that "all little Black girls, when they reached puberty level, leave this school."

For Lomax and his daughter, the experience wound up being a creative learning experience. "I helped to negotiate and nurture my child through a difficult racial experience, but one which did not traumatize her," said Lomax. When parents don't deal with it, "it is one of those layers of unhealed wounds for that child, because she will then say, 'I didn't get invited to the party because I am not worthy. I am unworthy because I am Black.' You can't allow her to run the risk of feeling something is wrong with her because she is Black. As long as it is an integrated environment, people are going to assault you because you are Black. What you have to understand is it is their problem, not yours. I told her, 'No one is ever to try and restrict you or hurt you. You must stand up and fight back.'" His daughter encouraged her schoolmates to talk about the experience and "she and all the girls cried. She got mad. Her classmates responded, but they had to deal with their mommies who told them not to invite [the two girls] in the first place."

Lomax noticed that "even though the kids who are in the second generation after integration are taking it for granted, it is not satisfying emotionally to them. . . . My daughter has said to me, 'I want to go to a public school, not private. I want to go to a public school where there are more Black people than this one.' It means she won't ever be enchained by the myth that it was something that she missed and she was excluded from it. She saw it, looked at it, found it unsatisfying, and sought something else." In assisting his daughter to negotiate race relations, Lomax views his role "not as an authoritarian parent, but an authority, like a reference book. You can go to that authority and get some information that can be helpful."

More parents have also begun to look at integration, and finding it unsatisfactory, they have begun to check their "reference book" about whether to send their children to White schools. Like Lomax, their "reference book" has added new data, causing them to rethink the integrationist hypothesis. Laura Price, a gynecologist, said, "My children were exposed to a predominantly White educational system very early. Many times I thought maybe I pushed them into it too early. Oftentimes, they were unhappy and wanted to change schools. Some emotional disturbances did occur. I was so set on offering the best academically successful environment." Although her children are grounded in the Black church and the community, their White educational experience left a legacy of unhappiness. Laura went to a predominantly White medical school, but she believes that because she had the "highest positive exposure to blackness" during her formative years, she was able to cope more successfully. "It was so entrenched in my brain, heart, and soul that Black is great that I was able to cope with integration better than my children," said Laura.

More parents, like Laura Price, have begun to evaluate the quality of education in a predominantly Black versus a White setting. During the sixties, there was a strong belief that integration offered the best academically successful environment. The Talented One Hundred, who came of age or who were young adults during the Civil Rights movement, are now questioning the negative impact of integration on their children (though 36 percent said the ideal educational setting for their children is a racially mixed one). Sixteen percent would like their children to be educated in a Black school at certain periods in their lives and to attend a predominantly White or mixed school at other points in their educational cycles, usually graduate school. Many parents expressed interest in their children attending a Black college. Jacqueline Fleming's *Blacks in College* supports the notion that the Black college is more nurturing; Blacks do better academically in Black colleges than in White colleges and universities, and their graduation rate is higher.[19] (I might add that 34 percent of the Talented One Hundred preferred a Black educational setting from kindergarten through college for their children.)

The Talented One Hundred who preferred a Black or a racially mixed educational setting at different stages of their own and their children's lives seem to look nostalgically on the era of segregation. While pointing out its negative aspects, they were quick to note the positive ones. Priscilla King and Jack B. Lane echoed the sentiments of many individuals when they described the advantages of the segregated system in the South. Said Priscilla, who is in her early fifties, "I am very glad I was raised in the South and had Black teachers. The teachers encouraged your success and encouraged you to feel good about yourself. There was a sense of Black pride. We sang the Negro National Anthem and did things relevant to Black people. The teachers were involved with you, not only at school, but also outside the classroom. So I never felt inferior to anybody."

Jack B. Lane also felt his Black teachers had a positive influence on him at a very early age.

> Most of my teachers would come from out of town. They would spend the week in the community, and then would go back to town. I guess for the first time you saw people with an education. They paid attention to us. They encouraged us. During Negro History Week, we had to cut out pictures from Black publications—*Jet, Ebony, Pittsburgh Courier,* and the *Afro-American*—of famous Black individuals, like Booker T. Washington, Ralph Bunche, George Washington Carver, Marian Anderson, or Willie Mays. The act of participating in Negro History Week, putting together

a scrap book, and having the teacher say, "You can be like these individuals," inspired me. If these people could do it, then you can make a contribution.

When I asked the Talented One Hundred who were their greatest influences outside the family, the largest number of them indicated their teachers. It is interesting to note that White teachers had little or no positive impact except in the case of a few persons who attended predominantly White schools or had mostly White teachers. One of these exceptions was Tony Michaels, the only Black student in his class, whose White teacher told him she expected him to be "better than the rest" of the students. Jonathan Mobutu's White second-grade teacher told him he could grow up to be president. And Sheridan Williams remembers her White teachers were supportive. But for the most part this pattern did not prevail.

Since the number of Black teachers is declining significantly and the population of all minorities is rising, it is important to ponder the implications for Black students. According to a 1987 survey by the National Education Association, only 6.9 percent of the country's public school teachers are Black. By the turn of the century, minorities may make up more than 40 percent of the public school enrollment, while comprising less than 5 percent of the teachers.[20]

David Benton, a forty-seven-year-old artist, never had a Black teacher in school. "Knowing what I know now and having gone through such an experience, I would opt for a Black institution because of the added positive role models." He is thoroughly amazed that he has come through such an experience and "has a wholesome attitude about blackness."

Looking at the impact of integration and the declining number of Black teachers, Teresa Stanfield, a college administrator, lamented, "When we had a community in which Black adults could band together and protect our youngsters from the psychological effects of racism, there were many good things about it. Now we are in a situation where that can't be. I don't know what is going on in public schools. I think [Black students] have a sense of inferiority. They do not feel good about themselves, even though they may show bravado."

The Talented One Hundred are rethinking the educational process and are beginning to encourage their children to attend Black colleges. Walden Wilmington, a geneticist, thinks it is important for his thirteen-year-old daughter to attend a Black college in order to reinforce her cultural heritage. Students can also develop leadership qualities in Black colleges. "There is no affirmative action program. A Black college is affirmative. You can do anything you want," asserted Tony Michaels. Leo Aramis equated the Black university with the church. "The Black university is a place like a Black church. Black folk have an opportunity to be somebody.

You might have been a janitor all week long, but on Sundays you were a deacon in the church. You might have cleaned floors all day long, but you might be a missionary in the church. It is good for your self-esteem and community. This sense of community needs to be gained before you get out there in the marketplace." Perhaps the sense of community gained while attending a Black college is the reason why Thomas B. Thomas, in his late thirties, will make a deal with his children when they are ready for college. "I have a deal. If they go to my Black alma mater, they will have a free ride. If they go to another Black school, they will be provided with 50 percent of their tuition. And if they go to Harvard, they will not receive anything."

Most individuals I interviewed were not as adamant as Thomas, who had all-White teachers in a predominantly Black school in Cleveland. He is strongly in favor of Black colleges.

> When I arrived on campus, it was the first time I had seen any Black people in such prominent positions. The only Blacks I had seen who wore suits during the day were one Black lawyer and one Black doctor in town. When I went to a Black college, I saw this group of people who were dressed up when they went to work. And they were teaching people. . . . I had never been in that atmosphere. It was a unique experience, because for the first time, I saw how people were walking around and talking about how great it was to be Black. I had never been around a group of people that felt so good about themselves and what they were able to do. And most importantly, they were interested in explaining what atrocities had been committed on Blacks. We met some very powerful people on the campus; people who knew so much about being Black in this country and what we have to do to improve our plight.

Prior to entering a Black college, Thomas B. Thomas felt that "if you put Black folks and White folks together, Whites will outscore Blacks." He also believed "Black always meant bad. Black cat meant seven years of bad luck, and bad guys wore black hats. I knew everything good was White and everything bad was Black." His parents did not challenge this assumption. Having grown up in the oppressed rural South in the thirties, they, too, were "children of bondage."

Despite the fact that many of the Talented One Hundred are encouraging their children to attend Black colleges, others continue to hold negative perceptions of Black schools, even when they graduated from Black colleges and universities and found the experience nurturing. When Judge Roscoe Champion, speaking before the Jack and Jill, an organization for children of professional Blacks, asked how many children were going to college, all raised their hands. When he asked how many had any Black schools under consideration, no one raised a hand. He asked parents of the children to stand if they had attended an all-Black school. "All the parents had gone to Black schools, and their children did not have any Black schools under consideration. The kids sensed something was wrong with that. The kids said, 'Black people who went to Black schools were not successful,' even though two mayors had just spoken before them and now a judge. The kids felt bad. Their parents came up to apologize, not knowing they had done that to their children." He thinks "most Blacks who went to all-Black schools do not attribute their success to them. They say they made it in spite of the Black school. They say, 'I overcame an inferior education and made it.' We don't feel a sense of obligation to convey to our children that they can get a quality education. Instead, we want to convey to them we overcame a poor education, so the children begin to look at White schools. Black education is regarded as inferior. We are not grateful. When you finish a Black college, it is like you are saying, 'I went because I didn't have the opportunity, but if I had a chance, I would have gone to another school.'"

Opponents of Black colleges, Jacqueline Fleming noted, argue that "the poorer resources of Black colleges intellectually undermine the students attending them. Segregated institutions are anachronisms in contemporary American society and have outlived their usefulness." The proponents of Black colleges, however, point out that these colleges are "places where Black students can learn without the constraints of minority status or the tension engendered by the hostile undercurrent in Black/White interactions."[21] Jacqueline Fleming's research supports the strengths of the Black college in educating Black youths and the historical role it has played in producing Black leaders.

Another concern surfaced in my talks with the Talented One Hundred: Which environment better prepares students for coping in a White society? Thirty-six percent and 4 percent, respectively, preferred a mixed environment or predominantly White environment for their children. Overwhelmingly, the major reason was to give them a "competitive edge" in negotiating in a White world. But defenders of Black colleges, like Thomas B. Thomas and Kelly Smith, argued that White universities do not provide Blacks with the necessary coping skills. Said Thomas:

> The people I've met who have gone to White schools (there are exceptions) who have all the credentials and names behind them seem to approach life with their hands out, like "someone owes me something, because I am a graduate of Yale. And I am entitled to all rights and privileges pertaining thereto." So, therefore, when they walk out and say "I am from Yale," they act as if the corporation will fold over and offer them a job. There is a direct correlation between performance and pay. I don't care where you went to school. If you get on the job and you don't perform, you don't stay very long. It's the real world out here and they

want something for what they put out. So I've got friends and associates from major universities unemployed because their attitudes are such that "I am entitled to," rather than "give me a chance and I'll make sure that I'll do what I am supposed to. Let me in the door and the job will get done. It has been instilled in me that I have to perform and to be better." You get this at a Black school. At the White school, it seems to me that they are trying to avoid you. The majority of Black students don't go back to their White class reunions. Who are they trying to reunite with? There is nobody with whom to reunite, except a few who banded together because they had to unite against the numbers. There is value to Black colleges and universities.

Kelly Smith agreed with Thomas. She also felt that one's coping skills are different if you grow up in a White environment. She cited examples of two friends who had grown up in a White community. One attended Yale as an undergraduate and went to Harvard Law School. And the other attended Harvard as an undergraduate and went to Yale Law School. The former worked for a senator and a major corporation, but when he moved to the South to work, she said, "he was disillusioned. He could not do well in that environment because of discrimination. His coping skills were at a minimum. This guy thought he was just as good and equal as Whites, and they were going to deal with him that way." The latter friend was "unemployed for two years," said Kelly, "because he was unable to cope in the real world. He internalized his failures."

Sharon Georgia, a civil rights attorney who has counseled upwardly mobile Blacks, observed that Blacks who lack a strong racial awareness and coping skills are more likely to internalize acts of racism and corporate politics as personal failures. "I've heard Black clients say 'I am just as smart' when they do not get the position. They are psychologically unable to handle it, because some Blacks truly believe being Black does not matter in the organization."

> I find that Blacks in White organizations who understand who they are and what it means to be in an organization don't suffer those kinds of consequences. They don't have to see a psychiatrist and psychologist or don't have ulcers. They move with the flow of things. They say, "I know what I am in this organization. I know I am good. I'll play the game and I'll fight to go on." It's people who don't understand who they are that internalize racism, have psychological problems, and end up getting into trouble on the job. The higher you go up in the system, the greater the pressure. If you don't bring some guns to fight that, they'll kill you off, and they will render you impotent by making you dysfunctional.

In summary, Black professionals who live as well as work in predominantly White environs are more likely to become socially isolated from the

Black community. Since there is continuous discrimination on and off the job, this isolation creates stress. Living in a predominantly White community also disrupts the Black professionals' traditional supportive familial, friendship, and organizational ties that could buffer them from stress. To cope with the stressful impact of social isolation and color barriers, the Black elite maintain contact with family, friends, and social organizations like the church within the Black community.

The perception that as Blacks move into the mainstream, their political consciousness becomes more class-linked than race-linked is not supported by the comments of the persons interviewed. The Talented One Hundred have a strong concern for issues that impact upon the Black masses. They understand that group mobility is bound by the color line and not the class line in America.

The Black elite who live in predominantly White settings are concerned about the quality of the educational and social environment of their children. When Black children are in predominantly White settings, there is a battle for their hearts and minds. The continuous exposure of children to such Eurocentric values as individualism conflicts with the need for a collective racial consciousness.

SIX

Gender Politics—Through the Eyes of Black Women

Yvonne Walker-Taylor reminisced:

> In the beginning, I didn't like being a girl. I had discovered at the age of five that people would come into my father's home and would ask, "Is this your only child?" "Yes," he would say, and they would say, "Oh, what a shame! It's not a boy." I heard that so much I began to feel totally inferior.
>
> One day I was sitting under the steps, my favorite spot, waiting for my father to come home. If I got hurt, I began crying when he came down the street to get his sympathy. I was consoling myself when he came up, and he said, "Baby, what are you doing?" I said, "I am trying to kiss my elbow." "Why are you trying to kiss your elbow?" he inquired. "The kids told me if I could kiss my elbow, I could turn into a boy." My father took me on his knee and told me that he loved me just as I was, and I didn't need to change into anything.
>
> When I was old enough to understand, he constantly reinforced and increased the philosophy that, "You are a woman; you have brains, so you can do anything you want to do!"

"Never underestimate yourself," said the seventy-one-year-old Walker-Taylor, the first woman president of Wilberforce University, one of the oldest Black colleges in the country. At the tender age of five, Walker-Taylor was precocious enough to understand the consequences of sex and gender on her life chances. But, too often, when the impact of racial oppression is examined, Black females and males are grouped together, muting these differences despite the fact that each experiences oppression differently.

Since Blacks were brought to this country, the Black woman has embodied the contradictions of both her gender and her race. In *Women, Race and Class,* Angela Davis notes that during the nineteenth century, when femininity meant embracing motherhood and being a homemaker, this did not extend to Black women. They were "breeders" and "sucklers" for Whites. Their offspring could be "sold away like calves from cows." Black women were homemakers, but outside their homes as cooks and servants for Whites. They also tilled the soil alongside Black men. Black women were not too " 'feminine' to work in coal mines, in iron foundries, or to be lumberjacks or ditch-diggers." [1] Thus, while White women were viewed as the "weaker sex," Black women needed to be strong to survive the hardships of slavery. As the "weaker sex," White women were desexed, idealized, and placed on a pedestal of purity, while Black women were dethroned and sexualized. Black women were, therefore, available sexual objects to White males. In addition to the physical punishment of lashings and mutilations endured by both Black men and women, Black women were often raped.

Historically, the gender roles and stereotypes of Black and White females in the United States have been in opposition. Black women have been portrayed as Aunt Jemima,[2] who is strong, domineering, matriarchal, and sexually uninhibited, while, in contrast, White women have been stereotyped, particularly in the South, as sexually restrained, gentle, and docile. Since there are so many contradictions and myths inherent in the gender role and image of Black womanhood, I shall examine the drama of sexism and racism through the eyes of Black women. While I recognize the plight of Black manhood in this society, it will not be the primary focus of this chapter.

Sexism and Racism

How does one distinguish between racism and sexism? According to Yvonne Walker-Taylor,

> It is hard to distinguish between the two. You never know if White men discriminate against you because you are Black or because you are a woman. It would be interesting to be a man for a little while to see if it's the same thing. As a category, women are discriminated against. I find there are similarities between the way women are treated, whether Black or White. But we have a double jeopardy.
>
> For instance, when I attended my first conference of academic deans, I noticed that the nuns in the room could command attention. They raised their hands and would be recognized. "Sisters, you have something to say?" they [White male deans] would ask. I noticed this particularly if they wore habits. They don't think of the nuns as women; they are desexed, and their opinions are respected.
>
> When I wanted to make a comment, I was overlooked. I was the only

Black face at the conference. After I had been dealt by for two sessions, I said, "Wait just a minute." I stood up. I have always been outspoken. I said, "Sir! I am completely visible. Of that I am sure, because I am the only Black face here. So I know you see me. I want one good reason why you won't recognize me so I can say what I have to say." He said, "I wasn't aware." [She imitated his "hem haw" embarrassed response.] "Well, thank you very much. I may be heard now."

I have fought for everything I got. This is what I meant by double jeopardy. It is a constant fight. You can never relax and say I don't have to fight. A man will not pay you any attention if you don't command and demand attention. I don't mean being a jackass. I mean dealing with it in a respectful and dignified way. One thing that will disarm a man is respect.

Thirty-seven percent of the Talented One Hundred are women. Like Walker-Taylor, "they can never relax," knowing they have to fight on two battlefronts. But they cannot clearly identify the enemy—their race or their sex. Hence, the overwhelming majority of the women of the Talented One Hundred recognize the confluence of both race and sex as salient variables in their professional and social interactions. As Crystal Miller acknowledged, "It is hard to distinguish, because the Black woman is in a particular kind of category that carries with it a lot of historical baggage. Her experience in the United States has been unique. I can't separate them. They are intertwined."

Even those, like Teresa Hale, who attempt to distinguish between sexism and racism by looking "at the language, the underlying assumptions and consequences," still conclude "that sometimes the situation is confounded by a combination of both racial and sexual components, making the distinction extremely difficult."

The appointment in the late 1980s of the Reverend Barbara Harris, the first female bishop in the worldwide Anglican communion, illustrates the confluence of sexism and racism. Though her sex appeared more salient in the controversial appointment, much was made of her race. Indeed, they are interactive. Black men and women are still the last to be hired and the first to be fired. They are underrepresented in senior level positions, particularly Black women, who represent, for example, only 1.8 percent of the officials and managers of major corporations, according to the Equal Employment Opportunities Commission. Black men represent 2.7 percent and White women comprise 21.1 percent of officials and managers.[3] Even among *Black Enterprise* magazine's "25 Hottest Black Managers" in corporate American in 1988, not one woman was listed. According to the magazine, women comprised less than 1 percent of the 125 final candidates. Only one or two of these women headed major divisions and had a direct impact on the financial status and direction of the company.[4]

Although Black women are underrepresented in high level positions, it would be unfair to ignore or underestimate the changes in their occupational distributions. In 1940, 60 percent of working Black women were employed as domestic workers, compared with 11 percent of working White women, who were mostly poor European immigrants. Presently, more than 50 percent of working Black females hold white-collar positions, which are primarily clerical.[5] Between 1970 and 1985, the most significant changes took place in the occupational distribution of employed Black women. In 1970, for instance, 42 percent of all employed Black women worked in service jobs, dropping to 30 percent by 1985. In contrast, technical, sales, and administrative occupations rose from 26 to 38 percent. In 1970, Black women represented 12 percent of managers and professionals, compared with 18 percent of White women; in 1985, Black women comprised 17 percent of managers and professionals, and White women, 24 percent. Between 1980 and 1985, the percentage of Black women managers and professionals remained the same, while that of White women managers and professionals increased slightly by 2 percent.[6]

A *Black Enterprise* survey of its readers indicated that sex and race are important variables in explaining these variations in the percentage of Black managers and professionals. While it appears from the survey that Blacks are much less affected by sexual discrimination at work now than in the past, most of those who reported such discrimination were Black women. Forty-five percent of the women stated they had encountered sexual discrimination, compared with only 15 percent of the men. Also, a larger percentage (57 percent) of women in the poll stated they had encountered racial discrimination. The survey suggests that as both Black men and women move up the corporate ladder, they encounter increased resistance and are perceived as posing a greater threat, particularly the Black male.[7] The traditional role of the man as the breadwinner has made the Black man more of an economic threat to the White man.

John P. Fernandez's study on *Racism and Sexism in Corporate Life* further supports the *Black Enterprise* survey that Black male managers at the highest levels are likely to feel greater obstacles in the workplace.[8] Fernandez's research is illuminating, particularly since he looks at the following groups by race and sex: Asians, Blacks, Hispanics, Native Americans, and Whites. While each minority group in this country has encountered discrimination, it has differed in kind and degree. The history, skin color, and size of the minority group are salient variables in predicting the treatment of each group by Whites. Fernandez believes that the "greater burden of racism appears to have fallen upon the Black race for a number of reasons: the bitter legacy of slavery, its darker color, its larger numbers, and its location throughout the country."[9] Fernandez's study found that Blacks are the most critical of discrimination in the workplace, followed by Hispanics, Asians, Native Americans, and Whites. With regard to women, Black women were the most critical of discrimination in the workplace, followed by White, Hispanic, Native American, and Asian women.[10] Since Blacks are at the bottom of the social structure, it is not surprising that they are the most sensitive to inequality in corporate America. In particular, Black women are sensitized to racial and sexual discrimination.

Let us look, for example, at the corporate life of Dira Ridley, a Ph.D. research physical chemist in a Fortune 500 consumer products company. Her story of working in corporate America in the late 1980s reveals racism and sexism in the workplace. Dira feels that she is quite competent.

> I think I am good, and people say I ought to be section head. But I've heard my manager say in performance appraisals that I work too hard, and I shouldn't work as hard. I should waste more time. It means to go around and talk. They are trying to delay a promotion for a Black woman. But I never want it said that I didn't work hard enough.
>
> I am opinionated and would not hesitate to tell anyone exactly what I think. If a White male said it, then, it would be great. It shows leadership. I get back I shouldn't have said that. I am aggressive. Aggressiveness in a man is exactly what they want. Yet, they assign me certain projects because I am aggressive and outspoken. On the one hand, it is good for the assignment, but on the other hand, it is bad because I am a woman. A White woman was also told not to work as hard and burn herself out on a project she had initiated, because they would have to promote two women. They want to delay my promotion.

Though Dira Ridley's primary task is to unravel the scientific mystery of how certain compounds and elements react in the laboratory, she is also forced to unravel the mystery of the social elements of racism and sexism operating in the world of work. Said Dira:

> I have individuals who report to me and who also report to White males, and their response in getting things to me is slower than getting things to the White males. I grant that our styles are different. It is tough when I look at things with a single variable faction to try to assess whether something is due [to my being] Black, especially as a female. My guts tell me it is because I am Black. White women have moved quite well in this company to the same degree as White males or even Black males—all more than Black women. White women have more project responsibilities and people responsibilities than Black women. To me, it implies that in order for Black women to be hired, they have to be better than White women and men. That is a fact. The reason we have not advanced is due to color.
>
> We wanted to know why Black women were not moving up the corporate structure and why their attrition rate was higher than other

groups. We were not adjusting; there were disparities among Black women. So we obtained data to show that there was a different standard used for Black women and other groups. Blacks were not progressing as readily as others. We now have in place an accountability program that addresses the kind of training given to Black women and how they are progressing. We are actually meeting with people at two or three levels up from where we are to discuss our progress in the company and what we really want.

We have within our company a Black Managers' Association. We have put into place accountability for assignments, training, and progression of that assignment for every Black woman within the research and development arms of the company. There are periodic meetings, enrichment programs, management training programs, and stress management for Black women.

This study was initiated after I joined the company in 1982. I was a charter member. We had to issue a letter to which we had to affix our signatures, putting our jobs on the line. Within the research and development arms, there were twenty-five of us and twelve of us originally signed the letter.

We put this program into effect last year. Now it has become a model, not just for developing Black women, but people. And it has been implemented throughout the company. And that is an enormous contribution. We've helped a number of Black women to be promoted. If a Black woman is going to move in this environment, the time is right to do that.

Despite some progress made by Black women in her company, Dira thinks the lack of upward mobility is also influenced by a comfort factor.

They don't ask Black women what kind of career they would like, and what kinds of support they need to develop their careers. This comfort factor was not in place with White males to think that a Black woman would want anything but a job at an entry level. With the new program we initiated, they are becoming sensitized, and hopefully, they can see the Black woman not as a liability, but as a help to them, and their careers will also progress.

Meanwhile, they are less likely to take you under their arm to be mentored and that's what you need. They have great people who work in this company. Anybody who works with this company can be a CEO. Whites were in the top 10 percent of their classes; Blacks were also in the top 10 percent of their classes. The people who succeed in this corporation are the ones who take an interest in certain people. White males tend to mentor White males, and they tend to act like them. In the 1970s, Black males also organized in this company and since it is consumer product oriented, the company cannot afford adverse publicity. Hence, it was a politically astute decision to advance Black males and reward Whites for mentoring them as well as White women, who are moving along with the women's movement. So all of these things have permitted everyone to advance, except Black women. Black men are more likely to have rapport with White men. They are more predominant in management positions than Black women. This company is conservative. Hence, if a Black man plays tennis with a White man, there is no question about that. If a Black woman does the same, the connotations are enormous for the Black woman. We need to create a corporate environment where Black women can be mentored without the other connotations attached.

One of the "other connotations attached" to the entry of Black women into this new egalitarian setting is the notion of White males' sexual attraction to the Black female because of her sexually unrestrained image. This was the reason why Teresa Johnson, whose interest is Black Women Studies, became so concerned about the plight of Black women. She remarked:

One of the things that was so amazing to me as a Black woman is the sense that somehow we are close to being whores. For this reason, I got interested in Black women. The ocean is important to me, so in college, I used to walk near the lake, and inevitably, I got these sexual calls from White men. I was sixteen years old, with pigtails. I can't remember the exact names I was called, but they were names that had to do with whores and sluts by White males. I was out there as a sexual creature in a way I knew young White girls were not. That was something I also felt consistently even when I was in graduate school in New York at Columbia. I would walk into a hotel to rest with my suit and the whole thing and would get that look. "Hey girl, what's you're doing?" It was perfectly clear I wasn't a prostitute. That happened then and it is still happening now. I went to a conference last year, and for the entire three days, there were White men who assumed I was a street walker or a call girl.

Whether the Black woman is in the professional or social arena, this image prevails. Dira Ridley, along with other professional Black women in her organization, is working to shatter this perception as well as others through organizing. In working with senior executives in organizations, she said, "we are hoping to make it profitable to mentor Black women." Dira Ridley would like to be a vice president in the company. She asserted, "For a Black woman to even think she can become a vice president of the company is clearly shooting for the moon. Not only has a Black woman just risen to the head of research in the company, but she is also the highest ranking Black woman. She is only one level above me. The vice president is at least four to five levels from me. My task in getting there is to convince a predominantly White male organization that a Black woman can do it."

In coping with racism, Ridley believes it is essential to have "internal personal goals and to work toward them." She said, "While you may not achieve them, continue to make strides, feeling happy as you move toward those goals. You check the small challenges off. The goal is the moon. You may never get to that goal, but you are satisfied that you are moving in that direction."

Contrary to experiences like Dira Ridley's is a perception that Black women have an advantage in the marketplace over White men, White women, and Black men. Cynthia Fuchs Epstein, in "The Positive Effects of the Multiple Negative: Explaining the Success of Black Professional Women," suggests that sex and racism can sometimes operate as an advantage if employers wish to hire a Black woman to fill the affirmative action goals of race and sex.[11] For most of the women I interviewed, this perception is merely an illusion. Aretha Shield articulated well the majority view, saying, "For every door that opens, ten doors close in my face."

"This double-minority status has worked against Black women like a double-edged sword," said Vanessa J. Gallman, an editor at the *Tallahassee* (Florida) *Democrat,* who wrote about this work myth in *Essence* magazine. "On the one hand, we face both racism and sexism in the job market, since most employers haven't given a second thought to affirmative action. On the other hand, our double status distorts what few gains we have made, leaving only stereotypes and misconceptions about what we can't change and what so many claim is an unfair advantage."[12]

The literature does not support the notion that it is an advantage to be a Black woman. Black women are still at the bottom rung on the economic ladder. They earn less than Black men, despite a pervasive sentiment that Black women are more readily hired and promoted than Black males.[13] There is a sense, as expressed by Veronica Pepper, a psychologist, that "Black women are less of a threat than Black men to White men, since women, in general, are given more latitude because they are not taken as seriously." This, too, can be a double-edged sword. A study of biracial groups concluded that Black women are perceived differently in the sexual role than White women and differently also in the racial role than Black men.[14] White society has "historically allowed more assertive behavior from Black women, because Black women are considered to be less dangerous."[15] Even though collectively they may be less of a threat to White men than Black men, the women interviewed believed that White men were personally threatened by them. "White men are most threatened by me," said Stephanie Tahara. "Therefore, I am reluctant to express myself fully. When I do that, I get chopped up. I have to mask my intellect and other being."

The entry of new recruits who are different from others in professional and social situations may pose a threat to those around them. Said Diane Earlinger, who is the only female, the only Black, and the youngest manager in an international agency, "I am different from others in my setting. It's not only unusual to be a Black, but also a woman pathologist. There is a level of discomfort when you are not an old White male. Old White males are accustomed to interacting with old White males. They are uncomfortable when you come from a different perspective. They don't know what your motivations are. There is no level of trust, irrespective of competence."

Whether the Black woman is less threatening to the White male than the Black male is merely one of many polemics in Black/White interactions. Perhaps Teresa Hale best summed up the feelings of many of the female Talented One Hundred when she noted that whether the contact between Black females and White males is on a professional or personal level, "racism and sexism can be so intertwined, one could be overwhelmed by critical analysis and fine distinctions. The task is so exhausting that I limit these relationships to the greatest possible extent."

This avoidance by Teresa Hale may be understandable given the historical reality of Black female/White male encounters in this country. I discovered, however, in the process of interviewing, that there is still another avoidance in Black/White dynamics. The Talented One Hundred females tended not to acknowledge the silent tension of racism underlying Black/White sisterhood. Perhaps it is because theirs is a fragile bond collectively, although individual Black women reported deep friendships with White women.

Black/White Sisterhood: The Fragile Bond

It was Sojourner Truth who challenged the myth of the weaker sex in 1851 at a women's rights gathering in Ohio. With her voice roaring like the mighty water of the ocean, she electrified the audience with the frequently quoted refrain, "Ain't I a woman?" noting:

> I have ploughed, and planted, and gathered into barns and no man could head me! And ain't I a woman? I could work as much and eat as much as a man—when I could get it—and bear the lash as well! And ain't I a woman? I have borne thirteen children and seen them most all sold off to slavery, and when I cried out with my mother's grief, none but Jesus heard me! And ain't I a woman?[16]

The echoes of her mid-nineteenth century refrain can still be heard by women of color in the twilight of the twentieth century. Sojourner Truth's words confronted not only sexism, but the racism and classism inherent in the earlier and the contemporary women's movements that have characterized the fragile bond of Black/White sisterhood.

Unlike contemporary Black women, Sojourner Truth and her nineteenth century Black sisters were pioneers in the struggle for racial and sexual equality. These women understood the confluence of race and sex.

The voices of contemporary Black women, however, have been largely silent. This impelled Bell Hooks, in *Ain't I a Woman?* to remind Black women that Sojourner Truth's refrain at the women's convention in Akron, Ohio, one hundred forty years ago is applicable today.

> At a time in American history when Black women in every area of the country might have joined together to demand social equality for women and a recognition of the impact of sexism on our status, we were by and large silent. Our silence was not merely a reaction against White women liberationists or a gesture of solidarity with Black male patriarchs. It was the silence of the oppressed—that profound silence engendered by resignation and acceptance of one's lot. Contemporary Black women could not join together to fight for women's rights because we did not see "womanhood" as an important aspect of our identity. Racist, sexist socialization had conditioned us to devalue our femaleness and to regard race as the only relevant label of identification. . . . We were asked to deny part of ourselves—and we did. Consequently, when the women's movement raised the issue of sexist oppression, we argued that sexism was insignificant in light of the harsher, more brutal reality of racism. We were afraid to acknowledge that sexism could be just as oppressive as racism.[17]

The few women of the Talented One Hundred who participated in the women's movement noted, like Bell Hooks, that they were met with "hostility and resentment from White women."[18] Listen to Stephanie Tahara, a county administrator in California, describe her experiences with a local chapter of the National Organization for Women.

> I was attending a N.O.W. meeting with a friend, and I noticed there was a coolness toward us. If it were a group of Black women, there would have been a sense of joy in joining in the fellowship. That warmth wasn't there with us. But they were more relaxed with one another. I sensed a wariness with us because we were two Blacks out of thirty. You got the sense they were asking, "Why are you here? We said this was a woman's group, but don't get crazy. We are not sure about you. Are you here to mess up something?" I do know there was a distance, and we weren't included in the sisterhood.

Hooks believes, "White women liberationists saw feminism as their movement and resisted any efforts by non-White women to critique, challenge, or change its direction."[19] Teresa Johnson's involvement with the women's movement lends credence to Hook's perception. Teresa, who is presently involved in Black women's groups, was at one time active in N.O.W. When I asked what happened, she sighed and said, "What a question!"

I worked hard to have good relationships with White women, and I think some I have managed to work well with. But often, it is difficult. I don't think they realize their sense of privilege as Whites. White women do not want to deal with our issues. Of course, they will deal with women like me who are academically successful, because there is a liberal feeling you ought to be included.

But I have to continually push the issue of Black women's concerns. I say to them, "If you are going to talk about the feminization of poverty, the people who are the poorest in this country are Black mothers." I take out the statistics and say, "If you want to do something, you have to start with this." There is a resistance among White women. Some don't understand the issues. Even when some try to understand, the terms they put it in indicate they are living in another world. Since I deal with Black women in my academic field, many White feminists would say I am not dealing with the issue of sexism. They view it as being diluted with race. We exist in categories. They are arguing who is pure.

I wrote a paper on where do I belong—Black Studies or Women Studies? I get the question from both sides—Black men and White women. You are supposed to exist solely in this category of fact. I've gone to many meetings where White women will say my race is not a central issue to the women's movement. The movement also assumes you exclude Black men. How can you not talk about Black men or men of color and not be concerned about them?* Some White women will say you are dealing with race. How can you not deal with race when Black men are viewed as sex objects in this society? "Isn't that sexist?" I asked them. Still they want to deal with that issue as only a category of race, so they can go ahead and deal with their own thing. We've had to do a lot of educating on that issue and around other political issues, like what is a woman's issue? Anti-apartheid is a woman's issue. Unemployment is a woman's issue. Are women of color being hired to the same extent as White women? For Black women involved in women's issues, we find ourselves educating on every front and it gets to be tiring. It suggests why Black women need one another. There are so few of us in positions where we can do that kind of educating. The problem of race and sex is so incredibly complicated. Until we straighten it out, it won't be a healthy country.

While the largely White middle-class women's movement in this country has conveniently used race to help define and clarify the problem of the movement, Jerrie Scott, a linguist whom I once interviewed about Black women and feminism, noted that the women's movement has not recognized "race in the solution of the problem, or recognized the contributions

---

*Clyde W. Franklin II notes a similar argument is made about men of color in predominantly White male groups. See Clyde Franklin II, *Men and Society* (Chicago: Nelson-Hall, 1988.).

of Black women to women's liberation." Stephanie Tahara concurred with Scott's analysis.

> In the early 1970s, I experimented in sisterhood and I could clearly see White women were as racist and threatened as anybody else. For example, the county commission on the status of women hired a director from South Africa, and now what does that tell you! She is still there. She has been protected and cared for by the power structure. The woman is exceedingly condescending. We were always at war with her. A friend of mine is on the commission, and she could see how they made decisions about women of color. She gleaned they despised them. If you bring up an issue from a racial perspective, they freak out. We were holding hearings on sexism and the media, and I decided I was going to testify. I talked about ethnic stereotypes in the media. It went beyond the sexism issues, and the White women were saying that I, along with other Blacks and Japanese, was being disruptive and negative. I pointed out that just the previous week on TV, I had seen only Asian whores, Black whores, or maids. I said, "Can you deal with that or not? If you can't deal with that, get out of my face." I should not get out of the arena; these White women should, because they are phonies. The White man does not pretend to be your friend; I know he is the oppressor. But here comes some person talking about sisterhood, and they don't have the slightest idea what it is about. They want to embrace me, saying we are in this together. No, stay away from me! The White man will say I know I am going to rip you off and you know it.

Black women achievers feel keenly this double sting of racism and sexism. Some of the females of the Talented One Hundred find it difficult to reconcile their common interests with White sisterhood because of racism. Said Marla Robinson, director of a state civil rights commission, "I have thought about joining N.O.W. I am concerned about environmental issues, nuclear issues, day care issues, and the comparable worth issue. I think it is important for Black women to be part of an organization doing that kind of thing. But right now, I can't hold their hands and sing the Sistersong."

Stephanie Tahara's experience with N.O.W. suggests that White women may not be interested in their Black sisters "holding their hands and singing the Sistersong."

> White women indiscriminately support each other. Their agenda says we don't care whether [you are] Republican or Democrat. I heard it from a N.O.W. political caucus. Although they indiscriminately support one another, they will not support Black women. And that's not vicious, just smart. They are saying the power needs to be contained within a certain group of women. Yet, I don't understand how they can support all

women. I don't suspend my intellect. I want to know what is a woman's position on important social issues.

I interviewed Lena Faulkner, a candidate for a major political office. She did not receive support from N.O.W., the League of Women Voters, or any of the major organizations headed by White women, although her agenda strongly supported women's issues.

Perhaps Bell Hooks' statement merits further investigation. She concludes in *Ain't I a Woman?* that Black feminists who participated in the movement found that sisterhood for most White women did not mean "surrendering allegiance to race, class, and sexual preference, to bond on the basis of shared political belief that a feminist revolution was necessary so that all people, especially women, could reclaim their rightful citizenship in the world." She asserts that the feminist ideology of White women was elitist and racist. While the ideology gave "lip service to revolutionary goals," it was "primarily concerned with gaining entrance into the capitalist patriarchal power structure."[20] Statistics confirm that White women are ahead of both Black females and males and other women of color in their race to the top of the workplace. For example, of the women corporate officers in Fortune One Thousand firms in 1986, 96.7 percent were White, 1.9 percent were Asians, 0.9 percent were Black, 0.5 percent, American Indian/Eskimo, and none were Hispanic.[21] It is in this arena that the reality of the White feminist ideology clashes with that of men and women of color. Since there are more White women than Black men and women in the United States, it is expected that they should move in greater numbers into positions of power. However, many Blacks believe this rapid mobility has been at their expense, since the affirmative action programs, used to advance racial minorities, have also included White women.

Numerous Blacks strongly disagree that White women should be considered as a minority. "The White man is going to hire the White woman as a minority. I dislike White women piggy-backing and moving up, and we don't have sense enough to do something. Nobody seems to be complaining about it. Since the Reagan era, there is an arrogance that you dare not question it. There is an attitude that I can do anything I please and you better stay in your place. I didn't see this attitude very much in the 1960s. It's what my mother and aunt experienced in the 1950s, but I certainly see it in the 1980s," said Marla Robinson, a forty-three-year-old administrator from the Midwest.

For many, race is seen as a greater barrier to overcome than sex. Edward W. Jones, Jr., who writes about Black managers in corporate America, said, "If the comfort level is a big factor in an invitation to enter the executive suite, it is understandable that White women will get there before Blacks. After all, the mothers, wives, and daughters of top officers are

White women, and they deal with White women all their lives—but only rarely with Black men and women. And they are likely to view White women as being more their own social class than Black men and women."[22]

Marla Robinson feels keenly the double sting of sexism and racism:

I feel if I were a White female, I would be further ahead careerwise and moneywise. There are no questions about that. I know it. I have looked at people who have started with me. Considering what I've done and what we each had to offer, they have advanced more rapidly than I. [How does it make you feel? I asked.] It makes me feel like shit. I have become so hostile. It's a new feeling for me. At each stage of life, you take on new battles. Your exposure is so different; you have more insights and your focus becomes less general and more specific. So at this point, I really have a lot of hostility toward White women.

Although Robinson was initially hesitant to discuss the tension between Black and White women, she was among the first of the Talented One Hundred women to openly and candidly talk to me about it. Therefore, when I interviewed Crystal Miller, a former director of the Women's Studies Resource Program at a major university, I was particularly interested in her experience. Miller left her position over four years ago, but her memories of her tenure are still vivid.

Black women were very much a majority. We were one of three centers who had a truly integrated staff. I won't say we dominated, but we were truly more than half. We also had one or two Chicanos and Asians from time to time. The staff would change frequently. I felt White women on my staff and those in the university who were not on my staff had the greatest trouble in accepting supervision from a Black woman. It was very difficult for them. They were not accustomed to it. They resisted any suggestions and corrections I made. One person just didn't do her best work. She tried to find another job, circumventing me and going to the administrator to whom I reported, hoping to discredit me. She bad mouthed the center, was not supportive, and made what we were doing look bad. I think we were doing exciting, wonderful things, and it became a major center in this region of the country.

There were always good and supportive faculty to work with, but there were others who had the "Miss Ann Syndrome," where some White women consciously or unconsciously expect a Black woman to serve [them]. In a professional sense, the person who serves becomes the staff person. If you are in a meeting you are expected to take minutes or follow through on all the nitty-gritty details. Since I was an administrator as well as faculty, they expected me to do that. It was indicated who was supposed to carry out details. They would say you are so able as an administrator. I may be wrong, but I equate that with the Black mammy servant that can always take care of everything. She can do it all. So let her do it. She is strong and able. She can take care of the kitchen and the children. This mammy role is transferred to the professional world. It is that kind of thing, and for that reason, that some people were really quite surprised and distressed when I left the position. Colleagues assumed, for some strange reason, that this was supposed to be my career, but I never saw it that way myself. My leaving to some was like losing a good servant. I am sure they didn't say that consciously. But I see them unconsciously feeling Mary Jane is leaving as if no one else will do the job well. I think that kind of attitude is exacerbated by the color line in this setting.

When Crystal Miller said the "mammy role is transferred to the professional world," it represents an amalgam of the past and present in the workplace, a painful reminder to Black women of the intertwining of classism and sexism in the United States as symbolized by the relationship between "Mary Jane" and "Miss Ann." Until recently, the majority of Black women in the United States worked as a "Mary Jane," the domestic, serving "Miss Ann" and her family. These memories are still fresh for the Talented One Hundred—no less than 36 percent had mothers who were employed as domestics or service workers, 24 percent and 12 percent, respectively.

Dorothy Bolden, founder and president of the National Domestic Workers' Union, senses, like Crystal Miller, that the symbols of "Miss Ann" and "Mary Jane" are deeply woven into the Black/White female socioemotional interactions, which are inextricably linked to the power struggle of class and race. Bolden, who started organizing Black domestics in Atlanta in the late sixties, said, "When I was invited to speak before several White women's groups, I heard more of 'I thought my maid was happy and pleased.' How could she be happy when she didn't have a good pair of shoes, when she had to wear men's pants, and when she had to take care of her children, too, on $25 or less a week!"

When the regional director of the women's bureau in Atlanta wanted to set a salary of $12.50 a day for domestic workers in 1969, Bolden organized the workers. Speaking before the director and an audience of domestics and their white employers, she led the protest, saying:

> Nobody can set a salary for me if I have to get on my knees to clean a bathroom and to wipe around the commode, inhaling the piss of her husband who missed the commode and having the piss to dry on the floor. When I put water on it, I refreshen it up and I have to clean it up with a rag. I don't think anyone can set my salary.

Whether professional or domestic, as Crystal Miller and Dorothy Bolden note, Black women may still be viewed as a strong, reliable source of cheap labor for the families of White women of privilege. Even when Black women and White women meet as equals in the professional arena, there is still a clash of race, class, and often culture, as Teresa Johnson pointed out:

> I have never thought of myself as someone who needs to be taken care of. Although sometimes I might think of myself as wanting to be cared for, I grew up with a sense of handling my own life. It doesn't have to be through a man. I think this is true for Black women here as well as the Caribbean. I think for many White women, this is not true. So I think there is a difference in the way they are coming at the gender question. They are trying to build up a life for themselves rather than through the accomplishment of men. I am not idealizing Black women as strong, but we deal with other kinds of problems. White women spend a lot of time dealing with a sense of self-identity.
>
> The irony of the situation is that in mixed women's groups so many of the White women are married to men who are professionals. And between the two, they are making a whole lot of money. Many Black women are not. We are single mothers, working for ourselves.

In 1987, Reynolds Farley, University of Michigan sociology professor, using data from the census bureau, found that only 30 percent of Black women between the ages of fifteen and forty-four were living with a husband, compared with 55 percent of White women in that age bracket. According to the study, Black women also delay marriage longer and are more likely to divorce than White women.[23]

Teresa Johnson sees Black women and White women as having different priorities. "When White women would say, 'Let's have a meeting,' I would say, 'I have to go home.' They can often set meetings at various times, because they have a maid to do their work. And we can't do that." When a Black woman can afford domestic help, like Diane Earlinger, she may be unable to obtain it. She reported that several Black domestics refused to work for another Black woman, even though she would pay more and would treat them better. This reflects an ingrained sense of inferiority toward themselves and other Black women. For some domestics, it is more prestigious to work for a White female.

Though race, class, and culture may collide in the workplace and the social arena, Black women, such as Crystal Miller, often feel a kinship with individual White females. However, collectively, this kinship is like that of a distant cousin. Remarked Miller, "I feel a kinship or sisterhood with some individuals, but not in general. Because of my experience at the women's center, I assume that kind of sisterhood has to be proven. Prior to holding that position and when I was younger, I was more willing to give people the benefit of the doubt. Now I don't always make those assumptions. I can't help but be more cautious than before."

There is still another reason why many Black females express wariness toward their White sisters. Their fragile bond of sisterhood has been further weakened by the complex and sensitive issue of sexual racism and interracial relations between Black males and White females and between Black females and White males. Here, the ambivalence, contradictions, myths, and stereotypes unfold on the racial stage, playing themselves out in complex scenes.

Black/White Sexual Relations

Since the 1967 U.S. Supreme Court ruling that struck down laws prohibiting interracial marriage, there has been an increase in these unions. Although interracial unions are still a very small percentage of all marriages, one can gauge this increase not only by statistics but also by the amount of attention given this topic in the popular literature, particularly Black periodicals like *Essence* and *Ebony*. Black men are more likely to participate in interracial unions than Black women. Seven out of ten of these unions involve Black men and women of other races, primarily White.[24] Many people believe that because Black men and White women have been historically denied access to one another, the attraction between them increased. This attraction is supposedly heightened by racist sexual myths—the myth of Black male supersexuality and the myth of the sexual purity of White females. This increase in relations between Black men and White women has exacerbated the tension between Black women and White women, between Black men and White men, and between Black men and Black women (particularly college-educated Black women).

According to the American Council on Education, the enrollment of Black men in U.S. colleges and universities declined by 34,000 between 1976 and 1986, the largest decline for any racial or ethnic group. The percentage of Black men, ages eighteen to twenty-four, in college, declined from 35.4 percent in 1976 to 27.8 percent in 1987.[25] This pattern has repercussions for the marriage potential of college-educated Black women, because the number of available Black males is further reduced.

Many Black women feel rejected by Black men who date or marry White women. For instance, when Leslie Glouster, a health administrator, attended the annual meeting of the National Medical Association, the Black medical organization, she and other members were invited to tour the homes of several prominent Black doctors in the city. She observed, "In every home we toured, we were greeted by a White woman [wife] at the door."

The sting of rejection Black women feel is heightened by the Black male's rationale for choosing a White mate. The White female is seen as more physically attractive, less domineering, and more intelligent and supportive. Many Black males have internalized negative images of Black women and have accepted these positive stereotypes of the White female.

Black women, on the other hand, have not generally dated or married outside their race until recently. Since the Black female has been viewed as a sexual object and in the slavery era was sexually abused and raped by White males, theirs is a history of negative familiarity. Hence, Black women have been reluctant to establish interracial relations. This pattern, however, is changing, according to the U.S. Bureau of the Census. In 1987, there were 56,000 Black women married to White men, 11,000 more than in 1980.[26] As more Black women enter the workplace as equals, they consider White males as partners. This pattern is motivated particularly by the shortage of Black males, though some women may also be attracted by the power of White males and the belief that White men treat them better. Despite the recent trend, Teresa Johnson thinks the Black female/White male relationship is more difficult than the Black male/White female, because "the Black woman carries the culture, and there is all that history of slavery that comes to mind."

Many Black males react strongly to this new trend, even when they approve of Black male/White female relations. They feel they are losing control over their women. Since the trend of Black female/White male egalitarian interaction is so recent, it is not clear how White females may react, or whether it will increase or decrease the tension between Black women and White women.

There are many motivations for interracial unions. While some are based on mutual attraction and respect for one another, others may be motivated by racist sexual myths. In an *Essence* magazine discussion of interracial relations between Black men and White women, one fifty-year-old college professor was quoted as saying,

> I grew up in Alabama where to look at a White woman could mean trouble. I always wanted to know what they were about. Then with the television telling you every day that they were the most desirable women in the world, I always wanted to own one. Now when I go home and my wife meets me at the door, or brings me something to eat, I feel that I am just as well off as any White man. I know it sounds a bit out of left field, but I am satisfied in America. I have what the White man says is the best there is.[27]

Still others might see, as Crystal Miller suggested, an advantage in interracial relations. Since a White mate does not experience discrimination, you don't have two people who have wounds to deal with. The impact of racism on a Black couple imposes a tremendous stress on their relationship.

While there is now a greater tolerance for interracial relationships in the society, there is still a strong resistance by Whites. And to many Blacks, like Jonathan Mobutu, it also poses a psychic dilemma; there is a higher comfort level dealing with one's own race. Others do not object to interracial relations as long as the couple is aware of its motives. "And that's where it is difficult," asserted Teresa Johnson. "Are they really seeing each other as individuals, or are they seeing each other through stereotypes? I think that is the problem."

Sexism in Black Male/Female Relations

In addition to sexism and racism encountered by Black women outside the home, they must also battle sexism on the homefront. Although historically the Black male/female relationship has been more egalitarian than that of Whites, Black males have been socialized to accept the patriarchal value of male dominance, even when they could not exercise it. Hence, Black females first experience sexism in the home or within the Black community.

Diane Earlinger's first encounter with sexism was in her home. In the mid-sixties, Diane, a gifted student, wanted to attend a medical school away from home. Her mother, a housewife and former home economics teacher before marriage, and her father, a civil engineer, decided that there were not sufficient funds to send both son and daughter away to school. It was more important for Diane's brother "to have that advantage." Diane felt sacrificed. "I was not angry at my parents, though I might react differently now. It was disappointing to me that I didn't go away to school. Clearly my level of achievement in high school was such that I had an opportunity to go to the best White Ivy League schools," lamented Diane. Even though she was a talented student, she could not apply to the National Medical Association, a Black organization, because fellowships were awarded only to Black men. Despite the fact that Diane successfully completed a high school that prepared students for professional careers, when she asked for literature on medicine, she said, "the counselor gave me a carton full of literature on nursing. When I graduated from medical school, I sent him an invitation, along with a picture, and he came. He said he was glad I had not listened to him." (The counselor was White.)

Like Diane Earlinger, Laura Price, also a gifted student, first felt the sting of sexism in the home. When Laura expressed interest in attending medical school in the early 1960s, her mother, a director of Christian education at a Baptist church, supported her aspirations. But her father, a minister, did not. Remarked Laura:

The sons were the ones you pushed, and the daughters were to be sweet and pretty and to finish high school and that's all they had to do. If they went to college, they were to teach school and work in the church. He was very enthusiastic about getting my brother into medical school, but didn't do the same kinds of things to get me in. When I got in, he was very surprised. Yet, he didn't deny me my tuition, books, or anything I needed. However, he would have been very happy if I had done a little less. It was my mother who emphasized if you have the ability, you can do anything. If you want to specialize after medical school, you can. On the other hand, my father said, "It's okay if you want to go to medical school and that's a little unusual to start with, but you don't have to specialize."

Unlike Diane Earlinger and Laura Price, who grew up in middle-class families, Laverne Townson, a forty-three-year-old bank manager who lives in Africa, came from a working-class background. Her father, a clay-mine worker, did not encourage her to attend college. But her mother, a domestic, gave greater encouragement to Laverne to attend college than her sons. She wanted her daughter to be independent in case her husband "turned out to be no account." For Black women growing up in the South before the Civil Rights movement, the only alternative to domestic or service work was to teach. Hence, daughters were often encouraged to attend college more than sons. Being a teacher as opposed to being a domestic would protect them from sexual harassment of White males.

In general, Black women attended college in greater numbers than Black men prior to the Civil Rights movement. Since 1976, Black male enrollment has dropped by 7 percent, while Black female enrollment has increased. This pattern is not only likely to exacerbate the existing tension between the sexes, but, more importantly, it will have an impact on the gender competition in the marketplace.[28]

The examples of Diane Earlinger, Laura Price, and Laverne Townson illustrate the sexist attitudes within the family. As women move outside the home and into the workplace, sexist attitudes and behaviors continue to prevail. They are particularly pronounced with successful women who have moved into the traditional male purview. A good example is Yvonne Walker-Taylor, the first woman president of Wilberforce University, a small African Methodist Episcopal institution in Ohio and one of the oldest Black universities in the United States. When she sat under her doorsteps as a five-year-old, trying to kiss her elbow and turn into a boy, Walker-Taylor may have sensed the beginning of a long journey—her "Struggle Against All Odds."

As president, the outspoken and energetic Walker-Taylor has waged many battles with the bishop of her district, who is the chairman of the board and quite influential in the operation of the university. When I interviewed Walker-Taylor in her Wilberforce office prior to her retirement in January 1988, she spoke candidly about her presidency.

> The bishop is so against me. He came into this district the first board meeting to get rid of me. That's a known fact. This man has a reputation of not wanting women in high places. He does not want to ordain women. It's a part of his pattern. He came in and told me, sitting right here in this office, that the only reason I was president of Wilberforce University was because my father was the president, and they wanted to give that honor to his daughter. He said, "I was against it, but I went along with it. So I made up my mind that when they assigned me to this district, you were going to have to go." I said, "So it took you three-and-a-half years to do it, didn't it?"
>
> Even though the bishop was talking to me this way, I would say, "Oh, bishop, I am so sorry to hear you say that. It really breaks my heart because of my father, who died in 1955. I wonder what he would think of you. You said you knew him and respected him." [Her voice trailed off.] I said, "Bishop, you have a daughter or don't you care about any woman at all? Bishop, I am going to fight you as long as I can, because I plan to remain president until 1988." [Laughed and lowered her voice.] He said, "No," and I said, "Yes." But there was never one time he could say I didn't respect him. I said, "I respect your position. My father was a bishop. I respect all bishops. But I do not respect your ideology. I will never embarrass you, but don't press me too hard because I have the ear of the church and you know that, sir."
>
> "Yes," he said, "some of my colleagues have been after me about me being on you." I said, "They see the unfairness of what you are doing. But my father taught me to love my enemies. So I rather translate that into respect, because I could never love you. Love means more, and I could never give you that. When you and I meet publicly, we will put up our little fronts, and to me that is a bit of hypocrisy, but in our church, it is necessary. And it will make me a bigger person, because everyone knows what you are doing. The fact that I can smile and you can hug me in public and kiss me on the cheek with your Judas kiss does a great deal for me in the eyes of the church." I said, "Sir, I may someday be elected to the Judicial Council, and I may see you down the line. One never knows." We parted and he went and announced my retirement. [At the General Conference of the A.M.E. Church held in Fort Worth, Texas, in July 1988, Walker-Taylor became the first woman elected to the Judicial Council, the highest judiciary body of the A.M.E. Church. The nine-member council is an appellate court elected by the General Conference.]
>
> How I hung on those three-and-a-half years is just the way I am telling it. Every board meeting he would try to get a search committee to look for a president. I would "sir" him to death and ask on what grounds. Fortunately, the board of trustees thought I was doing a magnificent job. He was the only one, except there was another person who supported him. And he was a chauvinistic guy who graduated from Wilberforce in

1932 and should have been off the board a long time ago. He stayed on my case like the bishop. But I am smarter than the bishop. I know I am. He does not know anything about the operation of the school, but I never threw it up in his face. I let him stumble into mistakes, and I'd say, "Sir, if you did this, it might straighten it out." He would do it and things would smooth out. And he'd say that worked, so I would get through that board meeting. But I would always provide a little snag, and he would have to come to me to find out what you have to do about it.

As a Black woman, you have to be better then everybody. You have to stay way ahead, and you have to have enthusiasm for life. You can't keep me down long. Oh, Lord, yes! That bishop would call me sometimes and my secretary would come in and I was sitting here like I was under the desk. I could be so low. It doesn't last long. I snap right out of it. It is faith in the fact that my destiny is in the hands of the Lord and no man can stop me from that which is to be mine. I should have been president a long time ago, but each step of the way I got slapped down.

"I am tired and worn out with the fight. I am seventy-one years old." Her youthful looks belie her age. "I took on this job when most people had retired." Looking at her watch, she remarked, "The average person would be packing to go to New York and I am sitting here talking with you." Walker-Taylor had a speaking engagement that same day in New York. She described herself as having boundless energy.

For Laura Price, like Walker-Taylor, sexism did not stop at her father's doorstep; it followed her into the medical profession. Although she owns her medical building and her patients are women, she still must interact with male colleagues. As the only woman officer of her local Black Medical Association, she found that it was necessary to remind her male colleagues that women are qualified to serve as officers in the organization. Said Laura, "Where are the women being nominated for these committees? We've had rapid growth of Black female doctors in this city. So it is past time for a woman to hold an office. They have us on committees, but they didn't have us holding office. They are aware now when nominations come through that it would be a good idea to put a woman's name on it. If I am on the committee or out in the audience, I will say, 'Where are the women?'"

Teresa Johnson, the first woman appointed to the Afro-American Studies department at her university, could repeat Laura's refrain, Where are the women? "I was the only woman for a very long time. I was practically invisible to the men. When I was coming up for tenure, they didn't even know it, because I was not taken seriously. I was not that important in the realm of things."

Though she was ignored, her presence was not totally invisible. When Johnson was appointed to her faculty position in Afro-American Studies, she received anonymous hate mail in her campus mailbox from Black men, claiming she was taking away their jobs. Reflecting upon the men's attitude, Teresa pointed out that "Black women were involved in the Civil Rights struggle; however, there is a division when it comes to jobs and positions. There is less emphasis on togetherness. I felt isolated and disappointed in our men."

While Teresa Johnson faced harassment from Black men about taking jobs away from them, Diane Earlinger encountered sexual harassment. Diane once served as a faculty member at a Black medical school but left because the environment was not nurturing and was overtly sexist. Diane was propositioned to have sex, even though she was married to a physician. "I never encountered that among my White colleagues. So I reacted with a great deal of haughtiness and arrogance. There were consequences. I was not promoted. It was a ghastly experience. I am not generalizing about the experience. But I hear Black women in similar environments tell the same story. I had only one experience, but I prefer not to think that it is typical," said Diane.

Too often, sexual harassment is a reality, especially where successful Black women are socially isolated from supportive networks of other women. Jonathan Mobutu observed that in higher education, "Black males tend to be called on to support both Black males and females, because of the nature of sexism and division of social walls which makes Black men more available. Black women have families and more responsibilities of child rearing and cannot be as flexible. . . . So I wound up having to spend a lot of time supporting Black women. I prefer to see them use a Black woman as a role model. I find that to be a difficult type of role. Some Black males might use the needs of Black women to exploit them," noted Mobutu.

The dimensions of sexual politics are endless. When women leave the workplace, sexism again follows them back to their doorsteps. Bebe Moore Campbell, in *Successful Women, Angry Men*,[29] shows that the power struggle continues in the two-career marriage. While many men give lip service to equality of the sexes, their behavior suggests they have not been fully liberated. In addition to their careers, women continue to perform the traditional household tasks and to assume more responsibility for child rearing. For women, there is an ongoing tension between career aspirations and familial duties. And Black women are doing a double balancing act, walking both the racial and sexual tightrope.

When Teresa Johnson was married and had a small child, life was difficult. Said Teresa:

> Having a child and being a faculty person, most men can't understand that at certain times, you have to go home. You got a baby to pick up.

There is very little consideration of being a mother. I told my male colleagues [when her child was a baby] that you have a wife. While you have
somebody to pick up [your child], I am expected to do that. The men
wanted you to give all to the job. It didn't have to be that way. It could
have been arranged otherwise. Men have privileges because they have
wives.

Diane Earlinger agreed that balancing career and family duties poses
overload dilemmas. "As a woman, you really don't have the luxury to say
at some appropriate point and time that you can take a hiatus from your
career. This usually means no coming back, because it is assumed that you
are not serious about your career. So at certain periods of time, it meant
not doing certain things well either professionally or personally. The personal obligations of women are very different from men."

Single women do not escape sex role stereotyping. They also have to
deal with the attitudes of their partners toward their careers. They have to
prioritize, deciding whether their career goals or their relationships are
more important. Teresa Johnson, forty-three years old, finds younger men
and women are more accepting, personally and professionally, of parity.
But she senses from men her own age a message about her career which
indicates, said Teresa, "I am not really real. I am just putting on. I am
trying to be an ambitious, successful woman—the big Black woman. I am
not really involved in what I am doing. I am just trying to be secure."

Whether the Black woman achiever is single or married, her race and
sex interface in perplexing ways, contributing to confusion, contradictions,
and dilemmas of status. Since she occupies a marginal position in society,
chances for isolation are increased.[30] For the Black woman elite, class, culture, race, or sex may stand between her two worlds. Consequently, she
finds herself on the edges of both, often operating without an anchor,
which contributes to her social isolation. There is, said Diane Earlinger, "a
lack of nurturing of Black women."

There are fewer support systems. Very often, you find other Black women
are antagonistic, and in some ways envious and jealous because you've
accomplished things they may have wanted to, but haven't. Seemingly
there is no desire to be supportive of people who have made it. There are
no exchanges of services like car pooling.

I've become very isolated in many ways and have generally tried not
to depend on other people to be supportive. And that's when you go into
the superhuman role for women who are not given any relief on the domestic side, and who have taken on the professional obligations and responsibilities as well. One becomes very lonely and isolated, and at some
point, I miss the social interaction I would like to have with other Black
women.

Diane also feels isolated from the women of her profession, because of the low percentage of women in the field of pathology and the kind of institution in which she is employed. An attempt was once made to establish an organization of Black women physicians. She was actively involved, but it fizzled. Said Diane, "The young, unmarried women were different from the older married ones. One of the first activities was a lingerie party to which lots of single men were invited. It was difficult to relate to something like that, and I considered it inappropriate under any circumstances. I was on the planning committee to develop a charter and purpose, not to plan a lingerie party." She has made several attempts to participate in women's organizations, but has found them unsatisfactory because of petty jealousy.

Similarly, Yvonne Walker-Taylor has not found support from other women. She thinks "women are jealous and they dislike for the sake of disliking. When women get in high places, they don't pull one another up. . . . My preaching is you reach down and bring somebody up. I wanted another woman to take my place when I leave the presidency," remarked Walker-Taylor.

Marla Robinson's experience has been different from that of Yvonne Walker-Taylor and Diane Earlinger. Although she lost friends as she moved up the career ladder, she remarked, "I am finding more beautiful Black women who are appreciative of me as a person and proud of me. I don't know if it's because we have matured or because we believe that if we don't support one another, no one else will."

Perhaps Black males and females are both beginning to understand that their destinies are linked. Recently, Teresa Johnson observed signs of change in her Afro-American Studies department. "There is much more information and knowledge, and it has gotten better. It hasn't happened easily. But there is more of an awareness to have both points of view in the department. I sense there is a change. What the power structure has set up, we should not necessarily be imitating. Since there are so few Black faculty, we need one another," said Teresa.

If Black men and women do not recognize they "need one another," they have failed to understand how they are inextricably linked in the struggle against oppression. Moreover, this sexual politic saps energy from the racial struggle, thus creating social isolation and additional stresses. In struggling alone, the Black woman is often victimized by her own strengths. Said Jerrie Scott, a linguist, "The woman is burdened down and feels she must save the world, save the children, save the Black man, save the White man and woman, save everyone except herself."

Historically, the Black woman has been in a peculiar position in this society. While she has generally accepted the dominant patriarchal values of this society, there are conflicts when she attempts to live up to the expectations of the Black male and the larger society. Similarly, Black males, having also accepted the dominant patriarchal values, find they, too, are caught in a double bind. In trying to meet the expectations of society and the Black female, they also get confusing and mixed messages and may be unable to live up to these demands. For both males and females, this dilemma creates conflicts in life expectations, which result in tension between them. This energy could more effectively be directed toward support for one another and not toward support of traditional values. There is a need to redefine the traditional dominant patriarchal values, so males and females can be a resource for one another. Increasingly, seminars on Black male-female relations have begun to address these issues. Black male research institutes are also emerging, like those at Albany State College and Morehouse College, which examine the present and future status of Black men. This growing awareness should reduce tension between the sexes, creating a more supportive environment in predominantly Black, mixed, or White settings.

In the next chapter, we will look at how Black men and women cope with oppression and social isolation in this society.

SEVEN

Styles of Coping

> . . . Out of the huts of history's shame
> I rise
> Up from a past that's rooted in pain
> I rise
> I'm a black ocean, leaping and wide,
> Welling and swelling I bear in the tide.
>   Leaving behind nights of terror and fear
> I rise
> Into a daybreak that's wondrously clear
> I rise
> Bringing the gifts that my ancestors gave,
> I am the dream and the hope of the slave.
> I rise
> I rise
> I rise.
> —*Maya Angelou*

Racial discrimination is a major stressor in the lives of the Talented One Hundred. Faced with an ongoing onslaught of oppression, what makes them rise? Do they still hear the voices of their parents reminding them, "You got to be somebody?" "You have to get an education." "Remember, a little learning is a dangerous thing; you must continue to learn." "If you acquire knowledge, no Whites can take it from you." "The fight today is with the mind and not the body."

The Talented One Hundred continue to achieve their goals, climbing mountains as academicians, as corporate executives, and as entrepreneurs. They maintain a steady pace by holding on to external and internal support systems in the face of adversities.

Bruce P. Dohrenwend and Barbara S. Dohrenwend, social scientists, have hypothesized that upwardly mobile individuals are more likely to have "achievement-related stress—events that exert pressure on the individual to change his customary activities to a new set of higher status activities," for example, entering a high status occupation. Lower status individuals are more likely to have "security-related stress—events that exert pressure on the individual to change his customary activities to a new set of lower status activity," for example, losing a job.[1] The stressor is the source or cause of strain, while stress is its effect.

Dohrenwend and Dohrenwend's idea of stress is relevant to upwardly mobile Blacks. Since there are achievement-related stresses that are caused by the social isolation of Blacks in pursuit of their goals, what is the price of their success?

Social isolation of upwardly mobile Blacks can lead to internal stress, which often manifests itself in physiological disorders, for example, hypertension and/or behavioral disorders, even suicide. In his research on suicide, sociologist Robert Davis notes that suicide has increased significantly for young Black males between the ages of twenty to thirty-four,[2] the category that is characteristic of the talented and highly educated. Robert Staples, sociologist and author of *Black Masculinity*, maintains that "for the Black college student or graduate, the cause of suicide may be related to the high expectations he has for success and the frustrations encountered in overcoming the persistent barriers against reaching his potential that result from racism."[3] Other studies have reported similar stress patterns, as manifested in alcohol abuse and health problems, among Black men.[4]

Though stress is a major factor in the lives of the Talented One Hundred, initially they did not report that it had any effect on their health. Males consistently rated their health as excellent or good, despite specific physiological disorders. Only after extensive probing was I able to obtain the following account of Ferdinand Hamilton's health. Said Hamilton, who is in his sixties, "I feel good, but my health is probably marginal. I've had five major operations in the last five years. I had a ruptured esophagus which poisoned my body. I had two major operations within two weeks. I had a pecan shell lodged in my throat. I had three ribs removed. I had problems with my arteries, and I had a six-way bypass on my heart. But I still walk seven miles a day."

Males were more reluctant to disclose health problems than females. However, both men and women tended to deemphasize negative health problems. (Their reaction is in sharp contrast to that of welfare recipients, who are more likely to highlight any health concerns, even minor ones.)[5]

Despite economic backgrounds, racism is a major stressor in the lives of Blacks and affects their health status. When racism is interwoven with sexism, there is an additional stress factor for Black women.[6] One can only speculate whether the stress resulting from social isolation led to the emotional collapse of Sheba, my brilliant friend, or to the suicide of Leanita McClain, a talented young journalist. An article entitled, "To Be Black, Gifted, and Alone," by Bebe Moore Campbell, is based on recollections about Leanita McClain, the first Black to become a member of the *Chicago Tribune's* editorial board, thirty-two years old and winner of several top awards in journalism, and interviews with Black women corporate executives. Before committing suicide, McClain wrote of her social isolation: "I have fulfilled the entry requirement of American middle class, yet I am left, at times, feeling unwelcomed and stereotyped.[7]

The way Campbell summed up the plight of executive Black women validates the sentiments of the Talented One Hundred, particularly the women. "Corporate racism, they expected. What was unexpected was the various degrees of culture shock, isolation, and alienation that Black women experience as they attempt to acclimate professionally and to assimilate their culturally distinct selves into organizations that reward uniformity."[8]

Individuals react differently to the negative stressful emotional impact of racism and the resulting social isolation. Some are proactive, others are reactive. Those persons who are proactive incorporate racism as a major impediment in their lives, but they accept some responsibility for overcoming it. On the other hand, persons who are reactive blame themselves for the negative emotional stress emanating from race or else they blame the system. At one extreme of the continuum, individuals who fail to incorporate racism as a factor in their lives are more likely to internalize negative stress and engage in self-blame. For example, if an individual who is competent fails to receive a promotion, that person is likely to blame him- or herself instead of the discriminatory system. At the other extreme of the continuum are individuals who not only incorporate racism as the overriding factor in their lives, but view it as the sole cause of any negative stress. Hence, they are more likely to engage in system-blame. To accept total self-blame or to attribute total system-blame for the stressor of race can lead to reactivity.

Roscoe Champion cautions us "to be realistic about the nature of the society we live in," noting:

> Race is a factor in America. Sometimes it is obvious, sometimes not. Don't become so sensitive to it that you'll have a chip on your shoulder and you'll allow your anger and bitterness to sway your judgment. You have to confront it—sometimes head on—and sometimes you circumvent it. The situation dictates the strategy. But don't let it turn you into a bitter person where you'll use racism as a crutch for your failures in society.
>
> The main thing for a Black man or woman not to do while growing up in this society is become so sensitive they allow the problem to control

them. I see people get bitter—outstanding, brilliant Black people. When they start to allow race to eat at them to the extent they see race in everything, they start faulting White people for everything, even when they have control over some things. Any Black man's failures are justified in terms of race. They get so bitter, claiming that all White people are no good. A Black moderate is an Uncle Tom. It eats away at them. They lose their perspectives and their personalities change. They grew up in this society, and they know racism is out there. So why let it take hold of you and destroy you or neutralize you. Then no one respects you. They start talking crazy. For instance, if you make a decision from the bench, they'll say, "White people got to him." Those people are unrealistic.

The overwhelming majority of the Talented One Hundred, like Roscoe Champion, successfully manage their stressful emotions by becoming actors in the situation rather than being acted upon—defining the situation rather than being defined by it. Growing up in the South was enough for Vernon Jordan, a lawyer and former executive director of the National Urban League, to act against racism and the anger and pain caused by it. "My victimization by the process of desegregation was sufficient incentive to act." When Jordan was struck down in Fort Wayne, Indiana, by a racist assassination attempt, it did not embitter him. Recalled Jordan.

> I spent ninety-eight days in the hospital. It took me out of commission for ninety-eight days, but it didn't affect my life otherwise. I am not one to carry around anger and resentment, because I think they are negative. Therefore, you put whatever effort behind you and move forward. I don't think you should get angry. You should get even. I don't think you can outwit the opposition by being angry at the opposition. I think you have to outwit the opposition by being smarter than the opposition.

Blacks overwhelmed by anger frequently become cynical, which can lead to a passive world view. "The problem with cynicism is that it is as debilitating as naivete," claimed Warner Babbitt.

> If you constantly look at the limits of proscriptions, the tendency is to behave within those parameters. If you choose instead to look at the possibilities, however impossible, the possibilities may become realistic. You'll find a way of getting around those limits. I choose for my basic sanity to do the latter and build around limits.

The Talented One Hundred have chosen "to build around limits" of racism. They exhibit a high level of self-efficacy. Albert Bandura, a psychologist, has described this concept as the ability of people to "produce and regulate events in their lives."[9] The Talented One Hundred indicated they have a high degree of control over their lives; the more objectively successful the individual, the higher the sense of self-efficacy. (In contrast, welfare recipients have a more passive world view, a sense of inefficacy.[10])

Unlike individuals who have a low degree of self-efficacy, which can lead them to place the onus of responsibility for their failures on the system or on themselves, individuals with a high sense of self-efficacy are likely to see self-responsibility and system-responsibility as interfacing. While acknowledging that a racist system contributes to constraining opportunities and producing negative stress, they incorporate both self- and system-responsibility for overcoming barriers to opportunities.

Michael Lomax eloquently articulated the need to acknowledge both self-responsibility and system-responsibility as dimensions in coping effectively with racism.

> I've begun to understand more strongly that as a people, we have internalized the negative images Whites have about us to the extent that we have low self-esteem. And that low self-esteem affects behavior. If you don't think well of yourself because you are Black, that can affect your academic performance, job performance, and personal relationships. I think it has affected me. The more I come to understand that it is not just the White man with his foot on my neck but my internalizing some of the negatives about myself as a Black that has really liberated me from that chain psychologically. I've been able to deal more forthrightly with myself and the areas in which I want to compete. I've been able to deal forthrightly with Black and White people. I think a lot of Black people have not recognized there are two sets of change—the external and internal change.
>
> We need to recognize that we have to fight a battle on more than one front of racism. We need to recognize that a lot of our problems are internal to us and to the group, and we should focus on that. Too often we say, "It is 'The Man.'" What we don't see is our adaptations of negative values, and we got to confront ourselves. I have a hard time blaming teenage pregnancy and drug abuse on "The Man." Certainly racism is involved, but there are individual and social issues which must have a dimension to the solution which says the problem is inside ourselves.

In accord with Lomax, Robert Woodson claimed:

> A lot of our leadership is misleading our people into believing that because racism exists, ending racism has to be a precondition of our achievement. And therefore there is little you can do, because White people are responsible, and unless racism ends, we don't have any responsibility for ourselves. That is a destructive message that is being communicated to our young people. I think that needs to be challenged. The victimizer might have knocked you down, but it is the victim's responsibility to get up. It's not White people's responsibility to see that I get up; it's my

responsibility. These experiences of racism have made me tough and given me drive.

Woodson, fifty years old, developed this race lesson and drive for self-improvement while serving as a young man in the armed forces.

> After two years of running to bars and running around while in the army, I stopped and said, "I'm not going to be like a lot of Black people who say White people got their foot on my neck. The way not to become a part of that is to prepare yourself." I turned some of that energy and anger into achievement. I had more training than all the Whites in my squadron in missile science and technology. So they had to rely on me even though they outranked me, because I was the only one who knew how to run the dials. I learned from this experience that the way you get control and influence is through achieving.

Woodson adds that racism is inevitable, so we should expect it and incorporate it into our strategy for coping. "The race thing is less important than some of the class questions. Racism is a given. I expect White people to act like White people. When I go to a corporation, I see the whole workplace is White. I just expect it."

Personal Coping Styles on the Job

Since "racism is a given," the Talented One Hundred have developed a variety of personal and collective styles of managing the stressors of race as well as class, and sex, both on and off the job.

These styles include: being a race ambassador; being professionally competent and working hard; having self-knowledge; assessing the environment; being unpredictable; gaining knowledge for personal and social action; prioritizing battles; creating options; burning and building bridges; and using biculturality as a weapon against racism.

Being a Race Ambassador

Rosabeth M. Kanter examined the stressors experienced by "tokens" in *Men and Women of the Corporation*. She indicated that individuals identified as being categorically different are singled out as representatives of their category, as symbols rather than individuals.[11] Black professionals are mindful, whether at the conscious or subconscious level, of the implications of tokenism and have incorporated this race lesson into their coping modes. Jonathan Mobutu said that his "basic strategy for dealing with racism is knowing, as Langston Hughes [a Black poet] suggests, 'You are always an ambassador for your race.' I know whenever I am involved in something, the presupposition is going to be I am there as a token because I am Black." Therefore, Mobutu has to be better informed and better prepared than his White colleagues to receive some semblance of respect.

Inherent in being a race ambassador is the underlying assumption that Blacks have to be better than Whites to succeed in this society. Hence, the Black elite cope by being professionally competent and working hard.

Being Competent and Working Hard

"There is no substitute for being the best. There is no situation that is ideal, but you learn how to make the best of it. I was taught to get things done and do things right," said John Daniels, a corporate executive. His grandfather taught him this lesson early as an effective way to cope with racism. "I picked up from my grandfather that you should be as smart as possible, get as many tools or collect as many weapons [as you can] to help you to deal with racism."

Being better prepared than others helps Graham Boston, a renowned engineer/scientist, to reduce the risk of failure. "I don't like to take risks. Therefore, when I want something, I work hard at being better than anyone else, and that reduces the risk and gives me the opportunity to get what I want." Kelly Smith, a corporate executive, believes that "it is important to do the best you can at all times, because you never know who is watching you. This is an adaptive pattern, being the best and being persistent." After being denied a promotion by an immediate supervisor, it was a White CEO who noted Kelly's competence and recommended her to a higher position in the international corporation where she works.

Thomas B. Thomas's field is sales and marketing. To be successful, he acknowledged, "I have to be good at what I do. It requires preparation in this business as any other business. I stay up and study." Thomas's parents got him started early in a winning mode. He recalled:

My father was very athletic; and being athletic, you had to win if you were going to be recognized as the best. As a result, this attitude carried over to everything. My mother had the same kind of attitude, but she directed it toward education. Nobody was supposed to read better than you or write better than you, because you recognized the problem you would have coming home with less than your best on your report card. So you take the two attitudes of my parents and put them together, and they mesh in the competitive attitude which says whatever you put in front of me, I'll take care of it.

My father also told me that in sports you don't have any friends, because the guy across from you will knock you down if you let him. The same thing applies to business. I don't have any friends. I am only going to get where I am going by being the best. If I were to walk into any of my clients' locations, sit down and talk to them and not have the information already consumed in my brain and ready to give it back out to them, they would not talk to me. Even when I know more about their business than they do, they will turn around and give the business to one of their friends. I am not going to be their friend. We have zero in common. I don't go to church with them. The only reason they'll sit down and talk with me is because they know I am bringing something to the table. If they listen to me, they'll probably gain from that. That gives me the forum to do my song and dance. If I get that opportunity, I'll get the business, because no one else is going to be that prepared, that knowledgeable, and that ready to serve their clients.

While competence, commitment, perseverance, and hard work are effective coping strategies, many Black elite revel in the competition with Whites or with themselves to prove their capabilities. Said Jeremiah Moses, "When I walk into the room and see White people, I know I am superior. I know how to handle myself and don't have to worry about it. I have built myself up. Instead of having an inferiority complex, I have a superiority complex, because I can do it better. I like to match wits with them in whatever I do."

Earnest Ross "likes to match wits" with Whites, too, but unlike Jeremiah Moses, he carefully sizes up his opposition.

If I am next to you and you are next to me, the race is on. It has colored my whole career. I compete against those I know I can [beat]. You compete for something based on knowledge. If I sense a person's knowledge level is greater than mine, I would not compete. I have been able to get what I want by competing in this way.

For others, the process of professional competence becomes an endurance test to prove one's skills and intelligence against the most difficult odds. Dira Ridley feels, "It becomes a true test of putting my skills—intellectually and personally—to move up in that society. Now, I want to know how I stack up against the toughest odds imposed on an individual. That isn't to say I would move up quicker in a Black environment. I want to test my skills with those who have the power." Claude Kent is challenged to prove his professional competence when others define his limitations. "When someone tells me I can't do something, I show them I can. So discrimination makes me only more determined to be successful."

Thirty-four-year-old Walden House, who has a Ph.D. in biology and received all his educational training in a predominantly Black setting and who has always lived in a Black community, would "like to test his skills against Whites." House is not unlike Clifford Warren, who trained at a predominantly Black medical school in the 1950s and who received his earlier education in Black schools. Warren also wanted to test his knowledge and skills in the White world because of his lingering doubts about his competence: "I just wanted to test my knowledge as a physician in an all-White medical school. How did I know they weren't teaching me better medicine than at Meharry? I didn't know it as a young person, but I know now that I would have gotten a better education at a Black institution." When he performed better than his White colleagues as an intern in an all-White hospital, he was reassured of his Black education. Competing successfully against "the toughest odds" provides individuals with a sense of competence and self-efficacy. That competence is related to self-knowledge.

Having Self-Knowledge

Having knowledge of oneself is to assess realistically the strengths and limitations of one's ability to achieve goals. Yvonne Walker-Taylor's father advised her, "Never underestimate yourself and never overestimate yourself." She feels there are ways to judge that. "You should be able to evaluate yourself. If you are a big healthy girl, you are not going to be a ballet dancer. If you are not good in mathematics, you are not going to be an engineer. I've been poor in mathematics [laughs] so I never aspired to become a mathematician. But the things you are good at, know that you are good at them and do them well."

Graham Boston accepts challenges only when he feels he will be "good at them" and "will do them well." He remarked, "I tend to be cautious about the challenges I accept. I try to do things I think I can make happen. I am not a big risk taker. I am a slight risk taker. Now, what I do is work hard and plan it out and get in good shape, so when I start the task, I'll have the feeling I am going to make it."

Self-assessment of one's skills has a major impact on the ability to influence others. It is important, therefore, to understand the strengths and weaknesses of leadership styles which affect success. Are you primarily an entrepreneur, a manager, or a team player? Are you an expressive leader (inspire and motivate others) or an instrumental leader (task oriented)? Are you a brilliant creator, financier, motivator, organizer, or promoter?

Benson Robinson, a successful entrepreneur, attributed his success to the way he manages his employees, who are motivated to produce. "My management style has a lot to do with success. I make a point to say, 'Nobody works *for* me; everybody works *with* me.'" Benson, like countless others, also stresses that it is important to like what you are doing. His effective leadership style is *product-oriented* and *people-oriented*. Joshua Smith, also an entrepreneur, agreed that this is an effective management strategy. It is his reason for allowing employees to own about 25 percent of his company's stock. As stockholders, they will have a vested interest in the company's success.

Like Benson, Joshua is not only an entrepreneur but also a good manager. Still, he likes to surround himself with people who can challenge him. "It is a part of being able to accept one's strengths and weaknesses." Both of these men have a hiring policy that is more *merit-oriented* than *patronage-oriented*.

If one lives in an oppressive society, it is particularly essential to have knowledge of one's assets and limitations. Therefore, Commissioner Michael Lomax copes with the limitations emanating from oppression by being a political change agent. "I've come to understand where my strengths and deficiencies are and where my racial identity affects that and where it doesn't," remarked Lomax. Self-knowledge helps him to negotiate the system, but an ability to assess the environment is also required.

Assessing the Environment

Assessing the environment incorporates the rhythm of timing. For example, many of the Talented One Hundred were born during a time period when major changes were taking place in Black/White relations. Like Earnest Ross, they sensed the direction of the racial winds and prepared themselves to take advantage of forthcoming opportunities: "I was born at a time period when I could afford an education. I was born in a period where Black/White relations were beginning to open doors, and if you were fast enough, you could run through the crack."

For Ned McMillian, timing involves a sense of "when to hold'em and when to fold'em," an old gambler's analogy.

> It means where to be, when to talk, when to shut up, and what to say. The interpretation is based on what I know about you. Somebody might call me a nigger tomorrow, and I might hit him upside the head. You might call me a nigger the next day and I might not say anything. It's knowing that and trying to understand the psychology of the country, especially those in the ruling class.
>
> Timing is also knowing when to act politically.

Jefferson Barnes, a sociologist, acknowledged:

> I am regarded in some circles as political; that is, I carefully assess the political situation before I act and will tend to pursue a line of interest which I think I can win that doesn't override my being Black. Some of my colleagues know I get along with the chancellor. They say, "He is able to bring equipment into his department. Hey, wait a minute. That isn't the way it is supposed to be." They don't say and he is a nigger, too. They

don't say that. But they say, "How come? How does he get to be buddy with the chancellor?"

Assessing the environment involves understanding and evaluating the motives of individual actors in a variety of social settings. Elizabeth Wright strongly believes it is important to have a bird's-eye view of the social setting. "As a leader, you have to understand what you are dealing with. Why are individuals asking you to do certain things? Why are they coming to you? You have to keep your antennas out. People will use you as much as you will allow them to use you. Sometimes it's all right to be used, but know that you are being used. Don't let people use you in a negative way." Frank Russo, a health commissioner, "does not want to be used in a negative way" by his staff.

> Being unpredictable is one way of maintaining control in a predominantly White environment. My deputy knows some of the time she can make decisions for me. But on crucial issues, she tracks me down. I don't care if I am on an airplane to the moon. She does not want the responsibility of trying to figure out things. Never get yourself in a position where your second person is in command, particularly if they are White. Do not place yourself in a position where you are so matter-of-fact—so predictable—that they can almost do things for you without having your input.

Assessing one's environment means taking advantage of untapped opportunities and challenges. Walter Calvin, a director of a foundation, creates opportunities by using his position in the corporate world to gain status as a power broker in the Black community. He dispenses corporate funds to various organizations in the community. Yet, he also uses his clout in the Black community to gain leverage in the corporation. Veronica Pepper, who is in her fifties, said she opens up herself for things to come along: "I see everything as an opportunity. I embrace it and try to do it." While other faculty complain about the lack of resources for professional development and research at his predominantly Black college, Tefe Fusi, an African ethnomusicologist, "embraces opportunities by writing, lecturing, and touring during the summer." He views continuous education as a way to climb the ladder. In his culture, personal success is seen as collective success; his failure is seen as a community failure. As an immigrant in America, he believes that he sees as well as seizes opportunities where African-Americans do not. "With Black Americans, there is a feeling if you put a seed in the soil, it will grow. I have a feeling some think the seed grows by itself, and all they have to do is reap the harvest," asserted Tefe.

William Ofodile's cross-cultural research on minority immigrants, such as Africans and West Indians, and native minorities, supports Fusi's claim that they do well in this country. Since they voluntarily come to this country, they have better expectations for educational and economic opportunities. Thus, "immigrants tend to ignore or rationalize discrimination by saying if you come to my country, you can expect to be discriminated against," says Ofodile. "In my culture, if you are discriminated against, you can cite a proverb which says, as a stranger in a foreign land, you don't expect to be treated like at home. The same thing can be said of Africans and West Indians. Thus, race is less debilitating for immigrants in this country. When Black Americans go to Africa, they also tend to do well."

Jefferson Barnes agrees with William Ofodile that racial discrimination is less debilitating for Africans and West Indians.

> Blacks from the Caribbean and Africa are much more likely to handle racism with psychological agility than Blacks from the U.S. I find the Caribbean-born Black comes at the world with such a strong equilibrium and strong sense of self that the White man doesn't bother him too much. American Blacks are a peculiar phenomenon. They have spent a lot of time in this country and have got it [coping with racism] wrong. I think American Blacks are victimized, and victimized in a very important way by White people. They tend to do one or two things. Look around and say I think this world is an unjust place. The way you handle it is by seeing the world in terms of only connections—who you know—power, privilege, and money. And the other version is the world is a just place; and if you work hard and persevere, and if you compromise, you'll get to the top. In general, Blacks in this country make one or two of these mistakes. Either they see it as meritocracy, or they see it as a game. It is who you know, the "old boy network," suggesting you don't have to be good or competent. That is such a trick bag at such an intricate level that African Blacks and Caribbean Blacks don't get into. I see a central problem with Blacks handling racism. When they experience racism, as I said to you, they will experience it. It is inevitable. Their way of handling it is to say, you see, it is racism and it explains what happens to me, or they'll say that wasn't racism. What happened was not racism at all because I was competent or because I was incompetent. It is either good or bad. They don't see the textured nuances in which racism penetrates and interweaves into their lives and can't be separated in a simple binary fashion called it was or wasn't racism, or better yet, it was partly competence and partly racism.

Assessing the environment means understanding the rules of the game. Leo Aramis believes when you are a part of a minority group, "you have to understand the rules of the game for functioning in a racist society." He is critical of Black professionals who complain of isolation and rejection by White colleagues. They "cry about how hard it is to deal and function in society the way it is." He feels Blacks "overplay the stresses and strains" of racism. Placing the past "stresses and strains" in a historical perspective, Leo chides Black professionals, saying:

Wait a minute! They use to lynch our asses for eyeballing. They would cut out our hearts and throw us in the waters, just for mouthing back. Suddenly, we are going to talk about the stresses and strains of being in a corporate setting and White folks don't like us and are going to impede our progress. What in the hell do you expect? I think that's the whole thing about knowing your history and knowing where you come from. You'll have young folks who'll say this is not fair. Who told you it was supposed to be easy? It's not easy. No one said it was supposed to be easy. There was a lot more stress and strain on our forebears who were lynched, shot, beat up, and misused. That was serious strain, and we are not going through that.

Leo implies if Blacks understand the nature of a racist society, they don't aspire to be accepted by Whites.

I think a big problem of the 1960s is that a lot of us felt if we went to the right school, worked real hard, did all the proper things, drank the right kind of wine, read the right kind of books, and learned to play tennis and golf, we'll wake up one morning and be White. That is never going to happen, and as long as that's not going to happen, we have to realize that, understand it, and deal with it. I just work at my job. I don't have any need for acceptance and fulfillment there, because I don't expect it. If I get it, that's nice and extra. That's frosting on the cake, but the cake is my own knowledge of myself and what I deal with to sustain me. The cake is fine without the frosting.

We have to come in as adults with some sense of grounding—a sense of who we are and what is going on. If that is the case, we are not a token in a job. I've been the only Black person in the newsroom. It certainly would have seemed to be a token job, but I had a job, because I worked at that building. But I worked for the people for whom I was writing [Black people]. When you think you work for a company and are a part of it, being the only Black, you can feel very isolated. As Black professionals, we have to get the understanding that when we work at a job, we work for the "people." Isolation and discrimination will occur on the job, but you have to maintain a healthy attitude, have other kinds of outlets, or maintain contact with other Black folks to keep a center, so all that stuff will go over your head.

Judge Roscoe Champion understands how these rules of the game operate within the legal system. There are Blacks who are critical of some of his decisions, claiming sometimes "Whites have gotten to him." But he knows "there are certain parameters" within the system. "I can go to the left; however, if I go too far, I'll be removed. And Blacks won't even have a Black judge on the bench to be lenient at the same time we are trying to make the system responsive to our needs," said Champion.

Warner Babbitt cautions that Blacks who play by the rules of "corporate Uncle Tomism," that is, "laughing at jokes, trying to impress the supervisor, always being on hand, carrying the supervisor's coat, and making sure the CEO is happy," must understand the "rules of the game."

> You have some people who have gotten good at corporate Uncle Tomism, but they have not done the dual thing of making their mark as a real producer and bottomline contributor in the organization. So they are given the ceremonial things to do and not really brought into the real work like their White colleagues. So it has worked to their disadvantage. There are a few Blacks who have managed to use the cloaking mechanism and shocked White folks about what they could produce, and so they keep demanding to be rewarded for what they do.

Understanding the rules of the game gives the oppressed insights into the oppressor. These insights can be used as knowledge for personal and social action.

Gaining Knowledge for Personal and Social Action

"One thing that gives Black folks a leg up on White folks is we know us; we know them; and they only know them," asserted Leo Aramis. Jonathan Mobutu agreed and has used knowledge gained from being a token Black to be more effective as a change agent.

> Serving on different committees allows me to understand the governance of the institution and how it functions. When I sit on a search committee, I know how the politics of the search is going to be conducted. They are going to have a Black and a woman on the committee to show there was consideration for Blacks and women candidates. They are going to bring in the affirmative action officer to talk about affirmative action. I don't go in with any expectation that they are going to hire a Black officer. I am going in with the expectation to learn something about how the institution functions, so I can later use it to the advantage of Black people. So that's how I approach committee assignments; I don't accept them as an indication of how I am appreciated. It is a source of knowledge about how to change the institution.

Mobutu cited an example of how he plans to use his knowledge to "the advantage of Black people."

> From the search committee I serve on, I have just found that one of the things the president does to recruit some deans is offer them directorships

214

in major corporations. It is worked out through the alumni and the board of trustees. I always thought that, but this was the first time it was confirmed by the president's mouth. You pick up nuances that will be helpful. At some point if you ever wanted to recruit a Black person to get some of these directorships in the corporation, you can use that as leverage. But Whites think I am stupid and not supposed to understand that.

Bernie Roberts also has used his knowledge as a social researcher to change social policy and to reinforce a positive identity in Blacks. His research on the Black family has affected so many lives. "Black people were believing what White people were saying about them. They were developing a defeatist attitude and didn't aspire. I believe in knowledge for action. Many researchers don't see the impact of somebody using what they do. It is not where I am in the status order, but what I do for others that makes a difference," asserted Roberts.

Sometimes, knowledge is derived from painful lessons that one incorporates into a positive strategy for action. When Jonathan Walden, a thirty-nine-year-old charismatic minister, ran for public office and was defeated, he incorporated his defeat into a positive lesson that will help him with any future bids for a public office. He ran on a Republican ticket, but, he said, "the party did not do all it could to make me a winner. I learned to deal with them. I never let the experience get me down and get me to the point where I can't function. I try to learn from it and try to figure out how to do it differently."

Walden ran an unsuccessful race, but after losing, he was still interested in "figuring out how to do it differently" and deciding whether he should engage in another immediate political battle or wait until a more opportune time in the future. This process requires individuals to prioritize battles. To fight every battle requires an expenditure of energy. The Talented One Hundred have learned to pick and choose their racial battles.

Prioritizing Battles

"Don't pick unnecessary fights. Don't fight just to be fighting. Have some goals in mind. In the process, pace yourself. Don't become bitter and hostile. Fight in a loving way," said Jack B. Lane. Prioritizing battles involves not only how you choose to fight battles but also the timing. Timothy Brownlee knows that the key to his survival as a public administrator is "knowing when to hold them and when to fold them. Timing is really the key, and you need to have a sense of it. As a public official, you never give up your total heart. You never lay your heart out there. If you do, someone is going to step on it. You have to be impersonal."

When Judge Roscoe Champion became the first Black judge in his county, he "knew when to hold them and when to fold them." There were serious racial charges leveled against the court. Judge Champion wanted reforms; however, he decided not to take on the battle immediately after assuming office, but waited until he felt he would have an impact.

> Before I went on the court, there were reports that judges were not advising defendants. I never went in and said I believed what those people said, and that you are wrong and the bar association castigated you. I proved to them I was competent. They accepted me. I went back to the problem; I didn't fault them. I said let's make sure we are right. Let's have a record of it to protect us against unfair criticisms. You don't have to say you're racist or it was racist-inspired, but it becomes obvious.

Picking and choosing battles and deciding when to wage them is time-consuming. It is, therefore, not surprising that so many of the Talented One Hundred ignore, deny, or fail to recall racist incidents. To dwell on these incidents would render them dysfunctional, thus impeding reaching their goals. Nevertheless, when some battles become too much to fight, it is important to have options. According to Ned McMillian, "To be successful, you have to set goals and go after them, but always have an alternative position. Don't keep beating a steel wall if you can't get through it. If you can't go over it, go around it. If you can't get under it, then come back and get another start." Even though McMillian has a successful medical practice and is a professor of medicine, he is working on a Ph.D. in gerontology.

Creating Options

The Talented One Hundred believe in having options. In addition to their primary professions, 50 percent have a secondary profession and 9 percent have a third profession. When I interviewed Diane Earlinger in 1987, she was completing an M.B.A., even though she had an M.D. and was successful in her position as an administrator at a federal agency. Having alternatives is a successful coping strategy. The following vignettes illustrate how important this is to the success of the Black elite:

"I believe you should be multifaceted and you should do lots of things. You shouldn't be saddled with just one thing to do. I am interested in designing and completing a doctorate in finance or business administration," said Timothy Brownlee, a successful public official.

"When the chairman denied my promotion, even though the dean recommended it, I went on to the next objective. I have never been one to rely on a single occupation or objective," said William Long, a fifty-two-year-old professor in the school of architecture and urban planning at a large university. He has a photography studio and owns real estate.

"As a journalist, I develop employment on the outside. You have to broaden your audience outside the newspaper and use that reputation to go elsewhere or to enhance your reputation in the organization," remarked Warner Babbitt.

One can have options within one's profession too. "I never rely on more than 10 percent of my business from one contractor. So if there are cutbacks, the company will not fold," stated Joshua Smith.

Thomas B. Thomas, a director of marketing for a major company, stated:

> I am in a career that gauges everything based on performance—very little of it is personality or whether you get along with people. If I were in administration, I would have to be a nice, personable person. I chose to be in a setting where I would be paid in direct proportion to my value in the marketplace. So, when the company says this is what the objective is, I blow the objective clean out of the wall. When I walk in there and talk about something, I get listened to. If I didn't have any numbers, any dollars, nobody would listen. Some companies are market-driven and are strong on performance. Others are not market-driven and people work on a salary. Blacks have to select a company that is market-driven to give them leverage in the company.

Having options became the major motivating drive for forty-three-year-old Frank Russo. In fact, he claims it was his "guiding light" after his encounter with a racist incident during his childhood in a small southern town in the 1950s.

> When I was about ten years of age, I remember how my father and other elderly Black men had to respond in the presence of White people. It used to bother me so much. I remember when I was thirteen years old, I got into a fight with a White teenager, the son of a prominent doctor in town at a packing company where I worked. The White teenager was a supervisor, giving instructions to sixty-year-old Black males. It was driving me up the wall, the way he was doing it. It was humiliating for me to watch Black men I said "Yes Sir" to and respected having to lower themselves to a thirteen- or fourteen-year-old White supervisor. It was during that time I made the decision that I wasn't going to be in a similar position. That was my guiding light.

Frank Russo is a health administrator and he also practices medicine part-time and is employed part-time as an administrator in a county agency.

A couple of years ago, the division director called me at home and told me I had to quit my part-time job, because there was a conflict in regulations with the job I had. They knew I had that job when I took this one. What bothered me the most was that I was on my way to work that Friday night, and he told me I couldn't go. I didn't go, but reflected on it all night. I said to myself [voice rising] too long and too hard have I worked to be in the same position as my daddy, except that I am at a different level.

"I am going to tell you now and tell you later," said Frank Russo to the director, "I just bought a new car and a house. But one thing you need to understand is that I am not trapped. I have certain standards and certain options and if you try to bring certain things on me, I'll walk away from here."

I took another job after checking the rules and regulations for possible violations. I must establish the difference between my father and myself. I must have options, and my father had none, and that's what I am all about. I've gotten very anxious and upset when my options [were] limited. If you walk in here today and tell me I don't have a job, it will set me back a little while, but because of my other options, my family will still have all the basic things. I'll have to send my Jaguar back, but I'll get a Toyota. In six months, I'll have the Jaguar back.

It is important for the Black elite to be economically independent. Many of the Talented One Hundred own businesses or plan to have one in the future. Like Jonathan Walden, they feel that an "independent economic base is a critical viable option."

It allows you to speak out against racism. For me the church is that independent base of operation. It allows me to more freely express my convictions. However, it doesn't make much difference to me what's the setting. I will speak what I believe is right, and I'll suffer the consequences. But I refuse to allow anyone to seal my speech or to stifle in anyway the expressions of my convictions.

But unless you have options, Jonathan Walden cautioned, *don't burn your bridges.* He maintained, "I never move on without having something to move to. I've always had enough good sense not to burn my bridge before getting to the other side. I may burn it behind me, but not before I get to the other side." While some individuals burn bridges behind them, others want to build bridges between the races.

Building Bridges

Clarence Pinkney said that the way he copes as a corporate manager is by "bridging the gap between the powerful and the powerless." Some Blacks feel they can best assist other Blacks by building bridges between the races and by working within mainstream organizations rather than through separate Black groups. It is the view of Veronica Pepper, president of a predominantly White professional association in the behavioral sciences, that "Blacks should remain part of mainstream organizations. They should challenge the system to make it what it is. Blacks give over ownership to other people. They see someone else in control, but don't see themselves as part of that system."

Being a bridge builder has helped Veronica Pepper to successfully achieve her goals in serving Blacks.

> I've always been involved with helping Blacks, particularly children. One reason why I've been so successful in my organizational effort is that I've done less gesturing and polarizing and more problem-solving. I know what my objectives are, but I always think there is a confluence of interests. I always tried to speak to the interest of the people I serve—staff and others—who are going to try to bring about changes that will ultimately help Black constituents.

Sharla Frances, a chief administrator, agreed, saying, "Being in a mixed setting allows me to influence social policies. It is very hard to influence social policies from a predominantly minority view. You have to understand other people's needs and wants in order to be effective." Jack B. Lane sees merit in this position. But it is also the influence of his participation in the Civil Rights movement under Martin Luther King, Jr., that continues to motivate him to "preach about the building of the beloved community. . . . I go to meetings and try to deal with people on a level [where] they are," said Jack. He attends prayer breakfasts with White public officials, one of the few Black members of this elected body to do so. "I don't have any ill feelings or malice toward anyone, whether they oppose me or say all manner of things about me. I just don't have it. I don't have time for it. This is what the movement taught us. You don't have time for ill feelings, to hate, or to hold grudges. You don't have the energy for that. You have to go with the business of trying to make the society better."

While Lane is interested in "building a beloved community," others want to build individual bridges as a crossover to their personal acceptance and professional success. Bonhart Wheeler, a college professor in his fifties at a predominantly Black University, adopts the mannerism of middle-class Whites, which he feels creates greater acceptance and comfort.

> I find myself in situations where people tend not to relate to me as they relate to other Blacks, because of the way I carry myself. People accept me because I don't have many of the mannerisms of Blacks. Many Whites have not been exposed to Blacks who speak well, are composed, have self-

worth, and cannot be drawn into an altercation. When I see it, I rather enjoy it. I see people who never related to a person in such a way tend to change.

While Wheeler enjoys being accepted personally by Whites, Dira Ridley thinks it is professionally expedient to establish bridges of comfortability with colleagues.

If I really want to succeed in this world, which is a predominantly White world, with the power and money, I must be technically competent. But I must also make these individuals comfortable with me as a person. I can be the most brilliant individual in the world, and they know that, but I am going nowhere unless there is a gut level feeling that I am okay. How do you get their gut feelings to say that you are okay? Does it mean you have to change as a person? The answer is, "Not necessarily, as long as you are not radical."

You'll find among scientists that they are very similar people in their thought processes. Their economic backgrounds might vary. But they are very close in what they like, if they've been exposed to it. Exposure is the key thing. First, I have to get them to feel comfortable with me—gut feelings—and that isn't as hard as you might think, because our economic status is going to be similar. We can drink Perrier water, if you are exposed to it. So you begin to expose yourself to things they like and their life-styles. But at the same time, it is not becoming like them. You want to maintain your identity. I am Black, a Southerner, and my parents are not educated.

Sometimes establishing bridges of comfortability is merely a gesture of one's humanity to others. When David Benton, an artist, is not treated cordially by Whites, before reacting to their slights, he said, "I will say, 'Good Morning' to a surly waitress. I will do human kinds of things and then get the service or I will speak directly to the person about my mistreatment or speak to others who can do something about it. If I were in a public place, I would demand the service to which I am entitled."

Since the Black elite walk between two worlds, they find it is expedient to establish bridges of comfortability with Whites. But they also find it may be necessary to use their biculturality, as Jonathan Mobutu and Thomas B. Thomas do, in coping with racism.

Using Biculturality as a Weapon Against Racism

Jonathan Mobutu asserted:

When I am on a committee, a lot of the perspective I bring to bear is bicultural. Black students need someone with whom to identify. I try to show how Black colleges have helped students to achieve. I also use my influence in terms of Black repertoire. At a place like my university, if you have a certain style of communication, the message can be lost. One of the things you do is raise your tone and start speaking in an urban cadence and in an excitable way to get their attention. For example, resorting to linguistic patterns, saying "Hey man, let's be real!" "Are you serious?" or "Give me a break!" That is out of the usual repertoire. If I sit up and start staring, that projects another image of the bad nigger. So that will defuse any hostility that will come across. So you use that to control the situation in which you find yourself.

Thomas Kochman, in *Black and White Styles in Conflict,* supports the idea that different cultural patterns and styles of communication by Blacks are often interpreted by Whites as aggressive behavior.[12] But to defuse a racist situation, Thomas B. Thomas finds it is necessary to "lapse into an ethnic bag." Listen to Thomas "signify" on his colleague by putting him in the "dozens."

One day we were sitting in a roundtable discussion and someone asked for a drink of something. This Mormon guy said, "You can use my cup as long as you don't nigger lip it." So immediately I made my presence known. I said, "Why don't you bring things out front? What is nigger lipping it?" He stammered, "You know what that is, don't you?" "Why would I know what a derogatory term like that means?" I said, "I want you to demonstrate the technique you call nigger lipping," I said, "Go ahead. You're so smart. Go ahead." When he is backed into a corner, he takes a cup and sticks his bottom lip out and says, "That's what I am talking about." Then I said, "It looks just like something your mother would do, but it would not be with a cup." [Laughs] He was beet red.

Collective Modes of Coping on the Job

Though the Black elite have developed several individual modes of coping on the job, they believe that it is important, as Leo Aramis noted, to keep one's center by maintaining contact with other Blacks. Bruce P. Dohrenwend and Barbara S. Dohrenwend, in *Social Status and Psychological Disorders: A Causal Inquiry,* stated that the impact of race and class as major stressors can be reduced by mediating factors, both external and internal. The internal constraints refer to abilities, drives, values, and beliefs. External constraints are the social support network, that is, family, friends, and social clubs. While there are conceptual limitations of studies on social support, other researchers have stressed their mediating effects on stress.[13] Having a strong support network acts as a stress buffer in reducing the impact of social isolation.

Networking

In response to social isolation in predominantly White environments, networks of professional organizations have sprung up around the country to meet the needs of the Black elite, from artists to zoologists. The Black professional understands there is more power in collectivity than in individuality.

The Black artist in the United States, for instance, is "stereotyped and kept at the periphery of the art world," because of "exclusionism disguised as artistic judgment" and "outmoded definitions of Black art."[14] An *ART News* survey of thirty-eight artists, dealers, collectors, art historians, and museum curators "reveals unanimity on one point: the art world is not widely informed about the scope and quality of visual art now being produced by Black Americans."[15] Hence, Black artists are organizing locally and nationally to change their plight. Aretha Shield exemplifies this trend:

> I am a member of a Black artist group. I joined the group because I feel that it is important to take a stand in my community as a visible working artist. I was working in the community, but no one knew what I did. Now that I've joined [the group], more people are aware of my talents. I think sometimes the Black artist has more power working collectively than individually. We held an exhibition of Black artists' works at a national museum. Individually, we could not have had a show. Under the title Black, you can get more doors open rather than just being a Black individual, because museums want a Black show. But they are reluctant to feature an individual Black artist as an American artist.

Jonathan Mobutu has found that organizing Black faculty and staff at his university is an effective "strategy in dealing with racism," creating "centers of power."

> We have a Black faculty/staff organization that meets regularly with the president. The bureaucratic line may not give us the chance to have an impact through formal channels, but we do it through informal channels by using the Black party and the staff organization as a collective voice rather than an individual one. In the long run, it provides a vehicle for transformation, particularly since the university is under a desegregation order.

When Black professionals organize on the job, it might be necessary to use informal networks and go "underground," said Stephanie Tahara. "When you make a strong statement by being visible, you can become a target. You tip Whites off to what they need to do. So one of the things you can do is not make a strong visible statement but a strong invisible statement. So you strategize at somebody's house—you are taking care of business, and they don't know whom to pick on."

While organizational networks have flourished among Black professionals in predominantly White settings, some have emerged as primarily social networks. Teresa Hale meets weekly with a Black women's group to combat alienation and isolation. Her mixed professional memberships are for professional networking, growth, and development. Many Black professional organizations in actuality, however, serve dual needs. While observing an annual meeting of the Congressional Black Caucus, Diane Earlinger was able to understand, for the first time, why there was so much gesturing, posturing, and rhetorizing among Black organizations, and why there were so few concrete innovative strategies for achieving goals— there are too many unmet psychological needs. Robert Woodson, chairman of the Council for a Black Economic Agenda, who studies issues of economic, tax, and trade policies and their effects on the Black community, understands Diane Earlinger's concerns. Said Woodson, "Many of our politicians are lazy. They don't read or take the time to study. They would rather get up and talk about 'It ain't the man, it's the plan. It ain't the rap, it's the map.' If you got rhyming cliches, you can get over with a Black audience. [Laughs] We like being entertained; we don't like being informed." Perhaps, since so many Black elite who work in isolation have unmet psychological and social needs, these organizations serve as a latent function for their ego-enhancement and self-validation.

A parallel criticism is often leveled against the Black church, that is, the predominance in emphasis on spiritual fulfillment versus social activism and collective empowerment. Contrary to most Black ministers, who emphasize spiritualism, Joseph Lowery exemplifies ministers who fuse spiritualism with *activism*. He knows that a sense of personal efficacy is related to group efficacy. Individuals' racial identity, class identity, personal identity, support system, and world view influence "what people choose to do as a group, how much effort they put into it, and their staying power when group effort fails to produce results."[16] Hence, under Lowery's leadership, the aim of SCLC is to improve the Black community through organizing at every level to bring economic, moral, and political pressure in the public and private sector.

Although Black leaders have a similar goal—to empower the Black community—there are different strategies for achieving this end. Robert Woodson, a former resident fellow at the American Enterprise Institute and a Republican, stresses self-help and economic development through organizing low-income people in the Black community. He is critical of the traditional civil rights leaders and their tactics, claiming they do not benefit the poor. Joseph Lowery disagreed:

I reject completely Reagan's niggers who talk about self-help as though we never helped ourselves and as though government has no responsibility. Government is largely responsible for our predicament, and it has a responsibility to deal with it. And furthermore, government has the resources to deal with it. The private sector never moves until government provides the leadership.

Nobody has ever claimed marching was a total answer, even in the sixties. Marching was just one dramatic way of calling attention to the problem or forcing people to deal with the problem. And don't overlook the fact of giving yourself a good feeling that at least you started doing something about it. It is better than throwing a brick or better than sitting in a corner feeling sorry for yourself and letting anger turn inwardly. We'll never stop marching; we will always keep moving onward, bringing more pressure and trying to effect more change. But somehow, young people need to discover a wheel, and they got to find totally new ways of resolving our problems.

There are no new methods. The methods are as old as the problem is. The methods are economic, moral, and political pressure. You do it in coalescence in some instances, and you do it in Black power movements in others.

Mentoring

Leo Aramis believes that the Black elite need to "train their replacements" as another strategy to insure Blacks' progress. One way to accomplish this goal is through mentoring, said Elizabeth Wright, who is particularly interested in helping young women. "I feel strongly that you have a responsibility to help others achieve through mentoring. I got to where I am, because there were many people who helped me. We need to have someone to answer the questions for mentees in order to get them at a higher level earlier." Ned McMillian believes this way, too, and has "started a program on minority recruitment and training in medicine," while John Lamont, a scientist, is involved in a program to recruit and mentor science students.

Collective and Personal Styles of Coping Off the Job

Thomas Kochman notes that the behavioral, emotional, and verbal styles of the two races, White and Black, are in conflict.[17] Despite economic status, it is likely that Blacks more readily choose nontraditional modes of coping, such as religion and humor, while Whites are more likely to choose more traditional modes of coping, such as psychological counseling.

The Talented One Hundred have developed effective *external* ways of coping off the job—they maintain close contact with the Black community through familial, friendship, and social networks. They have also developed effective *internal* ways of relieving their stress through exercise, hobbies, music, meditation, and prayer. The Black elite come from diverse backgrounds. If they grew up in the segregated South, for instance, they may feel more comfortable maintaining a Black social network. This pattern was typical for most of the Talented One Hundred. Only a few individuals stated they felt closer to Whites, having lived and worked in predominantly White settings all of their lives. Most said they felt isolated in White environs, and maintained contact with other Blacks as a buffer against alienation, isolation, and stress.

When Frank Russo was a junior in college in the South, he had a summer job with the Interior Department in a town in Ohio where there were no Blacks.

> I didn't realize the impact it had on me until one weekend. I went to my supervisor and told him I just had to get away from there and go to the next town and spend the weekend. I had to see somebody Black. I went to a little town—Cambridge, Ohio. I was walking down the street and saw a Black family sitting on the porch, and I stopped to talk with them. This experience allowed me to reflect on blackness and whiteness and how important it is to be around Black people. I learned there was a type of conversation I missed. It was evident when I saw an old Black lady down by the creek fishing; I could talk to her about my mother's church meetings or frying fish. It didn't matter that we talked, just being in her presence was enough.

Jack B. Lane feels strongly that "it is important for a token Black to be anchored in knowing where he or she comes from and not losing contact with family, Black social organizations, or institutions and their own blackness. You have to be anchored in yourself, knowing that you are here in this position only for a season, but you do what you can to make a contribution. Be true to yourself. Be true to your people. Be true to the legacy and heritage. You got to reach back and do something."

Joseph Lowery thinks it becomes increasingly difficult for Blacks who live and work in a predominantly White setting to "be true to the legacy and heritage and to reach back and do something. I think it is more difficult for a person who is isolated in the workplace and lives in a White community. If he is isolated in the workplace and bought a house in Black suburbia, he is also cut off from working, poor Blacks, especially if he is not involved in the church. With a few exceptions, the Black church is heterogeneous [and] pluralistic, and if you are not active in the Black church, you can be far off from poor Blacks."

However, Lowery noted, "little by little I see them easing back into social activities and into relationships they are sorry were destroyed in the Black community. . . . I had a couple who returned to my church who, for almost four years, had belonged to a White church in the suburbs where they live. They want their kids in Sunday school, which will be their major contact with other Black kids."

The Black church serves many functions. It is not only a place to find spiritual fulfillment and to relieve stress from social isolation by connecting with other Blacks but also the traditional center for political and social activities. In the late 1980s, however, there appeared to be a shift in political and social leadership from the sacred to the secular sector. Lowery sees this trend as a temporary phenomenon. He thinks the Black church is crucial as a support base and as a place for making politicians accountable to the Black community.

> We are going to realize that there was a temporary shift from the Black church to Black politics, and now we are shifting back, because we realize two things: (1) politicians have to get their support from the church/ community; and (2) if we don't learn to hold Black politicians accountable, they'll learn to become as corrupt as White politicians. We have to keep Black politicians accountable and in close touch [with the Black community]. We cannot let them substitute Chamber of Commerce meetings for prayer meetings, nor can we let them substitute cocktails for community. We have to keep them close to where the source is. We can't let them just run back when they get in trouble or need to be elected.

While the Black church offers a refuge from the stresses of the workplace, it is also important to have a strong support network of family and friends. "You need an external base you can count on. Unfortunately, Blacks in the corporate world have very few they can count on in the organization," noted Kelly Smith. Thomas B. Thomas advised token Blacks who work in predominantly White settings to separate their professional and personal lives. "People have to separate the workplace from everything else. It is a place where you go to perform a task. When the task is over, your life starts all over again. If you try to incorporate your professional life with your personal life, and people don't accept you, then you are bent out of shape. Your performance will be poor. So if you separate your professional and social life, you won't have that problem of being isolated."

Jeanette Gear, a judge, agreed. "You have to always be on guard in the workplace, whether White or Black, because you are not certain about anything. You don't know if you'll have a job tomorrow. In the corporation, everyone is trying to get to the top. It is very difficult to relax at work. You need to find a group where you can relax and hang loose."

The Black Party: Stress Reducer

For many Blacks who live between two worlds, the Black party becomes the place to "hang loose." Like the Black church, the Black party is viewed as a stress reducer, while the White party is seen as a place for professional and business networking. Having grown up in a Black community, Warner Babbitt had to rearrange his thinking about parties when he started working in a White world.

> Basically, I thought you go to a party to have fun. I never thought you went to a party to make business contacts. I realized you don't go to a White party to have fun. You go to a party to be seen, make contacts, and get ahead. So parties among Whites are seen as business opportunities. In the environment in which I grew up, they were basically seen as social opportunities or a chance to have a good time. You have to rearrange your thinking, and that takes some doing.

For Jonathan Mobutu, who lives and works in a predominantly White setting, a Black party becomes a welcome relief from isolation and stress.

> We live in a college town, where there are not any traditional Black radio stations. What comes across the air is European music. There are a variety of social outlets that my White neighbors are comfortable with, such as receptions and get-togethers that are sterile in format. Whereas, in the background I've come from, there is a lot of noise, joking, and music that comes out of the Black experience. We try to recreate some semblance of that by having regular card parties among Black males or house parties among the professional Black faculty and staff where we can act the way we want to.
>
> In many of those parties, it is still politically appropriate to invite White people to come, because you want to maintain a useful relationship with your neighbors—so you invite them to come. They'll only stay for a while, and then we start to get down. Take, for instance, when we had a surprise birthday party for my wife, the neighbors were all invited, but they left after a couple of hours. Then we were able to have more of a traditional Black party. This is a typical pattern. I think Whites leave parties earlier. It is almost a ritual for them. For us, it is a stress reducer, a sense of fellowship, and interaction that we can't get on a normal basis. For them, it is a regular pattern at predominantly White institutions. You go to receptions all the time. The White party is just another formal ritual. Theirs is not a true friendship or camaraderie that drives professional Blacks to get together. For us, it is an experience to re-energize and to recreate the Black experience. There is also a performance mode to how parties are held in the Black experience. You are able to get down and act in ways that you wouldn't if you were in your formal role in a professional

setting. You would not find that in the White parties I attend where people have middle level ranks or above.

Male and Female Coping Styles

While the Black party is a stress reducer for both Black men and women, Mobutu senses there is a distinct difference between the way they cope with stress off the job.

> It seems easier for Black males to get together. We have luncheon meetings every couple of weeks, where we just shoot the shit and talk the stuff. We call it the committee, and it has no major function. There is a group of us who play bid whist every three weeks or so. We talk stuff, drink beer, and wine. We also compare notes about what's going on; we maintain an informal political network. We have a group of us who play racquet ball to get rid of some of that tension.

The women at the university where Mobutu teaches, on the other hand, do not appear to have similar outlets for their stresses. The diverse marital status of women at his college seems to affect their chances of socializing, because of the varying degrees of responsibility. In addition to their professional duties, women still have the primary responsibility of child rearing and housekeeping. Perhaps this is one reason why the Black women in my population expressed greater isolation than the Black men. The married women of the Talented One Hundred were more likely to become involved in their families as a means of coping with work-related stress. Single women used work as a way of coping. Both also found other outlets for coping with stress. Like Mobutu and his male friends, Elizabeth Wright, a college administrator, and her female friends "get a jug of wine and get together at a single girlfriend's house to play scrabble and discuss consultant work until the wee hours in the morning."

While males and females may have different social modes of coping on the job, they both have developed effective internal mechanisms for relieving stress. When Sharla Frances, a chief administrator for a major city, is "frustrated," she is likely to find herself walking in the woods or in a museum. "I like to be thoughtful, but share it with someone, so I share it with the artists through their works. I want to know what they are thinking and feeling." Having this "continuity snaps me out of a downfall. When I don't have it, I am hysterical," Frances said, laughing. Others relieve stress through exercise, hobbies, humor, music, meditation, and prayer. No more than 2 percent of the Talented One Hundred said they used alcohol in excess. And many indicated without my probing that they never used alcohol or drugs as a way of coping. But some individuals said they ate excessively, while others used humor to cope.

The Role of Humor

Humor is a common way to reduce stress. Many Blacks have historically used humor to deal with the contradictions inherent in oppression. Roscoe Champion tries to "laugh at things."

> I amuse myself about racial incidents. I just returned with a delegate from another part of the world. On this trip, there were Black and White people. Oddly enough, when the three Black people were talking, the White people who were part of the delegation would think something was going on. It's like we can't get together. When I go to a social function and Blacks fail to acknowledge other Blacks in the presence of Whites, I find that amusing. It's like they are saying White people are watching, and you can't say anything.

The Role of Spirituality

I found a strong spiritual orientation expressed through prayer or meditation among the Talented One Hundred which helped them to reduce stress and to keep moving. When I discussed my research for this book with Charles V. Willie, an eminent sociologist, he said, "I've been in the storm so long, give me a little time to pray." Prayer also helped Yvonne Walker-Taylor to cope with the bishop of Wilberforce University.

> It has been a matter of tenacity and a spiritual belief in God that helped me to cope. Religion is an outlet for my stress. It is the root of my being. It is the one thing that holds me up. I think a strong, spiritual background gives you that strong impetus and added confidence in self. So you got to believe somebody is with you, and humans aren't. They'll turn on you. But there's only one thing that will never fail you, and that's God. The stronger you believe, the easier it is to understand what's going on around us, and you can cope with the bad times.

Jonathan Walden's strong spiritual orientation also helps to sustain him in the fight against oppression.

> It is not God's will for us to be oppressed, though it might be His permissive will. If He is all-powerful, as we believe, He has the power to change the course of history anytime He chooses. Therefore, you flow with the way the world was created and use your belief in Him and His desire for you to move beyond your circumstances. Let no one tell you what to do [but God].

When Tefe Fusi, a Catholic, feels alienated in this country, he knows he is never alone because he retains his African spirituality.

229

In the African world view, everyone has access to the spiritual world. I've been through enough rituals to accept that fact and to believe in it, despite the fact that I am Catholic. So I rely very heavily on the belief that I am never alone, and that is also the main reason why people think I am arrogant. I have self-confidence that I am never alone, so I ignore things. It is not intentional. If something is going to happen to me, it is predestined to happen. So I derive my spiritual strength from that more than Catholicism. I believe strongly in the spiritual world and feel decisions will not materialize until that time.

When fifty-nine-year-old Lee Watson's "heart began to skip a beat," she returned to her strong Baptist upbringing. Lee humorously recalled:

Oh, my God! I've done all the planning and all this work and I built my retirement home and have accumulated all these assets. I plan to retire, and now I am going to die. We've always said religion is a Black man's opiate. I got down on my knees and prayed. "Lord, show me the way—you surely can't treat me like this. You are supposed to be a just God and here I am at the end of my life and I've stacked up all these rewards for myself and now I am going to die of a heart attack." I was okay, but just under stress. Now, when I feel stressful, I go through relaxation and deep breathing.

Joseph Lowery cautioned that Blacks have to develop a "Liberation Lifestyle" free of stress and grounded on strong spiritual beliefs to help them cope with racism in this society.

I have developed a Liberation Lifestyle. I do what I can, and what I can't do, I don't worry about—you incorporate that in your life. I believe God has called me to do things, and I see my ministry in perspective. I've learned not to change things I can't and not to worry about what I can't change. Leave it in God's hands. If I can't get to it, I hope the Lord will.

The Liberation Lifestyle is based on what I say is the admonition of the 1980s and 1990s, and that is, we must not fall victim to assaults from without or to our faults from within. A Liberation Lifestyle will make us free at last—not after death, but right now. The lifestyle is based on a thorough understanding of who we are, and that's spiritual. We are sons and daughters of God. We are sacred human beings with sacred personalities, infinite worth, and made in the image of God. Beyond that, we are not only the sons and daughters of God, but we are the sons and daughters of Mary McLeod Bethune, Frederick Douglass, Martin Luther King, Jr., Charlotte Hawkins Brown, and that gives us another strength, resource, and understanding beyond ourselves. So when we live that way, it frees us from self-hate, and we are free at last. We know who we are. We know the people who are trying to abuse us or assault us are ignorant and need our education. They are lost, and they need our salvation. Hence, that frees us from hate.

A Liberation Lifestyle helps us to develop our own sense of priorities and values, which we must develop before we can get the nation to develop its priorities. How do we use the resources we do have? What are our values? Are we still begging for what we need and buying what we want? Are we still more concerned with Chivas Regal than we are with endowments, insurance, owning our own home, and investments? Are we still more concerned about long cars than we are concerned about long hours of study and work to get ahead? Do we vote emotionally more than we do pragmatically? Are we free from apathy and lethargy in the political world? Are we free from a mixed priority which makes us get all excited about a presidential race that we can't win, and then stay home and not vote for members of the board of education, the city council, or the county commission, which we could win and could make an important difference in our lives? A Liberation Lifestyle makes us free from the dependence on alien substance. If we know who we are, what our priorities and values are, we don't need dope and alcohol. We don't need artificial means of feeling good. A Liberation Lifestyle means we don't want to be sexually irresponsible, because we are free from sexual exploitation. We are free from self-gratification that can only be realized by exploiting others. We respect women. We respect ourselves. It makes us free at last.

I think we always had this concept. We just didn't have it phrased and structured as we are trying to do now. It is more recent. It started in Montgomery in 1985 at our SCLC convention, and that is where I coined the expression "Liberation Lifestyle."

It ain't judicial or legislative; it ain't computers; it ain't science; it ain't high tech; it's spiritual, and we got to begin there.

Lowery's Liberation Lifestyle is a positive concept that can elevate Blacks to a newfound sense of collectivity and clarity of identity. It is evident from the literature and from the views of the Talented One Hundred that stress can be meliorated if Blacks are grounded in an Afrocentric orientation. Social isolation is less likely to occur when one maintains a strong race orientation and a weak class orientation; when one is culturally and structurally segregated in a dominant society; when one has supportive Black networks and linkages with the Black community; and when one has effective internal coping resources and responses. Conversely, social isolation, greater stress, and lack of identity clarity are more likely to occur when one maintains a strong class orientation and a weak race orientation; when one is more culturally and structurally integrated into the dominant society; when one lacks supportive Black networks and linkages with the Black community; and when one lacks effective internal coping resources and responses.

In summary, this chapter addresses how the Black elite manage the negative emotional impact of racism. While some individuals are proactive, others are reactive. Individuals who are proactive incorporate racism as a major impediment in their lives, but they accept some responsibility for overcoming it. Individuals who are reactive accept only self-blame for the negative emotional stress resulting from race or they blame only the system. The Talented One Hundred have developed a proactive posture to racism. They use a variety of personal and collective modes of coping on and off the job to mediate the negative stress of race, along with class, to assist them in continuing as successful actors in reaching their goals. The literature, as well as the collective experience of the Talented One Hundred, has shown that by maintaining a supportive network of family, friends, and peers, Black individuals can reduce social isolation in White settings.

In the next chapter, we move beyond the color line to envision the Black elite as important players on the global stage.

EIGHT

Beyond the Color Line: An Alternative Vision

"What does Jesse Jackson want? What does Jackson really want?" Over and over, that question has been asked during the presidential campaign, as if there were a mystery shrouded in the answer.

But there is no hidden agenda, no secret ambition, no private deal. The agenda from the beginning has been peace, justice, and jobs. The ambition has been to unite our constituency. The deal has been to capture the nation's imagination and find common ground for change. . . . People have crossed ancient lines of race, religion, and region to come together. They may be Black or White or Brown, but however different their numerators, the denominator is the same.[1]

Jesse Jackson articulated and raised the aspirations of African-Americans. He also captured the imagination of factory workers, farmers, housewives, the unemployed, Chicanos, Native Americans, and the liberal, educated segment of the population to find "common ground for change" in the 1988 presidential campaign. Friends and foes of Jesse Jackson cannot deny the influence of his simple messages, "Down with dope, up with hope! We don't need workfare, we need fair share!" His antidrug message, along with his economic violence and pro-worker populist themes, affected the direction of the Democratic party and the presidential election of 1988. In addition, Jackson's concern for the self-determination of Third World nations and global oppression has inspired a new vision of this nation and of oppressed peoples of the world.

Often, it is the oppressed elite who live between two or more social worlds, but have transcended both, that lead the way to a new social order. Martin Luther King, Jr., the slain civil rights leader who inspired Jesse Jackson, is another example of the Black elite who pointed the way to a different social order. The Civil Rights movement motivated other disenfranchised groups, such as White women, Orientals, Hispanics, the Gray Panthers, and Gays. "They have gotten great benefits from the movement," said Michael Lomax. The student movement in China, suppressed by the government, is an example of its global inspiration.

Instead of expending negative energy on the impact of oppression, intellectuals like Jackson and King use their duality as a positive source of energy to fuel the creative process leading to social change. Their dual consciousness has given them a special way of viewing the world and special insight into understanding the larger socioeconomic processes of society. Too often, the creative process arising from the double-consciousness has been deemphasized because many believe that the conflicts arising in the Black elite living between two worlds require an expenditure of negative energy.

The personal and collective energies that the Talented One Hundred expend daily in dealing with racism can more effectively be utilized in their professional and personal development. John Hope Franklin, Black historian, reminded us that these wasted energies are "desperately needed to solve the major problems of peace and survival" in the world. Having a dual consciousness "takes part of your validity," said Johnson Longworth, an artist. "We've got to have double values, and that's schizophrenic. In school, you have no courses in double values and no courses in justifiable schizophrenia. It's the tragic reality of being Black in America, and nobody wants to hear your story."

Michael Lomax agreed with Johnson Longworth that the double-consciousness is "a source of conflict." It is not, however, solely a tragic reality for Lomax. He thinks conflict can be creative.

It [double-consciousness] can be both conflictual and creative. It can be a source of conflict if you don't recognize it; you are pulled in two different directions. We ought to be in conflict, because we are in an inherently conflictual situation. What we have to do is acknowledge it and guard how and why it is pulling us. If we do that, we can't stop these inherently conflictual situations from recurring, but we can use them and negotiate them in ways which are positive. It really is for me a matter of perspective. The situation doesn't change, but how I see it changes.

I gave a speech, and I was asked to talk about the Democratic party and social issues. I was following Jesse Jackson on a program, and he has been threatening Democrats for the last four years about what we can do on these social issues. The Democratic party wants to hold on to Black people, but not scare off White people. That is an inherent conflict.

I can be threatened by this conflict, or I can see it as an opportunity. I can say to the Democrats, "This is an opportunity for all of us to rethink our relationship, to debate, and to struggle with it. Go through the fire of that debate. Either we melt or we come out stronger, like steel, tempered and bonded more closely." I can see the process as a conflict or as a dynamic opportunity to reach a stronger resolution.

Even when the double-consciousness is a "tragic reality," Michael Lomax searches for a larger meaning in this reality. He poignantly reflected that:

> Maybe what we should recognize is that the conflict we feel as Blacks in a White society is really a symbol of the conflict the individual has in contemporary society. It is a world in which conflict exists. It is one symbol, one element of it. While it does alienate us as individuals, it is that conflict and also that requirement to find peace with that conflict that binds us together. If I don't find that in it, I am going to go crazy with it. I got to find my own mechanism for balancing conflict with the need for harmony, individually and collectively.

When Lomax, as a Black elite, views his duality as a creative stimulus, he has the potential for positive social action. W. E. B. Du Bois, in his formulation of the "Talented Tenth," also envisioned the role of this educated elite as "global citizen." This global citizen, he noted, would be an important change agent in transforming the larger social structure culturally, educationally, and politically.[2]

As an international citizen, this new man or woman of color understands racial oppression in a broader context. Having traveled extensively, the Talented One Hundred have experienced their linkage with other Blacks throughout the diaspora and are working to end global racism and human oppression.

Global Racism and Human Oppression: The Black Elite as a Change Agent

Living outside the United States gave Laverne Townson, a bank manager in Nigeria, a different perspective. She began to understand the linkage of global racism and economic oppression of Blacks throughout the diaspora and also the role of the United States media in stemming the flow of positive information about Third World countries.

> I think more globally about the problems of the Third World. In Nigeria, there is a need to project an image of Africa over colonial masters, and there is a view of South Africa and the United States as imperialist countries. You get a different perspective on the news. I have a better sense of how things operate in the United States being on the outside and looking back. The United States is more inward looking. It doesn't care about

other countries, particularly the Third World. Once you are outside the United States, there is a whole new world out there. You get an idea of what is happening in Africa, Europe, and other parts of the world. In the United States, the news you get is that the United States is the center of the universe.

Others have also begun to "think more globally about problems of the Third World." They have started to link their destiny with that of peoples of African descent throughout the diaspora. When one travels around the world, it is an inescapable observation that there is a correlation between color and social and economic oppression. The darker a group's skin color, the more likely it is that the group occupies a lower position in the social order. Yet, this observation is rarely articulated by leaders of African descent. They ignore the fact that one of the most significant "consequences of colonialism was its creation of races and racism through weakening the relevance of other human distinctions."[3] Yet, ethnic distinctions are real and remain strong, impeding a global and racial consciousness. These distinctions are fertile ground for former colonial powers to exploit—dividing and conquering peoples of African descent as well as other Third World people. This divide and conquer mentality is manifested in the United States in the tension between the Black middle class and the underclass. Globally, this divide and conquer mentality is salient in the tension between African-Americans and West Indians and African-Americans and Africans.

Black ethnic groups are treated differently by Whites in various countries, depending on their status as native-born, immigrant, or visitor—or as Aretha Shield said, "Whether it's your Black or my Black." If the group or individual who receives favorable treatment does not understand that the individualization of racial experience is a part of a global pattern, then a vision for the development of a global racial consciousness—so necessary for changing the conditions of racial oppression—is merely a distant dream.

My Black or Yours?: The Development of a Global Racial Consciousness

In the early seventies, Aretha Shield, a thirty-seven-year-old, fair-skinned African-American artist, was studying in England. One day while Aretha was working on an art project, she said a White female invaded her workspace, treating her discourteously. "When I opened my mouth, she found out I was a Black American. Apologizing, she said, 'I thought you were West Indian.' I was accepted because I was not *their* Black."

Teresa Hale, a fifty-two-year-old African-American psychologist, identified with Aretha Shield's experience. She spent three years in Paris,

France, in the late 1950s, where she was treated differently from the native people of color—the Algerians. She recalled, "My one-to-one experiences were positive. . . . [But] France was at war with Algeria and dark-skinned people could at times be indiscriminately rounded up and jailed—mistakes to be ironed out later. As a foreigner, it was the first time I ever felt American."

Walter Calvin, also an African-American, was not only glad to "feel American" but to be an American and an honorary White in South Africa. Being American perhaps saved his life. Calvin, a senior vice president for external affairs for a multinational corporation, has traveled thousands of miles from the rural South to South Africa, but his racial tracks are still the same. Listen to his story.

> I shall never forget an incident I had in South Africa. A White colleague and I were out driving one morning. The traffic was heavy, so we decided to walk the streets of Johannesburg, South Africa. We went across an area which was a university jogging track. After jogging for about fifteen minutes on the track, I suddenly heard catcalls and very foul language. I wondered about whom they were talking and at whom they were hollering. I looked up and about ten Afrikaners were jeering and sneering at *me*. I did not realize at the moment that particular university was an exclusive all-White Afrikaner university; therefore, no Blacks were allowed to do anything on campus unless they had a special pass—let alone jog on the track. One thought ran through my mind while jogging—you learned in the South that you don't run from White people; you don't let them know your fears. You may have them, but you don't show them. I didn't show them. I kept jogging until I finished. When I finished my exercise, I walked straight up the steps and passed this crowd of Afrikaners. I spoke impeccable English, and then they realized I was Black American, which made it all right for me to jog on this track. Had I been a Black South African [voice rising], they would have been perfectly in their rights to do whatever they chose to do, including detaining me and beating me until the police came. The police would have done serious harm to me.

He related another incident that occurred while he was on business in South Africa:

> When I took a Black South African couple from Soweto to dinner in Johannesburg, the maitre d' of the restaurant said, "You can come in, but your friends cannot eat here." And of course, we left. Again, it showed that even as a Black American, I am considered in that instance as an honorary White. But my Black South African friends, who are identical to me in terms of color, physical make-up, and everything, because of their language differences and birthright, weren't able to be seated with me. Discrimination against my brothers is discrimination against me.

Calvin correctly concluded that "racism is not peculiar to the United States; it is an international phenomenon." Tefe Fusi, an African ethnomusicologist, also discovered the international "race track." He candidly admitted that prior to coming to this country in the 1970s, he got negative information from Whites in *his* country about African-Americans.

> I got the message constantly from Whites before coming here that, "Your own people over in America do not want you." When I was at home, I associated a lot with White, educated Americans. And all they would tell you about Black people is negative stuff. Blacks are lazy and don't want to work. All Blacks do is wreck their own communities, rape White women, and steal. This is the kind of image that is created for you. So they told me what to avoid and what not to in America. I was told to go to a White church. I also had a White host family.

Like Fusi, Black Americans learn very early from their geography and history classes and from the media in this country the negative concept of Africa as a backward continent. Those who grew up with the Tarzan and Jane movies were firmly grounded in the erroneous notions that Africans swung from trees, lived in grass huts in the jungle, and grunted because they were too ignorant to speak a language. Most Black Americans, until recently, were ashamed to identify with Africans. (The recent name change, from Black to African-American, is a symbolic gesture of this new identification with Africa.) Not knowing that Black Americans had learned negative stereotypes about Africans, Fusi was baffled upon his arrival in this country when Blacks did not extend open arms. After reflecting on this puzzlement, he recalled that Black Americans—particularly fair-skinned ones, whom he referred to as "disappointed White folks"—who came to his country, were reluctant to associate with Africans. Fusi began associating with more African-Americans. "Then," he said, "I began to see myself in the role of an African-American. My consciousness was heightened. By associating with some responsible people from the Black community and discussing problems, [I] began to change my whole concept about the Black experience in the United States."

On the other hand, prior to coming to this country, William Ofodile, an African, had a favorable view of African-Americans that was influenced by an uncle who was a missionary. He came to the United States in the 1960s. He said:

> I was curious why there was no more mixing between Blacks and Whites. I asked in my White church why there were mostly White and mostly Black churches. The janitor in my church was Black, so I would talk with him. He took me to his church. I found differences and would go and spend Sunday afternoon with Blacks. I found out Africans did not asso-

ciate with African-Americans, and I began to look into the reason why. The mostly White host families arranged different affairs for them. Africans had strong stereotyped ideas about Black Americans, and Black Americans had [stereotypes about Africans]. I was involved in both worlds. I think it occurred because of the sheltering of Africans by White host families. This is how I developed my research interest in this area.

When Prince Albert, a sixty-one-year-old British-educated West Indian artist, came to the United States in the 1960s, he, too, was welcomed by Whites, but felt distant from African-Americans. Prior to coming to this country, he had, like Fusi, heard many stereotyped notions about African-Americans.

> The propaganda had been so heavy against Blacks in the United States, I was completely undermined into thinking no Blacks were capable of the English usage and kinds of expressions of philosophical thinking, until I read James Baldwin and heard M. L. King's speeches. So while in my thirties, I read James Baldwin; this event gave me self-confidence and made me overcome my respect for Europeans and their propaganda.

From my own observation, Africans and West Indians appear to hold more positive views toward one another. While Prince Albert's views about African-Americans were negative before learning about their achievements, he did not have these attitudes toward Africans. His identification with Africa and other Third World people emerged from another important event in his life.

> The event which most influenced my life was World War II. I remember when Italy invaded Ethiopia, a member of the League of Arabs, but no one did anything. There was a newspaper clipping which showed the Pope of Rome blessing the Italian troops who were boarding ships about to go into slaughtering of the Ethiopians. My father told me it was because they were Black. Shortly after, I was amazed to see the world go to war because of the Poles. It made me think that things were divided that way against Blacks. During the latter [part] of World War II, when the world died for freedom, where did the French get the guns in six months to kill Vietnamese? The Belgiums were in the Congo, and the Dutch [were] in Indonesia, killing Third World people.

These examples illustrate how the global pattern of racism manifests itself. In giving preferential treatment to immigrants and visitors of African descent over native-born Blacks and those from former colonies, Western colonial powers individualize a group's experiences, creating divisions. These divisions, along with negative stereotyping and real ethnic and political distinctions, make it difficult for people of African descent to see

239

their global interests as linked along racial lines. Alur Nod, African president of an international organization, who marched with Martin Luther King, Jr. in the South and who dined in Atlanta's restaurants before African-Americans did in the early 1960s, is working to bring about an international perspective. He said:

> We Africans and Black Americans don't know one another. We need to know more about one another and to get together to do things. We have a very long way to accomplish the goal to develop our own societies. Blacks, whether it's Africans or Black Americans, beg for [their] rights or [their] own destiny. We should put our money into the Black community to do things for ourselves. We don't always have to say we consume billions of dollars. We need to say we have to produce for our consumption. Black entrepreneurs are not likely to go to England or Italy to do business because of racism. The only place they have to go is the Caribbean or Africa. We also have to educate our children to be constructive and to learn about their history and culture, like the Jews. The Jews train their kids in the synagogue. Jewish boys grow up knowing they will always be pro-Jew, for their survival. We have to do the same thing. Our people have died in Mississippi, South Africa, and everywhere.

Whether in Alabama or South Africa, Blacks have begun to recognize their common linkage. They are interested in addressing global racism in the international arena, and they are concerned about global inequities in wealth and human rights, political oppression, and imperialism in the foreign policies and practices of the United States and other countries. Perhaps the Black experience "helps us to better understand the lot of the Hindu lower caste in India or the Black in South Africa," said John Daniels, a corporate executive.

Global travels have also allowed Blacks to see first hand the disparity in wealth between rich and poor. Wherever they have traveled, the Talented One Hundred have been struck by the social oppression of others— Catholics in Belfast, Northern Ireland; Jews and Christians in Russia; Palestinians in Israel; and Blacks in South Africa. Traveling outside this country has given them a broader perspective and understanding of issues. This was summed up by Leo Aramis, a journalist, whom I interviewed in my office at Central State University in Wilberforce, Ohio, in 1987.

> It gave me a perspective that's necessary. If there is a riot in your office right now, folks on the first floor would say there is a riot on the second floor. Folks in administration would say Wesley Hall. Wilberforce would say Central State University. Columbus would say a riot in Wilberforce. And California would say a riot in Ohio. But folks in Europe would say that there is a riot in America. It is a perspective that is really important. We don't have it, but we need to get it.

Having gained an international perspective, the Talented One Hundred are clamoring to be heard on global issues, such as human oppression and human rights.

The Issue of Apartheid in South Africa

John Lamont, a physicist and a progressive Democrat, was concerned about global human oppression, applauding our government when it speaks out against that oppression. He was disturbed, however, when this government did not speak forthrightly to the issue of apartheid in South Africa: "That's racism. We don't have that international view. We don't look upon South Africa in the same way as Nazism in the 1930s." (Let me add that the U.S. government and other world leaders were slow to speak out against the Nazis in the thirties.) Hence, there is a strong position among the Talented One Hundred that calls for greater involvement of the United States and other major world powers to bring pressure against the government of South Africa for its policy of racial oppression. Dira Ridley said, for example, "The power structure of the United States, Europe, and major corporations should take a stand if they are benefiting from the country. My company is no longer involved in South Africa." Teresa Johnson agreed that "the United States could do a lot more, but they don't because they are sleeping in the same bed"—the same bed of human oppression.

Stephanie Tahara understood the parallels between South Africa and the United States. But she was more interested in addressing racial oppression in *this* country.

> I am not indifferent to South Africa; but I don't worry a lot about it. I don't see South African apartheid as unrelated to America's apartheid. I am not one to go looking for trouble when it is right here in front of our doorsteps. Our energy needs to be directed towards apartheid here. When you lynch somebody in San Jose and you lynch somebody in Johannesburg, South Africa, it is the same. I've said enough.

Albert Sungist, a radical Democrat, realized, too, that there were parallels between South Africa and the United States, and he wanted this government to be involved in ending apartheid. Yet, he was also wary of what its role might be and said, "If the United States doesn't play a role in speeding up the demise of apartheid, it should get out the way and not prop up South Africa."

In contrast to Sungist, Ruth Shelly, a Democrat with an eclectic political orientation ranging from moderate to radical, felt, "The United States should not get involved, because it is always on the side of the devil." Kufra Akpan, a radical Democrat, agreed that the United States should not be involved. He advocated instead that "there should be an all-out war and destruction by the ANC [African National Congress], with no negotiations. How are we going to end racism there when we haven't ended it here?" Unlike Akpan, Pat Robinson had some doubts about a civil war. He has visited South Africa. A liberal Democrat, he was "uplifted" when he saw "the brave people" fighting the system. "It is a very intimidating system. Whites have military power, and they will kill you. So I don't see a civil war. Blacks aren't allowed to have guns, but they'll kill them anyway."

Since a civil war would be extremely costly to Black South Africans because of the differential in military capabilities, Jonathan Mobutu strongly advocates that Black Americans should play a role in ending apartheid. "Black Americans must take an active role through Trans-Africa in attempting to change government policy. Black students in colleges must spearhead divestment efforts, along with Black professionals." This fight against the apartheid government of South Africa symbolizes a developing global consciousness among peoples of African descent. Randall Robinson, an African-American who heads Trans-Africa, is in the forefront of the South African movement. In general, it is a movement about which the Talented One Hundred feel passionately.

While most of the Talented One hundred support divestment and call for economic and political sanctions by the United States and other countries, a few see divestment and economic sanctions as imposing a hardship on South African Blacks, as the U.S. government and many multinational corporations claim. Vernon Jordan, a liberal Democrat, said, "I am opposed to divestment, and I am for sanctions." On the other hand, John Daniels, also a liberal Democrat and a corporate executive, is more ambivalent about the effects of divestment on Black South Africans: "I have mixed feelings about divestment. I am concerned about the short-term effects and its economic impact on Black people. Yet, the long-term effects of divestment will free them."

Roscoe Champion denounced the argument against sanctions as paternalistic. "It bothers me when corporate executives tell us what's best for South Africa. People must make short-term sacrifices, so they won't suffer later." Champion also said, "It is interesting that no civil rights leaders have gone on record boycotting corporations." Yet, he understands their reasons: "Life is full of contradictions. How can a civil rights organization attack a corporate giant when the company is contributing over $100,000? Money still controls. You'll be biting the hand that feeds you. The hand that feeds you realizes that and puts you in that position. There is a lack of critical examination of such issues in the Black community." This lack of critical introspection gives rise to a reactive posture of inaction.

Robert Woodson is one who asks critical questions that go beyond the issue of race. "When I think about apartheid, I ask what will be the model after apartheid—Detroit or Atlanta?" Judge Pat Robinson, a liberal Democrat who was arrested in South Africa by Blacks, felt that Woodson raised an important question. Said Robinson:

> My experience in South Africa was one of the most remarkable experiences I've had. I went over there for eighteen days at the invitation of the Black Lawyers Association in Africa. I got arrested. It appeared in the paper. What makes the story interesting is I was arrested by Blacks. Everyone assumed I was arrested by South African Whites. I had attended a trial in one of the independent homelands, and they didn't know who we were, and I got arrested. The remarkable thing about that experience was that it showed a real example of the oppressed imitating the oppressor. Their laws are the same as South Africa's laws. They are paranoid and thought I was a Communist, and I was questioned about being one. The trial I went to see of this young kid was like the trials of South Africa. It was amazing.

Woodson also raised penetrating questions about human rights in the African diaspora.

> Bill Keyes [a Black Republican] is really castigated for representing South Africa, but a prominent civil rights leader could represent the Duvalier government in Haiti and be treated with respect. Under Duvalier, Blacks suffered just as much as Blacks do under Botha's regime in South Africa. Both regimes, as far as I am concerned, are the same. We can't have two standards of justice. Idi Amin was one of the worst tyrants I've ever seen, killing thousands of Blacks. But the Black leadership was reluctant to say anything against him. Other African nations sat back and watched what happened. What will happen when an Idi Amin type gets in power in one of these cities and every time Whites assault him, he says, "Racism"? There is a cadre of Blacks who will insulate this person. Who will then hold this person accountable?

Woodson called attention to the oppression of Blacks by Blacks, a human issue that people of African descent are reluctant to address. It is like airing dirty linen in a global arena, thus providing fuel for former colonial powers to say that Blacks are incapable of governing themselves. Calling attention to oppression by a Black leader suggests that the failure of one Black is symbolic of the failure of all Blacks. Yet, to ignore oppression by Blacks is a reactive response, creating an atmosphere which tolerates a high level of oppression. This high tolerance level is manifested in the statement, "I'd rather be oppressed by Blacks than Whites." Laverne Townson, who lives in Nigeria, has heard this statement repeatedly expressed among Nigerians. But others feel, like the wife who is physically abused by her husband, it is *more* painful to be oppressed by one's own group. But any form of oppression is dehumanizing. This sentiment, expressed by some Nigerians, suggests a tragic state of human affairs—one in which any form of oppression is tolerated. Blacks must develop an internal vehicle for sanctioning those who violate human dignity, whether in Nigeria or New Jersey.

Only by refusing to tolerate oppression, whether based on age, class, race, ethnicity, sex, or gender, can we realize our full potential as humans and understand our connectedness with all humanity. "To be a world citizen," Sheridan Williams, professor, playwright, and poet, reminds us, "we have to reach out to a person that is hungry. We have to reach out to a human heart to ease the pain, whether on a psychological or social level. We have to reach out and say the sun is shining regardless of race, and hopefully someone will reach back." The sun did shine brighter when the world community reached out to thousands of starving Ethiopians who were suffering from a long drought in the 1980s.

The African Drought and the Politics of Hunger

In a vast outpouring of concern and generosity, the world community responded, although slowly at first, to the drought-stricken Ethiopians when famine reached an epidemic level. Food and relief supplies were airlifted to Ethiopians, whose plight had received attention around the world. However, other countries, like Chad and Mozambique, were also deeply affected by the drought. If the drought trend continues, it is estimated that at least thirty other countries would be threatened by famine.*

Though the immediate cause of the African famine is drought, other factors aggravate the problem, such as poverty, overpopulation, abuse of the land, official mismanagement, and civil strife. The world community responded to the African drought problems with short-term solutions. After visiting an Ethiopian refugee camp, John Daniels became aware of the need for a long-term solution. He was also better able to understand the politics of hunger as employed by Africans and the Western world. He recalled the old adage, "Teach a person to fish, and that person can eat for a lifetime."

For many of the Talented One Hundred, technology is one solution to the drought problem. Physicist John Lamont, for instance, is disturbed that "we haven't been able to bring our technology to bear on human is-

---

*In the early 1990s, the drought is still threatening many African countries, such as Ethiopia and Sudan. According to a *Washington Post National Weekly* article (December 31, 1990–January 6, 1991, p. 10), "just two years after famine and famine-related diseases killed 250,000 civilians in southern Sudan, the country faces another famine . . . that may affect as many as 8 million of the nation's 22 million people."

sues. We have [only] been able to separate technologically affluent societies from impoverished societies." The new global man and woman of color are aware of this linkage between science and technology and the politics of control. They understand that technologically superior nations can maintain control over less advanced nations for the scarce resources of the earth. The drought issue is an example of the Western powers' *unwillingness* to bring their superior technology to solve human issues in the Third World. Diane Earlinger understands the politics of hunger and how technology is used as a weapon of control by the West:

> We need technology to address the issue of the drought. However, some Whites are content to see Black folks die. Although they [Whites] are the majority in this country, they are the minority worldwide. It is clear we have no such thing as a domestic economy; it is a global economy. So Whites would just as soon see these people die. Africa has one of the highest population growth rates, so it is a political situation.

Pat Robinson thinks it is also racial. "If it happened to Whites, European countries and the United States would do something about it." Tefe Fusi believes Western governments are trying to create a "world welfare system." He and others also feel that the African drought is being used by the West to attack the Marxist government in Ethiopia. In addition, Fusi said, "every time any newly independent government becomes self-sufficient, the Western countries, particularly the United States, start to cry wolf—Socialist, Communist, Marxist."

In contrast to Earlinger, Robinson, and Fusi, Robert Woodson did not see the African drought issue as racist or as a political weapon used by the West against Marxist governments. Rather, it is the result of internal problems, and thus, the solution must be internal. Woodson castigated African leaders for contributing to the drought because of their extreme military spending, an issue for which many of the Talented One Hundred criticized African leaders. According to Woodson:

> The drought is caused by mismanagement, not racism in the West. If you look at the budget of most African countries, 60 to 70 percent of the budget is consumed through military expenditures, even when they are not at war with anybody. So the question is, Why are they spending so much on military hardware? Many are doing it to protect the ruler against his own people. If you are spending money on hardware, you are not spending it on land control. We are not supposed to talk about it, because Blacks are doing it. In a country like Nigeria, AT&T went to build a phone system, but they had to pay out so much to bribe officials, there was nothing left to install the damn phone system. [Laughs]

Alur Nod, an African president of an international organization, disagreed with Woodson, saying, "No one has control over the drought. It's purely climatic conditions. I don't think it has anything to do with the government."

Whatever the causes of the drought, Jonathan Walden, a moderate Republican, thinks "there is still a disparity on the part of African leaders" in addressing the drought issue. "African leaders must come together for the relief of African nations. They must put energy into a mixed effort to care for their people and to eliminate the problem that exists in the homeland," he stressed.

Alur Nod said his organization is "working to eliminate the problem in the homeland":

> As president of a world organization, I am working to create better economic and commercial relations with Africans and other Blacks throughout the world to solve problems. We are working with Blacks in this country to transfer their scientific and technological skills to solve problems in African countries. We have to help ourselves. While Whites will rob you and come to get your diamonds and gold, they will try to prevent you from self-development. If you are hungry, anyone can feed you and thus control you. It is advantageous for the United States to see people starving. The people who give the food get the publicity. If you are strong and want money to study agriculture, the United States and other Western countries will say no. But if you are starving, they'll put you on TV with flies on your face. The American people will feel sorry, saying, "Look at those savages." We must help ourselves!

Jonathan Mobutu also thinks Africans throughout the world have a role to play in the solution of problems facing the continent of Africa. For African-Americans, there is a role to play in the transfer of technology. "African-Americans must develop independent linkages with African governments that would allow the transfer of skills. This can be done through historically Black colleges and Black churches."

Even when Third World nations know they must help themselves, the Talented One Hundred are disturbed by the low priority given to the welfare of the people and to developing human resources, whether domestically or internationally by these nations. When the U.S. government, as leader in the technological community, does not use its vast resources for the long-term solution of the African drought problem, it also indicates human welfare and resources are not high priorities. Instead of placing so much emphasis on developing technologically advanced weapons for military defense, the U.S. government should reorder its priorities. Most of the Talented One hundred feel, as Vernon Jordan does, that "the best defense is a strong domestic policy." As global citizens, the Talented One Hundred speak to the issues of nuclear disarmament and defense.

Nuclear Disarmament and Defense

John Lamont stated:

> Nuclear disarmament is a central issue of our age. I was in the military when [Robert] McNamara was the defense secretary. He had a civilian background. While others looked upon nuclear weapons as bigger weapons, he was aware of the consequences of nuclear war. The political system has been defined by nuclear weapons. We have had a nineteenth century political philosophy and twenty-first century weapons. We have been lucky.

Kelly Smith said we have been lucky that we have not killed each other, and "we should try to disarm as much as possible." Vernon Jordan disagreed, saying, "I am not for total nuclear disarmament." For Robert Woodson, nuclear disarmament is an irrelevant issue: "I don't get worked up over it," he said. Nor does Stephanie Tahara. She sees the nuclear disarmament issue as a "White man's game."

> They didn't invite me into the discussion about what I think. I am buying into the power elite. I am not horrified by the world coming to an end. What does disturb me is when children begin to say they have no future. My daughter is concerned about what is going to happen because of the pollution from nuclear energy and how it will shorten her life. Through the eyes of a child, you can share some guilt about the collective state the world is in.

In contrast to Jordan, Tahara, and Woodson, the majority of the Talented One Hundred believe strongly that there should be an arms treaty to reduce nuclear weapons. Jonathan Mobutu aptly summed up their feelings about nuclear disarmament: "There should be a movement toward an arms treaty that significantly reduces nuclear weapons. It should be followed by a reduction in defense expenditures and a shift toward increased social expenditures." Michael Lomax agreed that there should be a reduction in military defense and a higher priority placed on "human defense."

> I am a loyal American. I believe in a strong defense, but I believe there is waste. We need to bring the deficit down. We need to invest in other programs. I see defense as people, and we can't separate our defense from what we are doing with the most important resource—humans.

Pat Robinson was equally critical of this country's defense policies and the waste.

> I am not saying we don't need a defense. But I am appalled when people get upset over welfare fraud on the front page, and on the back page, you

read where Lockheed sold the government screws for millions of dollars. The military establishment is one of the scariest institutions in this country. They buy juntas off in different countries. Everything is at the expense of social programs.

John Lamont also thinks the military establishment is out of control. "The government has gone crazy. We need to come to some redefinition of what it means to be secure." For most of the Talented One Hundred, security means having an adequate defense. However, an adequate defense does not mean "we need a weapon reserve to kill people five to ten times over," said Dira Ridley.

Diane Earlinger saw a silver lining in the military build-up in this and other countries that might impel international heads of state to give serious consideration to military spending. She pointed out that the economy of the Soviet Union was in such shambles that it will be necessary for the country to address nuclear disarmament. "Glasnost is the only way to deal with the economic issue because the Soviet Union can't support its population," said Diane.

While there was general consensus among the Talented One Hundred that there should be a reduction in military defense and increase investment in human resources, Robert Woodson noted that often there is an inconsistency in ideological orientation and attitudes. "It is interesting that Black leaders say they are adamantly opposed to defense. However, when asked if a naval yard should close down in their district, they will tell you no. It's okay to talk in pejorative terms about these issues, but when you become very specific, they'll say, 'Oh, no, not my district.'" Diane Earlinger, who has a liberal political orientation on domestic policies, but a more moderate posture on foreign policies, has changed her views on defense.

> There was a time in the not too distant past when I could in no way justify the money this country invested in defense. But when you look at the defense budget, most of it is personnel. Blacks have been able to achieve a greater degree of equality in the military. But I still have great problems with money being spent on defense when there are so many health problems. I am more ambivalent in my reaction now.

While it is true that Blacks have made greater strides in the military, said Mobutu, "they are still underemployed in these military industries. These industries tend to be located in predominantly White areas. The technically trained people are disproportionately White."

Like Earlinger, Kufra Akpan, a radical Democrat, was ambivalent in his values and his attitudes about the military establishment. When I asked Akpan if he experienced any conflicts as a military officer and a history professor with Black nationalist leanings, after a pause, he responded:

Since the world is the way it is, we need to have a defense. But I wish there was a second defense for peace. I wish we would put a significant portion of our resources into reducing conflict. It presents lots of problems ideologically for me. It could make me feel like another mercenary, but I have been able to rationalize my way out of the contradictions by arguing [that] this position helps me to make educational opportunities available in terms of scholarships and jobs for young people. When I send them to a recruiter, it is a contradictory function, but I am comfortable with it.

While others may not experience the conflict on a personal level, as Akpan did, some of the Talented One Hundred experienced it at the collective level. They wanted to reduce military expenditures, yet they saw defense as necessary. "There is too much spent on defense, but the only way to maintain peace in the world is through control. The only thing people respect is power," said Frank Russo.

David Benton, an artist and a liberal Democrat, questioned the ascendancy of the military industrial complex in America, with its continuous drift toward war. He viewed the government as having lost sight of the greater interests of the people. "We need individuals who are concerned with humanity. We don't need people who like to play cowboys and Indians and use defense as a power leverage. It's my perception that people behind those guns are using them as penises." Joseph Lowery agreed with Benton: "It is time to reorder our domestic and foreign policies. Both are inextricably related. We need to stop exporting war over peace and justice. We have to commit ourselves to full employment, tax reform, etcetera. And we need a national leadership that can give us such policies."

Some Black elite viewed themselves as part of that cadre of national and international leaders that will shape domestic and international policies for the twenty-first century. Among the Talented One Hundred are individuals—like Michael Lomax and Jonathan Mobutu—who see themselves as liberators for this new social order.

The Black Elite as Liberators

Martin Buber, existential philosopher, has stated that one who is to be the liberator "has to be introduced into the stronghold of the alien." Freedom movements seek "a kind of liberation which cannot be brought about by anyone who grew up as a slave, nor yet by anyone who is not connected with the slaves; but only by one of the latter who has been brought up in the midst of the aliens and has received an education equipping him with all their wisdom and powers."[4] Living between two social worlds has given the Black elite insights into their social existence that transcend the ordinary consciousness. Instead of viewing themselves as marginal people of color within the context of the American society, they see themselves within the larger, global context where people of color are the majority. They have the opportunity, therefore, to become world citizens and lead the way to an alternative social order. The Black elite's experiences have not been so restrictive that they cannot fantasize about a new vision or "see their duality as a creative process and as part of the human condition," remarked John Daniels. He understands his duality "in terms of the human experience—the laughter, tragedy, love, and all the rest." This "laughter, tragedy, and love" is what Joseph Lowery referred to as "dark joy," a term coined by Lerone Bennett, author of *Before the Mayflower*. It is this "dark joy" which helps "Blacks make it in this world and better understand the lot of others," asserted Lowery.

> I don't think White folks got the joy of the struggle we have. They don't have the blessing of soul and experience. They can't pass on to the world the "dark joy" that has characterized the Black experience. We are sad; yet we are happy. It's what the White folks couldn't understand about the Black family. I don't know whether you read in the newspaper where I made a statement about Mayor Andrew Young calling Alice Bond.* He was reflecting a sensitivity that Black officials have to bring to public office.
>
> We were shut out so long that they didn't care what happened to us until Blacks came into office. All Black officials should have a sensitivity to their constituency, which should far surpass what White people have, because we know what it means to be down yonder in the valley where you couldn't hear nobody pray. We've been excluded, so we know how important it is to be included. We have been uncared for, so we know how important it is to be caring. So we bring a perspective, a feeling, and an experience nobody else has. Who else can feel like that? White folks can't even sing spirituals because they don't know what they are talking about. How can they sing "Swing Low, Sweet Chariot, Coming for to Carry Me Home." [He sings it.] How are they going to sing that? How are they going to sing, "I Got Shoes"? When the slaves sang that, they didn't have shoes. But they knew they were children of God, and all God's children have shoes. They were defiant; they were forgiving. They were joyful, sad, and that is what I mean by "dark joy." There is a sadness about our experience that we've overcome because of joy. Our hope is a part of that joy. Our struggle is a part of that joy. Our love for each other is a part of that joy. That is why we have to turn *to* each other and not *on* one another. We are doing too much turning on each other.

Having experienced this "dark joy" and using it creatively, some Talented One Hundred are stepping onto the global stage as collective actors

---

*The ex-wife of Julian Bond, the former Georgia state Senator and civil rights activist, whose marital dispute received national attention in 1987.

for oppressed peoples of the world. They view their Afrocentric perspective on humanity as an important counterbalance to the Eurocentric perspective, which deemphasizes human concerns and needs. Not incorporating an Afrocentric perspective into domestic and foreign policy has been one of the high costs of racism for Whites in America. They have failed to benefit from cultural diversity.

In our multiracial and multiethnic society, we tend to focus on the divisiveness in diversity rather than on the strengths. This is a point that Michael Lomax so eloquently reiterated:

> We've spent a lot of time in this country divided by race, ethnic group, and class. We are hostile toward one another. We've done a better job than some other multiracial societies. Japan has a sense of unity because of one race, and they work together to knock our socks off. This country has to find strength in its diversity. We are never going to be a homogeneous nation, and so we must have room for that diversity and pull together as one nation. If we do that, we will have different attitudes toward dropouts and teenage pregnancies as lost resources . . . We need to focus on being an inclusive rather than an exclusive nation.

In not recognizing strength in diversity, as Michael Lomax pointed out, this society fails to recognize the full potential of groups who can contribute to improving the quality of life for all Americans. Whites and others who promote racial oppression or other forms of social oppression also deny themselves "the full range of choices, experiences, and resources that could be theirs."[5] The Afrocentric perspective offers a rich tradition from which to view the world. Its holistic approach to health and life is the East's gift to the West. The Afrocentric holistic approach to medicine, for instance, is changing Western medical practices, which are based on the separation of mind and body. Thus, diverse cultural and social interaction can be beneficial for the development of society.

In a world that is increasingly global, where noncolored people are in the minority, cultural diversity is functional. White racism is particularly narcissistic because it promotes isolation from all peoples of color. It also inhibits intellectual growth among Whites and other people by promoting contempt, fear, and ignorance of other racial and ethnic groups. Hence, racism distorts the views of Whites and does not allow them to reconcile their own economic, political, and social interests and needs with the needs and interests of all people.

The value orientations of this society promote democracy and equality as well as racism. But democracy and equality are incompatible with racism. This leads to a distorted reality for Whites, resulting in moral ambivalence and a social blindness that dulls the senses. When the senses are dulled to racial oppression, one looks, but does not see. One tastes, but

251

does not savor. One touches, but does not feel; hears, but does not understand. A good example was Lee Atwater, chairman of the Republican National Committee and President George Bush's campaign manager of 1988, who heard and played Black blues but did not understand the rhythm of Black people or dance in step with their tune.

After the presidential election, Lee Atwater was appointed to the board of trustees of Howard University, a predominantly Black university in Washington, D.C. The students protested his appointment. He resigned, appearing slighted by their rebuke. In his first meeting with the student protesters, he told these bright, young students how much he liked rhythm and blues. Like the plantation slave master, he expected that their pent-up frustrations would be released on the academic plantation by "playing them a tune." He thought students would forget to ask his position on such issues as affirmative action, the extension of the voting rights act, and the African National Congress. He thought they would forget the issue of Willie Horton. Horton, a Black and a convicted murderer, was furloughed from a Massachusetts prison while serving a life sentence. He traveled from Massachusetts to Maryland and assaulted a White couple in their home, raping the woman. As the campaign manager for Bush, then vice-president of the United States, Lee Atwater used Willie Horton as a campaign issue to galvanize Whites. This issue played to the worst fears of Whites—Black crime and Black male supersexuality deflowering White womanhood.

Thus, when the senses are dulled because of moral blindness, "Whites become untrue to themselves and untrue to the world,"[6] writes Robert Terry, a White author who studies the negative impact of racism on White people. They start operating as inauthentic persons in inauthentic organizations.[7] For Terry, "racism leads to a false consciousness or an ungrounded solution. Either one forces us to live in an illusionary world that is dangerous to others and to ourselves. Our supposed strength defeats us. Our supposed wisdom becomes our ignorance and leads us to judgments that negate our short- and long-term self-interest."[8] He concludes that the negative impact of racism on Whites clouds their "capacity to make accurate judgments. . . . We [White people] cannot be with and for ourselves or each other if we do not know who we are and what we are about. Thus racism forces us into inauthenticity and denies humanity to ourselves and those we touch."[9]

If Whites are to achieve authenticity, they must start thinking about the meaning of their whiteness, accept responsibility for their whiteness, and act to bring about solutions to the resulting moral ambivalence and social blindness.

The U.S. Constitution starts out "We, the people," but this document did not include Black males and females nor White females, among others.

Now, in the twilight of the twentieth century, when the changing winds of human liberation are sweeping across the global village, from Eastern Europe to South Africa, "We, the people" can choose to translate this cornerstone of democracy into an authentic reality that includes Black, Brown, Red, and Yellow males and females. "We, the people" can also choose to continue with inauthentic institutions that lead to alienation of the oppressed. But both alienation and inauthenticity lead to dehumanization of the oppressor and the oppressed.

There is a way out of this quagmire. The new global man and woman of color want to define a new America and a new world for the twenty-first century. Michael Lomax and Jesse Jackson remind us that "We, the people," which must include males and females of all races, have an opportunity to create a new social order. "It is an opportunity for all of us," said Lomax, "to rethink our relationship, to debate, and to struggle" with the dehumanization of racism. We can choose, Jackson stressed, to "cross ancient lines of race . . . to find common ground" for social change, or we can continue to allow the color line, as Langston Hughes noted, "to fester like a sore" and to "sag like a heavy load" on the nation until it explodes. Each generation of Blacks does not have a choice to allow the nation to continue to sag or to explode. They must continue to carry the torch through the night, lighting the way to the dawn of a new day. Only through collective power can we make America and the world ours in the twenty-first century.

The new man and woman of color want to move beyond race and become actors in the international arena. As global citizens, the Talented One Hundred recognize a common linkage with Blacks throughout the African diaspora. Hence, they address the issues of apartheid and global human oppression. They also address the issues of nuclear disarmament and defense. A dominant Afrocentric perspective emerges which emphasizes human needs over military defense, and peace and justice over war. When an Afrocentric perspective is excluded because of racism, there is a high cost to Whites. They fail to benefit from cultural diversity, and they suffer from a distortion of reality, which leads to their inauthenticity and dehumanization.

APPENDIX A

Exemplary Visionaries: A Candle of Collective Consciousness and Collective Action

Four visionary standard-bearers paved the way for the demise of the color line in the twenty-first century. Each confronted the brutal pain and reality of the color line. Each successfully coped with it by taking a proactive stance. Yet, while each of the four standard-bearers has developed a strong collective consciousness, their paths to achieving a new social order differed.

Jeremiah Moses, the servant of the people, chose the public arena as an elected official to bring about social change. Having a strong racial consciousness, Moses employed his political astuteness to work tirelessly to improve the social and economic conditions of oppressed people in his local community as well as nationally and internationally. Though Moses was very political, when addressing the needs of diverse constituents, he was always guided by his strong racial ethos. He said, "Whatever deal I cut, I want to bring something back for Black folks."

Like Moses, Dorothy Bolden, a woman of vision, who rose through the ranks of the masses, uses her strong racial consciousness as a guide for changing the conditions of oppressed people, particularly working women. A former domestic, Bolden parlayed her expressive powers and her ability to organize workers and negotiate with her White employers into organizing and negotiating better working conditions for domestic workers on a national level.

Vangie Watkins, the social conscience of the Black community and a grass roots leader in Atlanta, on the other hand, is interested in empowering and raising the political consciousness of the Black masses to effect change on their own behalf. She is particularly critical of Black establishment leaders who are interested in protecting the status quo and who are primarily concerned with their own self-aggrandizement.

While Vangie Watkins is the social conscience of Blacks, Jack B. Lane is the social conscience of the global village. As a civil rights activist and an elected public official, he is concerned with building bridges between different ethnic and racial groups. He envisions a "beloved community" for the twenty-first century where justice and peace are priorities.

Though the four exemplary visionaries have taken different paths in coping with the color line, they are connected by their collective consciousness. In moving beyond their personal successes, each has used creatively the psychic pain of the color line as a change agent for collective action.

I now turn to the social backgrounds of the four standard-bearers and look at how significant life events and racial experiences influenced their styles of coping.

Jeremiah Moses: The Servant of the People

My father taught me to stand up for my civil rights and to face racial injustice wherever it faced you.

Social Background and Personal Influences

Jeremiah Moses, a sixty-five-year-old businessman and public official, was born in a small town in the Midwest in the early 1920s. He moved to Detroit with his parents, Jeremiah Moses, Sr., a college-educated businessman and civic leader and Jane Moses, a domestic with an eleventh grade education, before the family settled in an integrated midsize midwestern community in the 1920s. Jeremiah graduated from a predominantly Black university in a Southern state with a major in business. As an only child, Jeremiah grew up in a closely knit, religious household, attending his Baptist church every Sunday. His father was the most influential person in Jeremiah's life, instilling in him a strong work ethos. "I am a workaholic. I work seven days a week. There is no holiday, no basic starting time, and no basic quitting time." His father also instilled in him a strong racial consciousness. Jeremiah recalled an incident during his childhood when his father and mother, who were then employed as private household workers for a wealthy family in Detroit, stopped at a restaurant on the way home from work. When the owner of the restaurant said, "We are not going to serve you," his father insisted on being served, saying, "Oh yes you are going to serve me. [Laughter] I remember my dad flying through the air," said Jeremiah. "He always fought for his civil rights. My father taught me to stand up for my civil rights and to face injustice wherever it faced you."

Jeremiah was also strongly influenced by Representative William L. Dawson of Chicago, Illinois, one of the first Black congressmen since Reconstruction. Dawson reinforced the work ethic Jeremiah had learned from his parents. But most importantly, he influenced him politically. "He was an organizer and he made people responsible for producing." Jackie Robinson, the first Black baseball player in the major leagues, was also his idol. "I admired him for his football and baseball abilities," said Jeremiah, himself a former football captain and basketball star. Robinson and Jeremiah eventually met and became friends. At one point in their friendship, they decided to go into business together. Jeremiah admired Robinson because "he was a hustling type individual with a strong Black identity." "If a person didn't work, they didn't influence me," asserted Jeremiah.

Significant Life Events

After graduating from college, Jeremiah worked in the family business started by his father in 1932, and for a Black newspaper, prior to being drafted by the army in 1942. Fighting in a segregated army had a traumatic impact on young Moses. But first, he recalled the incident which led to his being drafted.

> A friend and I had gone to McCrory's, a dime store in the [Midwest]. We were refused service. We filed a suit. After I filed suit, I got a notice to go into the army. I always felt that was the reason I was called so quickly, because I had a plate and eight screws in my leg from a football injury. Ordinarily, they wouldn't have taken me with such a disability. The racial discrimination was outstanding in the army. There were White and Colored toilets on the Post. Black soldiers could not go in the main PX. I saw German prisoners and White WACS sitting at the counter drinking cokes, and I was denied the opportunity.
>
> While stationed in Anniston, Alabama, I became a marked man when I refused to get off of a segregated bus. If you wanted to go to Birmingham, you had to catch the bus in Anniston. When the bus arrived, there were always separate lines. First, White women soldiers, White men soldiers, White women civilians, and White men civilians. Second, there was a line with Black women soldiers and then the Black men soldiers. If you got to town at noon, you'd be lucky to catch the bus at 7 or 9 P.M. [Laughed] I said I would not do that anymore. I was first in the Black line. When the bus driver opened the door, I got on. The White driver told me to get off. I told him I was not going to get off. He let me stay on the bus. When I came back to the bus station about 3 o'clock in the morning, I wanted a coke. The [Blacks'] counter was closed, so I stepped up to the White counter to get a coke. Somebody

said, "That's that smart nigger." Two Whites came up and jumped me. There was a big riot with the soldiers and the police department. From then on, I became a marked man in Anniston. When I left the army base near Anniston, I went to Germany. The boat was segregated. Black troops were on one side and White troops were on the other.

In 1945, Jeremiah returned from the army. Back in his community in the Midwest, he again went to work in his father's business, and he also began his involvement in politics. Jeremiah's future looked bright, but his experiences in the army had left him embittered. He recalled:

When I returned from overseas, I was bitter. Bitterness had overtaken me. I was working in my father's business. If a White salesman would come to our place, I would let him sit all day long, or after he had sat for three or four hours, I would say I don't want anything. Hate was all over me. I was building up hate on top of hate, which was not giving me the results or the benefits I wanted.

One day Jeremiah made an appraisal of himself, saying:

I figured I had to use Whites instead of being used. My hatred was consuming me, and I was being used and didn't know it. I was not accomplishing anything for myself, or for the people I represented, or my family. I made up my mind to cut out the hate and work within the system to get everything I could out of the system. [Laughter] If I did that, I would be doing more towards my goals than following the line of hate, getting revenge, and pushing people around.

This turning point in 1945 eventually catapulted him into national prominence.

Coping with the Color Line

When Jeremiah was at a crossroad in moving from the role of victim to victor in 1945, he developed an effective strategy that assisted him in becoming a positive change agent. "I would sit quietly, get to know my subject, then think out my strategy, and move decisively to gain something when I moved," said Jeremiah. He used this strategy well for over forty years, "to serve the people." His service to others is his idea of success. Even when Jeremiah was the only Black serving on a committee or the only Black member of an organization, he still maintained a strong racial consciousness. "If you are the only Black in an organization, it is still your responsibility to go in there and bring something out for Black people," said Jeremiah.

He castigates Blacks who are placed on committees or who are in token positions "but do not bring something back for Blacks."

They get in these meetings and Whites start calling them by their first names and insinuating to them that if more Black people were like them, we wouldn't have a problem. Whites say to them that you are highly intelligent. When people start believing in that and don't take the part of a Black, then we've lost some gains. When I talk to Black leaders, I say to them, "The only reason you are placed on the committee is because you are Black." When you fail to carry out your function as a Black, hell yes, you are a token. Whites are being kind when they call you a token, because you are not fulfilling your part. They expect you to perform your duties as a Black. If they were in similar circumstances, they would do the same. But if you don't, they'll be just as happy with you.

Jeremiah has an independent economic base, which allows him to speak out earnestly on controversial issues without repercussions. He thinks Blacks who occupy positions in the "White man's structure" and "who are fearful to speak out" should not accept the responsibility of committee assignments.

"To be an effective token, you have to learn the agenda, know the subject, and ask pertinent questions," said Jeremiah. He cited an example of a person who was appointed to an important health district committee:

This person didn't know anything about the affirmative action of the combined health district. If I were on that committee, I would know the structure of the organization, the structure of employment, and know the services, goods, and output. I would also want to know how Blacks fit into each category of the organization. So if they are working on a committee, for example, that produces $2 million a year, and Blacks are not getting any of it, they need to find out why and start building on that. A token Black can do that and it is expected. Being the only Black may be difficult, but if you observe, listen, and speak at the right time, it can be done.

For over forty years, Jeremiah observed, listened, and spoke at the right time. He told me how he became a member of the Rules Committee, and he cited an example of how he coped when he sat on that committee as a state representative.

I was the first Black to sit on that committee in the House of Representatives. This committee determines which bills can come to the floor. It controls the floor. [How did you get on that committee? I asked.] I got on that committee by maneuvering. There was a guy who had been on that committee for seven years, and he wanted to become a county treasurer. Another guy was running against him and I had the Black vote to make or break both of them. I told him he had to deliver me the Rules Committee, and I would deliver him the Black vote. I was not only the first Black to sit on the committee, but the first freshman representative.

There was a bill in the Rules Committee pertaining to Blacks. Since the committee members had been so much in the habit of not having any Blacks, they spoke before they thought. "We don't want to give those Colored people that." Then they said, "Oh my God!" They apologized. I said, "That's not enough; we have to get the bill." I made them apologize by producing the bill on the floor. I didn't get the satisfaction of "cussing" them out, but I did get something for Black folks. I left the conscience on them. But if I were in my bag a few years before, I would have been "cussing," fighting, and talking about them, but I would not have gotten the bill on the floor. That is a shining example of keeping cool, taking advantage of your situation, and making it produce for you.

One of the many causes Jeremiah championed was prison reform. As the only Black member of a National Correctional Task Force Committee, he discussed his strategy to achieve prison reform and Black employment.

When the committee discussed prison reform, they worried about prisons near cities. I was able to push the advantage of having prisons near cities. It lowers Black unemployment. But there are some Blacks who oppose prisons near the city. They don't understand how it lowers unemployment. Prisons are at least 50 percent Black. And you can see to it that Blacks get medical care, education, and job training. If prisons are located in rural areas, where guards are uneducated and racially biased, reform is unlikely. They will not get any kind of mental rehabilitation, because they are so brow-beaten while they are in prison. It becomes another step, not in rehabilitation, but a step that is more detrimental to them.

What the public got to realize is that 98 percent of everybody who goes to prison will walk the streets. What you want to do is make sure the streets are safer for people when they leave prison than before entering. I sat in those meeting by myself and pushed the prison reform from the level of treatment resources, rather than emphasizing how it would help Blacks. It was my strategy to bring something back for Black folks. I wanted to increase the employment in correctional institutions from 3 percent to 30 percent of Black guards. Again, I would not speak on every item about prison reform. I would speak on issues of concern and save my strength to speak on those topics. When we sit on committees, we need to pick our subject, hold it, and speak on that subject that will benefit us the most—rather than speak on every subject. Even when I know it will benefit Blacks, I bring a general perspective.

Jeremiah's achievements in the Black community are numerous. As a Democrat who is liberal on social issues but conservative on fiscal matters, he has pushed through legislation on minority set-aside programs, sponsored a bill calling for divestment of corporations from South Africa, organized the Black-elected Democrats of his state, and was a key player for Jesse Jackson's presidential campaign bids.

Although Jeremiah always "brought something back to the Black community," he could "cut a deal" that benefited not only both his Black and White constituents, but also his city, county, and state. "I don't mistreat Whites. I play politics with them. Sometimes I give them something when they need it, and then chalk it up. I'll go to them when I need something," said Jeremiah. "I demand respect. I didn't go into politics for Whites to love me. I respect my White colleagues, but I don't play with them." Having the respect of both the Black and White community, he wielded his clout around his state and the nation. He worked tirelessly as a "servant of the people" seven days a week. "There were no holidays, no basic starting time, and no basic quitting time." Quitting time finally came for Jeremiah in 1988.

Jeremiah Moses fought a continuous battle, because, he told me, "We are not truly free until all of us are free." The people's voice is silent now, but the candle of his collective spirit continues to burn brightly for the many lives he touched.

Jeremiah was one of the most effective power brokers in his city and state until his death in 1988. He was "a race man," championing the Black cause, but governors, senators, and presidents also sought his advice and favor. After spending six hours with Jeremiah, I understood why he was respected by both the Black and White community. He was a fighter, waging a personal battle against racial oppression. He was also waging a personal battle against a terminal illness when I interviewed him in November 1986. The illness had weakened his diminutive stature, but had not diminished his fiery spirit.

During the course of my six-hour interview with Jeremiah, there were repeated breaks as he took care of his business clients' and constituents' needs. The interview took place primarily while riding around in his car. When we stopped at a restaurant for dinner, his constituents nearby—professionals, workers, the unemployed, welfare recipients—called out admiringly, "Jeremiah! Jeremiah!" or "Moses! Moses!" It was clear they felt that he could help part the color line and deliver his people from the sea of oppression.

Dorothy Bolden: A Woman of Vision

I eat civil rights. I sleep civil rights. I dream civil rights. I wake up to civil rights and I'll never give it up. My civil rights are still tingling my toes. When it does that, you don't get rid of it. It is instilled in me. It is like I've been bitten by a flea. Civil rights got in my blood stream, and I can't run it out.

Social Background and Personal Influences

Dorothy Bolden, founder and director of the National Domestic Workers of America, was born in Atlanta, Georgia, in the 1920s. Her father was a chauffeur with an elementary education, and her mother was an elementary school teacher with a twelfth grade education. He had left his father's rural sharecropping farm to seek work in Atlanta. Dorothy's mother, who taught school in a rural community, eventually joined her husband in Atlanta. They had two children—Dorothy and her brother.

At three, Dorothy lost her eyesight when she fell, knocking "an eye nerve out of place." Eventually, her "eye nerve fell back into place," and she started to school when she was eight years old. In the eleventh grade, Dorothy began to have trouble again with her eyesight, so she dropped out of school and started working regularly as a domestic.

Dorothy's parents had a major influence upon her strong racial consciousness. She recalled these memories of her parents:

> My father had great pride in being Black. My daddy was a handsome man. He walked with great pride and dignity. He was a Black man who didn't change his walk or status when he got around White people. He walked with his shoulders up straight and never pitied himself. He instilled this pride in me. He would always tell me I was just like him, and I was the apple of his eye. He wore fine suits, and he knew how to negotiate with White folks. My mother and father were my strength in helping me to act independent. They would say, "If you have only five cents, you act like you got more. If you eat bacon in the morning and evening, you go out and make people think you ate steak. It is not their damn business what you ate; you just go out and look good, so nobody will know your worries or troubles. It is no use telling it to them, because nobody is going to help you."
>
> My mother was one person who would fix a meal for you, feed you, and show you how to get on your feet, and then say, "Now you are out on your own. Now dammit don't come back here asking me for nothing else." [Laughs] This is what I say now to the women household workers. My mother was also a person of courage. She was strong and never let a man rule. She would tell my father, "Hell, if I work, I got a voice, too, and nobody is going to mastermind mine. You mastermind yours, and I'll take care of mine." Hearing that from my mother made me strong. My mother would always tell others, "If you make Dot mad (referring to me), she'll curse you." I have always been that way. I am going to do all the talking. Being a Black woman, I had to be talkative. People pretty much will knock you down or sit you down if you are not strong enough

to stand your ground. The Black woman's mouth is the only thing she got. I don't think any man wants to deal with the mouth of a Black woman. She can out talk anybody if she makes up her mind. The Black woman has had to do that in order to survive.

While growing up in Atlanta, Dorothy and her brother were nurtured not only by their parents, but also their two grandmothers and a grandfather. One grandmother was a sharecropper; the other was a teacher and her husband, a preacher. "I saw the differences between the two grandmothers," said Dorothy, "but it didn't really worry me. I had all these parents who could give me wisdom. God let me sit at their knee and listen to it." She spent much of her time with them during her early childhood, since she was unable to attend school until the age of eight.

Dorothy had much time to "bow down and listen" to her grandmothers and grandfather while riding the train from Atlanta to the rural towns of Madison and Social Circle, Georgia. She would discuss with her grandparents what she wanted to do when she grew up.

I always wanted to be a missionary worker. And my grandfather would tell me how to go about being one. Although I wanted to go to school to learn to be a missionary, my grandfather assured me it was not necessary, because that gift comes from Almighty God. He told me to just keep on going, and with my positive attitude toward people, I'd be fine. I never met a stranger, and I loved helping people. I told him you need an education to help people. He said, "Not all the time. It is not a requirement. Your job is to get somebody else to take care of the writing part, the book part, and every other part. Your part is to go out and help the people." And that is what I've been doing all my life. My grandfather gave me answers when I asked questions. I liked to be around older people, not younger people, because they could answer the questions I asked. My father always told me, "If you don't know, ask and it will be given to you." As a child, everybody told me I was a little before my time.

Significant Life Events and Racial Experiences

Although Dorothy worked full time as a maid when she dropped out of high school, she started working as a maid when she was nine years old. During the Depression she went to work to assist her parents. Black men who were chauffeurs and butlers made only $7.00 a week, and the domestics were making only $3.50 a week. At nine, she went to work for a Jewish family. She remarked:

I was trained by Jews. They would give you a meal and would give you something to carry home and $1.50 a week. I would wash diapers and nurse the babies. I didn't do much cleaning. I would watch their babies for them. You would work for neighbors and kinfolks and still end up with $1.50—no more or less. I wondered sometimes why they were using me. I always said if I ever get up off my knees, I promised God that I am going to stand tall and strong. [You had to scrub the floors on your knees, I asked.] I did.

When Dorothy started working full time as a maid after dropping out of school, she earned, like other maids, $3.50 a week.

That was the best we could do. We thought we were making something. But we were going from sun up to sun down. They would give you the leftover food and clothing their children didn't need, and they would buy new ones and give you the old ones. It was a form of payment. We really thought that was helping us to get bacon drippings to bring home to put in the collard greens. We realized that we weren't making anything, but what could we do about it? We were scared to tell another maid, because she might go back and tell "your madam."

For a time, Dorothy lived with an aunt in Alabama. She remembered vividly one racial incident that she encountered while working there as a maid.

I went to work for a week with a lady, but she didn't want to pay my $10.00. So I reached at her to whip her. Fearing for my life, my aunt put me on the train back to Georgia. She feared I would be hanged.

After Dorothy became "a grown girl," she would alternate between public and private employment.

President Franklin Roosevelt had started social security, and if I didn't work in public employment, I would not get anything when I got old. So I worked six months as a household worker in a private home and six months as a waitress or elevator operator. I started to travel to the North to work in places like New York, Chicago, and Detroit. Whites would offer me $75 to work for them a month. I would negotiate my living arrangements, my clothes, and my salary. I would not go unless I had a round trip ticket. [Laughed.] After ninety days, my mother knew I would come up the street. My husband was in the army, and we had a son. I would always tell my mom to call to tell me to come home and that my son needed me. He was not sick, but he missed his mother. I would get on the Dixie Fly [bus] and come rolling back to Georgia. I would dress up that night like Miss Sheba Webe and go down to Auburn and ball awhile. [Laughed.] We'd go from cabaret to cabaret until it was time to get up and go to work.

Going from cabaret to cabaret was not only a stress reducer, it was here that her collective consciousness was heightened. Said Dorothy:

I got a lot of experience going to the cabarets. The most experience I got with my people was while sitting on a cabaret bar in Chicago. I used to love to sit on the bar and feel the vibrations coming from my people. I could feel the vibrations like it was a spiritual thing. I felt the ignorance and intelligence mixing, but they were all kinfolks whether they were from the North or the South. There was a certain essence that gave me a special feeling about my own people. If you analyze the backgrounds of our people, you get to wondering about them. The only values we had at that particular time were having clothes, dancing, and balling. We were locked into a system of slavery.

While the cabarets heightened her consciousness, Dorothy learned as a household worker to wear the mask with her White employers to improve her own working conditions.

I learned how to change my personality to get what I wanted. I was very charming when I wanted something, and very nasty when I wanted to leave the job. I could always get a job. I knew how to talk to get what I wanted. I didn't beg or use any pressure. I would say in a nice way, "Darling, I can't live on this. I got a son I got to support. I am not asking you to break your rules, if you can't afford it, just let me know, and I'll work for somebody else." They'd say, "No, I don't want you to leave, Dorothy. I'll see what I can do."

Coping with the Color Line: A Vision for Collective Action

In 1968, Dorothy Bolden had a dream about helping to improve the socioeconomic status of domestics.

I promised God that I would do a great deal for domestic workers. I wanted them to have insurance benefits. Domestic laborers never had any benefits. It hurts so bad to see a Black woman who has worked so hard all her life, while birthing her children, but when she dies, her family has to beg to bury her. It is a hurting and heartbreaking feeling. My eyes fill with tears when I think about some Black women who have been buried in that way.

Dorothy's dream was not only about organizing domestic workers, but it was a dream that was in conflict with her family life.

I saw the dream to organize the domestic workers so beautifully; but I had to give up my family. My children were still in school. I thought about it and cried. I said I got to help my husband. I prayed to Jesus, telling Him my family might not understand what all I am giving up. I love my children, but I love you most of all. I talked with my ninety-four-year-old grandmother, and she told me whenever God puts you on a task, you do it. She said, "He is not going to leave you. He'll feed you. He'll take care of you and supply the everyday needs. It may not be the riches and glories of other people, but you'll be well taken care of." I went to sleep. In my dream I was frightened to give up my children. I had lost three children through death and that's a hurting thing. So I didn't want to lose them. My success in organizing was based on my children not going astray and not giving me any worries or problems.

Dorothy's dream did not mean she would physically leave her family. It meant less quantity time would be spent with the family. She found much support from her husband. This dream represented a turning point in Dorothy's life. She did not give up being a maid. She not only continued to use her expressive powers to improve her family's economic status but she employed her negotiating skills to organize domestics. She wore the mask when she organized NDW.

The last job I got before organizing the NDW, I negotiated a bonus once a year, and they wouldn't have a child unless they asked me. I got a bonus for each child they had. The children became so attached to me they called me "Mama." I had control over the household checkbook. I knew how to get [my employer] to go out of town with her husband and that would give me five or six hundred dollars for the benefit of my children. I didn't have to fix lunch for myself. It was ordered from one of the finest restaurants on Peachtree Street in Atlanta. They would buy my clothes, pay for my hairdo, and work shoes. I had three two-week vacations each year. I did all the hiring. I didn't do any housework. There were people hired to do that. I managed the house. All of this fell in line for me to set up the National Domestic Workers of America.

Everything I did was set up from this lady's house. I first got her organized with a schedule to participate in volunteer work, and that gave me a chance to get organized by way of the telephone. The household workers were calling to speak to me. If her husband called, I would tell him the phone was busy, or one of the children had taken it off the hook. Sure enough, when he asked the information operator, the phone would be off the hook.

Just when they had their third child, I finished organizing NDW and got my bonus. I told them I was going home to enjoy my own children, and I didn't want their children too attached to me. I said, "It would be very embarrassing to have your oldest boy, your girl, and baby son to call me Mama in public." I said that would not be nice. [You played on the racial issue? I asked.] Yes, I used the race issue. But they agreed. I left. Now she walks up to me and tells me how proud she is of me.

"When I dream, they are reality dreams. A dream is an idea; a vision is a reality," said Dorothy. In 1969, her dream became the National Domestic Workers. She remarked, "My grandmother gave me good advice. She lived long enough to see the organization established." Dorothy does not take credit for the success of the movement.

> The women caught a good grip of what I was doing in weekly meetings with them. They handled it so beautifully, like God just gripped the spirit of their heads and said, "This is what you do." Everyone cooperated. So I won't say it is my success, but I'll say it was their success, because I never negotiated anything with their employers. I taught them how, but they did it. I am successful to God, and He made me very successful to Him. Anybody can look at my charter to see it said no monetary gains. You see, money changes the attitudes of directors. I didn't want anything to change me from what God had instilled in me, and that was to help those women. I dreamed about it. I cried about it.

After organizing, Dorothy was reluctant to become president, but she was urged to do so by the domestics. Since it was shortly after King's death, she felt obligated to provide leadership to maintain morale. She remembers that in 1968 the women were making only $25 a week.

> I got their salaries up to $50 a week. They made $15 to $25 per day. A lot of employers didn't want to pay that. But I would say to the maids, "Let your employers know how worthy you are. Let them know this is the time you have to go home, so you can be with your children, and tell them you are not going to leave them any more by themselves." These are the things I talked about, for example, being too late when you cook dinner for your children at 10 or 11 o'clock in the evening. Tell them you are tired of that. Since I was a maid at the time, it built up their courage. My maid job got so demanding, I had to quit. I had to go out and explain to White organizations and White churches about NDW. I didn't bite my tongue; God was with me. But when I went into some of those places, I wondered if I'd get out alive. I would tell White women employers, if they couldn't pay Black women, don't hire them.

Mrs. Bolden has worked tirelessly on behalf of upgrading "household technicians'" economic and social status. She teaches them to be proud of their work. "You are a servant; you can make a profession of it."

Postscript

In over twenty years since organizing the NDW, Dorothy Bolden has achieved international acclaim. She was appointed to serve on a women's committee in 1970 by President Nixon and continued under President Jimmy Carter's administration. Her political influence is felt in Atlanta. Atlanta politicians know it is politically expedient to incur Mrs. Bolden's favor. They know she is "looking over their shoulders," keeping them accountable.

When I asked Mrs. Bolden how she would like to be remembered, she said, "I would like to be remembered as a Christian, striving and trying to help someone and loving to do it—not for the benefit of money, but for the benefit and love of God. I want to be a servant to humankind."

Mrs. Bolden, a most memorable woman, was interviewed in December 1987 at her office in Atlanta, Georgia. She concluded her interview saying, "People say I can't continue to do this work because of my age. I got arthritis, but I tell 'old Arthur' [arthritis] to move on. I got to go today. I can't stay here and moan with you. When I get to hurting, I walk fast and that hurt leaves. It ain't going to slow me up."

Vangie Watkins: Social Conscience of the Black Community in Atlanta

> I don't devote too much of my attention to White folks. In the 1960s, I addressed the Black issue to Whites, but I don't feel the need to do that anymore. It is important to get Blacks to understand who we are and where we are. If Blacks are able to understand and appreciate our accomplishment and beauty throughout humankind, there is no reason to be ashamed. We are unique, beautiful, and awe-inspiring. If it is so significant and so important that White folks got to spend twenty-four hours a day trying to stay on top of us, we are powerful within ourselves.

Social Background and Personal Influences

Vangie Watkins was born in Fort Worth, Texas, in 1935. During the late 1930s, her father, a professor with a master's degree in biochemistry at Fisk University in Tennessee, and her mother, a homemaker with a bachelor's degree in music, migrated to the West Coast. Vangie reflected on her upbringing.

> My father dreamed California would be better times. It was the ending of the Depression and the beginning of World War II, and going West was the thing. People in California had equality. But when he sought work, the only job he found to support the family was as a porter on a train. My father was a hard worker and committed to his job. He was the controlling force in the formative years of my sister and me. He read, watched news, and talked about world events. My perspective on race came from my father. He was very dark and my mother was very fair-skinned. My father, an Alabama boy, thought that was a good move to marry a damn near White girl from Fisk University. It was the era of marrying a person lighter than you to increase your stature in the com-

munity. Being poor, my father had struggled to get through Fisk University. On the other hand, my mother, a light-skinned girl, came from a well-to-do family whose folks could afford to send her to college. Her father was a minister and her mother had a master's in mathematics and was an accomplished pianist. So there was a class and color thing with my parents. My father talked about racism, segregation, body burnings, lynchings, and beating folks up. He let us know that he had come from some real bad experiences, and they still exist. We should strive for the best and take advantage of the educational system.

Both parents equally influenced me. They taught me to be independent. They validated me as good or bad, but they let me choose. I came up with the liberal upbringing of my father and that came out in me.

I grew up in a White community in Berkeley, California. I had one West Indian dance teacher, the most dynamic Black woman I ever met. She introduced me to dance, music, and jazz. From her I got an appreciation of Afro-American culture. The other influence in my life outside the family was my White Girl Scout leader. As the only Black girl in the troop, she opened up doors for me and suffered indignities for doing so. I learned to be confident and not afraid from her.

Significant Life Events

Vangie attended the University of California at Berkeley, in the 1950s, but did not complete college. It was at the university that her political consciousness was raised. She became involved in several movements and causes.

As a student at Berkeley, I was a part of the student movement when the silent generation came alive. So that dovetailed into my involvement with the Black Panthers, the Civil Rights movement, and the Muslims. I never wanted to be a Muslim, but I respected their approach, philosophy, and emphasis on good health. I was involved with the Black Panthers. The Panthers were out in the streets telling folks they had rights. They stressed not being afraid, self-protection, and basic rights, so I had no problems with what they were trying to do. As a Panther, I was followed by the police, because I had a big Afro and looked like Angela Davis. I knew I was followed, but it didn't bother me. I felt proud.

The fierce determination, courage, commitment, and hard work that she learned from her parents, Girl Scout troop leader, and the Black Panthers have helped to sustain her as a change agent.

Since moving to Atlanta in 1973, Vangie has been actively involved as a grass roots volunteer in organizing the Black community, pressuring the city and county governments to become more responsive in the delivery of services, and in implementing constructive policies that have an impact on the community.

Coping with the Color Line

Although Vangie Watkins addresses the issues of both class and race, she speaks out fervently against Black leaders who are not responsive to Blacks and who are not dealing with pertinent issues facing the Black community. She advocates collective empowerment as a means of influencing Black leaders and the larger society to respond to the needs of the Black community. As a radical Democrat, she has worked relentlessly, organizing around many issues in the Black community, such as: getting a regional library in the Southwest community of Atlanta; obtaining better social services and police protection; and requiring better planning and zoning of commercial property. She is also concerned about such issues as the quality of education, drugs, poverty, and teenage pregnancy.

Vangie works within the system as an active member of the State Democratic party and the Fulton County Democratic Committee. Yet, at the same time, she serves as the social conscience of the party.

Vangie sees two Atlantas—the chamber of commerce image of the great mecca of the South and the poor inner city. She reminds people of the gap between the two.

> People hear so much about all the buildings going up in downtown Atlanta, and they hear about beautiful southwest Atlanta where black officials live. But, if you look behind the glitter and glamour, you can come up with some indicators that may not be to the liking of the chamber of commerce and officials in the Atlanta area. Atlanta is the second poorest inner city next to Newark, New Jersey. I am concerned about what is happening in the Black community. The educational system is about 65 percent Black, and the school board is largely Black, but we have Black kids who can't read and write. They are not able to compete in the job market.

Vangie is critical of Black establishment leaders and their civil rights tactics. She calls for the leaders to use empowering tactics that are more relevant to the 1990s.

> What were the sixties about in Atlanta? We are riding on Martin Luther King, Jr.'s coat tail; we are saying this is the birthplace of King. King was not accepted in Atlanta when he was here. He was doing his work outside of Atlanta because he would have caused a shake-up here. There were a few people in Atlanta who were elitist and didn't want him to mess up anything. King was martyred after his death; then Atlanta claimed its own. Now we have the King Center and mausoleum, and it is like the Taj Mahal. It is sacred with an eternal flame, and we have money given to the center. I feel sometimes we have things whipped out to keep us in line.

They are used as control. The whole Civil Rights movement in Atlanta is used to keep niggers in line. Instead of truly educating Blacks to understand the reason for their lack of power to bring about change, Black leaders wait until there is an issue like teenage pregnancy and dope in the project. They then go out and march for a day.

We use civil rights tactics and methods that are appropriate for the 1960s. We march down to city hall, rant and rave, sing songs, and somebody gets up to make a grand speech or two. We go home and do nothing. This does not give folks an understanding of the political process and how it works. How do you learn about the political process? How do you involve yourself in the political process? What buttons do you push?

You've got to be able to simply not say I know the mayor or councilman and I rub elbows with them. When you are included in the crowd, you feel you have something to lose. So you are afraid to speak out, because you might not be invited to the next affair. Certain gratuities are used as control mechanisms. Maybe that is okay for some people, but I am not willing to give up my ability to speak out. I am not willing to sacrifice my respect in the community to go to somebody's dinner.

Vangie feels that the predominantly Black elected officials in Atlanta are also more responsive to White leadership than to the Black community that elected them.

I don't understand the role of Black elected officials in Atlanta. Are they still the token or the spook who sat by the door? I have to constantly block them from doing something in a detrimental way to the Black community. You see this headline in the newspaper? [She showed me the paper.] It is about the councilmen who were treated to a trip to Las Vegas for their vote on a landfill in the Black community. When a community changes its complexion to Black, even though the economic and demographic data are the same, we have to defend ourselves against poor planning decisions, poor zoning decisions, and the lack of services for our tax dollars.

When I address these issues, the officials see me as a troublemaker. If they can isolate me, I am nobody and I am crazy. They also postpone meetings with me and postpone acting on issues. For example, in our protest to get a library in the community, we started out with two hundred people. Each time we protested, we lost people. It is their strategy to isolate me and to say I am not truly representative of anybody or anything. Therefore, I don't have to pay attention to you. But it doesn't stop me. I have to prove that they are liars. Just recently I got a councilman for my district to vote my way on the issue, "Should property owners who own commercially zoned property have the right to have mini warehouses?" These mini warehouses are restricted to industrially zoned property, and they wanted to put them in the Black community.

Vangie is concerned, too, that Black leadership does not address serious social issues facing the community from an Afrocentric perspective. Too often, she claimed, they have a reactive posture to social issues.

> I am concerned that Black leaders do not address Black issues in the Black community. If Jews can address Jewish issues, if Italians can address Italian issues, and if Orientals can address Oriental issues, then what's wrong with Black folks addressing their issues and being proud that we are Black folks? When we don't address issues, it hurts us. Teenage pregnancy is hurting Black girls; drugs are hurting Black boys. Are we ashamed to admit the impact of AIDS on Black youths? We are afraid to say we, as Blacks, have problems because of what Whites might say. We are trying to be so positive that we fear talking about issues. Since there is so much negativeness about being Black, we are afraid and ashamed to say we got more problems. We want to make progress in society, so in order to do that, we put things under the bed or in the closet, and close the door on them rather than deal with them. Some problems, like teenage pregnancy, dope, and AIDS affect all of us, but we need to deal with these problems from a Black perspective and to say we don't care who knows we have them before we can adequately wipe them out.

How Vangie Uses Religion to Fuel Her Social Consciousness

While growing up, Vangie Watkins did not belong to a religious organization, although she did attend many different churches. Recently, she has become a member of the United Methodist Church. Religion has not only become a source of emotional support for her, but she also uses the message of Christianity as a vehicle for raising the collective consciousness of Blacks.

> Before I joined the church, I made a commitment to use the individual Jesus Christ as a mentor. I looked at it from both an earthly perspective and a spiritual perspective. I still have problems dealing with this heaven, but I look at Christ as a person who had a simple moral philosophy that He used as a guide in His behavior with everyday people. Christ was saying that all people are the same. And if they truly believe in their goodness, it is within them. They are worthy and have a life to live and contributions to make. Their penny is no less valuable than somebody's used dollar, and whatever gifts and talents they possess are needed, necessary, and even more valuable than somebody else's gifts and talents. So what I try to do is to go to church to use those messages as a confirmation to keep my foundation strong. I go back every Sunday to refuel my tank, so that I can have energy on Monday through Saturday to talk to people about how beautiful they are, what they are here for, and how they have as much right to be here as I have. They are no less important than the

mayor, the governor, or the president. When the day comes and we all get to go, we are all equal, aren't we?

When I am told by people—"Look at you and your successes in organizing"—I tell them, "You can do it too." I say to people if they are interested in making sure they get good programs and services from their tax dollars, they have to demand it. It is not given to you. They got to go downtown to city hall and shake cages and rattle some bones. They also have to come out of their community. They got to ask, "Why do Whites have gorgeous neighborhoods, clean streets, tutorial programs, etcetera?" Blacks can't say Whites have it and Blacks don't have it because we are Black and accept that.

I am trying to say to people that they don't have to come from a certain family or certain class to be worthy and accepted. Jesus was not sanctioned by the political leadership of his day. It is counterproductive for Blacks to look to leadership that has been sanctioned by the White establishment. If Black leaders have bought into the process, what price have they paid? What games are they running politically, educationally, and socially? What is the message? Do they abide by it? Do I disagree? Do I challenge it or have a right to? I know the process and the requirements, but other Blacks should also know them. We have only had a few Black aggressive champions like Martin Luther King, Jr., A. Philip Randolph, Paul Robeson, and James Baldwin to stand on their own, but something always happens to them in America.

Vangie is very concerned that Blacks do not build on their struggle against oppression. She posed the question, "Why do we reinvent the wheel each generation? Why don't we draw on what has gone before us?"

Postscript

When I interviewed Vangie in December 1987, she told me she planned to run for a seat on the city council in Atlanta. In her 1989 bid for a city council seat, she lost.

Jack B. Lane, The Preacher of the Beloved Community

My life has been sailing against the current.

Throughout this book, more of Jack B. Lane's life history has been given than that of Jeremiah Moses, Dorothy Bolden, and Vangie Watkins. Therefore, his story here is a brief summary of the influence of the Civil Rights movement on his commitment to build a beloved community that embraces all humankind.

Social Background and Influences

The sensitive forty-seven-year-old Civil Rights activist and public official grew up in the segregated South in a supportive household with parents, brothers, sisters, and various relatives. His family knew there was something very special about him. As a child, he always wanted to preach about the "beloved community," sometimes extending it to all living things. "This may sound strange or crazy to you," said Jack, somewhat self-effacingly:

> I grew up with the idea of wanting to be a minister, and one of my uncles had Santa Claus bring me a Bible for Christmas. So the family started referring to me as "preacher." I lived on a farm, and I had the responsibility to take care of the chickens. I used to preach to the chickens, and on one occasion I tried to baptize one. When a chicken would die, we had a funeral. My younger brothers, sisters, and cousins were mourners. We had a chicken cemetery and a chicken burial, and I would preach the funerals. I would also preach to the chickens at night when we closed them up.

Jack eventually went on to get a degree in religion and philosophy at a predominantly Black university. Although he never became an ordained minister of a church, he remained the preacher of the "beloved community."

Significant Events and Racial Experiences

In college, Jack participated in the Civil Rights movement. He was the only member of his family to become involved. His parents were initially very frightened for young Jack. They warned him to be "careful" and his mother cautioned him "to be particular when he traveled from school to home." He should "look in the closet and under the bed." But they were also fiercely supportive and proud of his participation. In the movement, he worked directly with Martin Luther King, Jr., and came under his personal influence and his philosophy of nonviolence. This was the turning point in Jack's life.

> It created for me, like so many people, a new sense of values, and that's what I think happened to many of us. There was a revolution of values and ideas. You come to that point where you see people as people, as human beings. And you even forget to a significant degree about race, color, and whether someone was born on this side of the track or the other side of the track. Seeing people as people, you try to move and create what Martin Luther King, Jr. called the beloved community—the

open society and the sense of family—and that's what we are—the extended family.

Jack has spent his life working towards the beloved community. It has not been easy. There were always skeptics, Black and White, who claimed it could never happen. "People said we couldn't talk the talk; we couldn't walk the walk. Governor George Wallace said we'll never make it in our march from Selma to Montgomery, but we made it. We got a voting rights act. We ended the era of segregated public accommodation."

Jack proved "through creative effort, by sticking together, and by developing a sense of solidarity, we could overcome." When he first ran for public office, some people told him he couldn't get elected. His opponent was "too well known and had too much money." But, Jack said, "my life has been sailing against the current." People told him he couldn't win his present position. He said, "I drew on my inner resources and inner strengths. It was the only thing I really had. I say to young people today, 'You can make it. You can do it. Don't sit back and say you cannot make it. If you believe in yourself, you can do it.' I've been blessed by coming under the influence of Martin Luther King, Jr. and the influence of the discipline of nonviolence."

Since his Civil Rights days, he has steadfastly worked for world peace and social and economic justice, making the impossible happen in creating "the beloved community."

W.E.B. Du Bois said, "The problem of the twentieth century is the problem of the color line." In the twilight of the twentieth century, Dorothy, Vangie, Jack, and Jeremiah are exemplary visionaries, paving the way for an alternative social order. Their bright candle of collective consciousness should help light the way to the demise of the color line for the twenty-first century.

APPENDIX B

Summary of the Social Background Characteristics of the Talented One Hundred

This study consists of 63 percent male participants and 37 percent female participants.

Six percent of the participants were under 35; 35 percent were 35–44; 33 percent were 45–54; 18 percent from 55–64; and 8 percent over 65.

Thirty-eight percent of the participants grew up in the South; 32 percent grew up in the North Central region; 12 percent grew up in the Northeast; 6 percent grew up in the West; 6 percent grew up outside the United States; and 6 percent lived in different regions of the country.

The birthplace of participants included the following states: 6 percent from Alabama; 2 percent from Arkansas; 3 percent from California; 7 percent from Kentucky; 16 percent from Georgia; 2 percent from Florida; 4 percent from Indiana; 4 percent from Illinois; 2 percent from Kansas; 3 percent from Louisiana; 1 percent from Maryland; 1 percent from Massachusetts; 16 percent from Ohio; 2 percent from Oklahoma; 1 percent from North Carolina; 5 percent from New York; 1 percent from Pennsylvania; 2 percent from South Carolina; 1 percent from Tennessee; 4 percent from Texas; 6 percent from Virginia; 2 percent from Washington, D.C.; and 3 percent from West Virginia. Three percent of the participants were born in Africa; and 3 percent were born in the West Indies.

Seventy-one percent of the participants grew up in a Black setting; 15 percent in a White setting; and 14 percent in a mixed setting.

The educational attainments of the participants were as follows: 32 percent held doctorate degrees; 27 percent held masters degrees; 11 percent held medical degrees; 6 percent held law degrees; 13 percent held bachelors degrees; 7 percent had attended college; and 4 percent held high school diplomas or less.

The educational attainments of the participants' parents were as follows: less than high school graduate—47 percent of fathers and 45 percent of mothers; high school diploma or equivalence—20 percent of fathers and 26 percent of mothers; junior college—6 percent of fathers and 4 percent of mothers; bachelors degree—8 percent of fathers and 13 percent of mothers; masters degree—9 percent of fathers and 7 percent of mothers; doctorates—2 percent of fathers and 1 percent of mothers; professional degrees (M.D., J.D., D.D.S., etc.)—4 percent of fathers. Data were not available for 4 percent of the participants' fathers and 4 percent of the participants' mothers.

The occupational attainments of participants' parents were: professional, technical, and kindred—23 percent of fathers and 23 percent of mothers; managers and administrators—5 percent of fathers and 2 percent of mothers; sales workers—4 percent of fathers; craftsmen and kindred workers—4 percent of fathers and 2 percent of mothers; operatives—15 percent of fathers and 3 percent of mothers; laborers—21 percent of fathers and 2 percent of mothers; service workers—13 percent of fathers and 12 percent of mothers; private household workers—24 percent of mothers; farmers—7 percent of fathers; and homemakers—25 percent of mothers. Occupational data were not available for 8 percent of the participants' fathers and 7 percent of the participants' mothers.

The personal income range of participants was: 64 percent earned over $50,000; 18 percent earned between $35,000 and $50,000; 12 percent earned between $20,000 and $34,999; and 6 percent earned $20,000 or less.

The marital status of participants was as follows: 10 percent were never married; 20 percent were divorced; 2 percent were separated; 65 percent were married; and 3 percent were widowed.

The political orientations of the participants were as follows: 5 percent were conservative; 28 percent were moderate; 38 percent were liberal; 13 percent were radical; and 14 percent had diverse orientations, depending on the issue. Data were not available for 2 percent of the participants.

The political party affiliation included: 67 percent Democrats; 5 percent Republicans; 26 percent of the participants declared themselves as independent; and 2 percent belonged to a third party.

Church membership of participants included: 16 percent A.M.E.; 37 percent Baptist; 8 percent Presbyterian; 2 percent Unitarian; 2 percent C.M.E. and 2 percent United Methodist; 2 percent Congregationalist/Episcopalian; 2 percent Catholic; and 29 percent other or do not attend.

The participants were employed in the following sectors of the economy: 22 percent were in government; 17 percent were in the profit sector; 9 percent were in the private nonprofit sector; 14 percent were self-employed; 4 percent worked for private colleges/universities; 31 percent worked in public colleges/universities; and 3 percent were retired.

The racial composition of business contacts of the participants was as follows: 12 percent were Black; 26 percent were White; and 60 percent were mixed. Data were unavailable for 2 percent of participants.

The racial composition of the social contacts of participants was: 62 percent Black; 4 percent White; and 34 percent mixed.

Participants would prefer the following ideal employment setting: 27 percent would prefer Black; 6 percent would prefer White; 48 percent would prefer mixed; 19 percent had no preference.

The ideal racial setting for participants to live would be as follows: 37 percent would choose a Black neighborhood; 2 percent would choose a White neighborhood; 45 percent would choose a mixed neighborhood; and 15 percent had no preference. Data were not available for one person.

The ideal educational setting for participants would be as follows: 34 percent would choose a Black setting; 4 percent would choose a White setting; 36 percent would choose a mixed setting; and 25 percent would choose a variety of settings, depending on the stage in their life cycle. Data were not available for one person.

The most important influence within the family for participants was the mother (43 percent); 18 percent of participants were most influenced by the father; 29 percent were equally influenced by both parents; 4 percent were most influenced by grandparents; and 6 percent by other relatives.

Three of the most important influences outside the family were teachers and other role models in school, such as counselors and coaches, 48 percent; Black role models, 16 percent; and ministers and the church, 9 percent. Twenty-seven percent of the participants were influenced by family, friends, and other individuals, such as neighbors and prominent Blacks.

APPENDIX C

Names, Principal Professions, and Types of Organizational Affiliations of Those Interviewed for This Volume

Names in this list, with the exception of those cited in the prologue, have been changed.

Name	Principal Profession	Type of Organizational Affiliation
1. Kufra Akpan	Professor	Public college/university
2. Prince Albert	Artist	Self-employed
3. Lisa Allen	Professor	Public college/university
4. Leo Aramis	Journalist	Private, for profit
5. Warner Babbitt	Journalist	Private, for profit
6. Jefferson Barnes	Professor	Public college/university
7. David Benton	Professor	Pubic college/university
8. Jeraldyne Blunden	Artist	Private, nonprofit
9. Dorothy Bolden	Social activist	Private, nonprofit
10. William Holmes Borders, Sr.	Minister	Private, nonprofit
11. Graham Boston	Scientist/engineer	Government
12. Lula Brown	Social activist	Retired
13. Timothy Brownlee	Public official	Government
14. Walter Calvin	Manager	Private, for profit
15. Elam Coke	Dentist	Self-employed
16. Cassie Cooper	Administrator	Private college/university
17. John Daniels	Manager	Private, for profit
18. Duane Dennis	Broker	Private, for profit
19. Diane Earlinger	Manager	Government

Name	Principal Profession	Type of Organizational Affiliation
20. Lena Faulkner	Manager/political activist	Private, nonprofit
21. Ronald Fellows	Manager	Private, for profit
22. Sharla Frances	Administrator	Government
23. Tefe Fusi	Professor/Administrator	Public college/university
24. Jeanette Gear	Public official	Government
25. Sharon Georgia	Lawyer	Government
26. Leslie Glouster	Health Administrator	Public college/university
27. Dick Godfather	Administrator	Government
28. Teresa Hale	Psychologist	Public college/university
29. Ferdinand Hamilton	Administrator	Public college/university
30. Walden House	Professor/Scientist	Public college/university
31. John Hubbard	Professor	Private college/university
32. Bernice Jackson	Social work administrator	Government
33. Roger Johnson	Politician	Government
34. Teresa Johnson	Professor	Public college/university
35. Vernon Jordan	Lawyer	Private, for profit
36. Hosea Kelly	Professor	Public college/university
37. Claude Kent	Professor	Public college/university
38. Ethel King	Journalist	Private, for profit
39. Priscilla King	Social work administrator	Private, nonprofit
40. John Lamont	Professor/scientist	Public college/university
41. Jack B. Lane	Politician	Government
42. Michael Lomax	Politician	Government
43. William Long	Professor	Public college/university
44. Johnny Longtreet	Politician	Government
45. Johnson Longworth	Professor	Public college/university
46. Joseph Lowery	Minister/social activist	Private, nonprofit
47. Ned McMillian	Physician	Self-employed
48. Tony Michaels	Manager	Private, for profit
49. Colbert Miller	Physician	Self-employed
50. Crystal Miller	Professor	Public college/university
51. Jonathan Mobutu	Professor/administrator	Public college/university
52. Jeremiah Moses	Politician	Government
53. Alur Nod	Administrator	Private, for profit
54. William Ofodile	Professor	Public college/university
55. James Paschal	Entrepreneur	Self-employed
56. Veronica Pepper	Professor	Public college/university
57. Clarence Pinkney	Manager	Private, for profit
58. Laura Price	Physician	Self-employed

Name	Principal Profession	Type of Organizational Affiliation
59. Dira Ridley	Scientist	Private, for profit
60. Bernie Roberts	Social researcher	Self-employed
61. Benson Robinson, Sr.	Entrepreneur	Self-employed
62. Marla Robinson	Administrator	Government
63. Pat Robinson	Public official	Government
64. Earnest Ross	Professor	Public college/university
65. Frank Russo	Health administrator	Government
66. Ruth Shelly	Educator	Retired
67. Aretha Shield	Artist	Private, nonprofit
68. Joshua T. Smith	Entrepreneur	Self-employed
69. Kelley Smith	Manager	Private, for profit
70. Robert Snow	Lawyer	Government
71. Renee Stone	Professor	Public college/university
72. Teresa Stanfield	Administrator	Public college/university
73. Ellen Strawberry	Administrator	Private, nonprofit
74. Bernice Sumlin	Educator	Retired
75. Albert Sungist	Administrator	Public college/university
76. Stephanie Tahara	Administrator	Government
77. Thomas B. Thomas	Manager	Private, for profit
78. Laverne Townson	Manager	Private, for profit
79. Jonathan Walden	Minister	Private, nonprofit
80. Yvonne Walker-Taylor	Administrator	Private college/university
81. Clifford Warren	Physician	Self-employed
82. Vangie Watkins	Social activist/General clerk	Private, for profit
83. Lee Watson	Administrator	Public college/university
84. Bonhart Wheeler	Professor	Public college/university
85. Sheridan Williams	Professor	Public college/university
86. Walden Wilmington	Professor/scientist	Public college/university
87. Booty Wood	Musician/performer	Self-employed
88. Robert Woodson	Social activist/ Community organizer	Self-employed
89. Elizabeth Wright	Administrator	Public college/university

Notes

Prologue

1. Everett V. Stonequist, *The Marginal Man* (New York: Russell and Russell, 1961), p. 222.

2. It is not possible to compare this distribution directly with national averages. The Talented One Hundred were asked to indicate their annual income at the time of the interview. Given that the interviews spanned a two-year period, there is no common reference point to examine the income distribution at a given point in time, for example, 1986.

3. Martin Kilson, "Black Bourgeoisie Revisited," *Dissent* (Winter 1983), p. 87.

4. Barney G. Glaser and Anselm L. Strauss, *The Discovery of Grounded Theory* (Chicago: Aldine, 1967).

5. Bart Landry, *The New Black Middle Class* (Berkeley: University of California Press, 1987); Daniel C. Thompson, *A Black Elite* (New York: Greenwood Press, 1986).

6. Gordon W. Allport, *The Nature of Prejudice* (Reading, PA: Addison-Wesley, 1954); T. W. Adorno et al., *The Authoritarian Personality* (New York: Harper, 1950); Gunnar Myrdal, *An American Dilemma* (New York: Harper and Brothers, 1944); Robert K. Merton, "Discrimination and the American Creed," in Peter I. Rose, ed., *The Study of Society,* 2nd ed. (New York: Random House, 1970), pp. 449–457.

7. Joe R. Feagin and Clairece Booher Feagin, *Discrimination American Style,* 2nd ed. (Malabar, FL: Robert E. Krieger Pub. Co., 1986).

8. Stokeley Carmichael and Charles V. Hamilton, *Black Power: The Politics of Liberation* (New York: Vintage Books, 1967), p. 4.

9. Albert Memmi, *The Colonizer and the Colonized* (Boston: Beacon Press, 1967), p. xiii.

10. James B. Stewart, "Psychic Duality of Afro-Americans in the Novels of W.E.B. Du Bois," *Phylon,* 4 (1983), 93–107.

11. W.E.B. Du Bois, *The Souls of Black Folk* (New York: Fawcett, 1961), pp. 16–17.

12. Ayi Kwei Armah, "Fanon: The Awakener," *Negro Digest,* 18 (Oct. 1969), p. 4.

13. Memmi, *Colonizer,* p. 107.

14. Ibid., p. 120.

15. This definition of racism is in the tradition of such scholars' works as Robert Blauner's *Racial Oppression in America* (New York: Harper and Row, 1972); John R. Feagin and Clairece Booher Feagin, *Discrimination American Style: Institutional Racism and Sexism,* 2nd ed. (Melbourne, FL: Robert E. Krieger Pub. Co., 1986); Stokeley Carmichael and Charles V. Hamilton, *Black Power: The Politics of Liberation* (New York: Vintage Books, 1967); and James Jones, *Prejudice and Racism* (Reading, PA: Addison-Wesley, 1972). See also Sunera Thobani, Shyrel Smith Hosseini, and Richard H. Ogles, "Towards a Further Demystification of the Racist, Patriarchal, Imperialist World System," *Human Affairs: International Journal of Social Studies,* 14 (1988), 3.

The concept of race has been used in many ways to refer to linguistic categories (Aryan, Russian speaking), to religious categories (Hindu, Jewish), and to national categories (Germans, Poles). Because such varieties of categories have been considered races, they reflect the arbitrariness and artificialness of racial designations. The official classifiers isolate certain social categories, based on an arbitrary selection of physically or biologically transmitted characteristics.

Race is, then, a social creation, not a biological fact. It is a sociopolitical category based on certain perceived inherited physical characteristics. These characteristics are isolated, and their importance, as differentiating features, is overemphasized in different societies. For example, Julian Pitt-Rivers, in "Race, Color, and Class in Central America and the Andes," in John Hope Franklin, ed., *Color and Race* (Boston: Beacon Press, 1968), pp. 264–281, noted that in much of Latin America, skin color and the shape of the lips are less important differentiating criteria than hair texture, eye color, and stature. In the United States, skin color and the shape of the lips are important. However, whether one's phenotype is closer to White is not an issue in this country. A person is Black if one has known Black ancestry—one-fourth, one-eighth, one-sixteenth, or too minute to be discernible. This classification of race is so entrenched in the United States that the Census Bureau figures are based on it.

16. William Julius Wilson, *The Truly Disadvantaged: The Inner City, the Underclass, and Public Policy* (Chicago: University of Chicago Press, 1987).

Chapter 1: The Color Line as Reality: Race Lessons, Patterns, and Propositions

1. John Hope Franklin, ed., *Color and Race* (Boston: Beacon Press, 1968), p. x.

2. Michael T. Martin and Howard Cohen, "Race and Class Consciousness: A Critique of the Marxist Concept of Race Relations," *Western Journal of Black Studies,* 2 (1980), 84–91.

3. Robin M. Williams, Jr., *American Society: A Sociological Interpretation*, 3rd ed. (New York: Knopf, 1970).

4. William E. Cross, Jr., "Black Family and Black Identity: A Literature Review," *Western Journal of Black Studies*, 2 (1978), 111–124.

5. James B. Stewart, "Psychic Duality of Afro-Americans in the Novels of W.E.B. Du Bois," *Phylon*, 44 (1983), 93–107.

6. See Frantz Fanon, *Black Skin, White Masks* (New York: Grove Press, 1967); James Weldon Johnson, *The Autobiography of an Ex-Coloured Man* (New York: Knopf, 1912); John Edgar Wideman, *Brothers and Keepers* (New York: Holt, Rinehart and Winston, 1984); Richard Wright, "The Ethics of Jim Crow: An Autobiographical Sketch," in Abraham Chapman, ed., *Black Voices* (New York: New American Library, 1968); and Roger Wilkins, *A Man's Life: An Autobiography* (New York: Simon & Schuster, 1982).

7. Martin Kilson, "Black Bourgeoisie Revisited," *Dissent* (Winter 1983), 87.

8. Zora Neale Hurston, *Dust Tracks on a Road* (New York: Arno Press and The New York Times, 1969), pp. 223–224.

9. James Blackwell, *Mainstreaming Outsiders: The Production of Black Professionals* (Dix Hills, NY: General Hall, 1981).

10. E. Franklin Frazier, *Black Bourgeoisie* (New York: Free Press, 1957).

11. "Race: More to be Done," *Hampton Roads Daily Press*, Jan. 13, 1991, H2.

12. Derek T. Dingle, "Finding a Prescription for Black Wealth," *Black Enterprise*, Jan. 1987, p. 39.

13. Elaine Pinderhuges, "Afro-American Families and the Victim System," in M. McGoldrick, J. K. Pearce, and J. Giordano, ed., *Ethnicity and Family Therapy* (New York: Guilford Press, 1982), p. 114.

14. Johnnetta B. Cole, "Culture: Negro, Black and Nigger," *The Black Scholar*, 1, no. 8 (June 1970), 41.

15. Kenneth E. John, "How Are Blacks Treated in Your Community?" *Washington Post, National Weekly Edition*, 2 March 1987, p. 37.

16. Cole, "Culture," p. 41. See also Francis Terrell and Sandra Terrell, "An Inventory to Measure Cultural Mistrust among Blacks," *Western Journal of Black Studies*, 5, no. 3 (1981), 180–185.

17. George Davis and Glegg Watson, *Black Life in Corporate America: Swimming in the Mainstream* (Garden City, NY: Anchor Doubleday, 1982).

18. Bart Landry, "Black Leadership: Possibilities and Limitations," paper presented at the Association of Black Sociologists, Atlanta, Georgia, Aug. 1988.

19. Al Karmen, "Just When Civil-Rights Activists Thought They Could Take a Rest," *Washington Post, National Weekly Edition*, 9, no. 15 (May 1988), p. 31.

20. Paul Ruffins, "Activists Fight Desegregation Rollback," *Black Enterprise*, Sept. 1988, p. 25.

21. Richard D. Hylton, "Working in America," *Black Enterprise*, Aug. 1988, p. 63.

22. Ibid., p. 66.

23. Zora Neale Hurston, *Mules and Men* (Philadelphia, PA: Lippincott, 1935), pp. 18–19.

Chapter 2: Manifestations of the Color Line:
The Impact of Violence

1. William Julius Wilson, *The Declining Significance of Race* (Chicago: University of Chicago Press, 1978), p. 151.

2. Charles Vert Willie, *Caste and Class Controversy,* (Dix Hills, NY: General Hall, 1979), p. 157.

For other critics of Wilson, see Harry Edwards, "Camouflaging the Color Line: A Critique," in *Caste and Class Controversy,* Charles Vert Willie, ed. (Dix Hills, NY: General Hall, 1979), pp. 98–103; Robert Hill, *Economic Policies and Black Progress: Myths and Realities,* Washington, DC: National Urban League, 1981); Alphonso Pinkney, *The Myth of Black Progress* (Cambridge: University of Cambridge Press, 1984).

3. Willie, *Caste,* p. 158.

4. Hussein Abdilahi Bulhan, *Frantz Fanon and the Psychology of Oppression* (New York: Plenum Press, 1985). p. 135.

5. Ibid., p. 136.

6. Ibid., p. 137.

7. Robert Blauner, *Racial Oppression in America* (New York: Harper and Row, 1972), p. 27.

8. Bulhan, *Frantz Fanon,* p. 140.

9. Abram Kardiner and Lionel Ovesey, *The Mark of Oppression* (Cleveland, OH: World, 1962).

10. Rosabeth Moss Kanter, *Men and Women of the Corporation,* (New York: Basic Books, 1977), p. 239.

11. Michael D. Woodward, "Ideological Response to Alterations in the Structure of Oppression: Reverse Discrimination, the Current Racial Ideology in the U.S.," *Western Journal of Black Studies,* 6, no. 3 (1982), 166–173.

12. Chukwuemeka Onwubu, "The Intellectual Foundations of Racism," *Western Journal of Black Studies,* 3, no. 3 (Fall 1979), 157–167.

13. Robert Rosenthal and Lenore F. Jacobson, "Teacher Expectations for the Disadvantaged," *Scientific America,* April 1968, p. 22.

14. Joe R. Feagin and Clairece Booher Feagin, *Discrimination American Style* (Melbourne, FL: Robert E. Krieger Pub. Co., 1986), p. 47.

15. Ibid., p. 52.

16. Daudi Ajani Ya Azibo (Donald Allen), "Perceived Attractiveness and the Black Personality," *Western Journal of Black Studies,* 7, no. 4 (Winter 1983), 229–238.

17. Richard D. Hylton, "Working in America," *Black Enterprise,* Aug. 1988, p. 63.

18. Sharon Collins, "The Making of the Black Middle Class," *Social Problems,* 30, no. 4 (April 1983), 369–382.

19. Bill Dedman, "Blacks Less Likely to Get Home Loans," *Dayton Daily News,* Jan. 22, 1989, pp. 1a, 10a.

20. Ibid, p. 10a.

21. See Calvin C. Hernton, *Sex and Racism in America* (New York: Grove

Press, 1965); Charles Herbert Stember, *Sexual Racism* (New York: Harper and Row, 1976).

22. Alfred Moss, *The American Negro Academy* (Baton Rouge: Louisiana State University Press, 1981).

23. James M. Jones, *Prejudice and Racism* (Reading, PA. Addison-Wesley, 1972), pp. 4–5.

Chapter 3: The Color Line Across the World of Work

1. Bart Landry, *The New Black Middle Class* (Berkeley: University of California Press, 1987), p. 88.

2. Joel Garreau, "The Integration of the American Dream," *Washington Post, National Weekly Edition*, Feb. 8–14, 1988, p. 6.

3. Landry, *New Black Middle Class*, p. 112.

4. Derek T. Dingle et al., "America's Hottest Black Managers," *Black Enterprise*, Feb. 1988, p. 81.

5. Derek T. Dingle, "Will Black Managers Survive Corporate Downsizing?" *Black Enterprise*, March 1987, p. 51.

6. Ibid.

7. Ibid.

8. Edward W. Jones, Jr., "Black Managers: The Dream Deferred," *Harvard Business Review*, May-June 1986, pp. 84–93.

9. Nathan McCall, "Making Fast Money in High Finance," *Black Enterprise*, Feb. 1987, p. 54.

10. Derek T. Dingle and Constance M. Green, "When the Tough Get Going," *Black Enterprise*, Aug. 1987, p. 50.

11. Jones, p. 86.

12. Ibid., p. 88.

13. Ibid., p. 86.

14. Rosabeth Moss Kanter, *Men and Women of the Corporation* (New York: Basic Books, 1977).

15. Richard D. Hylton, "Working in America," *Black Enterprise*, Aug. 1988, p. 64.

16. Ibid., p. 64.

17. Bebe Moore Campbell, "Black Executives and Corporate Stress," *New York Times Magazine*, Dec. 12, 1982.

18. Jones, "Black Managers," p. 85.

19. Derek T. Dingle et al., "America's Hottest Black Managers," *Black Enterprise*, Feb. 1988.

20. Jones, "Black Managers," pp. 91–92.

21. "Facts and Figures," *Black Enterprise*, Aug. 1987, p. 39.

22. "Facts and Figures," *Black Enterprise*, June 1987, p. 96.

23. Derek T. Dingle, "Finding a Prescription for Black Wealth," *Black Enterprise*, Jan. 1987, p. 48.

24. Sharon M. Collins, "The Making of the Black Middle Class," *Social Problems*, 30, no. 4 (April 1983), p. 373.

25. Ibid., p. 369.

26. "Fewer Blacks in High Positions," *Dayton Daily News and Journal Herald,* May 22, 1987.

27 Collins, "Making of Black Middle Class," p. 370.

28. Ibid., p. 371.

Chapter 4: The Color Line Across the World of Academe

1.William H. Exum, "Climbing the Crystal Stair: Values, Affirmative Action and Minority Faculty," *Social Problems,* 30, no. 4 (April 1983), 384.

2. Ibid., 385.

3. Shirley Vining Brown, "Increasing Minority Faculty: An Elusive Goal," *MGE Research Profiles,* 1, no. 3 (Princeton, NJ: Educational Testing Service, 1988), p. 1.

4. Ibid., p. 2.

5. Barbara Vobejde, "Blacks in the Sciences," *Washington Post, National Weekly Edition,* Aug. 15–21, 1988, p. 38.

6. Jewel L. Prestage, "Quelling the Mythical Revolution in Higher Education," *Journal of Politics,* 14 (Aug. 1979), p. 769.

7. Exum, "Climbing," p. 390.

8. Ibid., p. 391.

9. Edward Jackson, "Blacks on White Campuses: Problems and Perspectives," in Julia C. Elam, ed., *Blacks on White Campuses* (Lanham, MD: University Press of America, 1983).

10. Andrew J. Chisham, "An Assessment of the Role of Black Administrators in Predominantly White Colleges and Universities," in Julia C. Elam, ed., *Blacks on White Campuses,* (Lanham, MD: University Press of America, 1983), pp. 55–67.

11. Exum, "Climbing," p. 393.

12. Robert W. Stephens, "The Study of Music as a Symbol of Culture: The Afro-American and Euro-American Perspectives," *Western Journal of Black Studies,* 10, no. 4 (1986), 181.

13. Ibid., 182.

14. Russell L. Adams, "Evaluating Professions in the Context of Afro-American Studies," *Western Journal of Black Studies,* 5, no. 3 (Fall, 1981), 140.

15. Sam Hopkins and Ann Hardie, "Professor Denied Tenure Sues Emory," *Atlanta Journal and Constitution,* Dec. 24, 1988, pp. 1c and 4c.

16. Exum, "Climbing," p. 395.

17. Eloise Salholz, "Do Colleges Set Asian Quotas?" *Newsweek,* Feb. 9, 1987, p. 60.

18. Rosabeth Moss Kanter, *Men and Women of the Corporation* (New York: Basic Books, 1977), p. 240.

Chapter 5: The Color Line in Social, Religious, and Family Life

1. Ken Weber, "Young, Black and Bored," *Providence Sunday Journal Magazine,* April 12, 1987, p. 6.

2. Laura B. Randolph, "The Whitest State," *Ebony Magazine,* Dec. 1987.

3. James Blackwell and Philip Hart, *Cities, Suburbs and Blacks* (Dix Hills, NY: General Hall, 1982).

4. Beverly Tatum, *Life in Isolation: Black Families Living in Predominantly White Communities,* Ph.D. dissertation, University of Michigan, 1984, p. 225.

5. Robert Hill, *The Strengths of Black Families* (New York: Emerson Hall 1971).

6. Demitri B. Shimkin, Gloria Jean Louie, and Dennis A. Frate, "The Black Extended Family: A Basic Rural Institution and a Mechanism of Urban Adaptation," in Dimitri B. Shimkin, Edith M. Shimkin, and Dennis A. Frate, eds., *The Extended Family in Black Societies* (Chicago: Aldine, 1978).

7. Harriette P. McAdoo, "Black Kinships," *Psychology Today,* May 1979, p. 67. See also, Harriette P. McAdoo, ed., *Black Families* (Beverly Hills, CA: Sage, 1981) pp. 103–169.

8. Bebe Moore Campbell, "Black Executives and Corporate Stress," *New York Times Magazine,* Dec. 12, 1982.

9. John P. Fernandez, *Black Managers in White Corporations* (New York: Wiley, 1975), p. 25.

10. Daniel C. Thompson, *A Black Elite* (Westport, CT: Greenwood Press, 1986).

11. Lawrence E. Gary, "A Social Profile," in Lawrence Gary, ed., *Black Men* (Beverly Hills, CA: Sage, 1981).

12. Francis Fox Piven and Richard A. Cloward, *Regulating the Poor: The Function of Public Welfare* (New York: Pantheon, 1971).

13. "Facts and Figures," *Black Enterprise,* March 1987, p. 32.

14. Thompson, *Black Elite,* p. 112.

15. Gwen Ifill and Dan Balz, "Middle-Class Blacks Are Down Beat about the Campaign." *Washington Post, National Weekly Edition,* Oct. 3–9, 1988, pp. 6–7.

16. Robert Hill, *The Strengths of Black Families* (New York: Emerson Hall, 1972).

17. William D. Watley, *Roots of Resistance: The Nonviolent Ethic of Martin Luther King, Jr.* (Valley Forge, PA: Judson Press, 1985), p. 29.

18. Benjamin Quarles, *The Negro in the Making of America* (New York: Macmillan, 1964), p. 162.

19. Jacqueline Fleming, *Blacks in College* (San Francisco, CA: Jossey-Bass, 1984).

20. Charles Whitaker, "The Disappearing Black Teacher," *Ebony Magazine,* January 1989.

21. Fleming, *Blacks in College,* pp. 1–2.

Chapter 6: Gender Politics—Through the Eyes of Black Women

1. Angela Davis, *Women, Race and Class* (New York: Vintage Books, 1983), p. 10.

2. Sue K. Jewell, "Black Male/Female Conflict: Internalizations of Negative Definitions Transmitted Through Imagery," *Western Journal of Black Studies,* 7 (Spring 1983), 43–48.

3. Sharon R. King, "At the Crossroads," *Black Enterprise,* Aug. 1988, p. 47.

4. Ibid.

5. Ibid., p. 48.

6. "Facts and Figures," *Black Enterprise,* April 1987, p. 39.

7. Richard D. Hylton, "Working in America," *Black Enterprise,* Aug. 1988, p. 66.

8. John P. Fernandez, *Racism and Sexism in Corporate Life* (Lexington, MA: D. C. Heath, 1981), p. 61.

9. Ibid., p. 19.

10. Ibid.

11. Cynthia Fuchs Epstein, "Positive Effects of the Multiple Negative: Explaining the Success of Black Professional Women," *American Journal of Sociology,* 78, no. 4 (Jan. 1973), pp. 912–935.

12. Vanessa J. Gallman, "What to Say When Someone Tells You, 'It Pays to Be a Black Woman,'" *Essence Magazine,* March 1983, p. 89.

13. Karen Fulbright, "The Myth of the Double-Advantage: Black Female Managers," in Margaret Simms and Julianne Malveaux, eds., *Slipping Through the Cracks: The Status of Black Women,* 3rd ed. (New Brunswick, NJ: Transaction Pub., 1986). See also Francine D. Blau and Marianne A. Ferber, "Occupations and Earnings of Women Workers, in *Working Women: Past, Present, Future* (Washington, DC: Industrial Relations Research Association, 1987), pp. 55–59.

14. Kathrynn A. Adams, "Aspects of Social Context as Determinants of Black Women's Resistance to Challenge," *Journal of Social Issues,* 39, no. 3 (1983), pp. 69–78.

15. Edward D. Jones, "Black Managers: The Dream Deferred," *Harvard Business Review,* May-June 1986, p. 91.

16. Davis, *Women,* p. 61.

17. Bell Hooks, *Ain't I a Woman?* (Boston, MA: South End Press, 1981), p. 1.

18. Ibid., p. 190.

19. Ibid.

20. Ibid., p. 188.

21. "Facts and Figures," *Black Enterprise,* Aug. 1988, p. 43. See also Fulbright, "Myth," p. 36.

22. Jones, "Black Managers," p. 91.

23. "Blacks Have Less Incentive to Wed, Study Says," *Dayton Daily News,* March 17, 1989, p. 4a.

24. Orde Coombs, "Black Men and White Women," *Essence Magazine,* May 1983, p. 82.

25. Bill McAllister, "The Plight of Young Black Men in America," *Washington Post, National Weekly Edition,* Feb. 12–18, 1990, p. 6.

26. Laura B. Randolph, "Black Women/White Men: What's Goin' On?" *Ebony,* March 1989, p. 156.

27. Coombs, "Black Men," p. 138.

28. "Facts and Figures," *Black Enterprise,* April 1988, p. 39; McAllister, "Plight," p. 6.

29. Bebe Moore Campbell, *Successful Women, Angry Men* (New York: Random House, 1986).

30. Lois Benjamin, "Black Women Achievers: An Isolated Elite," *Sociological Inquiry,* 5, no. 2 (Spring 1982), 141–151.

Chapter 7: Styles of Coping

1. Bruce P. Dohrenwend and Barbara S. Dohrenwend, *Social Status and Psychological Disorder: A Causal Inquiry* (New York: Wiley, 1969), p. 133.

2. Robert Davis, "A Demographic Analysis of Suicide," in Lawrence Gary, ed., *Black Men* (Beverly Hills, CA: Sage, 1981), pp. 179–195.

3. Robert Staples, *Black Masculinity* (San Francisco, CA: Black Scholar Press, 1982), p. 32.

4. Lawrence E. Gary, "Health Status," in *Black Men* (Beverly Hills, CA: Sage, 1981), pp. 47–71; Frederick D. Harper, "Alcohol Use and Abuse," in Gary, ed., *Black Men,* pp. 169–177; Frederick D. Harper and Marvin Dawkins, "Alcohol Abuse in the Black Community," *Black Scholar,* April 1977, pp. 23–31.

5. Lois Benjamin and James B. Stewart, "Race, Illness Orientation, and World View as Linkages in Welfare Dependency," Mimeo, 1986.

6. *Report of the Secretary's Task Force on Black and Minority Health* (Washington, DC: U. S. Department of Health and Human Services, 1985); Ronald M. Andersen, Ross M. Mullner, and Llewellyn J. Cornelius, "Black-White Differences in Health Status: Methods or Substance?" *Milbank Quarterly,* vol. 65, supple. 1, 1987, pp. 72–99; Kenneth G. Manton, Clifford H. Patrick, and Katrina W. Johnson, "Health Differentials between Blacks and Whites: Recent Trends in Mortality and Morbidity," *Milbank Quarterly,* vol. 65, supple. 1, 1987, pp. 129–197; Harold W. Neighbors, "Improving the Mental Health of Black Americans: Lessons from the Community Mental Health Movement," *The Milbank Quarterly,* vol. 65, supple. 2, 1987, pp. 348–380.

7. Bebe Moore Campbell, "To Be Black, Gifted and Alone," *Savvy Magazine,* Dec. 1984, p. 68.

8. Ibid.

9. Albert Bandura, "Self-Efficacy Mechanism in Human Agency," *American Psychologist,* 37 (1982), 122.

10. Lois Benjamin and James B. Stewart, "The Self-Concept of Black and White Women: The Influences upon Its Formation of Welfare Dependency, Work Effort, Family Networks, and Illnesses," *American Journal of Economics and Sociology,* 48, no. 2 (April 1989), 165–175; Lois Benjamin and James B. Stewart, "Race, Illness Orientation and World View as Linkages in Welfare Dependency," mimeo, 1986.

11. Rosabeth Moss Kanter, *Men and Women of the Corporation* (New York: Basic Books, 1977), p. 214.

12. Thomas Kochman, *Black and White Styles in Conflict,* (Chicago: University of Chicago Press, 1981).

13. See James H. Geer, Gerald C. Davidson, and Robert T. Catchel, "Reduction of Stress in Humans Through Nonveridical Perceived Control of Aversive

Stimulation," *Journal of Personality and Social Psychology,* 16 (1970), 731–738; James W. Pennebaker, M. Audrey Burnam, Marc A. Schaeffer, and David C. Harper, "Lack of Control as a Determinant of Perceived Physical Symptoms," *Journal of Personality and Social Psychology,* 35 (1977), 167–174; Murray P. Naditch, Margaret A. Gargan, and Laurie B. Michael, "Denial, Anxiety, Locus of Control and the Discrepancy Between Aspirations and Achievements as Components of Depression," *Journal of Abnormal Psychology,* 84 (1975), 1–9; Jerry Suls and Brian Muller, "Life Changes and Psychological Distress: The Role of Perceived Control and Desirability," *Journal of Applied Social Behavior,* 11 (1981), 379–389; and Melvin Seeman and Teresa Seeman, "Health Behavior and Personal Autonomy: A Longitudinal Study of the Sense of Control in Illness," *Journal of Health and Social Behavior,* 24 (1983), 144–160.

14. Patricia Failing, "Black Artists Today: A Case of Exclusion," *ART News,* March 1989, p. 124.

15. Ibid.

16. Bandura, "Self-Efficacy Mechanism," p. 143.

Chapter 8: Beyond the Color Line: An Alternative Vision

1. Jesse Jackson, "What We've Won," *Mother Jones,* July/Aug. 1988, p. 22.

2. Rutledge M. Dennis, "Du Bois and the Role of the Educated Elite," *Journal of Negro Education,* 46, no. 4 (Fall 1977), 388–402.

3. Robert Blauner, *Racial Oppression in America* (New York: Harper and Row, 1972), p. 115.

4. Charles Vert Willie, *Race, Ethnicity, and Socioeconomic Status: A Theoretical Analysis of Their Interrelationship* (Dix Hills, NY: General Hall, 1983), pp. 253–254.

5. Joyce A. Ladner and Walter W. Stafford, "Defusing Race: Developments Since the Kerner Report," in Benjamin P. Bowser and Raymond G. Hunt, eds., *Impacts of Racism on White Americans* (Beverly Hills, CA: Sage, 1981), pp. 71–85.

6. Robert W. Terry, "The Negative Impact on White Values," in Bowser and Hunt, eds., *Impacts of Racism,* p. 134.

7. Ibid., p. 120.

8. Ibid., p. 134.

9. Ibid., p. 149.

Selected Bibliography

Adams, Kathrynn. "Aspects of Social Context as Determinants of Black Women's Resistance to Challenge." *Journal of Social Issues,* 39, no. 3 (1983), 69–78.

Alsop, Ronald. "Middle-Class Blacks Worry about Slipping, Still Face Racial Bias." *Wall Street Journal,* November 3, 1980.

Andrews, Gavin C., Christopher Tennant, Daphne M. Hewson, and George E. Vaillant. "Life Event Stress, Social Support, Coping Style, and Risk of Psychological Impairment." *Journal of Nervous and Mental Disease,* 166 (1978), 297–316.

Armah, Ayi Kwei. "Fanon: The Awakener." *Negro Digest,* October 1969.

Askenasy, Alexander R., Bruce P. Dohrenwend and Barbara S. Dohrenwend. "Some Effects of Social Class and Ethnic Group Membership on Judgments of the Magnitude of Stressful Life Events: A Research Note." *Journal of Health and Social Behavior,* 18 (1977), 432–439.

Azibo, Daudi Ajani Ya. "Perceived Attractiveness and the Black Personality." *Western Journal of Black Studies,* 7, no. 4 (1983), 229–238.

Back, Kurt, and Ida Harper Simpson. "The Dilemma of the Negro Professional." *Journal of Social Issues,* 20 (1964), 60–71.

Bandura, Albert. "Self-Efficacy Mechanism in Human Agency." *American Psychologist,* 37 (1982), 122–147.

Benjamin, Lois. "Black Women Achievers: An Isolated Elite." *Sociological Inquiry,* 52 (1982), 141–151.

Billingsley, Andrew. *Black Families in White America.* Englewood Cliffs, NJ: Prentice-Hall 1968.

Birmingham, Stephen. *Certain People: America's Black Elite.* Boston: Little, Brown, 1977.

"Black Plight, Race or Class?" *New York Times Magazine,* June 27, 1980.

Blackwell, James. *Mainstreaming Outsiders: The Production of Black Professionals.* Dix Hills, NY: General Hall, 1981.

Blackwell, James. *The Black Community: Diversity and Unity.* New York: Harper and Row, 1985.

Blackwell, James, and Philip Hart. *Cities, Suburbs and Blacks*. Dix Hills, NY: General Hall, 1982.

Blauner, Robert. *Racial Oppression in America*. New York: Harper and Row, 1972.

Blauner, Robert. *Black Lives, White Lives: Three Decades of Race Relations in America*. Berkeley: University of California Press, 1989.

Bowser, Benjamin P., and Raymond G. Hunt, eds. *Impacts of Racism on White Americans*. Beverly Hills, CA: Sage, 1981.

Brashler, William. "The Black Middle Class: Making It." *New York Times Magazine*, December 3, 1978.

Bulhan, Hussein Abdilahi. *Frantz Fanon and the Psychology of Oppression*. New York: Plenum Press, 1985.

Campbell, Bebe Moore. "To Be Black, Gifted, and Alone." *Savvy*, December 1984, 67–74.

Cannon, Mildred S., and Ben Z. Locke. "Being Black Is Detrimental to One's Mental Health: Myth or Reality?" *Phylon*, 38 (1977), 408–428.

Carmichael, Stokeley, and Charles V. Hamilton. *Black Power: The Politics of Liberation*. New York: Vintage Books, 1967.

Cheatham, Harold E., and James B. Stewart, eds. *Black Families: Interdisciplinary Perspectives*. New Brunswick, NJ: Transaction Pub., 1990.

Chimenzie, Amuzie. "Theories of Black Culture." *Western Journal of Black Studies*, 7 (1983), 216–228.

Cobb, Sidney. "Social Support as a Moderator of Life Stress." *Psychosomatic Medicine*, 38 (1976), 300–314.

Coles, Robert. *Children of Crisis*. New York: Dell, 1967.

Collins, Sharon. "The Making of the Black Middle Class." *Social Problems*, 30, no. 4 (1983), 370–382.

Comer, James P. *Beyond Black and White*. New York: Quadrangle Books, 1972.

Coner-Edwards. Alice F., and Jeanne Spurlock, eds. *Black Families in Crisis: The Middle Class*. New York: Brunner/Mazel, 1988.

Cortz, Dan. "The Negro Middle Class." *Fortune*, November 1966.

Cross, William E., Jr. "Black Family and Black Identity: A Literature Review." *Western Journal of Black Studies*, 2 (1978), 111–124.

Cruse, Harold. *The Crisis of the Negro Intellectual*. New York: William Morrow, 1967.

Dates, Jannette L., and William Barlow, eds. *Split Image: African Americans in the Mass Media*. Washington, DC: Howard University Press, 1990.

Davis, Allison, and John Dollard. *Children of Bondage*. Washington, DC: American Council on Education, 1940.

Davis, Angela Y. *Women, Race and Class*. New York: Vintage Books, 1983.

Davis, George, and Glegg Watson. *Black Life in Corporate America: Swimming in the Mainstream*. Garden City, NY: Anchor Doubleday, 1982.

Davis, Robert. "A Demographic Analysis of Suicide." In Lawrence Gary, ed., *Black Men*. Beverly Hills, CA: Sage, 1981.

Delaney, Paul. "Middle-Class Gains Create Tension in Black Community." *New York Times*, February 28, 1978.

Dennis, Ruth E. "Social Stress and Mortality among Non-White Males." *Phylon*, 38 (1977), 315–328.

Dohrenwend, Barbara S., and Bruce P. Dohrenwend. "Class and Race as Related Sources of Stress." In S. Levine and N. A. Storch, eds., *Social Stress.* Chicago: University of Chicago Press, 1970.

Dohrenwend, Bruce P. "The Social-Psychological Nature of Stress: A Framework of Causal Inquiry." *Journal of Abnormal Psychology,* 62 (1961), 294–302.

Dohrenwend, Bruce P., and Barbara S. Dohrenwend. *Social Status and Psychological Disorder: A Causal Inquiry.* New York: Wiley, 1969.

Dovidio, John F., and Samuel L. Gaertner, eds. *Prejudice, Discrimination and Racism.* Orlando, FL: Academic Press, 1986.

Du Bois, W. E. B. "The Talented Tenth: Memorial Address." *The Boule Journal,* 15 (1948), 3–13.

Du Bois, W. E. B. *The Souls of Black Folk.* New York: Fawcett, 1961.

Eaton, William E. "Life Events, Social Supports and Psychiatric Symptoms: A Re-Analysis of the New Haven Data." *Journal of Health and Social Behavior,* 19 (1978), 230–234.

Eisenberg, Bernard. "Kelly Miller: The Negro Leader as a Marginal Man." *Journal of Negro History,* 45 (1960), 182–197.

Elam, Julia C., ed. *Blacks on White Campuses.* Proceedings of a Special NAFEO Seminar. Lanham, MD: University Press of America, 1983.

Ellison, Ralph. *The Invisible Man.* New York: New American Library, 1952.

Ensel, W. M. "Social Support, Stressful Life Events, and Illness: A Model and Empirical Test." *Journal of Health and Social Behavior,* 20, (1979), 108–119.

Fanon, Frantz. *Black Skin, White Masks.* New York: Grove Press, 1967.

Farley, Reynolds. *Blacks and Whites: Narrowing the Gap?* Cambridge, MA: Harvard University Press, 1984.

Facts about Blacks. Los Angeles, CA: Jeffries and Associates, 1982–83.

Feagin, Joe R., and Clairece Booher Feagin. *Discrimination American Style: Institutional Racism and Sexism,* 2nd ed. Melbourne, FL: Robert E. Krieger Pub. Co., 1986.

Featherman, David L., and Robert M. Hauser. *Opportunity and Change.* New York: Academic Press, 1978.

Fernandez, John P. *Black Managers in White Corporations.* New York: Wiley, 1975.

Fernandez, John P. *Racism and Sexism in Corporate Life.* Lexington, MA: D.C. Heath, 1981.

Fleming, Jacqueline. *Blacks in College.* San Francisco, CA: Jossey-Bass, 1984.

Fogel, Robert W., and Stanley L. Engerman. *Time on the Cross: The Economics of American Negro Slavery.* 2 vols. Boston: Little, Brown, 1974.

Franklin, Clyde W., II. *Men and Society.* Chicago: Nelson-Hall, 1988.

Franklin, Clyde W., II. *The Changing Definition of Masculinity.* New York: Plenum Press, 1984.

Franklin, John Hope, ed. *Color and Race.* Boston: Beacon Press, 1968.

Frazier, E. Franklin. *The Negro Church in America,* 5th ed. New York: Schocken Books, 1964.

Frazier, E. Franklin. *Black Bourgeoisie.* New York: Free Press, 1957.

Frazier, E. Franklin. *The Negro Family in Chicago.* Chicago: University of Chicago Press, 1932.

Frazier, E. Franklin. *The Negro Family in the United States.* Chicago: University of Chicago Press, 1939.

Freeman, Richard B. "Decline of Labor Market Discrimination and Economic Analysis." *American Economic Review,* 63 (1973), 280–286.

Freeman, Richard B. *Black Elite: The New Market for Highly Educated Black Americans.* New York: McGraw-Hill, 1976.

Gary, Lawrence, ed. *Black Men.* Beverly Hills, CA: Sage, 1981.

Glaser, Barney G., and Anselm L. Strauss. *The Discovery of Grounded Theory.* Chicago: Aldine, 1967.

Glazer, Nathan. *Affirmative Discrimination: Ethnic Inequality and Public Policy.* New York: Basic Books, 1975.

Grier, William H., and Price M. Cobbs. *Black Rage.* New York: Basic Books, 1968.

Gurin, Patricia, and Edgar Epps. *Black Consciousness, Identity, and Achievement.* New York: Wiley, 1975.

Hare, Nathan. *Black Anglo-Saxons.* London: Macmillan, 1970.

Harper, Frederick D., and Marvin P. Dawkins, "Alcohol Abuse in the Black Community," *The Black Scholar,* April 1977, 23–31.

Henry, Charles P. "Ebony Elite: America's Most Influential Blacks." *Phylon,* 42 (June 1981), 120–132.

Hernton, Calvin C. *Sex and Racism in America.* New York: Grove Press, 1965.

Hill, Robert B. *Economic Policies and Black Progress: Myths and Realities.* Washington, DC: National Urban League, 1981.

Hill, Robert B. *The Strengths of Black Families.* New York: Emerson Hall, 1972.

Hochschild, Adam. *The Mirror at Midnight: A South African Journey.* New York: Viking Penguin, 1990.

Holahan, C. J., and R. Moors. "Social Support and Psychological Distress: A Longitudinal Analysis." *Journal of Abnormal Psychology,* 30 (1981), 365–370.

Hooks, Bell. *Ain't I a Woman?* Boston: South End Press, 1981.

Hoose, Phillip M. *Necessities: Racial Barriers in American Sports.* New York: Random House, 1989.

Hopson, Darlene Powell, and Derek S. Hopson. *Different and Wonderful: Raising Black Children in a Race-Conscious Society.* New York: Prentice-Hall, 1990.

Hughes, Everett. "Dilemmas and Contradictions of Status." In Lewis Coser and Bernard Rosenberg, eds. *Sociological Theory.* New York: Macmillan, 1976.

Johnson, James Weldon. *The Autobiography of an Ex-Coloured Man.* New York: Knopf, 1912.

Jones, Edward W. "Black Managers: The Dream Deferred," *Harvard Business Review,* May-June (1986), 84–93.

Jones, James. *Prejudice and Racism.* Reading, PA: Addison-Wesley, 1972.

Kanter, Rosabeth Moss. *Men and Women of the Corporation.* New York: Basic Books, 1977.

Kardiner, Abram, and Lionel Ovesey. *The Mark of Oppression.* Cleveland, OH: World, 1962.

Kilson, Martin. "Black Bourgeoisie Revisited." *Dissent* (Winter 1983), 85–96.

King, Michael. "Ambition on Trial." *Black Enterprise,* February 1990, 132–138.

Kochman, Thomas. *Black and White Styles in Conflict.* Chicago: University of Chicago Press, 1981.

Lacayo, Richard. "Between Two Worlds." *Time,* March 13, 1989, 58–68.

Landry, Bart. *The New Black Middle Class.* Berkeley: University of California Press, 1987.

LaRocco, James M., James S. House, and John R. P. French, Jr. "Social Support, Occupational Stress and Health." *Journal of Health and Social Behavior,* 21 (1980), 202–218.

Lazear, Edward. "The Narrowing of Black-White Wage Differentials Is Illusory." *American Economic Review,* 69 (1979), 553–564.

Mann, Coramae Richey, and Lance H. Selva. "The Sexualization of Racism: The Black as Rapist and White Justice." *Western Journal of Black Studies,* 3, no. 3 (Fall 1979), 168–177.

Marable, Manning. "Beyond the Race-Class Dilemma." *The Nation,* April 11, 1981, 417–436.

Marable, Manning. "Reaganism, Racism and Reaction: Black Political Realignment in the 1980's." *The Black Scholar,* 13, no. 6 (Fall 1982), 2–15.

Martin, Michael T., and Howard Cohen. "Race and Class Consciousness: A Critique of the Marxist Concept of Race Relations." *Western Journal of Black Studies,* 4, no. 2 (1980), 84–91.

McAdoo, Harriette P. *Black Families.* Beverly Hills, CA: Sage, 1981.

McAdoo, Harriette P. "Black Kinship." *Psychology Today,* May 1979.

McAdoo, Harriette P. "Factors Related to Stability in Upwardly Mobile Black Families." *Journal of Marriage and the Family,* 40 (1978), 761–776.

McAllister, Bill. "The Plight of Young Men in America." *Washington Post, National Weekly Bulletin,* February 12–18, 1990, p. 6.

McBride, David, and Monroe H. Little. "The Afro-American Elite, 1930–1940: A Historical and Statistical Profile." *Phylon,* 42 (June 1981), 105–119.

Memmi, Albert. *The Colonizer and the Colonized.* Boston: Beacon Press, 1967.

Moss, Jr., Alfred A. *The American Negro Academy: Voice of the Talented Tenth.* Baton Rouge: Louisiana State University Press, 1981.

Moss, James A. "Brashler's Black Middle Class: A Rebuttal." *The Crisis,* 86, no. 7 (August/September 1979), 307–310.

Moynihan, Daniel Patrick. "The Schism in Black America." *Public Interest,* 27 (Spring 1972), 3–24.

Myrdal, Gunnar. *An American Dilemma: The Negro Problem and Modern Democracy.* New York: Harper, 1944.

Nobles, W. W. "African Root and American Fruit: The Black Family." *Journal of Social and Behavioral Sciences,* 20 (1974), 52–63.

Onwubu, Chukwuemeka. "The Intellectual Foundations of Racism." *Western Journal of Black Studies,* 3 (1979), 157–167.

Park, Robert Ezra. *Race and Culture.* New York: Free Press, 1950.

Phinney, Jean S., and Mary Jane Rotheram, eds. *Children's Ethnic Socialization: Pluralism and Development.* Newbury Park, CA: Sage, 1987.

Pinderhughes, Elaine. "Afro-American Families and the Victim System." In M. McGoldrich, J. K. Pearce, and J. Giordano, eds., *Ethnicity and Family Therapy.* New York: Guilford Press, 1982.

Pinkney, Alphonso. *The Myth of Black Progress*. Cambridge: Cambridge University Press, 1984.

Pitt-Rivers, Julian. "Race, Color, and Class in Central America and the Andes." In

John Hope Franklin, ed., *Color and Race*. Boston: Beacon Press, 1968. Pp. 264–281.

Piven, Frances Fox, and Richard A. Cloward. *Regulating the Poor*. New York: Pantheon Books, 1971.

Pomer, Marshall I. "Labor Market Structure, Intragenerational Mobility, and Discrimination: Black Male Advancement Out of Low-Paying Occupations, 1962–1973." *American Sociological Review*, 51 (1986), 650–659.

Porter, Judith R., and Robert E. Washington. "Black Identity and Self-Esteem: A Review of Studies of Black Self-Concept, 1968–1978." In Alex Inkeles, James Coleman, and Ralph H. Turner, eds. *Annual Review of Sociology*, 15 (1979), 53–74.

Reich, Michael. *Racial Inequality: A Political-Economic Analysis*. Princeton, NJ: Princeton University Press, 1981.

Rosenberg, M., and R. Simmons. *Black and White Self-Esteem: The Urban School Child*. Washington, DC: American Sociological Association, 1971.

Sampson, William A., and Vera Milam. "The Intraracial Attitudes of the Black Middle Class: Have They Changed?" *Social Problems*, 23 (1975), 153–165.

Seeman, Melvin. "On the Meaning of Alienation." *American Sociological Review*, 24 (1959), 784–790.

Seeman, Melvin, and Teresa Seeman. "Health Behavior and Personal Autonomy: A Longitudinal Study of the Sense of Control in Illness." *Journal of Health and Social Behavior*, 24 (1983), 144–160.

Seyle, Hans. *The Stress of Life*. New York: McGraw-Hill, 1956.

Seyle, Hans. "Stress and Disease." *Science*, 122 (1955), 625–631.

Shimkin, Demitri B., Edith M. Shimkin, and Dennis A. Frate. *The Extended Family in Black Societies*. Chicago: Aldine, 1978.

Snyder, Mark. "Self-fulfilling Stereotypes." *Psychology Today*, July 1982, 60–68.

Stack, Carol. *All Our Kin: Strategies for Survival in a Black Community*. New York: Harper and Row, 1974.

Staples, Robert. "The Black Family Revisited: A Review and a Preview." *Journal of Social and Behavioral Sciences*, 20 (1974), 65–78.

Stember, Charles Herbert. *Sexual Racism*. New York: Harper and Row, 1978.

Stewart, James B. "Psychic Duality of Afro-Americans in the Novels of W. E. B. Du Bois." *Phylon*, 44 (1983), 93–107.

Stonequist, Everett V. *The Marginal Man: A Study in Personality and Culture Conflict*. New York: Russell and Russell, 1961.

Tatum, Beverly Daniel. *Life in Isolation: Black Families Living in a Predominantly White Community*. Doctoral Dissertation, University of Michigan, 1984.

Thompson, Daniel C. *A Black Elite*. Westport, CT: Greenwood Press, 1986.

Thornton, Jeannye. "The Quiet Power of America's Black Elite." *U.S. News and World Report*, April 6, 1981.

Valentine, Charles A. *Culture and Poverty: Critique and Counter-Proposals*. Chicago: University of Chicago Press, 1968.

Watley, William D. *Roots of Resistance: The Nonviolent Ethic of Martin Luther King, Jr.* Valley Forge, PA: Judson Press, 1985.

Wattenberg, Ben J., and Richard M. Scammon. "Black Progress and Liberal Rhetoric." *Commentary,* 55 (1973), 35–44.

Weiss, Leonard, and Jeffery Williamson. "Black Education, Earnings and Inter-Regional Migration: Some New Evidence." *American Economic Review,* 62 (1972), 372–383.

Welch, Finis. "Black-White Differences in Return to Schooling." *American Economic Review,* 63 (1973), 893–907.

Wideman, John Edgar. *Brothers and Keepers.* New York: Holt, Rinehart and Winston, 1984.

Wilkins, Roger. *A Man's Life, An Autobiography.* New York: Simon and Schuster, 1982.

Williams, Robin M., Jr. *American Society: A Sociological Interpretation,* 3rd ed. New York: Knopf, 1970.

Willie, Charles Vert. *Five Black Scholars: An Analysis of Family Life, Education and Career.* Lanham, MD: University Press, 1986.

Willie, Charles Vert. *A New Look at Black Families.* Dix Hills, NY: General Hall, 1981.

Willie, Charles Vert. *Caste and Class Controversy.* Dix Hills, NY: General Hall, 1979.

Wilson, William Julius. *The Declining Significance of Race.* Chicago: University of Chicago Press, 1978.

Wilson, William Julius. *Power, Racism and Privilege.* New York: Macmillan, 1973.

Wilson, William Julius. *The Truly Disadvantaged: The Inner City, the Underclass, and Public Policy.* Chicago: University of Chicago Press, 1987.

Woodward, Michael D. "Ideological Response to Alterations in the Structure of Oppression: Reverse Discrimination, the Current Racial Ideology in the U.S." *Western Journal of Black Studies,* 6, no. 3 (1982), 166–173.

Wright, Richard. "The Ethics of Living Jim Crow: An Autobiographical Sketch." In Abraham Chapman, ed., *Black Voices.* New York: New American Library, 1968.